The Films of ANDREI
TARKOVSKY

The Films of ANDREI TARKOVSKY,

A Visual Fugue

V I D A T. J O H N S O N,, and

G R A H A M P E T R I E

INDIANA UNIVERSITY PRESS
Bloomington & Indianapolis

Research for this book was supported in part by a grant from the International Research & Exchanges Board (IREX), with funds provided by the Andrew W. Mellon Foundation, the National Endowment for the Humanities, and the U.S. Department of State. None of these organizations is responsible for the views expressed.

The paper used in this publication meets the minimum requirements of American National Standard for Information Sciences—Permanence of Paper for Printed Library Materials, ANSI Z39.48-1984.

Manufactured in the United States of America

Library of Congress Cataloging-in-Publication Data

Johnson, Vida T., date
    Tarkovsky : a visual fugue / Vida T. Johnson and Graham Petrie.
      p. cm.
    Filmography: p.
    Includes bibliographical references and index.
    ISBN 0-253-33137-4 (alk. paper). — ISBN 0-253-20887-4 (pbk. : alk. paper)
      1. Tarkovskiĭ, Andreĭ Arsen'evich. 1932-1986—Criticism and interpretation.
I. Petrie, Graham. II. Title.
PN1998.3.T36J64 1994
791.43'0233'092—dc20   93-43589

    2 3 4 5 99 98 97

To Cathy and Dean
and
in memory of
Vida's father, the Russian scholar
Kiril Taranovsky

CONTENTS

PART THREE

Acknowledgments

We would like to offer our grateful thanks to the following, all of whom helped, in various ways, to make this book possible.

All those listed in the Works Cited as interviewees who kindly gave us their time and shared with us their knowledge of Tarkovsky both as a man and as a filmmaker. Those who provided invaluable assistance on our visits to Moscow in April 1989, September–October 1989, and May 1991: Naum Kleiman, director of the Film Center in Moscow, who made available to us the Center's facilities and films; Mariana Kushnerova, Director of the Tarkovsky Museum; members of the board of the Tarkovsky Society: Neya Zorkaya for inviting us to the Tarkovsky conference; Alla Gerber and Paula Volkova for making it possible for us to return to carry out our interviews; Irina Kobakhidze, Natasha Derevyanko, and Anna Mazurova, who translated for Graham Petrie.

Those who made it possible for us to see and re-see the films: Pam Engel of Artificial Eye, Kitty Cooper of Contemporary Films, and Ian Christie of the British Film Institute, in London; Vlada Petrić and Steve Livernash of the Harvard Film Archive; Jon Zemitis of the Broadway Cinema, Hamilton, Ontario; John and Isabel Flower and Dušan Puvačić, who provided videos; Elaine Burrows of the National Film Archive for providing facilities to make frame enlargements, and Jim Adams of the British Film Institute for his superb work on filming and printing these.

Vida Johnson would like to thank the following institutions and colleagues: for the financial support which made this project possible, the Jasper and Marion Whiting Foundation, the National Endowment for the Humanities, the International Research and Exchanges Board, and Tufts University for a Summer Fellowship as well as travel and research support and a sabbatical combined with a leave of absence; for logistical and moral support, Dean Mary Ella Feinleib, Provost Sol Gittleman, Professor Christiane Romero (Department Chairman), Professor David Sloane, and Professor Martin Sherwin.

Graham Petrie received a leave of absence from McMaster University to work on the book, and also financial assistance for a visit to Moscow. He would like to thank the Social Sciences and Humanities Research Council of Canada for its generous financial support of the project.

Andrew Horton and Dušan Puvačić read and commented on early drafts of some chapters, and Daniel Goulding offered valuable advice on an early version. We are especially grateful to Herbert Eagle for his scrupulous critical reading of the entire manuscript and his enlightening suggestions, many of which we have incorporated into the final text.

Special thanks to Catherine Gibbon and Dean, Kiki, and Kiril Johnson for enduring more than four years of Tarkovsky, and to Dean for his patient and expert assistance in the preparation of both the final text and its preliminary versions.

Stills and frame enlargements reproduced by permission of Artificial Eye

(*Ivan's Childhood, Andrei Roublev, Mirror, Nostalghia,* and *The Sacrifice*) and Contemporary Films (*Solaris* and *Stalker*). Production stills from *The Sacrifice* by Lars-Olaf Löthwall copyright The Swedish Film Institute.

A Note on References

The "Works Cited" at the end of the book is divided into three categories: primary published sources (works *by* Tarkovsky and interviews with him), secondary sources (works *about* Tarkovsky and general critical literature consulted), and interviews conducted by the authors with his coworkers, relatives, and friends.

The works *by* Tarkovsky include his Diary, his critical/theoretical work, *Sculpting in Time*, published scripts and articles, and interviews conducted with him. Items frequently referred to are cited in the text as follows:

Martyrolog: Tagebücher 1970-1986 (the German edition of his Diary) as *Martyrolog*.

Sculpting in Time as *Sculpting*.

Time within Time (the English edition of his Diary) as *TWT*.

Articles and interviews are listed under their published title and are referred to thus in the text. In cases where there may be some doubt as to the category in which a work belongs, the initials "A. T." indicate the Tarkovsky section.

The works *about* Tarkovsky, together with any other more general works referred to, are listed alphabetically by author or, in the case of collections of essays by various hands, by title, e.g., *Andrej Tarkowskij, Dossier Positif, Etudes cinématographiques, O Tarkovskom*.

A Note on Transliteration

In an attempt to make Russian words more easily accessible to the non-Russian-speaking reader, we have slightly adapted the system recommended by the Chicago Manual of Style: the United States Board on Geographic Names system. The Russian hard and soft masculine adjectival endings, which should respectively be transliterated -*yy* and -*iy*, have both been shortened to simply -*y*, primarily because English readers are already familiar with this form in first and last names: Arseniy Tarkovskiy is more commonly seen as Arseny Tarkovsky; *Sovetskiy ekran* appears as *Sovetsky ekran* to reflect the more familiar transliteration of journals such as *Novy mir* instead of the more confusing *Novyy mir*. Well-known Russian names are given in the form in which they have become familiar to English-speaking readers, especially in the United States: thus Tchaikovsky instead of Chaykovskiy; Chaliapin and not Shalyapin; Maria and Natalia, and not Mariya and Nataliya; Andrei and Sergei in place of Andrey and Sergey; the anglicized Alexei and Alexander are also found instead of Aleksey and Aleksandr. Soft and hard signs have simply been dropped, so *Sovetskaya kul'tura* becomes *Sovetskaya kultura;* these signs have no meaning whatsoever for the nonRussian speaker and their absence makes Russian words more easily recognizable, while the Russian speaker will not fail to insert the soft and hard signs where needed. Finally, the problem of the Russian letter pronounced "yo": the *e* with two dots above it is totally indecipherable to English readers. We will use the phonetically more representative *yo* in the transliteration of Russian words and of Russian references to Tarkovsky's film *Andrei Rublëv*. However, since the film's official English title is *Andrei Roublev*, we have chosen to use this spelling in our discussion of the film. The titles of all Tarkovsky's films are given as released in English: hence, *Mirror* and *Stalker* instead of *The Mirror* and *The Stalker*, and the Italian *Nostalghia* instead of *Nostalgia*. The two different translations of *Ivanovo detstvo*, as *My Name Is Ivan* (in the U.S.) and the more literal *Ivan's Childhood* (in Britain), have been noted, and the more accurate British version has been used.

Introduction

Russell Hoban's novel *The Medusa Frequency* contains, in the figure of the film director Gösta Kraken, a character based at least partly on Andrei Tarkovsky: in Kraken's films *Bogs* and *Quicksand*, we learn, "you can see his obsessions developing, his preoccupation with wetness and ooze as primal mindscape and his vision of a discarded world" (105). If, at least in some respects, it is easy to parody Tarkovsky, it is equally easy—and dangerous—to venerate and revere him. Toward the end of his life he set himself up in business, quite self-consciously, as a prophet and oracle and, by means of interviews, talks, films such as those made by Donatella Baglivo, and his book *Sculpting in Time* (especially the final, posthumously published chapter on *The Sacrifice*), succeeded to a remarkable extent in creating a framework which ensured that his films would be discussed and understood in terms largely established by him. This is not said in order to belittle him: he was—on the evidence of those who knew him and worked with him—a remarkable and charismatic personality, and—on the evidence of his films—a great artist and filmmaker, one of the finest working anywhere in the past three decades. He was not, however, without flaws, as either a man or an artist. The mythmaking that accumulated around him, first of all, and during his lifetime, in the West, and then, since his untimely death and the coming of glasnost, in the Soviet Union,[1] has made it difficult to look at his work objectively, without the stereotype of the persecuted and suffering artist (which he himself did much to encourage) blurring and even obscuring the focus of vision.

His films, in addition, have routinely been considered "obscure," "baffling," and "impenetrable," especially by American critics who have compounded the often very real difficulties by inadequate knowledge of the historical and cultural contexts that shaped them and by descriptions of their contents that are often woefully inaccurate. The tone for American criticism has generally been set by reviewers, writing about these long and complex films after only one viewing, and often seeing them in shortened and mutilated versions and with inadequate or misleading subtitling (British prints tend to have both fuller and more accurate subtitles and—with the exception of the initial release of *Andrei Roublev*—have always been more complete). Until 1980 *Andrei Roublev* was available in the United States only in a print that ran 146 minutes instead of 185; *Solaris* circulated for fifteen years in a print that was cut by 33 minutes and poorly dubbed into English; both *Ivan's Childhood* and *Nostalghia* are currently distributed in versions lacking important scenes (see our synopses of the films for details). The unfavorable early reviews that resulted, at least in part, from seeing the films in this way (the influential *New York Times* has been consistently hostile to Tarkovsky's work) ensured that, long after he was recognized in Britain and Europe as one of the major filmmakers of our time, Tarkovsky was still being treated in the United States as an obscure and incomprehensible phenomenon, the creator of tedious and (despite all the cutting) overly long works that made little narrative sense.

Although this situation is changing and, especially since Tarkovsky's death, his films have become a staple of art house revivals and college film courses, American criticism is still far from coming to terms with the peculiar challenges and rewards of his work. The impression that Tarkovsky is somehow more difficult and less accessible than comparable directors such as Bergman or Antonioni still persists—fueled by a backlog of never checked or corrected misinformation about what actually happens in the films themselves. Garbled versions of key incidents, scenes, and even whole plots, misidentification of characters (especially, but not only, in *Mirror*), misinterpretation or misunderstanding of historical, autobiographical, and cultural references are passed on, as if by osmosis, from one commentator to the next—with the director being blamed for the "obscurity" and "incoherence" that results.

If American criticism is perhaps most prone to this defect, British and other European critics, despite their enthusiasm for the films, are not exempt. Again, much that has been written or reprinted about Tarkovsky has been based on little more than a single viewing, and here, too, factual mistakes abound. With French critics in particular, blatant misreadings of what actually occurs on the screen are often used as the basis for elaborate interpretative edifices that utterly distort the meaning of particular scenes and even of a whole film. We have drawn attention to some of these problems in our own analyses of the films, as well as elsewhere,[2] and have no wish to belabor the point here; what matters is to recognize that Tarkovsky's films demand, and reward, careful, patient, and repeated viewings if they are to be properly understood, and—on the evidence of most published books and articles—too few critics have been willing or able to provide this.

One important element of our book, therefore, is the lengthy Appendix with detailed synopses of all the films except *Mirror* (which, for reasons explained in the chapter on that film, receives different treatment). These are based on multiple viewings of the films in the best available 35mm and 16mm prints and on video. The length, complexity, and ambiguity of the films make it easy to misinterpret or misremember many of the details; we thus see the provision of an accurate description of what is seen and heard in them as an essential prerequisite for later analysis, and even readers reasonably familiar with Tarkovsky's work are encouraged to consult the synopses in conjunction with the chapters on specific films.

It is not enough, however, to blame poor prints or hasty and inattentive reviewers for the widely shared feeling that Tarkovsky is indeed a "difficult" director. For Western viewers this results to some extent from lack of understanding of the specific cultural contexts within which the films operate, and a major focus of our work is to provide a greater insight into these and to see them not as barriers to understanding and enjoyment but as factors that enrich and deepen our pleasure in his work. Our analyses of the individual films begin with a "creative history" that attempts to give, as far as possible, an accurate record of the circumstances in which each one came into being, its problems or otherwise with the Soviet authorities (or, later on, Western producers), and its initial reception both in the Soviet Union and abroad.[3] We then examine each film in the context of Tarkovsky's own developing stylistic and thematic concerns, taking into account his strong sense of himself as a "Russian" artist, the heir to a rich cultural and spiritual tradition that he was determined to perpetuate and contribute to in his own work.

Tarkovsky is also one of the major stylistic innovators in film of the past thirty years, and his work can pose problems, not just to viewers accustomed to "classical" Hollywood narrative, but even to many familiar with the strategies employed by the European "art film" of the past three decades. Not only does he systematically subvert the narrative categories and structures (analyzed by David Bordwell and Noël Carroll among others) by which we have learned to "make sense" of most of the films that we see; his complex, non-linear narratives and multilayered subtexts defy easy understanding on any level and generally require more than one viewing before any really satisfactory intellectual comprehension can be achieved. Yet even on a first viewing—as the director himself insisted should be possible—a different kind of "comprehension," intuitive rather than intellectual, can be attained, and many readers must have shared with us the sense after an initial viewing of *Mirror* or *Stalker* that we may not really "understand" this work, yet we "know" and "feel" what it is about and that it speaks directly to us. We hope that we have managed to respect this sense of inner "knowledge" while making the films somewhat more accessible on an "intellectual" level.

The issues outlined in the previous two paragraphs provide the focus of Part II of our book, which consists of a film-by-film analysis of each work. Part I is based on extensive research in Soviet and Western sources and on almost fifty interviews with people who knew Tarkovsky well or worked with him in the Soviet Union or abroad. Its three chapters are intended to give a sense of his life and personality, the nature and organization of the Soviet film industry during his career, his working methods and his relations with his coworkers, his own aesthetic theories and their influence on his work, and his place within a wider spectrum of Soviet cinema. Here we cope with the fact that, although Russian critics show greater awareness than their Western counterparts of the personal, cultural, and historical contexts of the films, they are also more liable, especially in recent years, to succumb to a hagiography that attempts to establish him as the latest in a long line of suffering, misunderstood, and martyred artistic geniuses. While such an approach is understandable, given the nature of Tarkovsky's career and the political circumstances that inhibited open discussion of it in the Soviet Union until fairly recently, it too distorts the nature of his creative achievement.

In discussing Tarkovsky's working methods, we proceed from the premise that he was—as he believed the true filmmaker should be—the ultimate "author" of his works, but that he had also—like any other film director—to rely on the skills and commitment of many talented and creative collaborators in order to realize his vision fully. Where his own aesthetic theories are concerned, we recognize them to be firmly planted in a still-surviving Russian artistic tradition which is often at odds with contemporary Western thinking. We thus attempt to cope with Tarkovsky on his own terms, but without accepting his aesthetic position or his own analysis of his work as definitive or self-evident. Our critical position is eclectic rather than dogmatic; we are prepared to use any critical tools that serve to illuminate the work we are studying and have no desire to impose any one exclusive theoretical structure on his work. Interestingly enough, however, Tarkovsky's own currently unfashionable views on the role of the artist and his claims for the spiritual and religious dimensions of the work of art may be coming back into favor in the West, if George Steiner's *Real Presences* (University of Chicago Press, 1989) and Robin Wood's recent introduction to his *Hitchcock's Films Revisited* (Columbia University Press, 1989) are any guide.

The final section of the book provides an overall survey of the main stylistic devices, recurring image patterns, and themes which constitute Tarkovsky's "poetic world," pulling together material discussed or alluded to in the analyses of the individual works. Like David Russell in his perceptive review of Maya Turovskaya's book on Tarkovsky in the Spring 1990 issue of *Sight & Sound,* we believe that his "films together seem to resemble episodes in one great film . . . where themes, motifs and characters reflect each other, echo one another, suffer and commune together, like passages in some extraordinary visual fugue" (140). We have attempted to describe the essential qualities of Tarkovsky's films more comprehensively and more accurately than has been done in any of the published criticism to date—not by denying their very real difficulties, eccentricities, and strangeness, but by respecting these and attempting to understand them ourselves. Our ultimate goal is twofold: to peel back the layers of myth and misinformation surrounding Tarkovsky's creative life and work, and to provide a more detailed and richer analysis of his films by drawing on our combined knowledge of Russian and Western art, culture, and cinema.

This work is the result of a true collaboration, with both authors sharing the writing, critiquing, and editing of each chapter. Vida Johnson is a specialist in Russian language, literature, and culture with a particular interest in Soviet and post-Soviet film, and Graham Petrie is a film critic whose recent work has largely been concerned with what used to be called "Eastern European" cinema. Unless otherwise indicated, all translations from the Russian are by Johnson, and those from French and German are by Petrie. In some cases where the English subtitles for the films are inaccurate or inadequate, we have provided our own translation of the Russian dialogue.

The book is illustrated with frame enlargements, made with the kind cooperation of Tarkovsky's British distributors (Artificial Eye and Contemporary Films) and the British Film Institute. We have chosen this method rather than relying on the standard publicity stills for the same reasons that forced us to provide the lengthy synopses of the films themselves: the widespread inaccuracy of almost all the illustrative material that has appeared in print to date. *All* the books published on Tarkovsky so far, in whatever language, draw on the same restricted number of production stills, virtually none of which represent the image actually seen on the screen. Most are taken from a different angle, thus distorting the composition; some are clearly made from takes or even scenes not used in the finished film, or were obviously photographed *between* takes and have even less resemblance to the final product; some are both visually wrong *and* miscaptioned (this is true even of Tarkovsky's own *Sculpting in Time*).[4] In *no* instance is any acknowledgment made of this, leaving the innocent reader to assume that all these photos represent what they claim to represent—images from Tarkovsky's films—when in fact they contribute to a pervasively inaccurate visual record of the films themselves. For a director praised so highly for his visual qualities, the negligence evident here is little short of scandalous and, once again, our aim has been to set the record straight and to provide a clearer and more accurate understanding of a widely admired but still seriously misrepresented *oeuvre*.

PART ONE

ONE

A Martyred Artist?

Tarkovsky and Glasnost

On April 25, 1990, the influential newspaper *Literaturnaya gazeta* reported on its front page that the film director Andrei Tarkovsky had been posthumously awarded the Lenin Prize, the highest form of official Soviet recognition, for his "outstanding contribution to the development of cinema art, for his innovative films, which help to affirm universal human values and humanistic ideas." Few Russian readers could have missed the irony of this gesture, and most would point out that Russia and the Soviet Union have always tended to honor their artists only after they are safely dead! During his lifetime Tarkovsky had generally received grudging official recognition at home and had been in almost constant conflict with the bureaucracy over his films, even becoming a "nonperson" after his decision to remain in the West in 1984. In his notarized testament of November 5, 1986, Tarkovsky bitterly notes that, in connection with rumors of his impending demise, the Soviets have begun to screen his films widely and "are preparing my canonization."

Tarkovsky's rapid "rehabilitation" was due primarily to Gorbachev's policy of glasnost, which resulted in an almost immediate public reclamation of many persecuted and exiled artists, especially those who were no longer living. They presumably could not "object" to this belated recognition, and Tarkovsky in his testament perhaps expressed a common sentiment: "Neither dead nor alive do I want to return to the country which caused me and those close to me so much pain, suffering, humiliation. I am a Russian, but do not consider myself a Soviet." Solzhenitsyn and other living émigré artists had to wait another five years for recent official apologies from the Soviet government and reinstatement of citizenship.

Tarkovsky was correct about his canonization. The official recognition which had eluded him in life swiftly followed upon his death: a highly laudatory obituary signed by both Goskino USSR (the State Committee on Cinema) and the Filmmakers' Union of the USSR appeared in major newspapers on January 1, 1987 (among others *Literaturnaya gazeta* and *Sovetskaya kultura*). The leadership of both of these organizations had during 1986 been transferred from the conservative bureaucrats, who had often opposed Tarkovsky, to a liberal group more receptive to his work. Tarkovsky unfortunately could not take pleasure in the downfall of his old nemesis, Filip Yermash, the chairman of Goskino who resigned the day Tarkovsky died (London *Times*, January 3, 1987). A steady stream of publications on Tarkovsky has followed, particularly in the most prestigious film journal, *Iskusstvo kino*, the liberal *Kino* (Riga), and most recently in *Kinovedcheskiye zapiski* (literally *Cinema Studies Notes*).¹ Complete retrospectives of all his films, including the Western productions, were organized first at Dom Kino (the House of Cinema), the headquarters of the Filmmakers' Union, in April 1987, and then at the XV International Moscow Film Festival in July 1987. Since 1987 Tarkovsky's Russian films have frequently been on the repertoire in the major cities, Moscow and Leningrad, and are even on the film club circuit in the provinces, and his Western productions have also recently reached the screen. Elem Klimov, at the time the new liberal head of the Filmmakers' Union, may not have been joking when he conjectured at the first international conference on Tarkovsky in April 1989 that he may yet prove to be the most commercial Soviet film-maker. In April 1990 the Tarkovsky production of Mussorgsky's opera *Boris Godunov* (originally staged at the Royal Opera House in London) opened at the renowned Kirov Theater in Leningrad. A Tarkovsky society has been established, conferences have been held, books published. By 1990 he had become both an "industry" and a figure of mythic proportions.

Many factors apart from the tragic nature of his illness and early death (which many Tarkovsky admirers attributed to the stress resulting from the rough official treatment he received) conspired to elevate Tarkovsky to the status of martyr, prophet, and greatest modern Soviet filmmaker in his own country and abroad. From the banning of his masterpiece *Andrei Roublev* in the late 1960s, Tarkovsky's reputation as an original uncompromising artistic genius grew steadily as he continued to battle the conservative film bureaucracy during the period of "stagnation" in the 1970s; furthermore, in the early glasnost period of the mid-1980s the absence of new masterpieces and the "silence" of many talented filmmakers resulted in a kind of artistic and moral vacuum which Tarkovsky's films filled. His call for spiritual and religious rebirth and his vision of a technological apocalypse (especially after Chernobyl) have come to be seen as both timely and prophetic. One might even venture that the best film of the early glasnost period was *The Passion According to Andrei*, the original uncut version of *Andrei Roublev*, released in 1988 and awarded the Lenin Prize in 1990. However, the whirlwind changes of the early nineties—the liberalization and commercialization of the former Soviet cinema industry—have, for the time being, also marginalized Tarkovsky. Admitted to the pantheon of the great Soviet filmmakers (Eisenstein, Dovzhenko, etc.), his "difficult" films recognized as classics, Tarkovsky is honored for his contribution to Soviet cinema, yet he hardly wields any real influence on a new generation of filmmakers. But the myth of the martyred artist lives on.

Working in the Soviet Cinema Industry

When one compares Tarkovsky's fate with that of his most talented contemporaries, one sees that, unlike Sergei Paradzhanov, his closest competitor in innovative poetic cinema, Tarkovsky was never arrested and jailed. Even though most of his films ran into trouble with the censors, with the exception of *Andrei Roublev*, they were all released rather quickly, and even *Roublev* was "shelved" for only five years. In contrast, Andrei Konchalovsky's *The Story of Asya Klyachina* (*Istoriya Asi Klyachinoy*), made in 1966, was released some twenty years later. Tarkovsky's films were never butchered like Marlen Khutsiev's *The Lenin Gate* (*Zastava Ilyicha;* renamed *I Am Twenty* [*Mne dvadt-sat let*], 1962) or Igor Talankin's *Daytime Stars* (*Dnevnye zvyozdy*, 1968). (This is to Tarkovsky's credit, however, since he clearly withstood the bureaucratic pressure better than these directors.) But Tarkovsky's fate was not nearly as tragic as that of two extremely talented directors who were simply not allowed to film for many years. Alexander Askoldov's brilliant first and only film, *The Commissar* (*Komissar*), completed in the mid-sixties, was one of the last films to be unbanned more than twenty years later. His career was over before it had hardly begun, and Askoldov even lost out to Tarkovsky in the Lenin Prize competition for 1990. Kira Muratova, who directed two sensitive films about women, *Brief Encounters* (*Korotkie vstrechi*, 1967) and *Long Farewells* (*Dolgie provody*, 1969, released 1987), was for years simply unable to make films. Her recent film *The Aesthenic Syndrome* (*Astenichesky sindrom*, 1990) is a tour-de-force in which her pent-up talent explodes unevenly on the screen. For all these directors, the damage inflicted on their lives and careers can never be adequately compensated.

Tarkovsky complained bitterly that he was unemployed for most of his career in the Soviet Union, and many critics, certainly in the West, have taken his complaints at face value. In his 1983 letter to Goskino chairman Filip Yermash, Tarkovsky cites as his reason for wanting to continue working in the West the fact that in twenty-two years at home he was allowed to make only five films. But Tarkovsky *did* work in cinema for many of those years. He planned films, wrote scripts (for both himself and others), even staged a play (*Hamlet*), and unfortunately spent much time and energy fighting bureaucrats in an attempt to get approval for both scripts and completed films. But that, too, is part of a director's calling, and "difficult" or "uncommercial" directors elsewhere face similar problems. He was never reduced to laboring at odd jobs to pay the rent, but was instead surrounded by people who believed in his talent and were financially willing to help in hard times. (His wife Larissa was instrumental in coordinating these efforts.) Turovskaya offers in interview what will surely be seen as a highly controversial view: that Tarkovsky also by nature worked slowly and thus might not have made a significantly greater number of films, even given the opportunity. The long gestation period of each film and the endless rewrites of scripts support this contention.

There are perhaps two different ways of looking at the very real problems that Tarkovsky encountered with the bureaucracy, beginning with *Andrei Roublev*. Two diametrically opposed views are offered by the two Russian critics who "discovered" him, knew him well personally, and followed his career closely from its very beginning. In interview both Neya Zorkaya and Maya Turovskaya agree that Tarkovsky's life and career were changed by the five-year struggle to get *Andrei Roublev* released. Zorkaya thinks that this had a negative effect, preventing him from creating at the height of his powers, and making him hard, suspicious, and frustrated. Turovskaya posits that the struggle strengthened him, firmed his resolve, and made him uncompromising in questions of art. There certainly is a long-held view among Russian intellectuals that an artist must suffer for his art and that his best creations result from a struggle against dogma and authorities. Tarkovsky's first wife, Irma Rausch,[2] also speaks of Tarkovsky's growing self-confidence during this period and his conviction that he should film only what he wanted.

By refusing to accept Tarkovsky simply as a long-suffering and tragic martyr of a monolithic government-run cinema juggernaut, one can begin to explore objectively his real and substantial accomplishments in cinema. The question one should ask is not why Tarkovsky was allowed to make only five feature films in some twenty years in the Soviet Union, but how he managed to make *that many* films, considering the extent to which they diverged from the accepted thematic and stylistic norms of socialist realism. After all, he was making noncommercial films (labeled "difficult" in the Soviet Union) which certainly would have been hard to fund in the West, where the ideological Soviet censorship would (as he was to discover when he moved there) have been replaced by an almost equally deleterious economic "censorship." In order to comprehend the extent of Tarkovsky's accomplishments, then, one must first also understand the workings of the Soviet cinema industry.

An Overview of the Soviet Film Industry

For most of Soviet history the cinema industry was an important state-owned and state-controlled monopoly like all other Soviet industries. It had a highly centralized and rigid bureaucratic structure with economic, political, and ideological controls resting in the hands of the government and the sole ruling Communist Party. The history of Soviet cinema is indeed very closely tied to the establishment of the Soviet Union and the consolidation of power by the Communist Party. Whether or not Lenin himself ever called cinema "the most important art," this statement has throughout Soviet history become a kind of "mantra," repeated *ad nauseam* to reaffirm strong political and ideological control over films. Lenin and his Commissar of Education, Anatoly Lunacharsky, recognized cinema's potential for education and political propaganda among the barely literate and ideologically unconverted masses. A government decree in 1919 nationalized the existing privately owned cinema industry, and in 1922 Goskino (the Central State Photo-Movie Enterprise) was created under the auspices of the People's Commissariat of Education. For much of the 1920s, under the liberal New Economic Policy, private studios continued to coexist with state-run ones; but with the introduction of the first

Five-Year Plan in 1928, almost the whole industry came under government control. Over the years the name of the organization which ran the industry changed numerous times (although physically its headquarters were always located in the same place, at 7 Maly Gnezdnikovsky Lane in Moscow); each change usually signaled an attempt to increase and centralize control over all aspects of the industry, including, and most important, production and distribution. The organization went through a dizzying array of names—beginning with Goskino, then moving on to Sovkino, Soyuzkino, the Main Administration of the Movie-Photo Industry, the All-Union Committee on Artistic Affairs, the Committee on Cinema Affairs, the Ministry of Cinema, the Main Administration for Film Production under the Ministry of Culture—before finally, in 1972, ending up as Goskino again: the State Committee for Cinema under the Council of Ministers of the USSR (Gosudarstvenny komitet po delam kinematografii pri sovete ministrov SSSR).

In contrast to its earlier namesake, this Goskino was, until the perestroika (restructuring) of the late 1980s, a gigantic, centralized bureaucratic institution which controlled every aspect of the cinema industry: some forty studios in all fifteen Soviet republics, distribution, professional education (the renowned All-Union State Institute of Cinematography, VGIK), film research institutes, trade publications and critical journals (*Iskusstvo kino* and *Sovetsky ekran*), the central film archives (Gosfilmofond), the Central Film Base (the storage facility for "shelved" films and original copies of all films), a print-duplicating factory in Moscow, a script studio, the Theater of the Film Actor, and even a symphony orchestra (Golovskoy 11–13). Despite the recent rapid disintegration of this state-run monopoly and the rise of a multitude of private film-production enterprises, during Tarkovsky's time the dictum attributed to Lenin was in full force and Goskino in full control.

The increasing bureaucratic centralization of the cinema industry, most of which occurred in the 1930s, was accompanied by the tightening of ideological and political controls. After the Bolsheviks seized power in 1917, film was immediately used during the ensuing civil war (1918–21) for political purposes, as agit-trains crossed the countryside screening *agitki*—short documentary propaganda films glorifying the Communist cause. But the twenties saw much variety in films. Audiences flocked to see Charlie Chaplin and Mary Pickford, while Eisenstein and Pudovkin were creating odes to the Revolution. There was a great deal of formal and thematic experimentation in film as well as in all the other arts and, despite the revolutionary fervor, little overt systematic ideological control until the late 1920s. Then the need to unify the country behind a gargantuan effort to industrialize called for film and the other arts to extol the sacrifices which were to be borne by the masses. By 1932 socialist realism was proclaimed as the only accepted "method" in the arts, with the goal of "portraying reality in its revolutionary development." In fact this came to mean a simple style and narrative, a clear message, strong Communist heroes, and mass appeal. There was often little realism in the schematic, highly idealized heroes and improbable plots of most socialist realist literature and cinema. In his classic article "On Socialist Realism" the writer Daniel Sinyavsky (under the pseudonym Abram Tertz) pointed out the incompatibility of the terms "socialist" and "realism" and offered instead a more accurate designation—"Socialist Classicism."

Art was totally harnessed in the service of the state, and socialist realism remained the officially prescribed means of artistic expression (with a brief liberalization during the "Thaw" of the late fifties to the late sixties) until its resounding rejection in 1988. Yet, after *Ivan's Childhood*, each of Tarkovsky's films can be seen as an attempt to subvert socialist realism. In itself this challenge to artistic dogma was not unusual. What *was* unusual was that Tarkovsky was not supressed but was allowed to keep making films, albeit with great difficulty. After all, many writers who continued to experiment and reject socialist realism ended up writing "for the drawer." Their works either circulated in *samizdat* (hand-written manuscripts) or were published only abroad, often with dire repercussions: trials, imprisonment, and/or exile. Since writing is a solitary occupation requiring only pen and paper, it was clearly impossible for the state to totally suppress its production. But cinema requires funding, equipment, personnel—all of which have to be officially assigned after a film script has been approved. It would seem extremely easy to suppress ideologically unacceptable or "dissident" filmmaking. The fact that many films were produced and then "shelved," on and off from the 1930s through the 1970s, points to the much more complex, and perhaps even chaotic, workings of the cinema industry than would appear from merely a formal description of this highly centralized monolith.

The official structure of the cinema industry during Tarkovsky's career was as follows: the centralized governmental agency, Goskino, was headed by a chairman (in Tarkovsky's time Alexei Romanov [1963–1972] and Filip Yermash [1972–1986]) with a governing board (*kollegiya*) which included all the deputy chairs. These latter were the heads of departments (such as the Main Administration for Production of Feature Films), the editor of the journal *Iskusstvo kino*, the head of the Script-Editorial Board, a deputy chair representing the KGB, and a number of the most established directors, actors, and scriptwriters. Under Goskino were the individual studios such as Mosfilm, the largest and most powerful Soviet studio, where Tarkovsky shot all his films. Mosfilm's executive director and the deputy chair of Goskino, first V. Surin and then N. Sizov, played the dual role of capable administrator and watchful ideologue. Under him were a number of deputies—heads of departments such as production, personnel, and ideology, and the editor-in-chief of the Script Board—as well as a large Artistic Council (*khudsovet*) consisting of some 75–100 filmmakers, local party officials, and workers, making up a "democratic" advisory body which generally approved all films (Golovskoy 23–24). The Script Board, which considered drafts and complete scenarios, was a more professional body.

The actual production work at the studio was conducted through the creative "teams" (*tvorcheskiye obyedineniya*) which were introduced in the mid-1950s in order to streamline the production process. There were seven such teams at Mosfilm, each headed by a well-known director (like Sergei Bondarchuk), with a production manager (*direktor obyedineniya*) who handled business matters. There was an editorial department of five to ten editors, headed by an editor-in-chief—censors who were supposed to preview the film during production and hold the first official viewing of the finished film. But, as Maya Turovskaya points out, these "censors," mostly women, were generally very supportive of their directors, often making helpful suggestions to "save" a problematic film. She adds that Tarkovsky himself benefited from their favorable noninterference and was always in total control during the whole shooting and editing process. Each team also had its own editorial board and artistic council, both staffed by professionals. The advisory editorial board which read the scripts consisted of some twenty writers, scriptwriters, and critics—some of them hired from outside the studio on a part-time basis. The real creative discussions and decisions were supposed to take place in the artistic council (made up of writers, critics, directors, actors, and cameramen) which followed the film from script to finished product, approving the script, the sets, music, costumes, actors, and the completed film.

With all these levels of bureaucracy, it would seem that a director would have very little creative freedom. But in fact an established director such as Tarkovsky was able to choose his whole working group—cameraman, art director, composer, costume designer, actors, and even assistants—with the artistic council generally giving approval to his decisions. In any case, the unwieldy multilayered bureaucratic system simply could not and did not operate as planned. An example can be taken from the two most important steps in the life of a film: the acceptance of the script and the submission of the completed film. In their book *The Soviet Film Industry*, Paul Babitsky and John Rimberg describe ten steps a script had to pass through in the mid-1950s before receiving final approval: the script began with the editor of the script department at the studio, proceeded to the editor-in-chief, then to the editorial board, next to the studio's artistic council, and finally landed on the desk of the studio's director; he, however, could not sign a contract until the exact same process had been repeated at the higher body, the Main Cinema Administration (Goskino). At each step revisions could be demanded, and the process could take two or three years (Babitsky and Rimberg 110). Although some streamlining had occurred by Tarkovsky's time, the script still had to pass through several stages for approval both in the studio and at Goskino.

Neya Zorkaya described to us the actual process as it often happened in practice rather than according to regulations. The script was not simply an individual proposal for a film, which could be accepted or rejected with no consequences. Before it was written, a synopsis had to have been approved by the studio and, most important, included in its production plan; a script therefore had to be produced, and, moreover, by a certain date. But scriptwriters often worked down to the wire, facing the studio and Goskino with failure to fulfill the plan if the script was not accepted on time. Working against a deadline, everyone gave approval, sometimes without even reading the script! The film industry's spectacular growth in the late 1950s and 1960s also made complete oversight extremely difficult. While Romanov was a hard-working chairman who personally screened every one of the some 120 feature films released annually (denying approval to many), his successor, Yermash, often allowed films to be released without seeing them (Golovskoy 13–14).

Once the "literary script" had been passed, the greatest control during the preproduction period was exercised over the budget, which was negotiated through endless correspondence between the studio and Goskino, ending up with Goskino trimming a usually inflated studio proposal. Goskino could and did show its dissatisfaction with Tarkovsky by cutting back his proposed budgets, forcing him to cut scenes from his films, such as the opening Kulikovo Field battle scene in *Andrei Roublev*. But over the years Tarkovsky and his devoted crew learned to work within the modest budgets allotted him. And, in the now famous case of the reshooting of *Stalker*, he managed to get an extra 300,000 rubles for making what was practically a new film (see chapter 8).

During the actual shooting, however, remarkably little supervision was provided either by the studio or by Goskino. No one from Goskino was present to make certain that the director shot what had been approved in the script. Tarkovsky was famous for rewriting his scripts, so that the difference between what had been approved and what ended up as the final product was often substantial. On the set he was in total creative control, although financial constraints often made the work frustratingly difficult.

Tarkovsky's serious troubles usually began with the submission of the completed film, which, like the script, had to make its way through the studio bureaucracy and then all the way through Goskino to its board and chairman, who had to sign an acceptance (*priyomka*) and give the film a category for release.[3] Though this was a crucial step in the life of a film, it did not necessarily *guarantee* its release: the acceptance was given for *Andrei Roublev*, but after the scandal broke (see chapter 5) the film was shelved anyway. At almost any stage in the acceptance process, the director could be asked to make cuts or changes—as Tarkovsky always was—and the film could be held up. Here, unlike most directors, Tarkovsky was quite intransigent, managing to make only very minor cuts and still get the films approved. As the acceptance and the film's category also determined the scriptwriter's royalties and the financial bonuses and prizes to be awarded to the whole production team (which were not paid until the film had been released), Tarkovsky's insistence on the inviolability of his art took a tremendous emotional as well as financial toll on others beside himself, and his crews must have been devoted indeed to continue working for someone who was almost certain to have problems with every film he made.[4] No wonder he angrily complained to Yermash (letter of June 1983) that only *Solaris* had been awarded the highest category and a proper distribution, while all his other films were in the second category, and sometimes released in even fewer than the minimum number of prints for that category (A. T., *Le temps scellé* 232–33).

Stalker was released in 196 prints (*O Tarkovskom* 259) and sold about 3 million tickets (Golovskoy 61)—average for a new release. Considering the fact that *Stalker* was a "difficult" film which, if made in the West, would have played only in art houses, Tarkovsky should have been pleased that so many people saw his film. Even so, he clearly had a major problem in the distribution network, especially outside the major cities: upon seeing *Stalker* many distributors walked out shaking their heads as someone asked, "Who is going to see this garbage?" (*O Tarkovskom* 259). While the intelligentsia and educated, primarily urban, viewers flocked to Tarkovsky's films, the more philistine distributors (and Party officials in the provinces, who also had the right to pass judgment on the films shown there) mirrored the average viewer's demand for less challenging fare. And this had more to do with the realities of the marketplace than with ideology and censorship, even in the Soviet Union.

Although Tarkovsky over the years complained frequently about his treatment by Goskino and its chairman, he, too, exercised a form of "self-censorship" by never pointing a finger at the power which stood over Goskino—the Communist Party itself. In the whole Soviet governmental structure, real power always resided with the Central Committee and the First Secretary of the Communist Party. The two chairmen of Goskino in the 1960s and 1970s both came from the Party's Central Committee: Romanov from its Propaganda Department, and Yermash from the Department of Culture (Golovskoy 13–14). In the huge Central Committee apparatus, the film sector in the Department of Culture was charged with the day-to-day supervision of the cinema industry (Golovskoy 17), with the Propaganda Department keeping a close eye on it as well. Their assignment was to check the ideological content of films, and they generally played a role detrimental to artistic creativity. Since in the Party apparatus departments of culture with film sectors existed on the republic, district, and local (city) levels, they could, and often did, play a very meddlesome role in a film's life, holding up release or even banning a film in a city or region. Yermash himself complained that any local Party secretary could create trouble for a film if his mother-in-law didn't happen to like it!

Since the 1930s, ideology had always taken precedence over economic concerns in the cinema industry, which explains why films might be banned even at the expense of tremendous financial losses. In general, changes in Party leadership and periods of tightening and relaxation of ideological and political controls in the whole country were reflected rather closely in all the arts, and in "the most important of the arts" in particular. That the Secretary of the Communist Party himself would be concerned with any individual film was not at all strange if one considers historically the close oversight by the Party of the cinema industry. After hailing *Chapayev* as a great Soviet film, from the mid-thirties Stalin took an increasingly active role in cinema, personally becoming its main arbiter and censor. In the immediate postwar period (1946–53) he even became the main hero in numerous grandiose "artistic documentaries"—hideously artificial and bombastic odes to Stalinism—and the Stalin cult was further bolstered by biographical films about Russian historical figures (Kenez, chapter 11). In this "period of few films," if one discounts some thirty photographed concerts or theatrical performances, only 124 feature films were produced in the whole Soviet Union (Kenez 227). Soviet filmmaking reached its nadir and almost died in 1951 and 1952, with fewer than 10 true feature films produced.[5]

Stalin's death in 1953, followed by Nikita Khrushchev's denunciation of Stalinism at the 20th Communist Party Congress in 1956, initiated a political and cultural "Thaw" of unprecedented proportions. Without rejecting socialist realism, artists called for sincerity, truthfulness, and a more realistic portrayal of modest heroes and their daily lives. The cinema industry boomed. Studios and cinemas were built, scripts were commissioned, and many young (and not-so-young) directors were allowed to make their first films. In 1955 sixty-five feature films were produced, to increase to well over a hundred per year throughout the 1960s (Cohen 231, 459). The number of movie theaters doubled between 1955 (59,000) and 1965 (118,000) (Cohen 294).

Tarkovsky was indeed fortunate to have studied at VGIK (Vsesoyuzny gosudarstvenny institut kinematografii: the All-Union State Cinema Institute) from 1954 to 1960, and to have made his debut in the most liberal political and cultural climate since the 1920s. Meteoric success came in 1962, when he became the youngest Soviet filmmaker to receive a major international prize, the Golden Lion in Venice for *Ivan's Childhood*. Even though the film's complex cinematic style led to mixed reviews at home, international recognition immediately established him as a major director. But the honeymoon with the cinema bureaucracy was quickly over, as the Thaw itself was shortly to end. As early as 1962 Khrushchev was already trying to restrain the struggle for artistic freedom, singling out Tarkovsky's teacher Mikhail Romm for criticism and reminding everyone that films were first and foremost "an effective ideological weapon and a mass medium of education" (Cohen 291). Then Khrushchev was replaced in 1964 by a more conservative Party secretary, Leonid Brezhnev, and Tarkovsky's second film, *Andrei Roublev*, was caught in the increasingly conservative political climate and the tightening of ideological controls of the late 1960s: the film was almost released twice, but ended up "on the shelf" for five years.

One could argue that changes at the highest levels of the Party percolated down and affected every aspect of Soviet life, culture, and industry. Yet during what is now called "the period of stagnation" (*zastoy*)—which lasted into the early 1980s—despite all the official emphasis on stylistic and thematic conformity, Tarkovsky's original and daring films were not banned. Like Goskino or any bureaucracy, the Party apparatus was not a monolith carrying out one prescribed policy. In interview both Zorkaya and Turovskaya agree that one should not underestimate the chaotic unpredictability of the system, whether it be the Party or the cinema bureaucracy. There is often no logical explanation for why some films were banned and others not. Compared to those artists whose careers were decimated in the 1960s and 1970s, Tarkovsky seems to have been relatively fortunate after *Roublev*. Occasional support of influential people in the industry, particularly at the studio, continued interest from foreign distributors, and a series of foreign awards enhanced Tarkovsky's stature at home and thus played a substantial role in enabling him to go on making films during the period of stagnation, though his films were notoriously "difficult" and Goskino released them grudgingly and only after bitter and lengthy debates.[6]

Tarkovsky's career is in many ways a paradox: for every film after *Ivan's Childhood* he had to fight to overcome the obstacles that were continually put in his way in either the film's creation or its release, or both, and many cherished projects (especially Dostoyevsky's *The Idiot*) were never accomplished. Yet each film was finally released in a form that was essentially true to his original artistic intentions, and he remained a respected and admired figure within the film industry even as he complained vociferously of bureaucratic harassment—so much so that, according to Turovskaya, he was envied by less fortunate directors, even in the later stages of his career, as "the darling of Goskino" (Interview). What would Orson Welles have given (as some cynical Western commentators have mused) to have made "only" five films in twenty years—*all of them* with adequate, if rarely generous, budgets, shot under conditions of complete creative freedom, and ending up on the screen in a form that respected their original intentions rather than being mutilated, often beyond recognition, by outside hands! Tarkovsky certainly saw himself as a martyr in his last years and, whether consciously or not, helped to foster a myth of his own persecution that was rather uncritically accepted at face value by well-meaning foreigners (and is now being vigorously recycled for home consumption). Yet, even if one must reject the more extreme claims of martyrdom, there is no reason not to acknowledge the very real struggles and sacrifices he made for his art: despite the frequent bureaucratic obstacles placed in his way, and without compromising, he made in the Soviet Union five outstanding feature films, all of which can be ranked among the best in contemporary Russian—and world—cinema.

Tarkovsky in the Context of Soviet Cinema: 1960s–1980s

Tarkovsky's early films, *The Steamroller and the Violin* and *Ivan's Childhood*, can both be seen as belonging to Soviet cinema of the liberal Thaw period of the late fifties and early sixties. His diploma film, *The Steamroller and the Violin*, reflects the popularity of children's films in the early 1960s. *Ivan's Childhood*, at least thematically, fits one of the most popular genres, the war film, and benefited from the domestic and international successes of predecessors such as Grigory Chukhrai's *Ballad of a Soldier* (*Ballada o soldate*, 1959),

Mikhail Kalatozov's *The Cranes Are Flying* (*Letyat zhuravli*, 1957), and Sergei Bondarchuk's *Fate of a Man* (*Sudba cheloveka*, 1959). But *Ivan's Childhood* significantly expands the stylistic experimentation in "poetic cinema" of Mikhail Kalatozov and his cinematographer, Sergei Urusevsky, while harking back, like them, to the exploration in montage and mise-en-scène of the 1920s. While generally denying the influence of Soviet filmmakers in his work, Tarkovsky readily acknowledged, in interviews and his own writings, the importance of Alexander Dovzhenko, a "poet" who explored, through the long take, the purely visual beauty of the cinematic image. Moreover, while arguing against the intellectual montage of Eisenstein, Tarkovsky was clearly also well aware of his theories on spatial relations within the frame and between shots and on the use of sound, and was even influenced by them (especially in *Ivan's Childhood* and *Andrei Roublev*). While, at times, looking for stylistic inspiration in the experimentation of the 1920s, literature and film in the Thaw period rejected the rigid socialist realism of the 1930s with its stereotyped heroes, calling instead for sincerity, truthfulness, and depiction of real individual human beings. Turovskaya calls this the period of "the privatization of the hero" (Interview). Tarkovsky's Ivan is but one example, albeit the most memorable, of this new type of "hero": a complex, flawed human being at the mercy of forces beyond his control.

While *Ivan's Childhood* can readily be compared with other films of the period, with *Andrei Roublev* Tarkovsky embarks on such an original creative quest, both stylistically and thematically, that direct comparisons with other concurrent films initially seem unrewarding. This is not to say that Tarkovsky was the sole creative genius of the late sixties, as this period too was marked by numerous innovative films such as Konchalovsky's *First Teacher* (*Pervy uchitel*, 1965), Larissa Shepitko's *Wings* (*Krylya*, 1966), Muratova's *Brief Encounters*, Askoldov's *Commissar*, Abuladze's *The Prayer* (*Molba*, 1968)—to mention just a few—and most important, Paradzhanov's *Shadows of Our Forgotten Ancestors* (*Teni zabytykh predkov*, 1965). But these films represent parallel yet often quite different explorations in film language.

Andrei Roublev was certainly antithetical to contemporaneous historical epics with their pompous nationalistic fervor—such as Sergei Bondarchuk's *War and Peace* (*Voyna i mir*, 1967). But because of its monumental scope it couldn't easily be compared with the more personal, even intimate, films typical of the period. From the beginning it was a difficult film to categorize, both hailed and vilified—according to one of the best "sixties" critics, Lev Anninsky—for what it was *not*, rather than for what it was. In retrospect, Anninsky argues that *Andrei Roublev* was the quintessential sixties film, incorporating and fearlessly carrying to their extremes all of the sixties' concerns: the tragedy of the individual; rejection of stereotypes and canons; the attempt to combine the poetic and the naturalistic, documentary realism and intellectual analysis (Anninsky 190–96). It was a truly "national film" and a harbinger of the return to the Russian "soil" which was to become so popular in the village prose and films of the late sixties and seventies (199).

It is now widely recognized by Russian critics that, beginning with *Andrei Roublev,* Tarkovsky's work was misunderstood and criticized not only because of the increasingly conservative political and ideological climate of the Brezhnev era; he was a man ahead of his time, who refused to be constrained by existing stylistic and thematic conventions in pursuit of visions which were to prove quite prophetic. He broke the canons of existing genres: in *Andrei Roublev,* a monumental historical epic in its own way, he deflated the artificial, self-satisfied, and grandiose pomposity of that genre in Soviet cinema. Even when he worked within the fairly safe and popular science fiction genre, as in *Solaris,* he retarded the action with his long takes and slow camera movements, and subordinated the plot (where almost nothing *happens*) to his philosophical ruminations, once again frustrating the genre expectations of both viewers and critics.

In the period of stagnation, typified by mostly low-key realistic social melodramas, comedies, or screen adaptations of popular literary classics (a safe way of either avoiding political issues or examining them obliquely through "Aesopian" language), Tarkovsky's *Mirror* shocked audiences with its stylistic complexity and its unabashed subjectivity. Its only possible precursor was Igor Talankin's *Daytime Stars* (1968), which, like *Mirror,* mixed past and present, dream and reality, and was built on the principle of interior monologue (Zak, *Andrei Tarkovsky* 18–19). But Talankin's film was destroyed by editorial cuts (Demidova Interview) and pales in comparison with the more daring *Mirror. Mirror*'s true impact may be surfacing only now as filmmakers increasingly reject realistic linear narrative in cinema and experiment with the use of documentary footage in "fictional" films. *Stalker,* the last film Tarkovsky shot in the Soviet Union, brings to the forefront spiritual and religious concerns which the Polish director Andrzej Wajda describes as his "throwing down the gauntlet" to all of us who live in a technological, materialistic world. Among Russian film buffs, *Stalker* has become a kind of cult figure and film, foreshadowing Chernobyl and the ecological, social, and moral collapse of the Soviet Union.

It is ironic to note that, while viewers, critics, and film students eagerly embraced Tarkovsky in the glasnost period, his fellow directors have been more reserved in recognizing the significance of his work for Soviet cinema. Critics like Turovskaya and Zorkaya point out that in the close-knit cinema world there is much lingering envy and resentment of Tarkovsky's success abroad and what is perceived as his special treatment at home. Tarkovsky himself contributed to his lack of popularity among directors by his condescending attitude to contemporary Soviet cinema in general.[7] Only Paradzhanov and Ioseliani were deemed worthy of his attention. It is not surprising that Tarkovsky admired these two directors, with whom he shared an insistence on the primacy of the visual image, even if each developed that interest in parallel and distinctively different ways.

For many, even among his contemporaries, and especially for those of the new generation of directors who are eager to discover what they see as the

Hollywood formula for success, Tarkovsky seems to be a part of the creative rebellion of the past, not someone who can point the way in the insane, unstable, frighteningly free present they find themselves in. Only a handful of the currently working directors want to be or can be fruitfully linked with him, though many others freely acknowledge his importance as a moral examplar and praise his creative vision.

Two filmmakers who could be called "disciples," Ivan Dykhovychny (*The Black Monk* [*Cherny monakh*], 1988) and Konstantin Lopushansky (*Letters from a Dead Man* [*Pisma mertvogo cheloveka*], 1987, and *A Museum Visitor* [*Posetitel muzeya*], 1989), imitate Tarkovsky's cinematic style—the long takes, and the slow-moving camera lingering over the landscape—but fail to attain the organic inner unity of Tarkovsky's imagery. *A Museum Visitor*, Lopushansky's attempt to pay homage to Tarkovsky, specifically to *Stalker*, was an embarrassing failure at the XVI International Moscow Film Festival in 1989, where for the first time in the thirty-year history of the festival, a Soviet film failed to win the Grand Prize. With that film worshipful imitation reached a dead end. In his recent *Moscow Parade* (*Prorva*, 1992) Dykhovychny used Vadim Yusov, Tarkovsky's cameraman, to shoot a very different kind of film. Dykhovychny successfully exposes the horrors of Stalinism behind a lush, glittering, visually spectacular facade. Although any literal trace of Tarkovsky's style is gone, Dykhovychny has clearly absorbed his message on the importance of the visual image itself.

Alexander Sokurov, a talented filmmaker nurtured by Tarkovsky who is often seen as his main "disciple," rejects the idea of direct influence and resists any comparison of his work with Tarkovsky's; for his generation Tarkovsky was important as a "moral force," a kind of "prophet" who discovered the cinema's visual potential (Interview). Although Sokurov too makes considerable demands on the patience and visual acuity of his audience, and there is much that seems "Tarkovskian" about *Days of the Eclipse* (*Dni zatmeniya*, 1988) in particular, Sokurov's recent films—such as *Save and Protect* (*Spasi i sokhrani*, 1989) and *The Second Circle* (*Krug vtoroy*, 1991)—are clearly moving in thematic and stylistic directions of their own. For all his expressed desire to dissociate himself artistically from Tarkovsky, Sokurov still unquestionably seeks to play a very similar public role as a true "auteur" in a commercial and philistine cinema industry. With his dark hair, mustache, and piercing eyes, Sokurov has even begun to look like Tarkovsky!

Biography—A Russian Saint's Life?

The myth of Tarkovsky the martyred artist is supported by an idealized biography—a composite of facts often used to misinterpret or give a pseudo-biographical interpretation to his films. A limited nucleus of these facts is selected to piece together a portrait of a highly educated and cultured member of the Russian intelligentsia, a deeply spiritual person, who loved and revered his parents and coworkers—a myth uncritically recycled, for example, by Mark Le Fanu: "Andrei's own internal spiritual equilibrium seems not to have been affected by his parents' separation, for he continued to revere both with an intensity and honor attested to by numerous homages in his work" (16). Little is said publicly about his two marriages and relationships with his children. Family, friends, and coworkers who are writing memoirs stand in awe of Tarkovsky's persona, writing off any problems or negative traits to the mistreatment he suffered at the hands of the bureaucrats. In private, however, some who were close to him will talk of a brilliant, volatile, extremely complex individual with sado-masochistic tendencies who fought many of his personal demons on the screen. His bisexuality, for example, still remains a well-hidden secret in the extremely homophobic Russian society. Because Tarkovsky himself so frequently insisted that he was never able to separate his art from his life, a closer look at his personality, upbringing, and family history will surely yield a richer interpretation of his films.

Tarkovsky was born on April 4, 1932, in the village of Zavrazhye on the river Volga near the town of Yuryevets. He was born into an educated family, typically representative of the old Russian intelligentsia. His father, Arseny Tarkovsky, was an unpublished poet who made his living as a translator, while his mother, Maria Ivanovna (Vishnyakova), was to spend her life working as an editor for the First State Publishing House in Moscow. His parents moved to the country for the birth, since Maria Ivanovna's stepfather was a doctor who lived and worked in a large village. A diary she kept during the first few months of Andrei's life shows a happy family with a noisy, at times difficult, baby. The father described him: "eyes dark, blue-grey, grey-green, narrow; looks like a Tartar and a rat; looks angrily . . . A good mouth. . . . (*O Tarkovskom* 17). Both parents shared the care of Andrei, with his father even changing diapers! But this idyllic existence was shortlived, with the diary stopping in June when his mother ran out of paper and his father returned to Moscow to work. Tarkovsky's sister notes that their father left in early June, and could not return to the village anymore; the parents saw each other in Moscow only in the fall (*O Tarkovskom* 29). Numerous critics have pointed out that Tarkovsky's love of nature stems from spending his childhood in the country, but this period seems to have been quite brief: in the documentary by Donatella Baglivo, *Andrei Tarkovsky: A Poet in Cinema*, Tarkovsky relates that he spent the first two or three years of his life in the countryside and was to return for a time during the war. However, the Tarkovskys were clearly city people and, like so many Muscovites, guests summering in a countryside they loved and idealized.

When Andrei was four and his younger sister Marina just two, their parents separated and later divorced. Their father remarried while their mother never did, devoting herself to her work and her children. By all reports she was an independent, strong personality. When asked about the role women played in his life, Tarkovsky would point out that he was raised in a totally matriarchal household, with grandmother, mother, and sister. Relations between his parents seem to have remained cordial, and Andrei did spend time with his father, but the reason for the divorce was a taboo subject. His sister Marina recalls in interview that they never once talked about it! Although Andrei as a child may not have known the story behind his father's sudden abandonment of the family,[8] he must have become aware that his father was living with another woman, and, according to all accounts, Andrei disliked her intensely. He seems to have had more cordial relations with his father's third wife, Tatyana Ozerskaya, a well-known translator, but by the time his father married her, Andrei was almost an adult.

The major trauma of the young Andrei's life was quite clearly the dissolution of the family and an early childhood with a mostly absent father. During World War II the family moved out of Moscow to the provincial town of Yuryevets while Arseny was at the front. Tarkovsky himself recalls the war as a period of waiting for two things: the war to end and his father to come back (interview in Baglivo). Too young himself to fight, Tarkovsky belonged to a generation that admired the sacrifices of fathers who fought in the war, and when his own father came back, with a medal and without a leg, Tarkovsky must have shared his peers' love and pride. But there was no family reunion for the Tarkovskys. The fact that *his* father did not come back to the family must have been very painful. Neya Zorkaya relates that Arseny did not even come to the station to meet Andrei coming back from the wartime evacuation, and instead sent a friend who saw an angry, cornered "little wolf" (Interview 1991).

A family friend describes the young Andrei as restrained and cool with people, a loner; he was also touchy and stubborn, giving his mother "lots of grief" (*O Tarkovskom* 31). He was clearly an energetic (even perhaps, according to his sister, hyperactive), recalcitrant child, often rejecting his mother's attempts, so typical of the Russian intelligentsia, to cultivate in him an interest in the arts. As a teenager he studied, but then gave up music and painting, preferring to keep the company of local toughs, to play ball and get into fights (Marina Tarkovskaya Interview). His sister rejects the depiction of Andrei as a quiet, intellectual boy in Andrei Voznesensky's poem "White Sweater" ("Bely sviter," *O Tarkovskom* 37–39). Tarkovsky's youthful rebellion against the "cultured" matriarchal environment was to find its way into his diploma film, *The Steamroller and the Violin*.

Like most educated Moscow households, theirs was full of Russian classical literature (especially Pushkin, Turgenev, and Tolstoy, as well as children's writers like Marshak and Chukovsky), which Maria Ivanovna started reading to the children when they were very young. His sister remembers that the young Andrei was quiet only when reading. Their mother took them to concerts and opera, and Andrei developed a love of Tchaikovsky and Russian music, but then moved to Beethoven, Mozart, and, most important, Bach. Maria Ivanovna had apparently decided that Andrei would be an artist of some sort, and she spared no energy and expense, even during wartime, to prepare him for his calling. She herself had written poetry as a student at the Institute for Literature (called Advanced Literary Courses in the 1930s), but she never finished her education, and became an editor. According to Tarkovsky, his mother had completed her coursework but, because of family commitments, was not able to satisfy all the requirements to receive a diploma and, thus, had to give up her literary work (filmed interview in Baglivo's *Andrei Tarkovsky: A Poet in Cinema*). Perhaps for Maria Ivanovna her son was also meant to fulfill her own failed ambitions as well as to equal his father's creativity. Later in life Tarkovsky admitted that his mother was responsible for his becoming an artist, although as a child and probably even as an adult he must have resented her persistent, even oppressive, mentoring. Alexander Gordon, his friend and future brother-in-law, observed that there was an unspoken "cult" of Andrei at home, but that his mother was also a very strict disciplinarian (*O Tarkovskom* 46). From an early age the women's love that he found so stifling also convinced him of his artistic genius.

As a teenager and a young man Andrei seemed to prefer the company of his father: together they pored over art books which the father began to buy and listened to music from his wonderful record collection. Arseny also read his own poetry beautifully. Andrei idolized this dashing, handsome man, acquiring from him a taste for the finer things in life—fancy clothes, beautiful pens, and books. His sister states that he even imitated his father's handwriting. Yuri Kochevrin, Andrei's high-school friend, remembers him constantly carrying a collection of his father's poetry. To what extent the father truly reciprocated the son's adoration is not known, but in the autobiographical *Mirror*, the father is an absent and a distant figure whom the son clearly misses. There seems to be some disagreement even among family members and friends on the true nature of the father-son relationship. While his father kept supporting the family financially, his visits were generally limited to birthdays and other family occasions. Although Arseny Tarkovsky's third wife mentions in interview their frequent visits *together* to Arseny's first family and talks of a loving relationship between father and son, one might just wonder how much the young Andrei resented these visits by the father's new family. Again and again family intimates identify the main trauma of young Andrei's life as Arseny's desertion of the family. But Andrei did not seem to place the blame solely on his father, with whom he felt a closer personal affinity than with his mother: in the autobiographical *Mirror* the mother's aloofness, and her friend's accusation that she drove away her husband with her "emancipated ways," may be Tarkovsky's rationalization for his father's actions. Tarkovsky's mother was clearly a very strong, self-reliant, unsentimental woman and, although beautiful, some add "unfeminine" and "cold."

Unlike his father, Andrei's mother cared little for material things or finery, preferring to spend her meager earnings (and freelance supplement) on Andrei's lessons and theater. Marina, in interview, called her a "nihilist" (*nigilistka*), referring to the liberated nineteenth-century women who rejected their traditional female roles to become revolutionaries and terrorists and added (with both pride and consternation in her voice) that they didn't even have curtains in the house until she sewed them. Clearly very sensitive to appearances, Andrei must have been embarrassed by the family's relative, though genteel, poverty and their modest two-room communal apartment on the outskirts of town.

As a young man Tarkovsky became quite a dandy (*stilyaga*), dressing in a rebellious and hip fifties fashion of tight pants (worn short to show white socks), broad-shouldered jackets, and either very thin or extremely wide Hawaiian-design ties, professing a generally bored anti-intellectualism and a great love of American jazz (Rausch Interview, 1991). His first wife adds that since he didn't have the money for the complete "look," Andrei would pick individual pieces of outrageous clothing. Alexander Gordon remembers at their entrance examination into VGIK a young man wearing a bright yellow jacket standing off by himself with a copy of *War and Peace* under his arm (*O Tarkovskom* 41). His *stilyaga* stage may have reflected his desire to stand out of the crowd, to shock the staid Soviet society, as well as his family. Throughout his life Tarkovsky surrounded himself with beautiful objects, especially in his dacha, enjoying—whenever he could afford it—the life of a Russian country squire. Like his father, he was proud of his aristocratic heritage (they believed that the "Tarky" were princes in the Caucasus dating back to Ivan the Terrible's time) (Zorkaya Interview). Interestingly, Tarkovsky's sister Marina calls this a family legend, denying their noble roots, but points out that both grandfathers were highly educated representatives of the Russian intelligentsia. Tarkovsky could justifiably feel himself an heir to all the best in the Russian cultural heritage, although it was only upon enrolling in VGIK that he was to find his true calling.

After finishing high school, in 1951, Tarkovsky first entered the Institute for Eastern Studies, not only because he was interested in the East (as he was to remain all his life) but also because it was a prestigious, elite institution (Marina Tarkovskaya Interview). But his initial enthusiasm quickly disappeared when he was confronted with the prospect of pedantic, long-term study. He left the institute in his second year and, in desperation, his mother "exiled" him to Siberia to work on a geological expedition—without even a pair of warm boots, according to a friend of the family (*O Tarkovskom* 33). Although he was already experiencing trouble with his lungs, Tarkovsky did not get sick on the expedition; instead he remembered the months he spent in Siberia very fondly: there he had a chance to think about his future, and he came back with a determination to study directing at VGIK. Both parents supported him in his decision.

In 1954, out of some five hundred applicants, the famous director Mikhail Romm selected a group of fifteen to study under him. Besides his father, Romm was to be the other great influence and male role model in Tarkovsky's life (Irma Rausch and Marina Tarkovskaya interviews). While in the West Romm is best known for his films on Lenin and other orthodox socialist realist fare, he is perceived as a tragic figure by many Soviet film scholars. He was a true intellectual with broad interests, a brilliant teacher, and a great director who finally, past the age of sixty, was to undergo a total creative transformation, bursting out of the conformist Stalinist mold to make two powerful, humanistic films: *Nine Days in One Year* (*Devyat dnei odnogo goda*, 1961) and *Ordinary Fascism* (*Obyknovenny fashizm*, 1964). But Tarkovsky studied with Romm before the latter's creative "conversion." What could he have learned from the director of *Lenin in October*?

Romm's most important lesson was that it is, in fact, impossible to teach someone to become a director. Tarkovsky's fellow students—his first wife and his friend, Alexander Gordon—remember that Romm, unlike most other VGIK master teachers, encouraged his students to think for themselves, to develop their individual talents, and even to criticize his work (a process that backfired when his class mercilessly tore apart his film *Murder on Dante Street*: Rausch Interview). Tarkovsky flourished in this unconstrained creative environment, so unusual for the normally stodgy and conservative VGIK. Convinced of Tarkovsky's extraordinary talent, Romm was to be his ardent supporter until his death in 1971. In the often-told story of the first official screening of Tarkovsky's first feature film, *Ivan's Childhood*, Romm exhorted an audience of professional filmmakers and critics to recognize a new talent and to "remember the name: Tarkovsky" (Zorkaya, "Zametki" 144).

The almost instantaneous success of his first feature film made Tarkovsky a public persona, and the details of his private life become quite elusive. Little concrete biographical information has been published, and when it did appear, it was generally in the context of his work on a film, focusing—particularly in the foreign press—on his herculean struggles against an uncaring bureaucracy, his ability to persevere and to suffer for his art. Soviet criticism generally avoided all but the most basic biographical information. Even with the recent removal of all ideological and social constraints, Soviet critics have been reluctant to delve into Tarkovsky's personal life or his complex personality. While in the West the private lives of famous people are constant objects of scrutiny and gossip, much of it published in unsavory magazines, in the Soviet Union no such pulp magazines existed until very recently. Those friends, critics, and coworkers who had frequent contact with Tarkovsky and were witness to events in his private life have been reluctant to reveal all they know, whether out of natural reticence, personal loyalty, or the desire to maintain the public image of the great martyred artist. This certainly was true of almost all of some forty individuals we interviewed. Not many would go on record with negative characterizations, although privately some portrayed a much more complex and tormented Tarkovsky, reserving their bile for the controversial figure of his second wife.[9]

Tarkovsky's published diary (*Martyrolog* in German and *Time within Time* in English), edited primarily by his widow, contains well-expurgated selections from the voluminous diary (twelve large folios and four smaller volumes) that he kept from 1970 to his death.[10] Not only does she purposely omit information on Tarkovsky's private life, and his scathing characterizations of many of his contemporaries, but her stated goal is to counteract the "so-called friends and students" who she claims were distorting and falsifying the truth about Tarkovsky, and to let him speak to the readers in his own voice (*Martyrolog* 7). She was also outraged at some of the libelous accusations leveled at her—and also at Tarkovsky—by Shavkat Abdusalamov, the short-lived art director on *Stalker*, whose memoir appeared in the collection *O Tarkovskom* edited by Tarkovsky's sister, Marina (Larissa Tarkovskaya Interview). The long-standing rift between Tarkovsky's second wife (and Tarkovsky himself when he was alive) and his sister Marina,[11] between the keepers of the Tarkovsky flame (and fortune) in Moscow and abroad, has created a tense, competitive atmosphere in which the "truth" about Tarkovsky's personality, life, and work has become highly selective and subjective.

It is in this still unresolved and highly charged atmosphere that we attempt to objectivize the man and the myth, by focusing solely on biographical information which is in some way significant for his work. Clearly the major childhood trauma of his parents' divorce resulted in complex, often estranged relations with both parents. In a rare personal admission Tarkovsky writes in his diary in September 1970 that he hasn't seen his father for a long time, that he still feels like a child with his parents, who treat him as such. He loves them and they love him, but they are frightened and ill at ease with each other (*Martyrolog* 51).[12] Their differences were to remain unresolved even after his "confessional" film *Mirror*, in which, as Olga Surkova points out (188), Tarkovsky provides only the superficial facts of his biography and fails to delve into the internal dynamics of the family relations and problems, preferring instead to blame History, Fate, Original Sin. . . . But, instead of faulting Tarkovsky for not revealing the deepest recesses of his soul in the film, one might conclude that the film benefits from the broader vision, the shared "autobiography" of his generation with which we can all identify.

It is a well-known fact that the adult Tarkovsky followed in his father's footsteps by leaving his first wife and son (Arseny, born in 1962) and remarrying: he had married his classmate Irma Rausch in 1957 while they were still students at VGIK, but left her during the shooting of *Andrei Roublev* for Larissa Pavlovna Yegorkina, an assistant working on the film. Irma Rausch, by all accounts—including her own—was quite similar both physically and in personality to Tarkovsky's mother, with whom she remained on close terms even after the divorce. Both women were independent, self-reliant, emotionally reserved, even somewhat distant; Irma recalls her mother-in-law berating her for being the same kind of "fool" she had been in her own marriage. An early warning of marital difficulties to come may have been Tarkovsky's desire for Irma to become an actress, and not a director—which he did not consider a suitable occupation for a woman (Rausch Interview).

Tarkovsky's second wife, Larissa, may at first have seemed a welcome change from these disturbingly independent personalities,[13] becoming a caretaker even on the set of *Andrei Roublev* and nurturing him when he injured his leg falling off a horse, responding to his every whim. She continued to play this role throughout their life together, and he came in turn to depend upon her in all practical aspects of life;[14] yet he must also have deeply resented her total control, for, by all accounts, theirs was a stormy relationship on the set and off. Olga Surkova points out that significantly Tarkovsky chose not to deal with this relationship in his confessional *Mirror* (though Larissa does play the role of the unsympathetic doctor's wife in that film) and only in his last film presents a figure clearly modeled on his second wife. Tarkovsky married Larissa in 1970, and their son Andrei was born the same year. Repeating his father's actions, Tarkovsky was to have a complex relationship with his first family, visiting, but basically neglecting, his oldest son Arseny; he was to live out his days with his second wife, and even after his death, she remains the loyal guardian of his personal and professional reputation, attempting to control the "facts" of his biography and the shape of his posthumous career.

Although his relationships with his mother and his wives are clearly reflected in his films, Soviet critics have a tendency to carry the directly autobiographical correspondences too far. Olga Surkova points out that Tarkovsky, in fact, produces a pseudo-autobiography, creating an image of himself as an artist, but not trusting himself as a simple man (189). Quoting Writer in *Stalker*, she comments that Tarkovsky, in his own way, "preached vegetarianism, but dreamed about a piece of juicy meat." He would certainly not be the first artist who strove for a higher, spiritual existence only to be held prisoner of the flesh, tormented by questions of his own sexual proclivities. In his films women's sexuality is rather threatening, and women are presented in a positive light only in their nurturing, supportive roles of wife and mother.

The family relationship which is most significant for understanding Tarkovsky's creative drive is the one with his father. On a personal level he must have sought the love of a father who had abandoned him, and on a professional level he tried to emulate and compete with his father, becoming literally "a poet in cinema." There is in fact a closer relationship between Tarkovsky's imagery and his father's poetry than has been pointed out to date even by the observant Russian critics. Significantly, fame came to father and son in the same year, 1962, when the father's first book of poetry was finally published and the son's first feature film was released. Was Tarkovsky's intransigence in fighting for his films a response to his father's ineffectiveness in having his poetry published? Despite Tarkovsky's statements that his father was the greatest contemporary Russian poet, he was in fact only a very good poet, overshadowed by a slightly older generation whose truly great poets—Mandelshtam, Akhmatova, Tsvetaeva, and Pasternak—met tragic fates. Arseny was left on the sidelines, a survivor, who never seemed to have risked anything for his art— "the old maid of Russian poetry," as the critic Vladimir Solovyov unkindly, and perhaps unfairly, calls him. This seemingly harsh judgment can be understood only within the Russian context, where poets and writers, not only in the Soviet period but in Tsarist Russia, were honored for suffering for their art. Did Tarkovsky inherit his father's sense for self-preservation, at the same time that he fought so mightily for his films and willingly accepted the aura of martyrdom that has become inseparable from discussion of his films, both in the Soviet Union and elsewhere?

At this point it is worth noting that a composite Tarkovsky biography, created through interviews and published memoirs, begins to resemble, even in our own rendering, a kind of medieval Russian saint's life, with typical hagiographic elements: the saint's—here the artist's—special calling that is somehow presaged even in childhood, his extraordinary talents and abilities. In describing the young Andrei, family and friends focus on his perfect pitch, his far-ranging intelligence and talent, his interest in things mystical, and even a kind of sixth sense.

While the saint creates miracles, he must also suffer for this. Tarkovsky himself originally titled his diaries in Russian *Martirolog*:[15] "Pretentious and false as a title," as he himself acknowledged, "but let it stay there as a reminder of my ineradicable, futile worthlessness" (*Time within Time* 87— hereafter cited as *TWT*). This formulaic and aggressive self-deprecation is reminiscent of Dostoyevsky's Underground Man (from *Notes from the Underground*) and the spiteful narrator of *The Adolescent*. Despite the genuine sense of despair and frustration that emerges from the diary, it also chronicles an active and even privileged existence—especially in such areas as travel—and no doubt directors such as Paradzhanov, languishing in prison, or Askoldov, deprived of any possibility of making films, would gladly have exchanged Tarkovsky's martyrdom for their own.[16]

Once again, we are not attempting to deny the very real hardships and sufferings that Tarkovsky underwent in his later career, or to ignore the petty vindictiveness, jealousy, and hostility that he encountered from the bureaucrats with whom he had to deal. The cat-and-mouse game played with him over whether or not he would be allowed to make *Nostalghia* and the deliberate emotional cruelty inflicted on him in separating him from his son after his decision to remain in the West are certainly unforgivable and helped to fuel the sense of persecution that he experienced so acutely in the last years of his life.

Tarkovsky unquestionably *did* struggle, *did* fight the bureaucrats, *did* persevere against heavy odds in bringing his creative concepts to fruition. After the relatively quick completion of *Ivan's Childhood*, each of his films took years to realize (see the creative histories in the individual chapters), and many projects—potentially his best films—were stonewalled, such as Dostoyevsky's *The Idiot* and Bulgakov's *The Master and Margarita*. Yet those years were also filled with more awards and recognition abroad, if not at home, than any contemporary Soviet director had attained. In his diary Tarkovsky lists some twenty-three international prizes between 1961 and 1980. Some of his most highly respected awards include the Golden Lion in Venice for *Ivan's Childhood* (1962), the Donatello Prize (1980), and several different prizes at Cannes for *Andrei Roublev, Solaris, Stalker, Nostalghia*, and *The Sacrifice*.

At a time when travel abroad was reserved for officially approved artists, Tarkovsky, thanks to his international awards, was able to travel widely in the 1970s and early 1980s—to Italy, France, Poland, Sweden, Britain, and elsewhere. He was one of only a few directors allowed to make a coproduction in the West, and between 1979 and 1983 he made several trips to Italy planning and shooting a documentary, *Time of Travel* (1979), and then a feature film, *Nostalghia* (1983). By the late 1970s Tarkovsky was a highly respected, if controversial, director. He managed to stage *Hamlet* in Moscow in 1977, was allowed to reshoot *Stalker* (1977–78), and in 1981–82 lectured in the Advanced Courses for Scriptwriters and Directors at Goskino. And, though he complains in a letter to Yermash in 1983 that his films had systematically been denied proper theatrical distribution within the Soviet Union (*Le temps scellé* 232–35), they were nevertheless widely shown in other locations—including schools and film clubs with unlikely names such as the Aeronautics, Miners', or Construction institutes—as he notes in his diary after introducing the screenings or responding to questions afterwards.

The most obvious "persecution" occurred after he had finished *Nostalghia* and requested an extension on his visa and permit to work abroad. Although Larissa had finally been allowed to join him in Italy, their son Andrei and members of Larissa's family were denied permission to leave the Soviet Union. While waiting for the official answer, Tarkovsky pursued some of the many opportunities that were opening up for him in the West. He attended the Telluride Film Festival in Colorado as a guest, directed (with Claudio Abbado conducting) Mussorgsky's opera *Boris Godunov* at Covent Garden (which he was to reprise a year later), lectured on the Apocalypse at St. James's Church in London, and negotiated his last film, *The Sacrifice*. When official permission to work in the West was not forthcoming, he finally took a step he must have been considering for several years:[17] at a press conference in Italy in July 1984 he announced his intention of staying in the West, stressing that he was not a dissident and that his motives were artistic freedom and economic necessity. Committees were formed in the West to put pressure on the Soviet government to allow the family to be reunited, but this did not occur until after Tarkovsky had been diagnosed with terminal cancer in late 1985. Tarkovsky believed that he fell ill in order that he might be reunited with his son. He had just completed what was to be his last film, *The Sacrifice*, and was busily considering new film projects—*Hoffmanniana*, *The Temptation of St. Anthony*, a virtually wordless version of *Hamlet*, and even *The New Testament*.[18] He fought the cancer, undergoing painful chemotherapy, and when that failed, he sought alternative therapies, planning new films to the very end. He died on December 29, 1986, at the age of fifty-four.

Shaping an Aesthetics of Cinema

Tarkovsky's Pantheon

As a student at the Film Institute during the cultural and political "Thaw" of the later 1950s, Tarkovsky saw a fairly wide range of classic and foreign films, as well as the officially sanctioned and unofficial corpus of Soviet cinema. Titles and directors mentioned by his fellow students Irma Rausch and Alexander Gordon include American silent comedies, films by John Ford (including *The Grapes of Wrath*), *Citizen Kane* (which made a great impact), William Wyler's *The Little Foxes*, the French "poetic realists" of the 1930s, Jean Renoir and Jean Vigo, the major Italian neo-realists, and the "Polish School" of Andrzej Wajda and Andrzej Munk. The Moscow Film Festival of 1957 introduced a period of greater availability of recent work from the West, and Alexander Gordon remembers the late fifties as an exciting time, a real "cultural explosion"; they could now see the works of Picasso, see Paul Scofield on stage in *Hamlet*, and hear Beethoven's Seventh Symphony (Tarkovsky's favorite at the time) in the concert hall (*O Tarkovskom* 43). While Tarkovsky complains that they saw few foreign films at VGIK (*Sculpting* 90), as a film student and later a director he had ample opportunity to see "forbidden films" which were not in general distribution, and later, as his prestige grew, he was able to benefit from his own relatively frequent travels abroad in the 1960s and 1970s, both to accompany his films to festivals and on private or official visits to Italy, France, Sweden, and elsewhere. During the 1960s he became acquainted with major works of the French New Wave such as Godard's *Breathless* and Resnais' *Hiroshima, Mon Amour* (Gordon Interview) and, somewhat belatedly, with Bergman.

From the references to other filmmakers scattered through interviews, articles, and *Sculpting in Time*, it seems clear that he developed his own personal pantheon of great directors very early on and remained faithful to it throughout his career: the names that recur again and again are Bresson, Bergman, Fellini, Antonioni, Dovzhenko, Kurosawa, Bunuel, and Mizoguchi. Occasionally such figures as Cocteau, Renoir, Vigo, Chaplin, Welles, and Ford are referred to, and among his Soviet contemporaries he praised Paradzhanov and Ioseliani;[1] but the list of those for whom he professed genuine admiration does not extend much further than this. He maintained a love/hate relationship with Eisenstein, rejecting what he saw as his "despotic" attitude to his audience (*Sculpting* 183) and his cold intellectualizing of the image (118), though he expressed a somewhat reluctant respect for *Ivan the Terrible* (67)—and, as we point out in relation to *Andrei Roublev*, was perhaps even influenced by it. The overall taste expressed here is obviously for filmmakers who are serious, intense, committed, and uncompromising,² and whose work demonstrates an instantly recognizable personal style (see *Sculpting* 121)—the values that Tarkovsky associated with his own films. He had little time for cinema as a form of entertainment and despised the commercial aspects that he felt compromised its integrity as a serious art form, and thus remained indifferent to the accommodation between art and commerce, craftsmanship and enjoyment, that marks the best of Hollywood cinema (though, according to Ian Christie, he occasionally showed some curiosity about what was happening in that alien and uncongenial world: Turovskaya xv).

While he was happy on occasion to list his favorite directors on the same level of artistic achievement as the poets, painters, and composers he most admired (e.g., *Sculpting* 21), he also expressed doubts as to "whether up till now cinema can actually claim any authors worthy to stand alongside the creators of the great masterpieces of world literature" (173). Those whom he *was* prepared to place in the category of serious artists he called the "poets" of cinema, those who created their own inner world rather than simply recreating external reality. The need to listen to and follow their own inner demons made them relatively unpopular and even misunderstood, but they performed a far more valuable service to the audience than those who simply accommodated themselves to, and flattered, the taste of the mass public (from an illustrated talk given in Rome in 1982, reprinted in *Dossier Positif* 59; a videotape of this also exists).

Tarkovsky's specific comments on Bergman, Bresson, Kurosawa, Bunuel, et al. are always shrewd and suggestive, though they tend to be governed by what he sees as the similarity between their artistic practice and his own. In particular he admires their ability to create imagery that respects the reality of the material world and yet simultaneously transcends it: examples of this from Kurosawa, Bresson, Bunuel, and Bergman are given on pages 72–73, 110, 189–92, and 213 of *Sculpting* and on pages 60–61 of *Dossier Positif*. One of the extracts shown during his talk in Rome was the final scene of Antonioni's *La Notte*, which Tarkovsky describes as the only case he knows in cinema in which the act of making love is simultaneously a desperate necessity for the characters and an unbelievably beautiful spiritual gesture. On other occasions Bunuel is praised for his deep roots in the classical culture of Spain and his evocation of the essential elements of the national character (*Sculpting* 51), and Bergman and Bresson are admired for their subtle and evocative use of sound and music (159 and 162). Bergman is also singled out for the restraint and artistic honesty of his handling of actors and his ability to make them reveal the inner truth of their characters (146).

What Tarkovsky actually *learned* from them, however, is more problematic. Obvious affinities can be pointed out: Dovzhenko's long takes that create a palpable appreciation for the beauty of the natural world; Mizoguchi's serenely beautiful tracking shots and his presentation of the supernatural and the dreamlike as if they were indistinguishable from everyday reality; Antonioni's respect for real time in his lengthy sequence shots; the ability to move freely between reality and dream, memory and hallucination in such films as Bunuel's *Belle de Jour*, Fellini's *8½*, or Bergman's *Persona*; the sense of vivid, tactile reality that pervades every frame of Kurosawa's films; Bresson's transformation of the squalor and misery of his characters' lives (in, for example, *Mouchette*) into something radiant and luminous—but Tarkovsky was always wary of displaying direct indebtedness to any other director, and his films remain, as he would have wanted them to be, *sui generis*. This concern to avoid recognizable imitation of others even led him to apologize for a shot in one of the dream sequences of *Nostalghia* showing Gorchakov's wife and Evgenia embracing, because it derived too obviously from a famous shot of Liv Ullman and Bibi Andersson in *Persona*.

There are one or two surprising omissions in his list of favorite directors, however. Though he apparently admired *Hiroshima, Mon Amour*, he rarely, if ever, refers to Resnais in his writings—even though, as French critics such as Jean-Pierre Jeancolas have pointed out (*Dossier Positif* 102), *Providence* in particular offers a close analogy to *Mirror*, both in its overall structure and in its movement between present and past, dream and reality, memory and hallucination. *Last Year in Marienbad* likewise seems an obvious influence on his recurring use of a continuous panning shot that shows one character in several incompatible spatial positions, and on some of the compositions during Domenico's self-immolation scene in *Nostalghia*. Theoretically, he should also have been impressed by Miklós Jancsó's mastery of the lengthy sequence-shot, often lasting a full ten minutes; but, after seeing the Hungarian director's *Hungarian Rhapsody* and *Allegro Barbaro*, he dismissed him facilely as merely an "epigone of Sergei Paradzhanov" (*Martyrolog* 282: January 24, 1980). And, though he saw Stanley Kubrick's *2001* before making *Solaris*, he disliked the film intensely, finding it cold and soulless.

His travels and attendance at film festivals allowed him to meet some of his heroes. He became acquainted with Antonioni through their common friend, the scriptwriter Tonino Guerra, and also met Fellini in Italy, though on June 6, 1980, he is musing in his diary that both Fellini and Antonioni have succumbed to the lure of money and what he calls "fear": "Where have all the great ones gone? Where are Rossellini, Cocteau, Renoir, Vigo? The great—who are poor in spirit? Where has poetry gone? Money, money, money, and fear. . . . Fellini is afraid, Antonioni is afraid. . . . The only one who is afraid of nothing is Bresson" (*TWT* 256). He met Kurosawa in Moscow in December 1973, when the latter was working on *Dersu Uzala*, and felt that the Japanese director was being given a raw deal by the Soviet authorities—

no Kodak film and a bunch of "informers and cretins" as a crew (*TWT* 85). Surprisingly, however, given the intense mutual admiration between himself and Ingmar Bergman—he delighted in quoting in his diary all the complimentary things Bergman was reported to have said about his films, and Bergman, of course, went on record as calling Tarkovsky "the greatest"[3]—the two men never met, even though they had offices in the same building while Tarkovsky was shooting *The Sacrifice* in Stockholm. According to Sven Nykvist, they avoided one another out of shyness.

In his diary entry for January 3, 1974, Tarkovsky compiled for himself a questionnaire regarding his favorite books, writers, composers, colors, seasons, and so on, giving his own answers opposite each question. In response to "favorite Russian film director" he wrote merely "?—none" (somewhat unfairly, perhaps, given his admiration for Dovzhenko, Ioseliani, and Paradzhanov).[4] To "favorite foreign director" he replied "Robert Bresson" (*TWT* 89). He met Bresson too, of course, when both were given special awards at the 1983 Cannes Festival. While Bresson may appear at first sight to be the director to whom he had most affinity, the resemblance between them, as Barthélemy Amengual has pointed out in some detail, is more apparent than real ("Andreï Tarkovsky après sept films," in *Etudes cinématographiques* 157–77). Although in both directors, to use Tarkovsky's own words about Bresson, "precise observation of life passes paradoxically into sublime artistic imagery" (*Sculpting* 95), the means by which this is achieved are, as Amengual argues, totally different in almost every respect. He cites, among other things, the different treatments of space and time (Bresson fragmented, Tarkovsky unified), and points out that Bresson is compact, laconic, and elliptical, hastening toward a goal, where Tarkovsky is more expansive and contemplative, concentrating on the quest itself. Bresson's affinity is for the "dry" and the "sharp"; Tarkovsky's for the "damp" and the "soft." The beauty of Bresson's films is often abstract and cold, even "brutal"; Tarkovsky is more mystical and less rational.

Though it is possible to quibble with some of the details of this analysis, the general argument is convincing and suggests, once again, that, however much Tarkovsky may have admired other film directors, he went, in essence, his own way. Where he did not—as, it could be argued, is the case in *The Sacrifice*, where the influence of Bergman is particularly strong—the film perhaps suffers as a result. Andrei Konchalovsky has suggested in interview that in his final films Tarkovsky tried too hard to be like the later Bergman in incorporating complex philosophical concepts into his work; lacking Bergman's literary skills and his profound psychological understanding of his characters, he succeeded only in undermining his own major talent as a visual poet. Despite this harsh judgment, *The Sacrifice*, both stylistically and thematically, still remains a moving and characteristically Tarkovskian film, for until the end he continued to put into practice the almost unchanging theories on the art of cinema formed basically more than twenty years previously.

Tarkovsky's Aesthetics

From the very earliest stages of his career as a director Tarkovsky began to formulate a theoretical basis for his art that found expression in articles, interviews, published statements, lectures, and the diary that he kept from 1970 to 1986. The ideas expressed in these were reworked, often with little alteration, and added to for his book *Sculpting in Time*, first published in German in 1986 and appearing in English later that year.[5] Although this book is the most easily accessible source for English-speaking readers and will be referred to frequently below, it is important to realize that most of Tarkovsky's ideas about art and the artist, the role of the film director and the elements of cinema as an art, the nature of film imagery and the role of the film viewer, were established in more or less their final form by the end of the 1960s; *Sculpting in Time* and the later articles and interviews often simply repeat these, sometimes word for word.

An article from 1964, for example (A. T., "Tarkovsky"), already introduces some of his favorite themes: the need for film to separate itself from literature and the other arts; the nature of "poetic logic" in the cinema; the equality that should exist between filmmaker and viewer; the specific requirements of mise-en-scène; art as a combination of the "subjective" and the "objective," of "facts" and "feelings"; the "poetic concreteness" of dreams; the "harmony of feelings and thoughts" that produces masterpieces; and the role of the director in providing the overall unity of the finished film. The discussion of time in the cinema in *Sculpting in Time* (especially on pp. 62–78) is taken almost verbatim from his article "Imprinted Time" ("Zapechatlennoye vremya" 69–79); and pages 106–24 of the book, on the nature of film imagery, are derived from a discussion with the film critic Olga Surkova, in which the latter appears to provide some of the precise formulations which Tarkovsky uses as his own later on ("O kinoobraze" 80–93).[6] *Sculpting in Time*, then, is essentially a compendium of ideas developed, and to some extent modified and reworked, over a period of more than twenty years.[7] Yet the basic elements remain consistent throughout and provide valuable insights into what Tarkovsky considered to be the role of the artist and the nature and purpose of artistic expression. They can also be used, with appropriate caution, as a guide to what he considered to be the meaning and intention of his own films, which (with the exception of *Solaris*, which is virtually ignored) are discussed and analyzed in some detail.

The language itself of these last two sentences, however, suggests some of the problems that Tarkovsky's aesthetic theorizing presents in a critical climate that, in North America and Western Europe at least, is largely dominated by varieties of Deconstructionism, Marxism, Feminism, and Poststructuralism, all of which, in their different ways, deny many of the assumptions that Tarkovsky takes for granted. At first sight, Tarkovsky's free and unembarrassed use of such terms as "genius," "transcendence," "spiritual vision," "beauty," "truth," and "spiritual treasures of timeless significance" may seem to place him as the inheritor of a "Romantic" tradition that is widely regarded in the West as being outmoded and discredited. The thrust of aesthetic theorizing over the past decade has been to deny the notion of the artist as a shaping and controlling force, expressing in his or her work emotions and concepts that have some kind of universal validity. For the many critics today who espouse the notion of the "death of the author," the artist is little more than the conduit through which the "dominant ideology" of his or her time finds expression, a virtually anonymous figure[8] who is the prisoner of the language and artistic conventions of the time and of a set of political, cultural, and social codes that he or she can do little more than covertly and unknowingly endorse, however much the overt intention may be to challenge or destroy them: "books are material products and their authors servants of social power," as Terry Eagleton is quoted as reminding us (*New York Review of Books,* September 28, 1989: ll). Works of art, then—or "texts" as they are, significantly, more usually called today—tend to be studied not for what the artist can reveal to us but for the self-deceptions, contradictions, and delusions that they embody. "Meaning" resides not in what the artist thinks he or she is "saying" but in the variety of creative readings (and even misreadings) that the ingenious critic can impose, using the text as an often perfunctory basis.

In this context, Tarkovsky's thinking can be seen as merely quaintly and even touchingly archaic, the product of intellectual isolation in the Soviet Union from the mainstream of critical developments elsewhere. Yet George Steiner's *Real Presences,* in offering an assessment of current critical tendencies as they relate to more traditional views of art and the artist, intriguingly echoes Tarkovsky throughout, often virtually word for word. Although there is no indication that Steiner is even aware of Tarkovsky's written work, the similarity perhaps comes from recourse to a common heritage of some two thousand years of thinking about art. And not all important film critics today, of course, subscribe unquestioningly to the currently fashionable approaches—David Bordwell and Robin Wood are two who come to mind. Steiner's book, along with some others that have appeared recently—Noël Carroll's *Mystifying Movies* is one with specific relevance to film—may suggest a growing reaction against some of today's dominant modes of critical thinking and perhaps a partial and modified return to some of the values championed by Tarkovsky.

In any case, whether one considers Tarkovsky's ideas of art "old-fashioned," "misguided," or "prophetic," given that this thinking is inseparably intertwined with the films themselves, partly deriving retrospectively from the finished product and partly, and perhaps increasingly, helping to shape it, it is worth examining more closely both the validity (at least for Tarkovsky himself) and the sources of his ideas.

In a question-and-answer session conducted at the National Film Theater in London on February 8, 1981, Tarkovsky announced that his conception of the function of the artist was exactly that expressed by Pushkin in his poem "The Prophet" (*Dossier Positif* 57), a constant refrain in his writings and talks.

(The poem is printed in full in the chapter on *The Sacrifice* in *Sculpting in Time:* 221–22.) Throughout his career, he saw himself as the inheritor of a specifically Russian tradition of artistic genius with its sense of the artist's high calling and the sacrifice it entails. In Pushkin's poem the artist, "tormented by spiritual thirst," is painfully transformed into a prophet by a six-winged seraph who opens his eyes and ears to the wonders of this world, and is then commanded by God to "see and hear, be filled with My Will and go forth over lands and seas setting fire to people's hearts with The Word."[9]

The inspired artist, however, finds that his gift is a source as much of pain and suffering as of joy: "True artistic inspiration is always a torment for the artist, almost to the point of endangering his life" (*Sculpting* 188); "the artist cannot express the moral ideal of his time unless he touches all its running sores, unless he suffers and lives these sores himself" (168). Tarkovsky stresses that "the artist is always a servant" (of the divine, rather than of "social power") "and is perpetually trying to pay for the gift that has been given to him as if by a miracle" (38). "Talent," he writes in his diary for August 14, 1971, "is a misfortune," because it imposes duties and obligations and offers very few tangible rewards in return (*TWT* 40). It has nothing to do with self-expression, a concept which Tarkovsky despises, for "true affirmation of self can only be expressed in sacrifice" (*Sculpting* 38). The ideas of the "suffering" artist, of art as "sacrifice," and of artistic talent as a gift from God, already present in Pushkin's "Prophet," have been common themes in Russian intellectual thought since the nineteenth century, and Tarkovsky is simply expanding and reaffirming them.

Toward the end of his life, as, for example in an interview given in Stockholm in 1985 and later published in *Iskusstvo kino* ("Krasota spasyot mir"), these concepts became increasingly colored by a sense of being misunderstood and even persecuted: the artist—for Tarkovsky apparently an exclusively masculine figure—is, he claims, the true voice of the people and expresses the inner needs of society, but he is not accepted or recognized until after his death. (Once again this is an idea that has enjoyed greater currency in Russia than elsewhere.) The sense of "martyrdom" here is countered to some extent by his recognition that the artist is not inherently superior to other people, only more perceptive and better able to articulate what he perceives. He does not need to have a "mission," and his talent should be a source of humility rather than of pride.

Although Tarkovsky referred constantly to his own gifts in terms of "talent," he had no qualms about using the word "genius" in connection with the great artists of the past, while emphasizing that genius was indissolubly linked to "humility," "responsibility," "honesty," and "sincerity." "The true artist always serves immortality" and seeks out "absolute truth" (*Sculpting* 168), even if, as Tarkovsky acknowledges elsewhere (188), no one is ever in possession of the complete truth: "the genius is revealed not in the absolute perfection of a work but in absolute fidelity to himself, in commitment to his own passion" (56).

A concept of this kind is necessarily elitist, and here too Tarkovsky is unapologetic: "Art is by nature aristocratic, and naturally selective in its effect on the audience" (*Sculpting* 164), though he insists that it is not class-bound and is accessible to anyone prepared to make the effort to enter into communication with the artist. The latter, in turn, has a profound responsibility toward his public: "because of his special awareness of his time and of the world in which he lives, the artist becomes the voice of those who cannot formulate or express their view of reality. In that sense the artist is indeed *vox populi*" (164). (This concept of the artist's role must, of course, also be seen within the context of the Soviet system, where being an artist who "expresses reality" could be dangerous as well.) In the opening pages of *Sculpting in Time* Tarkovsky quotes extracts from letters he received from viewers of *Mirror* (which, of all his films, was the one most heavily attacked for its supposed incomprehensibility and elitism) and states that what gave him the strength to continue as a filmmaker at this particularly discouraging stage of his career was the realization that at least some people *needed* what he had to say, and that he had been able to make them "recognise a part of themselves that up till now [had] never been given expression" (12).[10] Audience reactions of this kind were particularly important to Tarkovsky, and he filled several pages of his diary with similar messages handed or sent to him after he had introduced screenings of his films at factories and workers' clubs.

Despite his stress on individual artistic genius and his claims for the universality of works of art in terms of time and space, Tarkovsky was also fully aware that the artist is "of necessity . . . a product of the reality that surrounds him" and is inevitably shaped by this: "Clearly each person expresses his own time and necessarily carries its laws of development within him" (*Sculpting* 165). And, although he emphasizes the artist's search for truth, he recognizes that the meaning and understanding of this truth is endlessly debatable and will differ for each member of the audience: "Only through the diversity of personal interpretations does some sort of relatively objective assessment emerge"; "in the multiplicity of judgements passed upon it, the work of art in its turn takes on a kind of inconstant and many-faceted life of its own, its existence enhanced and widened" (*Sculpting* 46). Here he is reacting against Eisenstein's aim to create "*a construction which, in the first place, serves to embody the author's relation to the content,* at the same time compelling the spectator to relate himself to the content in the same way" (Eisenstein 168) and sounds quite close to Mikhail Bakhtin's ideas of "polyphony" and to contemporary ideas on reception theory.

Tarkovsky's view of the purpose of art is conditioned by his view of the artist as a moral and spiritual mediator between the divine and the human: "the goal for all art . . . is to explain to the artist himself and to those around him what man lives for, what the meaning of his existence" (36); "art must carry man's craving for the ideal, must be an expression of his reaching out towards it; . . . art must give man hope and faith" (192). (Although the language here is uncomfortably sexist for a contemporary

English-speaking reader, the Russian in the original allows only the use of masculine forms. In any case, Tarkovsky clearly believed creativity to be a male prerogative.)

Art, then, has a moral and ethical function: it is a means to self-knowledge for both artist and audience, and it "has the capacity, through shock and catharsis, to make the human soul receptive to good.'" It cannot, however, *teach* anything—"in four thousand years humanity has learnt nothing at all" (50)—and it cannot *make* people good, which is where Tarkovsky deviates sharply from the dogmas of socialist realism with which some critics such as Ian Christie (Turovskaya xvi) have tried to link him. Art is also, and very importantly, a "meta-language" (40), a means of communication between human beings: "My childhood was like that," one of his correspondents wrote to him about *Mirror*. "Only how did you know about it?" (*Sculpting* 10).

"But art must transcend as well as observe; its role is to bring spiritual vision to bear on reality" (*Sculpting* 96). Throughout his book Tarkovsky instinctively and naturally writes about art in language appropriate to religion: "In art, as in religion, intuition is tantamount to conviction, to faith" (41). "The artist . . . tries to grasp [the life] principle and make it incarnate, new each time; and each time he hopes, though in vain, to achieve an exhaustive image of the Truth of human existence" (104). "Through the image is sustained an awareness of the infinite: the eternal within the finite, the spiritual within matter, the limitless given form. . . . Art could be said to be a symbol of the universe, being linked with that absolute spiritual truth which is hidden from us in our positivistic, pragmatic activities" (37). *Sculpting in Time* ends with these words: "Perhaps the meaning of all human activity lies in artistic consciousness, in the pointless and selfless creative act? Perhaps our capacity to create is evidence that we ourselves were created in the image and likeness of God?" (241–42).

The concept of the artist as a suffering, tormented, inspired genius is not likely to elicit much sympathy in a contemporary cultural environment dominated by a coolly intellectual, skeptical postmodernist sensibility, and Tarkovsky was inclined, in some of his public utterances as well as in his diary, to attempt to live up to a role that he had to some extent consciously created for himself. Stripped of some of the rhetorical excesses, however, which derive largely from a specifically Russian tradition of awe and reverence for artistic genius that has persisted longer there than in most other countries, he may serve to remind us, as does George Steiner in *Real Presences*, of some of the reasons why we turn to works of art, why, as Tarkovsky himself puts it, we "need" them: as a means of communication, of knowledge (of the self and of others), of understanding (of the world and our place within it), of transcendence (a word which Steiner, like Tarkovsky, seeks to rehabilitate). A position very similar to Tarkovsky's is expressed by the novelist Larry McMurtry: "Art . . . has always been reckoned to be one of the highest expressions of the human spirit, a force as old and as powerful as religion, and one which, like religion, has sustained and encouraged mankind in its struggle with the severities of human destiny. All people have needed art, sought art, loved art."[12]

Turning specifically to his chosen medium of film, Tarkovsky takes pains to dissociate it from other art forms, especially literature, and to try to define its essential characteristics, producing in the process (as do most other film-makers, poets, and painters who set up as critical theorists) what is essentially a rationale for his own creative practice. "The time has come," he announces near the beginning of *Sculpting in Time*, "for literature to be separated, once and for all, from cinema" (15). "Trying to adapt the features of other art forms to the screen will always deprive the film of what is distinctively cinematic, and make it harder to handle the material in a way that makes use of the powerful resources of cinema as an art in its own right" (22). A corollary of this position is an attack on the adaptation of what he calls "masterpieces" (as opposed to minor works like Vladimir Bogomolov's novella *Ivan*, the source of *Ivan's Childhood*) which exist perfectly in their own medium and would be destroyed in any attempt at transformation (15). This position, however, reflects a relatively early stage of his thinking, and as he became more and more convinced of the growing maturity of cinema as an art form, Tarkovsky clearly began to relish the challenge that he had previously contemptuously dismissed as demonstrating "indiffer[ence] both to fine prose and to the cinema" (15), for much of his later career was devoted to determined, though fruitless, efforts to film such works as Dostoyevsky's *The Idiot* and *Crime and Punishment*, Tolstoy's *The Death of Ivan Ilyich*, Mann's *Doctor Faustus*, and Bulgakov's *The Master and Margarita*. In *Mirror* (1974) he is already carrying on a dialogue with other art forms, poetry and painting, on equal terms.

Film, for Tarkovsky, is not a composite art, the amalgam of features of other art forms (64); it has its own characteristics and has at least the potential to be the "most truthful and poetic of art forms" (18). By "poetic" he seems to mean film's capacity for the associative linking of images (20) rather than the self-conscious creation of beautiful images, while "truth" is linked constantly to realism and simplicity: "To be faithful to life, intrinsically truthful, a work has for me to be at once an exact factual account and a true communication of feelings" (23). Even dreams in film should be "made up of exactly these same observed, natural forms of life" (71) and arise from "unusual and unexpected combinations of, and conflicts between, entirely real elements" which "must be shown with the utmost precision" (72). Unlike literature, "film does not have to use words: it manifests itself to us directly" (60). Like music, it needs no "mediating language"; it "allows for an utterly direct, emotional, sensuous perception of the work" (176). Nevertheless, this direct, unmediated reality is filtered through the subjectivity of the artist, though the moral integrity of the true artist, however, will ensure that this subjectivity is employed to good purposes, with "nobility" and "restraint" (27).

The specific quality of film, however, which distinguishes it from all other arts, is defined by Tarkovsky as its treatment of time: "For the first time in the history of the arts, in the history of culture, man found the means *to take an impression of time"* (*Sculpting* 62). *"Time, captured in its factual forms and manifestations:* such is the supreme idea of cinema as an art" (63).[13] Once again the essence of these remarks scattered throughout *Sculpting in Time,* and especially his continuing polemic against Eisenstein, can be found at a relatively early stage of his career; as early as 1962 he had inveighed against "intellectual cinema" and "intellectual montage" ("Mezhdu dvumya filmami" 83), and in an interview published in *Positif* in 1969 (*Dossier Positif* 86–94), Tarkovsky set out more fully the basic position that he was to reiterate, often with identical wording, in his book, his lectures, and later interviews. Here again the central issue is the basic realism of the film image: for Tarkovsky cinema could portray *real time* in a way that no other art could, and could also repeat that same, actual time, in exactly the same form, indefinitely. Editing, then, consisted in respecting the rhythm of life established in each individual shot, and not in distorting this by jumping back and forth between long shots and close-ups, or artificially speeding up the rhythm by rapid cutting between short pieces of film: the effects produced by these devices could be achieved, and far more naturally, by careful composition or by allowing the internal rhythm of the shots, and the sequence as a whole, to find its own inevitable pattern.

In setting out his own position, Tarkovsky tended to use Eisenstein as a straw man, accusing him of imposing a spurious rhythm on his films and failing to respect the integrity of each individual shot by being more concerned with creating an artificial "third" effect through the juxtaposition of two, often unrelated, images. In fact, of course, Eisenstein was extremely conscious of the integrity of each shot and had, in turn, accused Dziga Vertov of "neglect[ing] the inner dynamism of the shot" (quoted in Petrić, *Constructivism in Film* 52). What matters, however, is not whether Tarkovsky was fair to Eisenstein, but to realize that the concept of real time within the shot remained central to his filmic technique from *Andrei Roublev* onwards, reaching its perhaps inevitable culmination in the shots lasting six minutes or longer in *Stalker, Nostalghia,* and *The Sacrifice.*

Tarkovsky's insistence on the "reality" of the film image also accounts for the constant irritation he expressed when asked by viewers or critics to explain his "symbolism." Though he was perfectly capable, from a fairly early stage, of using the word "symbol" himself (he told Michel Ciment, for example, that the horses in *Andrei Roublev* symbolized life: *Dossier Positif* 91), he generally attempted to distinguish between the image, which was to be experienced directly, "on an emotional or even supra-emotional level" (*Sculpting* 40), by the viewer, and the symbol, which could be "deciphered" or "interpreted." Tarkovsky here seems to mean by "symbol" what Lotman would call either a "conventional" or an "iconic" sign, one with a fixed and restricted meaning (4–7). The imagery "natural to cinema," Tarkovsky tells us, has nothing to do with what he dismissively refers to as "poetic cinema," with its "symbols, allegories and other such figures" (*Sculpting* 66). He generally seems to attribute two central qualities to the film image: on the one hand it takes its basis in everyday reality, in "a specific, unique, actual fact" (72), while on the other the artist's own perception and presentation of this fact (107) gives it something of the quality of a "revelation" (41) that is *experienced* by the audience rather than consciously understood or interpreted. This allows Tarkovsky to make such comments as the following: "The moment a viewer understands, deciphers, all is over, finished: the illusion of the infinite becomes banality, a commonplace, a truism. The mystery disappears."[14] It also enabled him to insist, with total sincerity, that there was no "hidden, coded meaning" in his films (*Sculpting* 133).

At times, however, Tarkovsky hopelessly confuses his apparently clearcut distinction between the mystery and ambiguity of the image and the one-to-one "decipherability" of the symbol, by suddenly attributing to the symbol "inexhaustible and unlimited . . . meaning. . . . Symbols cannot be stated or explained, and, confronted by their secret meaning in its totality, we are powerless" (47—quoting the Russian poet Vyacheslav Ivanov's well-known Formalist definition of symbol). Tarkovsky does not, however, pursue the distinctions, for example, between the one-to-one correspondence of metonymy, synecdoche or even metaphor, and the multivalent symbol, so in the chapter on *The Sacrifice* added to the second edition of *Sculpting* and written shortly before his death, he returns to the equation of the symbol with a single, identifiable meaning, but now has no qualms about urging his readers to agree with him in interpreting that meaning rather than opting for an "inexhaustible and endlessly suggestive mystery": "the watering of the barren tree," we are told bluntly, " . . . for me is a symbol of faith" (223). From totally rejecting any symbolism or metaphoric meaning in the tree at the end of *Ivan's Childhood*, he now invites the reader to interpret the tree in his last film.

Much of this "theorizing" is obviously intuitive, however deeply felt, and it is probably sufficient to realize that his imagery, at its best, operates on the two levels that he himself defined: it represents a "specific, unique, actual fact" and also provides a "revelation" that can be "experienced" but not necessarily explained by the viewer. In between, nevertheless, some scope remains for "interpretation." When questioned, for example, about the dogs who appear in *Solaris, Stalker,* and *Nostalghia*, Tarkovsky tended to shrug off any notion of metaphysical significance—"It's just a dog," he told a Lithuanian critic who wanted to know what the animal in *Stalker* "symbolized."[15] In all three works, however, the appearance of the dogs is not purely random or fortuitous, for in each case the dogs possess the characteristic of somehow mediating between the world of present reality and the world of dreams and memory; they therefore can, and surely should, be "interpreted" on at least some level. And yet, at the same time, some of the scenes in which they appear, such as the swamp in *Stalker* or the hotel room in *Nostalghia*, have the authentic quality of strangeness and mystery that, rightly, defies attempts at specific explanation. In this respect, they are perhaps closest to what some

Formalist critics called "*affectual signs*, signs conveying an emotional 'attitude' toward the people or objects depicted" (Eagle 10).[16]

Although in practice Tarkovsky was usually prepared to offer explanations of his films on his own terms, his frequently expressed hostility toward interpretation of specific images may well derive from his antagonism toward Marxist theorizing and the dogmas of socialist realism (which ranked clarity, lack of ambiguity, and ease of comprehension among the highest virtues). A diary entry for March 10, 1973, explicitly rejects Marxist concepts of art as inherently class-bound and historically determined (*Martyrolog* 116—not in the English edition); for Tarkovsky part of the very essence of art was that it was "timeless" and enabled us to share and learn from the experiences of those living in different times and cultures from our own: "In terms of a person's spiritual experience, what happened to him yesterday may have exactly the same degree of significance as what happened to humanity a thousand years ago" (*Sculpting* 193). His dislike of "manifestos" (51) and "deliberate tendentiousness or ideology" (109) in art was not limited simply to Soviet culture, though it was there that his own work was most directly affected, but could also be applied to such classic artists as Raphael (50–51) who, in Keats's words, have "a palpable design upon us."

A final theme is the role of the film director and what Tarkovsky saw as "his" relationship with "his" audience. (Although women held many responsible positions in his productions, Tarkovsky viewed directing, as his first wife points out, as a purely male profession.) While fully acknowledging the essential contribution made to a film by the scriptwriter, director of photography, actors, composer, set designer, editor, and other collaborators, Tarkovsky insisted firmly from his earliest days as a filmmaker that the conception, realization, and final responsibility for the film should belong to the director alone (*Sculpting* 18, 33, 126). To a remarkable extent, he was able to achieve this, both assisted and hindered by the conflicting forces at work within the Soviet filmmaking system. Although he made far fewer films than he wanted to, he did, as he freely acknowledged ("Entretien" 36), make only those films that he was interested in making, and succeeded in having them released in a form that avoided any destructive compromises.

The qualities he ascribes to the filmmaker are essentially those of any other serious artist: moral and ethical integrity, sincerity, humility, the ability to observe the world around him attentively and respectfully and then transmute this observation through his own "subjective, author's vision [into] the stuff of art" and so create "that distinctive, complex world which reflects a true picture of reality" (*Sculpting* 33). Equally important, however, is that this vision should be shared with, and responded to, by an audience.

While admitting that the director inevitably controls the response of the spectator to some extent, especially through the imposition of a flow of time which the latter can only either accept or reject (120), Tarkovsky is eager to welcome the spectator as virtually a cocreator of the film. A diary entry for

January 24, 1973 (*TWT* 65), analyzes this process: he no longer believes, he writes, that because the final form of a film is fixed and unchanging, it will be perceived in basically the same way by all members of the audience. He now wishes to speak to each member of the audience individually, and the best way of doing this is to show as little as possible, thus forcing the spectator to engage creatively with the material offered and construct his or her own meaning by putting it together according to his or her own understanding of it. Rephrased in *Sculpting in Time,* this notion emerges as: "The method whereby the artist obliges the audience to build the separate parts into a whole, and to think on, further than has been stated, is the only one that puts the audience on a par with the artist in their perception of the film" (20–21). Without a responsive audience of this kind, filmmaking becomes meaningless: "I do nothing in particular to please an audience, and yet hope fervently that my picture will be accepted and loved by those who see it" (170). The desire for acceptance and love, however, should in no way induce the artist to make concessions to popular taste, and the acknowledged difficulty of Tarkovsky's films derives from his respect for his audience (174–75), his concern to stimulate and challenge them and to live up to the high standards of his calling, for "art ennobles man by the mere fact of its existence" (182).

THREE

Working Methods

The Collaborative Process

"When I hear people say in solemn
tones, 'Oh, you worked with Andrei
Tarkovsky,' I remember this cheeky little
chappie who was doing the most
outrageous things, pulling faces and
gamboling around."

—Susan Fleetwood, Interview

Working with Tarkovsky was not always "fun"—though this is a word
that occurs remarkably frequently in interviews and published reminiscences.[1] He could be moody, authoritarian, frustrating, ruthless, and endlessly demanding, yet, with very few exceptions, those who worked with him
were happy to continue to do so, and those who *did* break with him—either
by his choice or by their own—rarely lost their respect for him as a filmmaker
of exceptional artistic and moral integrity. Their views on him as a person
were not always so flattering.

Tarkovsky felt that his own kind of filmmaking and that of the handful of
other directors whom he unreservedly admired was as totally personal as the
work of a writer, painter, or composer, and insisted that the final responsibility for the completed work belonged to the director alone (see, for example,
Sculpting 125–26). As noted in chapter 1, the conditions of filmmaking in the
Soviet Union allowed him almost total freedom *while shooting*, and the subsequent struggle to have the work released in its intended form was one that he
undertook on his own; in Italy and Sweden he was lucky enough to work
with producers who respected his artistic intentions and allowed him almost
complete creative freedom in achieving them. Nevertheless, he did not make
his films singlehandedly and, like most other "personal" directors, he worked
best when surrounded by a team with whom he felt comfortable and whose
members were prepared to contribute their own very considerable creative
talents toward the realization of a vision that they too had come to share.
Though it was naturally easier to reach this goal in the Soviet Union, it was
attained to a surprising extent in Italy and, especially, in Sweden, where Susan Fleetwood spoke warmly of the "family" atmosphere during shooting.

What he found difficult to adjust to in Italy and Sweden was not so much
the size of the budget, for most of his Soviet films were made relatively

Tarkovsky "the cheeky little chappie." Copyright Swedish Film Institute.

Tarkovsky the "searcher." Copyright Swedish Film Institute.

cheaply even by that country's modest standards, but the constant account-ability as to how money and time were allocated. In the Soviet Union—at least from *Andrei Roublev* onwards—his films underwent a process of constant rethinking, rewriting, and recreation at every stage—preproduction, shooting, dubbing, mixing, and editing—that would have been intolerable in a more cost-conscious environment where every day's delay could add thousands of dollars to the film's expenses. The luxuries of being able to take a day or two off shooting in order to find the solution to a particular problem, to rehearse for two days and then shoot on the third, to scrap several weeks of work on a film and start again from scratch (as happened with *Stalker*), or virtually to rewrite the script of a film at the start of each day's shooting, may not compensate for everything that he endured at the hands of the Soviet bureaucracy; but they should certainly be placed in the balance to offset at least a few of his tribulations.

While Tarkovsky had a very clear idea of the ultimate goal that he wanted to achieve and was almost fanatically involved in every detail of the production, he was constantly prepared to improvise along the way and to accept suggestions from others that were in the spirit of his overall intentions. (The exception to this was *Ivan's Childhood*, where he was a young, nervous, and untested director and worked much more closely from a fully developed script.) Many of those who worked with him comment that he was always "searching," and almost all emphasize that, once he had come to trust them (not always an easy or inevitable process), he allowed them to find their own way and make their own decisions—providing, again, that they kept within the overall framework that he had established. Once these decisions had been reached, however, and the rehearsals had been completed, no changes or deviations were normally permitted during shooting.

The loyalty, devotion, and love of most of those who worked with him are clearly attested to in what follows, and many, including Susan Fleetwood, Alexander Kaidanovsky, Margarita Terekhova, and Nikolai Grinko, spoke warmly of the "love" and "kindness" that they received in return. The often unpleasant obverse to this, however, was the irrational possessiveness that Tarkovsky displayed over those who worked with him: he resented their working with someone else, even when he had no particular need of them himself, and in the privacy of his diary he could be scathingly hostile and cruelly unfair about those who he felt had "betrayed" him. Vadim Yusov, for example, the brilliant cinematographer of all his films through *Solaris* and a long-standing friend, was accused of being envious, uncooperative, ambitious, conceited, and untalented (*TWT* 72–73) once he expressed doubts about the moral and artistic validity of Tarkovsky's script for *Bright, Bright Day* (the origin of what was to become *Mirror*). His replacement on that film, Georgy Rerberg, in turn fell into disfavor and was dismissed during the shooting of *Stalker*—to the accompaniment of another barrage of insults in the diary (*TWT* 146). The vehement irrationality of these reactions is disturbing and hints at the paranoia that another former friend and colleague, Andrei Konchalovsky, diagnosed in his perceptive and, at times, less than flattering contribution to the collection *O Tarkovskom*. On the other hand, it may more innocently reflect another characteristic much commented on by those who knew and worked with him: his essentially childlike nature.

Actors

Despite criticism that he was unprofessional in working with actors (Konchalovsky, Yusov) and that he wasn't really interested in them (Turovskaya 27), Tarkovsky was, in fact, quite careful in his selection and handling of actors. Some of the highest praise he received during our interviews was from actors, many of whom loved and admired him. His leading actors gave outstanding performances. Not only did Tarkovsky "discover" Nikolai Burlyaev (Ivan in *Ivan's Childhood* and Boriska in *Andrei Roublev*) and Anatoly Solonitsyn, who acted in all his Soviet films after *Ivan's Childhood*, but he also inspired several actors—Margarita Terekhova (the wife and mother in *Mirror*), Natalia Bondarchuk (Hari in *Solaris*), Yevgeny Zharikov (Galtsev in *Ivan's Childhood*), and Nikolai Grinko (who acted in *all* of Tarkovsky's Soviet films, but most memorably in *Stalker*)—to give perhaps the best performances of their careers.

It is also true that professionally trained and established actors, especially in the Soviet Union, were often uncomfortable working with him because of his unorthodox methods. All actors interviewed agreed that Tarkovsky never really discussed a character's motivation, and those with a theatrical background—like Donatas Banionis (Kris Kelvin in *Solaris*) or Alla Demidova (the mother's friend, Lisa, in *Mirror*)—found this particularly frustrating. As Banionis put it, he didn't express himself in "the usual categories of causality but in images" (*O Tarkovskom* 133), while in Demidova's words he was "imprecise and did not explain anything." In *Sculpting in Time* (145) the director responds in kind, noting that he couldn't develop a working relationship with Banionis because he was an analytical actor, who "cannot work without knowing the whys and wherefores." He could not "accept that in cinema the actor must not have a picture of how the finished film is going to look," because "even the best director, who knows exactly what he wants, can seldom envisage the final result exactly" (*Sculpting* 145).

Tarkovsky was adamant in his determination not to have the actors "play" the roles (*Sculpting* 152). He would tell Natalia Bondarchuk (Hari in *Solaris*) to "live, breathe, not act," or Nikolai Burlyaev to "cry real tears, not onion tears" (Burlyaev Interview). At times, in order to keep the actors' reactions "natural" for a given situation, he would even not allow them to read ahead in the script in order to ensure that their responses would be spontaneous and unpremeditated—as was Margarita Terekhova's experience in *Mirror*. Natalia Bondarchuk relates in interview that Tarkovsky never assigned a task directly: "Instead he created a marvelous atmosphere and the actors didn't act, but meditated before the camera."

According to Demidova, this experience was inspirational only for those actors who could share Tarkovsky's intuitive approach to acting, who didn't demand or need explanations, who could "feel his pulse and share his worldview." Anatoly Solonitsyn became Tarkovsky's favorite actor because he didn't ask questions; he "knew the difference between theater and cinema," and was "highly strung and suggestible" (*Sculpting* 144–45). Alexander Kaidanovsky quotes Tarkovsky from the set of *Stalker:* "I don't need your psychology, your expressiveness. . . . The actor is part of the composition, like the tree, like water" (Interview). Donatas Banionis recalls that at times only the physical disposition of the characters seemed important to Tarkovsky. One could argue, however, that rather than simply downplaying the importance of the actor, Tarkovsky was attempting to balance his role with that of the setting in the overall composition of each frame.

That Tarkovsky took his actors seriously is demonstrated by his attentiveness to the choice of actor, especially for the lead in each of his films, and he would often alter his initial concept of the role to suit the particular actor he was working with. He took over *Ivan's Childhood* from another director only because he had in mind the actor for the leading role, and Nikolai Burlyaev recalls that he has never since done so many screen tests as he did for the part of Ivan. Tarkovsky probably had to convince the studio of his unusual choice of a sharp-featured, scrawny boy for the role of a typical youthful Soviet war hero. For the title role of *Andrei Roublev* he chose Anatoly Solonitsyn, an unknown provincial actor; both the artistic council and Tarkovsky's mentor, Romm, were against entrusting such an important part to an unknown, but, after several screen tests, Tarkovsky prevailed. Solonitsyn's brother tells a perhaps apocryphal but nevertheless revealing anecdote: that Tarkovsky took all photos from the screen tests to restorers specializing in medieval Russian art and asked them which one was Andrei Roublev; they pointed to Anatoly Solonitsyn (*O Tarkovskom* 112–13). For all his criticism of Eisenstein, Tarkovsky clearly borrowed his concept of "typage," selecting actors whose physical characteristics fit the part.

For his third feature film, after rejecting Natalia Bondarchuk as too young for the part of Hari and testing some thirty other actresses, he finally cast her in the role a whole year later. Susan Fleetwood was chosen to play Adelaide in *The Sacrifice*—partly because of her physical resemblance to Tarkovsky's wife—after he had tested actresses all over Europe. One could argue that, in the Soviet Union, because of the lengthy process for script approval for each of his films, Tarkovsky could take his time in selecting his actors. Yet under the more pressured conditions in the West, he seems to have been equally careful and selective.

Tarkovsky's coworkers note that his natural shyness and fear of strangers, combined with his reluctance to explain their parts in detail, made it difficult for him to work with new and unfamiliar actors. Favorite actors thus reappear again and again—Nikolai Burlyaev in *Ivan's Childhood* and *Andrei Roublev*, Nikolai Grinko in all five Soviet films, Anatoly Solonitsyn in four. When Solonitsyn was too ill to star in *Nostalghia*, Tarkovsky tried to get Alexander Kaidanovsky (from *Stalker*) approved for the part, but he was not given permission to go abroad. Tarkovsky finally turned to Oleg Yankovsky, a well-known actor who had played a small part in *Mirror*. For his two films abroad, Tarkovsky chose Erland Josephson, an actor he had known and liked from Bergman's films.

Although some actors describe the "fun" atmosphere on the set, the work itself was very serious, often tense, and physically and emotionally exhausting. Because he would do only one or two takes, the preparation for the shoot might entail endless rehearsals, complicated by Tarkovsky's often incoherent and overly philosophical musings, rather than specific explanations or directions for the scene. Andrei Konchalovsky recalls Tarkovsky talking so much to the actors on the set of *Andrei Roublev* that they no longer knew what or how to act! Along with his reluctance to be specific, Tarkovsky's intuitive approach to acting probably made him unable to explain exactly how one should act a particular scene. Nevertheless, he could tell an actor what emotion he wanted expressed, and the right actor could understand and convey this. For the "candle" scene at the end of *Nostalghia* Tarkovsky told Oleg Yankovsky that "one action can be experienced as if it is your whole life" (*O Tarkovskom* 251). In *Mirror*, on the other hand, he deliberately created tension between the actresses Terekhova and Demidova so that the frustration and bewilderment they felt would emerge all the more strongly on the screen (Demidova Interview).

The women seem to have gotten off easily compared to the treatment that the male actors were subjected to. Tarkovsky himself admits to pretending to be dissatisfied with Nikolai Burlyaev's acting in *Andrei Roublev* in order to keep him in the tense, insecure state that he needed for the role of Boriska (*Sculpting* 146). Natalia Bondarchuk remembers Tarkovsky swearing at Anatoly Solonitsyn and physically exhausting him, so that the mild-mannered Solonitsyn would become the nervous, irritable, and sleepless Sartorius in *Solaris*. Probably the longest preparation for a role occurred before the shooting of *Nostalghia* even began. Oleg Yankovsky reports that Tarkovsky purposely left him to cool his heels for a month in Rome, where he felt lonely and disoriented, before coming to see him and then saying with satisfaction: "Now we can film you" (Interview). Tarkovsky also did not use stand-ins, with the result that Nikolai Burlyaev had to swim through the cold river in *Ivan's Childhood*, and slide through the mud in *Andrei Roublev*, again and again. Burlyaev recalls that after one particularly hard day of shooting, Solonitsyn counted more than twenty bruises on his body (*O Tarkovskom* 92). Several actors called Tarkovsky a "dictator" on the set. Why then would the actors put up with his emotional abuse and the tiring physical work and all still confirm that they would work with him again?

While he could be a nasty, hard taskmaster, Tarkovsky could also be childlike, funny, kind, and tender, very solicitous of his actors while being highly possessive toward them. According to Yankovsky, he could inspire actors and pour energy into them. There was mutual love, respect, and trust—all words used by actors we interviewed. They admired his artistic integrity, recognizing that the perfectionism, intense concentration, and total devotion he demanded of them, he himself was willing to give. Once he had established a rapport with an actor and he or she knew—sometimes through "a kind of ESP" (a phrase used by both Susan Fleetwood and Oleg Yankovsky)—what Tarkovsky wanted, the actor was relatively free to work out the details. Tarkovsky liked to be surprised and would accept proposals to change lines (Terekhova in *Mirror*, Kaidanovsky in *Stalker*), add props or modify costuming, or even choreograph a whole scene (Fleetwood in *The Sacrifice*), so long as they fit into his overall concept of the role. When Rolan Bykov refused to go to a professional ballet master in preparation for his role in *Andrei Roublev*—arguing that the buffoon's dance was quite spontaneous and primitive—and wanted to write the song and choreograph the dance himself, Tarkovsky let him (*O Tarkovskom* 170–76).

It is perhaps surprising that both Western and Russian actors who worked with Tarkovsky often had similar experiences, and even use the same words in describing him on the set. Given Tarkovsky's reluctance to answer questions, lack of a common language with the actors was not much of a handicap, yet, faced with unfamiliar actors in *Nostalghia*, he seems to have done something new. Erland Josephson describes a mini-scenario he wrote and shot with the actors in full costume, in order to give them a sense of the task ahead. For *The Sacrifice* he revived the tradition of *Andrei Roublev*—long, inspirational instruction to the cast. Although not all the Swedish actors were mesmerized by the power of his spiritual vision, Susan Fleetwood found herself exceptionally moved:

> He spoke to us [the actors] for some time, very solemnly and very simply, and so movingly about how he wanted us to be like children, to drop all the ideas that we had before about how to act, just very simply be as children, allowing feelings and sensations to occur to us and to free ourselves to respond to them. He spoke about having faith . . . about mankind and faith, and this was really the essence of the story. But it was also about how we should work, so it was like a story within a story. He was terribly moved at the time he was saying it. . . . The atmosphere and the integrity of what he was trying to transmit to us there was the essence of what I held at the heart of me when we were working together. (Interview)

Cinematographers

However much Tarkovsky may have "loved" his actors, his closest creative collaboration was always with his director of photography. It was the remarkable visual qualities of *Andrei Roublev* that first drew the attention of Sven Nykvist and made him overjoyed to be invited to work with its director many years later (Interview), and most actors seem to have accepted, as Susan Fleetwood did, that the visual style of the film should take precedence over all other considerations. That this style is essentially Tarkovsky's own is confirmed by the fact that virtually any frame from *Solaris, Mirror, Stalker, Nostalghia,* or *The Sacrifice* could be instantly identified as being from one of his films, yet these films were shot by five different cinematographers: Yusov, Rerberg, Knyazhinsky, Lanci, and Nykvist respectively. Each brought his own special qualities to the film and made his own distinctive contribution to it, yet none of those we spoke to sought to detract from Tarkovsky's "authorship" in this respect—as is only too often the case when disillusioned cinematographers feel that they have been overlooked or neglected by critics who insist on praising the "visual style" of directors who may have shown no interest whatever in this aspect of their films.

Alexander Knyazhinsky, who shot *Stalker,* felt that Tarkovsky was one of the very few Soviet directors who understood that cinema was essentially a visual art and quoted him as saying that, if they got the images right, the film was sure to be a success. Sven Nykvist credited him with knowing a good deal about the technical side of filmmaking and with being very sensitive to light, though he had to be weaned away from what Nykvist felt was an excessive reliance on artificial light and accustomed to a simpler style of lighting. Ultimately, however, as Nykvist put it in an interview with Hubert Niogret for *Positif,* the lighting "was my domain" (Niogret 26). They found themselves on common ground in a dislike for bright "naturalistic" colors and engaged in long discussions as to how to achieve the desaturated color effects in *The Sacrifice,* with Nykvist finally adopting a method that he told us he had learned from John Huston,[2] who had used it in *Moby Dick.* Two dupe negatives, one color and one black and white, are made from a color negative and then married in the optical printer, progressively eliminating certain colors until the desired effect is achieved. The effect can be varied from one shot to the next, if necessary. This expensive process was used for some fifty shots of the night scenes in the film, in order to achieve a "magical, mystical" effect (Niogret 26). In *Stalker* the strange, almost-but-not-quite black and white scenes in the bar and the Stalker's house (of which Knyazhinsky was particularly proud) were created by printing a color negative in black and white. In both cases Tarkovsky knew the overall effect that he wanted, but trusted the expertise of his cinematographer to realize it for him.

In both *Stalker* and *The Sacrifice* much of the location filming was done at dawn or dusk (the former meaning 2:00 A.M. in Gotland in May) in order to take advantage of the special quality of the light at that time. Nature itself was often "improved" for visual effect (Tarkovsky treated nature like a set, according to *Mirror*'s set designer Nikolai Dvigubsky): leaves were painted gold in *Mirror,* trees were sprayed with water to make them show more black on film in *The Sacrifice,* and grass and trees were painted in *Stalker* to intensify the almost hallucinatory greenness of the entry into the Zone. By the time Tarkovsky came to make these films, he was far more self-confident and willing to trust his own judgment than when working with Vadim Yusov on *Ivan's Childhood*, where those arriving on the set for the first time, like the actor Nikolai Grinko, assumed that Yusov was the director (he sat there "like a tank" according to Rausch) rather than the nervous young man wearing a strange cap ("Talisman" 22). While Yusov always found Tarkovsky, to some extent at least, "unprofessional," he also recognized that this enabled him to take risks and make discoveries that a more conventional director might have shunned. From *Andrei Roublev* onwards he was fully in charge, searching for new modes of visual expressiveness, yet knowing, when it came to the actual shooting, exactly what he wanted.

Alexander Knyazhinsky, on *Stalker*, confirmed both the thoroughness with which Tarkovsky prepared the visual side of the film, often taking two days to set up a particularly complicated and lengthy shot before filming it on the third day, and also the fact that no deviation was permitted once filming began. One consequence of this careful preparation was that he rarely needed, in any of his films, more than one or two takes for any shot.[3] In Nykvist's case Tarkovsky suggested that they should spend a full year together discussing how to make the film, blithely ignoring the harsh economic fact that even artists have to earn a living in a capitalist society, and someone has to pay them (he similarly wanted two months of Susan Fleetwood's time and found it difficult to understand that she too would have to be paid for this). In any event the two men spent a rewarding month together, viewing each other's films and absorbing each other's filming styles.

Despite this, however, the first few days of filming *The Sacrifice* were unexpectedly tense because, as Sven Nykvist told us, "I was a little irritated because he was always looking through the camera. We were shooting exteriors and I didn't have so much to do and he gave personal instructions to the actors through the camera. He was always doing that and I was not used to it." When he finally confronted him over this problem, Tarkovsky explained that he didn't feel comfortable instructing the actors unless he looked through the camera, and that he needed to see the composition. After, as Susan Fleetwood put it, "sniffing one another out in an animal way," they came to a mutually agreeable compromise that allowed Nykvist to get on with his job and became extremely close, both personally and professionally.

Scriptwriters

Tarkovsky was the true author of all of his films. He shared the scriptwriting credits in five films (*The Steamroller and the Violin, Andrei Roublev, Solaris, Mirror,* and *Nostalghia*), and he has sole credit for *The Sacrifice*. Although his name does not appear in the credits of *Ivan's Childhood* and *Stalker*, that has more to do with the financial arrangements than with real authorship, and it is well known that in both of these films Tarkovsky changed the scripts significantly enough to upset the original authors. No matter who shared the task of scriptwriting with him, however, the result—as with the cinematogra-

Tarkovsky and Sven Nykvist on *The Sacrifice*. Copyright Swedish Film Institute.

phy—is something intensely and unmistakably personal. In interview Vladimir Akimov, a scriptwriter who knew him, hypothesizes that Tarkovsky needed a coauthor mainly in order to bounce ideas off someone and thus be able to make decisions. The coauthor was also a "control" figure who could provide some safeguards against Tarkovsky's tendency to discard something on a sudden whim or change his mind daily.

Tarkovsky's first scriptwriter was Andrei Konchalovsky, a fellow student and friend; they collaborated on Tarkovsky's diploma work and the first two feature films. On *Andrei Roublev* Konchalovsky's main task became endless rewriting and cutting during filming; in retrospect he sees their original work as "unprofessional": talented, full of "flights of imagination," a "poem" about Roublev, but not a script (*O Tarkovskom* 227). Although Tarkovsky was willing to agree to certain cuts and alterations, he remained adamant on others—relying, as in his work with actors, on his own intuition rather than on an ability to explain exactly what was right (or wrong) about them. Konchalovsky's frustration at this was intensified by Tarkovsky's reactions to his comments that the finished film was really far too long: already on the defensive against the authorities on this very point, Tarkovsky accused him of disloyalty and betrayal. From this point onwards they drifted further apart, both personally and in their aesthetic positions.

After Konchalovsky, Tarkovsky did not collaborate with any scriptwriter for more than one film. His relationships with his cowriters, especially when they were the original authors of literary works that he was adapting—such as Vladimir Bogomolov (for *Ivan's Childhood*) and the Strugatsky brothers— were often stormy and confrontational. Stanislaw Lem, though not directly involved with the script of *Solaris*, was far from happy with what resulted. Tarkovsky himself thought it difficult to separate the functions of the director and scriptwriter, for once the director takes on someone else's script, it inevitably changes: "It never materialises on the screen literally, word for word, mirrored; there are always distortions. Collaboration between screen-writer and director therefore tends to be beset by difficulty and argument. A valid film can be realised even when the original conception has been broken and destroyed during their work together, and a new idea, a new organism, has emerged from the ruins" (*Sculpting* 75–76). Bogomolov, Lem, and the Strugatskys, however, clearly did not appreciate having their works "destroyed."

The many problems on *Stalker* were compounded by Tarkovsky's desire—as with *Solaris*—increasingly to move away from the original science fiction concepts and premises of the original story (titled "Roadside Picnic"),[4] and by his insistence on endless last-minute rewriting. Boris Strugatsky quickly withdrew from direct involvement, leaving his brother Arkady to continue alone on location, flying regularly to consult with Boris in Leningrad. Arkady and Tarkovsky would work late at night rewriting, with the director turning up on set early in the morning ready to start work. The closing-down of production with the film half-shot gave an already dissatisfied Tarkovsky a golden opportunity to make even more extensive changes—on what, as Arkady observes sardonically, was supposed to be an accepted and approved script (*O Tarkovskom* 258)—once he received permission to resume working.

As in his dealings with actors, Tarkovsky found it difficult to articulate what he found wrong with Arkady's endlessly rewritten script, and, when asked how it could be improved, would say only: "That's your job, you're the scriptwriter, not I. Go and redo it. It must be ready tomorrow evening" (257–58). Finally, perhaps in despair, Arkady suggested jettisoning the science fiction element of the story completely. Tarkovsky looked at him "like a cat who had caught a canary" and remarked modestly that he *had* thought of suggesting this himself but had been afraid of offending them. If that, however, was what they themselves wanted. . . . Arkady promptly flew off to Leningrad, and within ten days he and Boris had produced what was now a "fable," with a fashionable Writer and an important Scientist being led into the Zone by the Stalker, an apostle of a new faith. Tarkovsky's words on approving this provide a somewhat ambiguous compliment to his cowriters: "For the first time in my life I have *my own* script" (259).

When Tarkovsky was cowriting original scripts, however, his relationships with his coauthors seem to have been less confrontational and, in fact, highly productive. Such collaborations produced what are often considered his best films: *Andrei Roublev* with Konchalovsky and the autobiographical *Mirror* with Alexander Misharin. *Mirror* was truly a joint effort—perhaps the most completely so of all Tarkovsky's films—in which not only the scriptwriter but the cinematographer, main actors, and set designer felt that it was *their* experiences and *their* reality, as well as the director's, that were being recreated for the screen. In a burst of combined creative energy, Misharin and Tarkovsky wrote the basic script for *Bright, Bright Day*—as *Mirror* was first called—in two weeks, swearing not to reveal who wrote which episodes. As usual much rewriting—both before and during filming—took place, and, as usual, Misharin felt that Tarkovsky knew what he wanted but was often unable to articulate it. As he describes it, the filming process sounds like a recipe for utter chaos, with the final script for each day's shooting being written on set, on little pieces of paper, while the cast sat around waiting, and Tarkovsky then rushing out to start filming each scene as it was completed (Interview and *O Tarkovskom* 60). Yet somehow it all worked and, unlike Arkady Strugatsky, Misharin felt that there was no disparity between what he had written and what finally appeared on the screen; the result, he told us happily, was like "one dream shared by three or four people" (Interview).

Set and Costume Designers

Tarkovsky claimed personal credit for set design on only one film, *Stalker*, after the original designer had been dismissed. From *Andrei Roublev* on, however, he made all the major decisions on sets and costuming, usually saying what it was he wanted and expecting his coworkers to come up with a satisfactory solution. On *Roublev* the aim was complete verisimilitude in the clothing and sets: "to reconstruct for a modern audience the real world of the fifteenth century, that is, to present that world in such a way that costume, speech, life-style and architecture would not give the audience any feeling of relic, of antiquarian rarity" (*Sculpting* 78). He succeeded so well in this that one complaint during the meeting of the artistic council to discuss the *completed* film was that the clothes were too drab and commonplace and should be changed! In *Solaris*, according to the costume designer Nelly Fomina, the intention was to avoid a futuristic and irrelevant exoticism, to suggest a certain timeless quality, and to provide the link to earth so central to the film's theme. The solutions to particular problems were left to the professionals, however: such as how to show Hari's frozen clothing in her suicide scene melting and returning to normal as she comes back to life. Here Fomina stiffened Hari's shirt with sugar water, and it was then thawed during the scene by spraying water on it.

For *Mirror* he used photographs of the clothes his mother wore when he was a child as the basis for Margarita Terekhova's costume in her role as Maria, just as he had the dacha of his childhood memories rebuilt as a major set for the film. The costume worn by the rich doctor's wife, also based on one that his mother had made, was intended to suggest a style of dress that was out of place in the general misery and poverty of wartime. The link between clothing and character became even stronger in *Stalker*, where the clothes for all three men were carefully chosen to suggest not just their different personalities but their contrasting approaches to their expedition: Professor is prepared for a lengthy outing, with warm jacket, hat, and knapsack, while Writer is in a rather long formal black coat and carries an incongruous and seemingly useless plastic bag. Stalker, meanwhile, who has visited the Zone many times and knows what to expect, wears old, dirty, but rugged pants and jacket.

Nelly Fomina, the costume designer on these three films, found him very different from most other directors, who simply accepted her sketches without much discussion; Tarkovsky would go over everything with her until she understood exactly what he wanted, though he would accept her suggestions if she could convince him that she was right. As with the camerawork, script, and acting, changes would be made right up to the moment of shooting, but normally nothing would be altered once filming began. Deprived of Fomina's services for *The Sacrifice*, Tarkovsky virtually designed Susan Fleetwood's costume himself, with her cooperation, being particularly concerned that her long, flowing dress should show off her legs and back to advantage. He also specified her hairstyle which, she was astonished to discover, was exactly that of his wife, Larissa.

His "hands-on" approach and constant rearrangement of sets and costume were not always welcomed by the technicians who had to keep an eye on mundane matters such as continuity, or who had spent hours or days preparing something that they were brusquely told was no good and would have to be replaced. An example of this can be seen in *Directed by Andrej Tarkovskij*, Michal Leszczylowski's documentary on the making of *The Sacrifice*, where the director cavalierly orders the removal of a huge tree that had earlier been placed, on his instructions, in front of Maria's cottage—to the obvious displeasure of those who actually had to shift it. His obsession with detail occasionally delayed the filming process, as when he insisted on using white birch logs for the wood pile at the Andronnikov monastery in *Andrei Roublev* rather than the grey aspen that had been provided, and everything came to a standstill while they waited for the birch to arrive (Ogorodnikova Interview). In the event, it made little difference, for the birch looked exactly like aspen on the screen.

In *Solaris* the sets, like the costumes, were intended to suggest the characters' longing for Earth in their alien environment. Once again Tarkovsky gave his art director (Mikhail Romadin) an overall idea of what he wanted, together with some specific instructions—such as the use of the Brueghel paintings in the library—and left him to provide most of the necessary objects and furnishings. Although the interiors of the space station are obviously sets, it is surprising to discover that most of the interiors in *Mirror*—even the present-day apartment with its courtyard—were also specially constructed for the film, and its designer, Nikolai Dvigubsky, like many others we spoke to, emphasized Tarkovsky's concern for textures and for subtle gradations of color within a particular scene. This can be seen too from Leszczylowski's documentary on the making of *The Sacrifice*, where Tarkovsky is seen making sure that even debris and mud have the right texture and are correctly positioned. He asks for black garbage bags to give more texture to Alexander's apocalyptic vision, and wades around in the mud rearranging rocks near the miniature house. His set designers were told that there was to be "no yellow" in the tree that was originally placed outside Maria's house (and then removed)—even though this scene was to be monochrome!

Susan Fleetwood perhaps best summed up the combination of exasperation and near-devotion that greeted Tarkovsky's constant changes of mind about what he wanted and his insistence on being involved in every aspect of the production, when she told us that Anna Asp and the others concerned with costume and set design on *The Sacrifice* "adored him in a way which knows he is a bloody nuisance most of the time, but that he is still wonderful." Most people, both in the Soviet Union and in the West, realized that they were working with someone special and that the results would fully justify the demands made upon them, however irrational or bizarre they might appear at the time.

Editors

Although Tarkovsky made the major editing decisions on all his films, he preferred—as with actors and other collaborators—to work with a known factor whenever possible, in this case Lyudmila Feiginova, who was assistant editor on *Ivan's Childhood* and editor on all his other Russian films. In almost every case there were rarely more than two or three takes to choose from; the major editing choices concerned the order of the episodes, and virtually no scene that had been shot was totally discarded. The main exception here was *Solaris*, where almost none of the material filmed in an elaborate, totally mirrored room was eventually used, while part of a night scene on Earth just before Kris's departure was also deleted. *Mirror*, according to Tarkovsky himself, went through twenty or more variants before it finally fell into shape, but here too the problem was the rearrangement of the scenes rather than choosing which to retain or to discard (*Sculpting* 116). According to Feiginova, it was she who came up with the crucial suggestion of moving the scene with the hypnotist and the stuttering boy from the middle of the film to its eventual position as prologue. Together they devised a system of summarizing the various episodes on cards and shifting them around to see how they would best fit together.

Again rather unusually, Feiginova was present at the dubbing and sound-mixing sessions for most of the films. The most complex task here was *Stalker*, where not only was the script constantly rewritten for each day's shooting, but all the dialogue was postdubbed and much of it rewritten yet again at this stage. Nikolai Grinko (the Professor) described Tarkovsky sitting in the dubbing studio, not even watching the screen, but paying intense attention to the intonation and rhythm of the speech and instantly correcting anything that sounded false (*O Tarkovskom* 105).

With the Soviet films there was almost always the additional problem of meeting the authorities' demands for changes and deletions once the director's final cut was completed. As a rule, he was willing to make cuts where he could be persuaded that they would be artistically beneficial or where they would not damage the artistic integrity of the work itself. Beyond that he remained totally intransigent. Rather like 1930s Hollywood writers and directors who coped with the Production Code by deliberately inserting irrelevant scenes that they knew would be cut, in the hope of diverting the censor's attention from other, more important ones, Tarkovsky would sometimes "throw a bone" to his own censors by deliberately filming some scenes at excessive length so that he could show his good will by shortening them (Yusov and Bondarchuk interviews).

Editing in the West presented rather different problems, now more rigorously tied in with time and with satisfying contractual obligations than had been the case previously. On *Nostalghia* Tarkovsky found that he had to wait till shooting was over before he could begin to edit, "something I had never done in Russia, where I had always edited as I went along. This had made it possible to prepare the next lot of filming, to clear up anything that had gone wrong, or to change things; in a word, the whole time I was filming I was dependent on the impressions of what had been filmed previously. In filming *Nostalghia*, this did not happen, and at first it was hard for me" (A. T., "Between Two Worlds" 78).

Michal Leszczylowski, editing *The Sacrifice*, found that he had to earn the director's confidence, but once this was done, Tarkovsky was willing to listen to him and to accept his suggestions. With a film containing as few shots as this one, (around 115 for a running time of 149 minutes) editing decisions mostly concerned where to begin and end each shot, though this apparently simple process could involve endless discussions. Two complete scenes were finally omitted: an expository one at the beginning that Tarkovsky characteristically felt made the family situation too "obvious" too soon, and one where Alexander writes his letter to his family. A major source of friction with his producer came when Tarkovsky decided that the film's "natural" length had to be 149 minutes—20 minutes longer than he had reluctantly committed himself to in his contract; but the director, who had battled Soviet bureaucrats for years, was not going to surrender here, and finally he had his way.

Composers

From an early age Tarkovsky exhibited a serious interest in music, to the extent of even considering professional training. Both composers who worked with him at home (Vyacheslav Ovchinnikov and Eduard Artemyev) agreed that he knew far more about the subject than most film directors and understood the "essence" of music. His taste remained conservative, centering initially around the standard late eighteenth- and nineteenth-century classics—Tchaikovsky, Beethoven, and Mozart—before moving to selected sixteenth- and seventeenth-century composers and, above all, Bach, to whom he would listen endlessly. He seems to have shown little interest in twentieth-century music as such (and had a particular dislike for Shostakovich and other Soviet composers), though Artemyev persuaded him to use electronic music in *Solaris, Mirror,* and *Stalker.*

Ovchinnikov, a friend who scored Tarkovsky's diploma film *The Steamroller and the Violin* and the first two features, was already known as a composer. For *Steamroller* Tarkovsky told him what the film was about and what kind of music he wanted; according to Ovchinnikov, he always knew where and why he needed music, thus making it difficult for the composer to experiment on his own, and would often use literary images to suggest the appropriate mood. Ovchinnikov was brought into *Ivan's Childhood* at a relatively late stage and—as is usual in filmmaking in the West—wrote the music after the film had been shot; with *Andrei Roublev*, however, he participated at the script stage and even wrote some music in advance, including a lengthy accompaniment to the planned but never-shot scene on the Kulikovo battlefield. Tarkovsky—on his own initiative and against Ovchinnikov's wishes—later transferred this music to the closing shots of Roublev's paintings. While admitting that the music works effectively in its new setting, Ovchinnikov was angry at being overruled and refused Tarkovsky's invitation to work on *Solaris,* thus incurring the familiar accusations of betrayal and disloyalty.

The choice of electronic music for *Solaris* was prompted partly by his new composer, Eduard Artemyev, who works extensively in this medium, and was not simply related to the fact that the film was science fiction. The electronic sounds were used as reminders of the alien setting of the space station, while costumes, sets, dialogue, and action reinforced the characters' inescapable links to Earth. Even the Bach Prelude that recurs throughout the film was electronically enhanced and reworked to emphasize this disharmony. Tarkovsky at first wanted to alter the classical music in *Mirror* in a similar fashion, then decided to leave the original scoring. According to Artemyev, the director's use of classical music (all of which he chose himself) was prompted by his feeling that cinema was a young art and needed to root itself in older, more established art forms (a similar reason might account for the constant references to literature and painting in the films).

Even more than *Solaris*, *Mirror* replaces a conventional musical accompaniment with the use of synthesized sound for what are primarily rhythmic purposes; as a result, sound mixing became an important and time-consuming element in the filming process. Surprisingly, given his close involvement in every other aspect of his films, Tarkovsky would leave Artemyev alone with the rough cut (and a clear idea of what he wanted) and then not even attend the sound recording. On *Stalker* this led to problems when Tarkovsky rejected the first soundtrack that had been prepared for the film, even though Artemyev thought he had achieved the synthesis of Eastern and Western cultures that they had discussed as an intellectual framework for the film as a whole (he had taken a medieval tune and rescored it for Eastern instruments). Typically, Tarkovsky told him only to "do it differently: that's your job." Finally Artemyev took one note of Indian music and then reworked it electronically. Though the taping was very expensive, they redid the music for the whole film.

Artemyev felt that Tarkovsky needed a composer only to organize the sounds for him, and that he used music as a last resort, when the visuals were not adequate on their own to convey everything he wanted. It is not surprising, therefore, that he moved progressively away from conventional scoring in his later films and toward emulating the overall practice of Bresson and of Bergman in such films as *Persona* and *Shame*, by using only carefully chosen sound effects and fragments of (mostly classical) music.

Producers

The role of the producer in the Soviet Union during Tarkovsky's career differed greatly from that of his or her counterpart in the West, and Tarkovsky's problems there were caused far more by bureaucrats and by ideological rigidity than—as would be the case with a similarly "difficult" director in the West—by the pressure to produce something entertaining and commercially viable. Budget constraints—though often very real—and the need to turn a profit were not the decisive factors that they are in a capitalist system, resulting in the situation alluded to earlier whereby, *while actually shooting his films*, Tarkovsky was remarkably "free" to work at his own pace, to rewrite and reshoot as he went along, and to make apparently outrageous demands and extensive last-minute changes that would have been intolerable in a system where "time is money."

Tamara Ogorodnikova, who acted as "producer" on *Andrei Roublev*, described her responsibilities as follows: the physical organization of the film, the allocation of the already agreed-on budget, and the safety of cast and crew. She acted as intermediary between Tarkovsky and Mosfilm where major budgetary decisions were concerned, such as the elimination, for financial or logistical reasons, of scenes from the original script; but she had no real power to stop him from constantly rewriting the script before filming or ordering lengthy delays in shooting while some prop or costume was altered in favor of something more suitable. While time and labor were relatively flexible items, she had no authority to call on additional funds, and they often had to resort to various ingenious devices to make the battle and crowd scenes look convincing. For the Tartar attack on Vladimir they were originally allocated the meager total of twenty-six horses and had to supplement them with ninety others borrowed from a hippodrome. It is a tribute to Tarkovsky's ingenuity under the circumstances that Western audiences often assume that *Andrei Roublev* was a far more expensive production than in fact was the case.

The relative freedom on set or location, of course, was fully balanced by the fact that the major production decisions—those that caused Tarkovsky the most mental and emotional anguish—were made either before or after shooting. It was there that he had to fight and resist in order to get what he wanted, or to agree to the least destructive compromise that he was prepared to tolerate. Yet, during shooting, he could feel that he was fully in charge, his every whim catered to by a devoted crew who were prepared to make considerable sacrifices to satisfy the artistic genius for whom they were working. While there is an element of deliberate caricature in putting it like this, there is also enough truth to help explain why Western producers, accustomed to holding a tighter rein over shooting, found Tarkovsky peculiarly exasperating to deal with.

According to Daniel Toscan du Plantier, the crew on *Nostalghia* initially resented what they saw as his authoritarian behavior—though they later came to understand and respect him. Anna-Lena Wibom, who produced *The Sacrifice* for the Swedish Film Institute, an organization that fully respects the idea of film as an art and has fostered the career of Ingmar Bergman, among others, for several decades, felt that he had totally unrealistic expectations and demands (deriving from his disdain as an "artist" for sordid financial details) and that his habit of improvisation made normal scheduling and budgetary decisions extremely difficult. She found it impossible to pin him down in advance or even to hold him to certain commitments he had already made—this being, perhaps, on his part, a natural defense mechanism after years of dealing with unscrupulous and unreliable bureaucrats.

Tarkovsky, in fact, may well have assumed that his prestige as an artist in the West would ensure him rather more preferential treatment than he in fact received. Despite his high critical reputation in Italy, France, Britain, and Germany, his films had been far from profitable, even on the art film circuit, and Daniel Toscan du Plantier, who helped finance *Nostalghia*, was perfectly realistic in seeing it as a "small" film that, over time, would earn back its modest costs and was being made for love of film as an art form rather than in the hope of making anyone rich. Tarkovsky, however, may have hoped for something more than this or have at least assumed that, in the prosperous West, he would be spared some of the humiliating and niggling restraints that he had been forced to endure at home.

An illuminating anecdote from Susan Fleetwood illustrates some of the almost comic mutual misunderstandings involved. Talking of the fleeing crowds in Alexander's dreams of nuclear disaster in *The Sacrifice*, she implied that Tarkovsky had wanted to summon up hundreds of extras at a moment's notice and was astonished to discover that they would all have to be paid and that the most he could get, after due negotiation, would be around forty (which Tarkovsky then made look like a hundred in the scene)—whereas, she said, in the world he came from, "they would turn out the Red Guard and it was done" (Interview). In actual fact, of course, the Red Army would be working for someone like Bondarchuk rather than Tarkovsky, and it was not so much his enjoying unlimited resources of this kind in the Soviet Union that was the problem as the hope that he—a critically acclaimed and admired figure—could at last be treated according to his merits and granted the privileges that he deserved. The result of his inevitable disillusionment was considerable friction between him and those responsible for handling day-to-day business on the set (Fleetwood Interview). When Anna-Lena Wibom was asked what his future prospects in the West might have been, her considered judgment was that, much as she liked and admired him, he could have survived only if he had learned, as Bergman had, to scale down the scope of his filmmaking, while developing a form that would still satisfy his artistic intentions. Having been forced—for different reasons—to do something similar in the Soviet Union, this would hardly have been a very attractive proposition for him, and a career in the West, if he had lived, might have proved ultimately as frustrating, in its own way, as anything that he had been forced to endure at home.

PART TWO

FOUR

Beginnings: *The Steamroller and the Violin* and *Ivan's Childhood*

The Steamroller and the Violin (*Katok i skripka*, 1960)

At VGIK (the State Film School), Tarkovsky worked on two collaborative student films, *The Killers* (*Ubiytsy*—an adaptation of a story by the ever-popular Hemingway) and *There Will Be No Leave Today* (*Segodnya uvolneniya ne budet*), an action story based on a real postwar incident. Tarkovsky and fellow classmate Alexander Gordon interviewed participants, visited military barracks, used real uniforms and armored vehicles, and shot on location to create a "docudrama" of a simple, self-effacing officer who becomes a hero by detonating German artillery shells found during the excavation of a construction site. Despite competition from a professional Lenfilm production of the same story, Tarkovsky's and Gordon's film was screened on Soviet television in April 1959 (Gordon Interview).

Tarkovsky's first independent directing project was his diploma film, *The Steamroller and the Violin*. As befits a graduation work, this film is clearly intended as a "calling card" to show off the young director's creative potential and technical virtuosity. His ambition can be recognized both in the length of the film (50 minutes rather than the normal 20, and in color rather than black and white) and in his presumptuous—and unsuccessful—attempt to obtain the services of the highly acclaimed cameraman Sergei Urusevsky, whose work on Mikhail Kalatozov's *The Cranes Are Flying* (1957) had brought him international renown (Yusov Interview). Many of his coworkers on the film were friends who would contribute much to the success of his early feature films: cowriter, Andrei Konchalovsky (who became a well-known director himself), cinematographer Vadim Yusov (*Ivan's Childhood, Andrei Roublev*, and *Solaris*), and composer Vyacheslav Ovchinnikov (*Ivan and Roublev*).

The Steamroller and the Violin (produced at the Mosfilm Studio's Department for Children's and Youth Films) combines relatively conventional thematic elements with both self-conscious stylistic bravura and early premonitions of the highly personal artistic and moral concerns that were to characterize all of Tarkovsky's later work. The film is the story of a growing friendship between a budding young musician, Sasha (six or seven years old), and Sergei, a steamroller driver working near Sasha's apartment building. Sergei protects Sasha from the tough kids who regularly bully him but also teaches him to stand up for others and be a man. While Sergei educates the boy in the basic realities of life, Sasha opens up the world of music to Sergei. The two arrange to see a movie together, but Sasha's mother insists on keeping him at home; he imagines a happy ending in which he joins Sergei on the steamroller and drives off with him.

The youth theme generally dominated Soviet cinema of the late fifties and early sixties, not only because of the influence of Albert Lamorisse's very popular *The Red Balloon* but because, in the "Thaw" period, films generally sought the fresh perspective and the innocent viewpoint of children not burdened by either ideology or life's tribulations. Diploma films about children were fashionable at the time, such as Konchalovsky's *The Boy and the Dove* (*Malchik i golub*, 1962)—best short film in Venice—Yuli Fayt's *Streetcar to Other Cities* (*Tramvay v drugiye goroda*, 1962), or Georgy Danelia and Igor Talankin's joint debut *Seryozha* (1960). Despite Tarkovsky's subsequent genuine contempt for socialist realism, *The Steamroller and the Violin* is perfectly orthodox in its depiction of the friendship between worker and artist, each of whom learns something new and valuable from the other, and its idealization of the brightly colored steamroller that is playing its vital part in creating a better society: images of urban reconstruction are situated at the center of the film. The fact that Sergei is a World War II veteran suggests that only through the sacrifices made by his generation can Sasha enjoy his relatively privileged existence and the luxury of art.

Stylistically the film is—with very few exceptions—more important in showing what Tarkovsky *could* do with camerawork, editing, sound, and music if he wanted to, than for significant anticipations of his later work. After the energetic opening sequence as the boy leaves his apartment, Tarkovsky sends him through the streets of Moscow to celebrate that vibrant city and demonstrate his own technical virtuosity in camerawork and in editing. As the boy stops to look in a store window, the camera tracks past him to a collection of mirrors that reflect multiple images both of himself and of the surrounding city. A complex montage of split-screen and other fragmented effects follows that clearly pays homage to Dziga Vertov's 1929 classic *Man with a Movie Camera* (*Chelovek s kinoapparatom*), though it also reflects a contemporary fascination with the life of the city later seen in such films as Marlen Khutsiev's *I Am Twenty* (1962) and Georgy Danelia's *I Walk about Moscow* (*Ya shagayu po Moskve*, 1964).

As the boy waits for and then has his music lesson, Tarkovsky experiments with both sound—wittily mixing diegetic and nondiegetic music and linking the formidable teacher to the relentless beat of her metronome—and editing, cutting closer and closer to his hero as the teacher repeatedly walks in front of the camera and briefly blocks out his image. Later, as the boy plays his violin and Sergei drives his steamroller, the harmony and understanding that the two have attained is reflected in the deliberate mismatching of image and music—the violin heard over shots of the steamroller, and the roar of the engine accompanying images of the boy playing.

Other virtuoso effects include the scene of the demolition of a building, conveyed through rapid cuts, hectic music, and swaying, erratic images as if from the perspective of the wrecking ball itself; and other point of view shots as one of Sasha's tormentors tries to show off by recklessly riding his bicycle—before ignominiously crashing and damaging his machine. A more interesting sequence, which heralds a later motif in Tarkovsky's work, has Sasha and his mother talking in front of a mirror, with the lack of communication between them suggested by the fact that the boy seems to be talking to her reflection rather than to her. Apart from examples such as this, however, the film's style is noteworthy for what Tarkovsky chose *not* to follow up on in his more characteristic later work: extreme and unusual angles, complex montage effects, and frequent use of fades and dissolves to signal changes of time and space. The film's chronology and its settings have nothing of the ambiguity even of *Ivan's Childhood*, much less a later work like *The Sacrifice*.

Though Tarkovsky seems concerned mostly to establish his technical credentials through his skillful handling of an uncontroversial subject—the friendship of a worker and a budding artist/*intelligent*—certain themes and image patterns that were to be central to his later work are clearly present already. Water is a pervasive element in almost all the important scenes: rain, as Sasha and Sergei are reconciled after a disagreement; the running water tap that is both seen and heard as the friends have their lunch; the flooded alleyways that precede a rainstorm and the puddles everywhere after it, especially in the final dream sequence; the reflections of steamroller, driver, and boy in a puddle as the two agree to meet again that evening. The theme of art, so central to almost all Tarkovsky's work, is introduced, lightheartedly perhaps as Sasha struggles unavailingly against his teacher's stultifying and restrictive discipline, more seriously as, allowed to express himself freely, he plays his violin to the enraptured Sergei.

Sasha's strained relationship with his domineering mother, and the clear lack of understanding between them, looks forward to *Solaris* and *Mirror*, while similar noncommunicative scenes in front of mirrors are found in both these films as well as in *Ivan's Childhood*. The film's ending—in which the tensions and conflicts are apparently resolved in a dreamlike reconciliation as the boy, wearing a red shirt, imagines himself joining Sergei on his red steamroller—foreshadows *Solaris*, *Mirror*, and *Nostalghia*, even to the extent, as Philip Strick has pointed out (*Monthly Film Bulletin* [May 1981]: 116), of anticipating the reunion with the father (here father figure) in *Solaris*. The strong mother and absent father have clear autobiographical roots as well. Both these examples also reflect another, perhaps more disturbing, aspect of Tarkovsky's work in the distrust and even hostility directed against the female characters: the music teacher and the mother display similar authoritarian features, and Sergei would clearly rather go to the cinema with Sasha than with his conniving female coworker; he looks around almost despairingly for Sasha as she waylays him and carries him off with her at the end of the film. The only "positive" female figure in the film is a little girl, a doll-like fellow music pupil to whom Sasha presents an apple. The strong male bonding between Sergei and Sasha is reflected in the relationships between Ivan and the other soldiers in Tarkovsky's next film and between Andrei Roublev and Daniil or Boriska, and (after much initial antagonism) in the understanding reached by the three men in *Stalker*. Where strongly positive male relationships do not exist—as in *Solaris, Mirror, Nostalghia,* and *The Sacrifice*—the heroes seem peculiarly lost and disoriented.

Although *The Steamroller and the Violin* would seem to satisfy the criteria for a successful diploma film of the period (orthodox subject matter as workers and artists cooperate to build the ideal socialist society, and judicious and unthreatening stylistic experimentation), some of the responses within the studio provide a foretaste of Tarkovsky's much more serious later conflicts with the bureaucracy. In *Tarkovsky: Cinema as Poetry* Maya Turovskaya notes that the young director was criticized for characters and casting that were too crude for a children's film, but that disagreements did not go beyond the confines of the studio as the film won praise in the press and Tarkovsky was recognized as a promising young talent (26). Yet the review of the film in the influential journal *Iskusstvo kino* is, in fact, both complimentary and critical. After describing the film and noting that it belongs to a minority of films *about* rather than *for* children, the reviewer praises the young director for his "good taste, light, unforced manner, and the ability to find expressive details" (Smelkov 26). He then berates Tarkovsky for occasionally not being original, for "quoting" Italian, French, and Polish cinema (the rainstorm scene, for example, clearly recalls De Sica's *Bicycle Thieves*). The reviewer here misses the self-conscious nature of the young Tarkovsky paying homage to his masters in the West as well as in the Soviet Union. The most serious criticism is reserved for the acting in the film: while the boy is natural, the steamroller driver is "posing, acting"—the fault of an inexperienced director who needs to improve his work with actors (26). Turovskaya comments that Tarkovsky's response to this criticism was brash, uncompromising, and undiplomatic—setting a pattern that was followed throughout his later career.

Ivan's Childhood (Ivanovo detstvo, 1962)

Tarkovsky saw his first feature film as ending a cycle in his life, an apprenticeship which consisted of his studies at VGIK, the making of his diploma film, and the eight months he spent working on *Ivan's Childhood* (*Sculpting* 15). This film was his "qualifying examination" which allowed him to work out his ideas about cinema art and to test his abilities as a director (27). Although in his book Tarkovsky does not mention that he took over the film from another director (E. Abalov), this fact made the working conditions for his first feature film even more difficult than normal. Much of the money allotted for the film had already been spent (Rausch Interview, 1989), and even though the losses were not carried over, there was clearly much psychological pressure to make them up. The Mosfilm studio officially shut down film production on *Ivan* (as the film was called) in October 1960 (Turovskaya 29) and was looking for another director. Tarkovsky's friend and cameraman, Vadim Yusov, gave Tarkovsky the news about the closing of the film and brought him *Ivan*, the novella by Vladimir Bogomolov, on which the film was based (*O Tarkovskom* 72).

Why was Tarkovsky interested in such a risky project? His first wife suggests several possible reasons: it was very difficult for young directors to find work, and Tarkovsky already had the cameraman (Yusov) and even the star, Nikolai Burlyaev, whom he knew from Konchalovsky's diploma film and who was the exact physical opposite of the cute, plucky youngster originally envisaged in the role. Tarkovsky himself states that he was attracted to this atypical war story by its avoidance of military exploits, and mostly by the warped personality and tragic fate of the young military scout (*Sculpting* 17). Luckily Tarkovsky had not been the director when the original co-scriptwriter, Mikhail Papava, attempted to give the film a happy ending, renaming it *A Second Life*, and allowing Ivan to survive the war, get married, and have a family. Bogomolov, however, insisted that his Ivan was a tragic hero who shared the fate of most young Soviet scouts during World War II (Turovskaya 31).

By June 16, 1961, the team of Tarkovsky, Yusov (camera), and Ye. Chernyaev (art director) was given permission to "return to work on the film *Ivan*" (Turovskaya 29). The shooting was completed by January 18, 1962, a rough cut was ready by January 30 (partly because Tarkovsky, following what was to become his usual practice, had begun the editing during shooting), and the film was approved on March 3, coming in 24,000 rubles under budget and even earning Tarkovsky official compliments for his technical handling of the production (Turovskaya 33). Eight months from start to finish for a full-length film was certainly to be a record for Tarkovsky. But these facts belie the difficulties which Tarkovsky experienced in making *his* version of *Ivan*. Tarkovsky had many arguments with the equally strong-willed Bogomolov over his downplaying of the story's detailed military exploits and his unwillingness to attempt to transfer its dry emotional texture and neutral, restrained style to the screen (*Sculpting* 18). By adding four "dream" sequences he "poeticized" the film, shifting the focus from the external reality of war to Ivan's psychological state. Although Tarkovsky's film still credits the original scriptwriters, Papava and Bogomolov, it was in essence so different that one must recognize Tarkovsky himself and his uncredited co-scriptwriter, Andrei Konchalovsky, as the real authors of *Ivan's Childhood*.

The film's tortuous path through the studio bureaucracy foreshadowed the difficulties Tarkovsky was to encounter in obtaining approval for all his later films. It was subjected to examination at thirteen separate artistic council meetings (Feiginova Interview), the last of which took place on March 1, 1962. Gathered at this meeting were established artists from the literary and film worlds, each of whom first complimented the film, especially the role of Ivan, and then requested some minor or, more often, major changes. Beginning with Sergei Mikhalkov, the head of the Writers' Union (and father of the directors Andrei Konchalovsky and Nikita Mikhalkov), many criticized the graphic documentary footage (omitted in the American version) of the burnt bodies of high-ranking Nazis (*Stenograma* 2–3). While admitting that there would have been no film without Tarkovsky, Bogomolov again enumerated all of Tarkovsky's military inconsistencies, and completely rejected the love angle in the story (39–51). As might be expected, Tarkovsky's strongest defender was his mentor, Mikhail Romm, who pronounced the film very "powerful." Romm both argued for and explained the necessity of the most controversial episodes—the love scene and the documentary footage—and warned about cutting any episode (21–29). From Tarkovsky's response it is clear that he was barely able to contain himself after three or four months of such discussions. Characteristically, he rejected proposals for cuts because he "didn't feel the need for them and therefore could not do it." He accepted the suggestion that he rest and think for a couple of weeks, but would not guarantee that he would change anything in the film (66–69). The general director of Mosfilm, V. N. Surin, even gave him a way out by saying that a director doesn't have to respond to all the criticisms, if he doesn't find it necessary to do so (71)! Two days later the film was approved.

Ivan's Childhood was to make a strong impact at a widely attended discussion on "The Language of Cinema," held over a number of days in March 1962 at the Filmmakers' Union. Mikhail Romm spoke confidently about a film practically no one had yet seen, as an example of truly contemporary cinema language. When *Ivan's Childhood* won the Golden Lion at the Venice Film Festival in the fall of 1962, it brought Tarkovsky international fame practically overnight. Newsworthy critical and political scandal was created when *Unita*, the hardline Italian Communist Party newspaper, attacked the film for being "petit-bourgeois." No less a cultural arbiter than Jean-Paul Sartre felt compelled to defend in print Tarkovsky's "socialist surrealism" and his depiction of a genuinely "Soviet tragedy" ("Discussion sur la critique à propos de *L'Enfance d'Ivan*").'

In the Soviet Union the film was recognized as an important new development in "poetic" cinema by well-known writers such as Konstantin Simonov (*Izvestiya* [May 25, 1962]) and in articles by Maya Turovskaya and Neya Zorkaya, the two young critics who were to become Tarkovsky's best interpreters. It immediately became the focus of the ongoing debate on the language of contemporary Soviet cinema and was seen by many as a quantum leap forward in its development. Critics pointed to the film's subjective camera and development of narrative by associative links, its interweaving of dream and reality, the original use of documentary footage, an unforgettable hero, the opposition of two worlds—internal and external—in war, and finally its deep humanism. Of all Tarkovsky's films this was the one that garnered the most press and the most favorable reviews (and at least five front-page articles in major newspapers that year); but it, too, had its share of negative criticism, primarily from those who tried to compare it too closely to the detached realistic account of war in Bogomolov's *Ivan*, or were too concerned about its pessimism, or did not understand its stylistic complexity. But for once, the critical voices were in the minority, especially after the film's resounding success abroad. After *Ivan's Childhood* no serious discussion of Soviet film could leave out the figure of Andrei Tarkovsky.

In *The Steamroller and the Violin* Tarkovsky had combined uncontroversial subject matter with conspicuous stylistic virtuosity, and to a certain extent this is true also of *Ivan's Childhood*: although the film stimulated a good deal of critical debate in the Soviet Union, it was essentially in tune with the personal, nonheroic mood of Soviet war films of the period. For Tarkovsky, Ivan is more victim than hero. While the film avoids the excessively chauvinistic patriotism of standard Soviet World War II epics, little sympathy is wasted on the Germans, who are a sinister off-screen presence. Ivan's hatred of the Germans appears fully understandable (even if it has warped his own personality), and his comments on their perversion of art and literature, though not necessarily Tarkovsky's own views, are allowed to stand without authorial qualification. The newsreel scenes at the end and the revelation of Ivan's execution (and those of countless others) link the Germans firmly to atrocities and mindless cruelty. By contrast the Soviet soldiers are simple, straightforward, and kindly, the officers fatherly and reassuringly competent. There is nothing here of the moral relativity that was beginning to creep into even American war films of the period, such as *The Young Lions* (directed by Edward Dmytryk, 1958) with its "good" and even sympathetic Germans, much less of the presentation of military authority as crazed, despotic, and incompetent in the films of Stanley Kubrick or novels like *Catch-22*.

For a "war" film, however, there is remarkably little action in *Ivan's Childhood*, and even the apparent "reality" of the war scenes appears—especially from the perspective of a knowledge of Tarkovsky's later work—remarkably stylized. The actual fighting is merely hinted at—indicated by off-screen sound, signal flares, and ruined buildings—rather than directly shown, while the landscape itself takes on an obsessive, hallucinatory quality, suggesting a mental rather than a physical reality, which is closer to that of the Zone in *Stalker* than to a conventional war movie. What made *Ivan's Childhood* truly different even from the revisionist war films of the "Thaw" period was Tarkovsky's visual and aural presentation, his insistent use of stylized, often expressionistic camerawork and sound to present the character's interior reality—primarily through dreams—but also to create a highly subjective external world as well.

Tarkovsky's addition of the dream sequences inevitably altered not just Bogomolov's plot—a detached, realistic account of Ivan's heroic missions, his relationship with the four soldiers/officers (Galtsev, Kholin, Katasonych, and Gryaznov), and his eventual death—but the whole concept of Ivan himself and our attitude toward him. The film opens with the sound of a cuckoo and a fade-in to the face of the twelve-year-old Ivan, seen first behind a tree trunk and then through a spider's web; next he is in the distance, behind the tree, which has been explored in close-up. The bright, radiant lighting and powerfully lyrical music help to create a mood of carefree happiness, though the spider's web, in retrospect, may create a sense of faint unease. A series of images—of Ivan's face, a goat's head, a butterfly—is followed by a tracking shot as Ivan appears to be flying, laughing and ecstatically happy. A cut to a helicopter shot from his apparent point of view shows a pastoral landscape with the camera moving toward a river and trees. The extreme long shot of the landscape suddenly gives way to a disorienting extreme close-up of what seems to be an earthen embankment. We are back on earth, examining with the boy the sunlight streaming through leaves, the butterfly, roots, and soil. He runs toward a woman in the distance, the image still bright and sunlit, and stops to drink from a bucket on the ground. Seen from a high angle, he looks up and says, "Mother, there's a cuckoo." A cut shows a smiling young woman looking down at him. As she wipes her forehead with her arm, the sound of gunfire replaces the happy, lyrical music. The camera tracks into her face as the smile turns to fear, and tilts sharply to the right as she falls. We hear the boy scream, "Mama!"

This dream, only belatedly identified as such, contains much of Tarkovsky's later work in embryo: the dream which begins as everyday normality, then (with the flying) becomes something obviously unreal; the motif of flight itself; the love of the natural world, trees, sunlight, birds, insects; the association of the mother with water; the sudden intrusion of violence into an apparently peaceful scene; and the use of autobiographical material. (Tarkovsky's sister Marina mentions in interview that one of his first sentences as a child was "Mama, there's a cuckoo"; the apparently irrelevant shot of the goat can perhaps be explained by the photograph of a goat among the scenes of his childhood in the German edition of his diary.)

When Ivan wakes from the dream he is seen in a dark, narrow, enclosed wooden room. He goes downstairs, shot from both very low and high angles, and is seen exiting through a door that is filmed at a tilted angle worthy of Orson Welles (*Citizen Kane* was one of the films most admired by Tarkovsky and his fellow students), with Ivan's face in disorientingly low-angled close-up. He walks across a barren landscape dominated by the windmill he has just left, past abandoned army vehicles with sunlight glinting through their ruined bodywork, as smoke drifts in the background and darkly ominous music dominated by harsh brass and drumbeats replaces the lyrical theme of the dream. Then he is a tiny figure wading through a swamp, surrounded by dead birch trees; the image is very dark, fitfully illuminated by signal flares, with menacing drumbeats continuing on the soundtrack; even the sun is shrouded. While it would be unfair to accuse Tarkovsky of "showing off" his technical virtuosity here (as could be said of many of the effects in *Steamroller*), he is clearly aiming both to impress the spectator right away and to create a mood that reflects the bleak and distorted perspective of his young hero. In the scene with Lieutenant Galtsev that follows, the high-contrast lighting is again very expressionistic, plunging the room into unnatural patterns of bright light and dark shadow, with Ivan himself lit so that his face and especially his eyes appear almost demonic.

From the very beginning Tarkovsky establishes powerful visual and aural contrasts between the worlds of dream and reality which constitute the film's dramatic center. While his shadowless dream world is bright, clean, full of sounds and images of the living beauty of nature, Ivan's "real" world is dirty, dark, deeply shadowed, distorted, with the mostly silent landscape burnt and dead. Although in the real-life scenes Ivan is an actor and not an observer and the story is not literally told from his viewpoint, he nevertheless is the film's "center of consciousness," whose psychological state effectively controls and intermingles the "real" and the "dream" worlds.

The scene that works best in presenting a subjective perspective on an actually occurring event—as opposed to the more obvious unreality of the dreams—is probably the one in which Ivan, left alone in the church/bunker as Galtsev, Kholin, and Katasonych go off to search for a boat, "plays" at hunting and capturing Germans. He is seen hoisting and fastening a bell that had been visible previously in the room; he then draws the knife that Galtsev has given him and crawls along the floor in semidarkness as if stalking someone. The lighting becomes arbitrary and unrealistic, sometimes following the direction of the flashlight he carries, and sometimes seeming to have an independent life of its own. German is heard, sounding like one of Hitler's speeches; we seem to hear the projection of Ivan's own thoughts here, as we enter into his consciousness: the sound is therefore diegetic. Meanwhile the nondiegetic music becomes dramatic and suspenseful. The circle of light from his flashlight picks up a scratched message on the wall: eight prisoners, none of them over nineteen, are about to be executed. German voices are heard, along with frightened cries, as well as the music; the message continues: "Avenge us!"

A series of rapid pans and swish-pans follows, moving in what seems a circular movement from Ivan's face to the flashlight, back to his frightened face, past an unidentified body on the floor, back to Ivan and his hand holding the knife, then to multiple reflections of the circling light and a brief glimpse of his mother's face, and back to Ivan now reflected in a mirror and brightly lit. (All this seems to be one continuous shot.) The music and sounds of sobbing continue and grow louder as the camera again picks up the reflected light and the mother's face before moving back to Ivan and then in a jagged motion up to the bell, which the weeping Ivan, in a cut to a high angle, starts to ring. The camera tracks out from the bell as the sound of cheering

An image of entrapment from *Ivan's Childhood.* Artificial Eye.

drowns out the earlier sobbing; Ivan moves away from the bell, though its ringing continues, and the unmotivated lighting effects also persist as he rushes around the room fighting an imaginary battle and calling on the enemy to surrender. He threatens a coat hanging on the wall, as the bell stops telling it, "You will pay for everything. Do you think I don't remember?" before breaking down in tears and collapsing onto the floor. The room is now completely dark, until a sudden explosion blows a wall open and reveals an icon of the Madonna and child, tilted over at an oblique angle.

This audaciously shot scene conveys more powerfully than any other in the film the terrible paradox of Ivan's situation: a lonely and frightened child still with many of a child's responses and emotions, yet thrust into a brutal environment that twists and distorts his feelings in a way that he can neither comprehend nor escape. Tarkovsky makes us share his responses through the subjective soundtrack and camerawork, yet also conveys his fear and confusion through the inconsistent and arbitrary lighting, alternating between subjective and objective throughout. We are simultaneously within the boy's mind and outside it, able to understand, as he cannot, the *meaning* of his confused and terrifying experience. The only false note, and one that Tarkovsky would probably have avoided later, is the nudging shot to the icon that closes the scene.

The major exception to the Ivan perspective—when he is both physically and emotionally absent—is found in the romantic interludes centering around the nurse Masha. Here the setting is provided by the dazzling white trunks of a birch wood and bright sunlight, suggesting a necessary relief from the grim realities of war and the persistence of normal human emotions even in this strained and unnatural atmosphere. These scenes are filmed with elaborate camerawork, many tracking shots, and a variety of low and high angles, as Captain Kholin first entices, then brusquely dismisses Masha. When he leaves, she wanders in a daze, the camera taking her point of view as if she were running, moving rapidly into and away from the white trunks of the birches. Later, after she has met her former school friend, her feelings for Kholin are again expressed through subjective camerawork as, to the accompaniment of richly romantic waltz music, the camera seems to sway and dance through the trees in her place. Although the function of these scenes in terms of thematic contrast is clear enough—just as it has denied Ivan his childhood, the war has made Kholin's and Masha's intimacy impossible—they are not particularly successful, largely because Kholin's motives are left extremely obscure. Is his flirtation simply part of a cynical sexual game, a testing of his control over women? Or, on the point of surrendering to his own baser impulses, does he gallantly refuse to exploit her naiveté and vulnerability? The obscurity here seems symptomatic of Tarkovsky's perennial problems in presenting positive love relationships.

Although Tarkovsky was rarely to resort in later films to the obtrusive lighting effects, self-consciously hectic camerawork, and extreme angles that characterize this film, they mostly work well within its deliberately stylized structure. Likewise, though some of the more obvious symbolism—such as the shot of Ivan surrounded by a circle of broken rafters that both recalls the very early shot of his face behind a spider's web and conveys the clear-cut idea of "entrapment"—would be eschewed by Tarkovsky later on, it does not seem badly out of place in this more overtly didactic work. His most characteristic and lasting innovations, however, are to be found in the "dream" sequences which enclose the film, dominating it both emotionally and aesthetically.

The second dream is more clearly signaled than the first, by the exhausted Ivan falling asleep (after his successful return from the German side) and by the sound of dripping water. The internal logic of this dream is much the same as for the opening, with a few moments of sunlit serenity and happiness, associated with the smiling, youthful mother and water, brutally ended by a gunshot and death. The third dream, of Ivan, his sister, and the apples, is the only totally happy one and is again signaled by dripping water, the lyrical music associated with the first dream, and Ivan being clearly drowsy, though not actually asleep. The dreamlike effect is accentuated by what was to become one of Tarkovsky's favorite devices, as a character is seen several times, in rapid succession, within the same camera movement, but with each appearance apparently "impossible" in terms of naturalistic time and space. Here, as Ivan offers the girl an apple, she moves into frame from right to left

Apples and rain in one of Ivan's dreams. Artificial Eye.

Ivan's final dream, with the beach and the dead tree. Artificial Eye.

and then off-screen; immediately reappears from the right and exits again; then reappears once more—each time with a more serious and intense expression on her face. The apples spilled from the back of a truck, the horse munching them, and the cleansing rain, all create a highly lyrical sequence—an obvious homage to Dovzhenko's *Earth*—and introduce one of Tarkovsky's favorite animals, the horse.

The fourth and final dream follows immediately on our knowledge of Ivan's death at the hands of the Germans. Once again there is sunlight, a smiling mother, and the "dream" music. Ivan is kneeling and drinking from a bucket on the beach; his mother picks up the bucket and walks away, then turns to wave to him. (She is alive once again, but this time is she saying farewell to him?) Ivan plays hide-and-seek with other children near a dead tree, then they mysteriously vanish (through a dissolve) and he continues the game with his sister. He chases her along the beach to the sound of the lyrical "dream/memory" theme, with the sun sparkling on the water behind them. He catches up with her and passes her, the camera moving with him to the sound of drumbeats as he runs into the water. There is a cut to a close-up of Ivan reaching out his arm (with the background now that of the beach rather than the open water) and then a cut to the dead tree, looming black and ominous ahead, with the camera tracking into it until it fills the screen and blocks out the sun and the image goes black.

Until the very last shot there is little "dreamlike" about this particular scene, which could be a purely naturalistic memory of normal childhood games. The earlier dreams signal their unreality at some point; here there are only faint hints of unease in the changing soundtrack, the vanishing children, and perhaps the sight of the dead tree itself—and, of course, and essentially, our own experience of the previous dreams, with the now familiar imagery of the mother, the water, the sister, and the beach, and our knowledge of Ivan's death. What gives the scene its terrible poignancy is its very normality and our realization that this is what a twelve-year-old should be doing instead of dangling from a meat-hook, after a brief life soured by hatred and deprivation. The scene raises a further question, however: Who is dreaming or remembering it? The earlier dreams are slotted naturalistically into the sequence of events, but this one takes place after the dreamer is dead. It is almost as if Tarkovsky transfers the burden of this dream onto the audience, forcing us to fill in for the experience that Ivan can no longer have for himself, and providing for us—but not for him—a sense of potential harmony and reconciliation that reminds us all the more cruelly of what he has lost. In this respect the impact is closer to that of *Mirror* or *Nostalghia*, where the main character too seems to have died before we are shown the final dream/fantasy/memory vision that seems to resolve the various conflicts that have previously tormented him, than to the more hopeful endings of *Andrei Roublev*, *Solaris*, *Stalker*, and *The Sacrifice*. Yet the sheer finality of the brutal cut to blackness that ends the film remains without parallel in Tarkovsky's other films.

Although the dream that opens the film is initially disconcerting, it is quickly integrated into the overall pattern in which the dreams provide both an illusory escape for Ivan from the terrible reality of his waking life and an explanation of his hatred for the Germans and his obsessive desire for revenge. It also functions, however, to introduce one of Tarkovsky's favorite narrative devices by forcing the spectator to participate, from the very beginning of the film, in interpreting the images on the screen: there is no immediate clue that we are witnessing a dream and, though the film as a whole is much less complex than anything Tarkovsky was to make later, the audience is constantly obliged to work to piece together the information with which it is presented. In his lectures some twenty years later, Tarkovsky told the young directors that a film's dramatic structure must take a "musical form" where emotion is evoked through the destruction of narrative logic. He reminded them that Chekhov, upon finishing a story, would throw out the first page, thus removing the motivation (*Lektsii* 61).

Where *The Steamroller and the Violin* had proceeded in conventional and logical fashion, signaling shifts in time and space by means of fades and dissolves, Tarkovsky resorts here to what was to become a characteristic technique of ignoring conventional establishing shots and the normal methods of indicating chronological links between scenes or conveying essential narrative information. The scene that follows the credit sequence of Ivan wading through the swamp opens on a close-up of a hand, and then the face of a sleeping young man (Galtsev), addressed as "senior lieutenant" by a soldier trying to awaken him to tell him they have captured a young boy. We piece together fragments of information as the scene proceeds, sharing the lieutenant's bewilderment at the boy's bizarrely authoritative behavior, and finally realizing that his claims to be treated with respect are to be taken seriously. As Ivan marks out the German positions with leaves and nuts, his actions, together with the sound of German on the soundtrack and the noise of marching feet—rather than any dialogue—inform us that he is an army scout. Only later, when Kholin arrives (and, incidentally, we see another side of the apparently savage, self-sufficient child in his obvious need for love and affection), do we fully understand the opening scenes in the windmill and the swamp.

Although *Ivan's Childhood* is, on the whole, far more linear in its structure than most of Tarkovsky's later work, he is already establishing a pattern of "retrospective understanding" in which often important narrative information is imparted obliquely, belatedly, and even grudgingly. It is only halfway through the film that we are told what had happened to Ivan's family (though his mother's death, at least, is clearly enough indicated through the dreams). The temporal relationship between scenes—as well as the time span of the main action of the film—is often left very vague: we are not told how much time elapses between Ivan's conversation with his "father figure" Colonel Gryaznov and his attempt to run away, or between the ending of that scene and the conversation between Galtsev and Masha.

More significant than these, however, and perhaps particularly disconcerting to a Western viewer, is Tarkovsky's apparently offhand attitude to
imparting crucial narrative information. Although the Colonel threatens to
send Ivan to military school and retrieves him when he attempts to run away,
Ivan is next seen, dressed in a scaled-down version of Kholin's military clothing, apparently ready to resume his duties as a scout—with no explanation as
to why this should be the case, unless Ivan has managed to talk his superiors
into keeping him on. Even more puzzling is the whole business of Ivan's final
expedition, which seems to be carried out in secrecy and without permission,
to either rescue the bodies of the executed scouts or take Ivan on another
(officially sanctioned?) mission, or both. Tarkovsky's disregard for conventional narrative and psychological motivation in his later films is notorious
and—in the context of these films—acceptable; within a more realistically
motivated film, however, it can often be unnecessarily confusing. Nevertheless, the sheer emotional power of the subjective inner reality Tarkovsky
visualizes on the screen makes the narrative almost irrelevant, clearly over-
shadowing its more pedestrian episodes.

Much of what has been written about *Ivan's Childhood* in the West takes
its starting point in Sartre's seminal essay (really an open letter) referred to
earlier. He writes eloquently about the way in which we perceive Ivan as
both an innocent child who needs love and a "monster" who has interiorized
violence and lives totally to satisfy his need for vengeance. Like the child
victims of the Algerian War he can no longer separate the horrors of daylight
reality from those experienced in his dreams. Sartre's two basic ideas—of the
child as monster and the division of the film into "two worlds" represented
by dreams and everyday reality—have been taken up in the West particularly
by Antoine de Baecque and Kovács and Szilágyi. In the Soviet Union, Maya
Turovskaya was contemporaneously writing about the conflicting duality of
Ivan's existence. For de Baecque Ivan inhabits his own private world, and
when he enters fully into it, as in the hallucination scene where he imagines
taking vengeance on the Germans, he becomes truly monstrous. Yet he is
simultaneously a victim and (for de Baecque at least) a martyr and saint (53–
54). The German critic Klaus Kreimeier agrees with him in seeing Ivan as the
first in Tarkovsky's long line of "mute, sick, deprived or murdered children"
who are nevertheless images of the Christ child—an idea which he sees reinforced in the documentary footage of the dead children of Goebbels (*Andrej
Tarkowskij* 94). Maya Turovskaya's main chapter on the film is called "A
World Cleft in Two," while the Hungarians Kovács and Szilágyi (chapter III)
see the creation of an alternative reality through dreams as a basic structural
principle, not just of this film but of all Tarkovsky's work.

In "A World Cleft in Two" (a reprint of an article she wrote at the time),
Turovskaya quotes (10) a passage from Viktor Shklovsky's article "Poetry and
Prose in the Cinema" and suggests that Tarkovsky's films—however irritated
he may later have become by the application of the overworked term "po-

etic"—share the qualities of "the cinema of poetry" in that "elements of form prevail over elements of meaning and it is they, rather than the meaning, which determine the composition." Although this is less evident in *Ivan's Childhood*, where the "prose" of plot and characterization still plays a major role, than in the films that were to come, there is enough evidence to suggest that "elements of form" would provide the most fruitful subject of the director's future explorations.

FIVE

Andrei Roublev

After the extraordinary success of *Ivan's Childhood*, Tarkovsky was clearly under much pressure, both internal and external, to produce a great second film. *Andrei Roublev*, which is often considered to be, along with *Mirror*, his finest work, is also his longest and politically most controversial, and the only one to go unreleased for several years. In what was to become his standard procedure, Tarkovsky did not wait to complete his first film before he submitted, in 1961, a proposal to the studio for a film on the life of Russia's greatest medieval icon painter, Andrei Roublev. Although Tarkovsky and his cowriter Andrei Konchalovsky "borrowed" the idea for the film from a fellow actor, Vasily Livanov, the script itself was their original creation. The contract was signed in 1962, and a film treatment approved in December 1963 (Turovskaya 46).

Tarkovsky and Konchalovsky worked on the script for more than two years, steeping themselves in medieval Russian texts and reading chronicles and saints' lives, as well as history and art books. Tarkovsky received permission to start work in April 1964 (Turovskaya 46), at the same time that the completed literary script for the film, titled *Andrei Roublev*, was published in the influential film journal *Iskusstvo kino*.[1] In the film world, where it stirred up lots of controversy, the script was immediately renamed "The Three Andreis."[2] Lively interest and discussion followed among historians, art specialists, critics, and ordinary readers. The script was unusually large: a comprehensive look at Russian medieval history including the Kulikovo Field battle (1380), Tartar attacks, pagan celebrations, monastic life, a buffoon's dance, struggles among the rulers, religious discussions, and the ever-present and constant hard work (Zak, *Andrei Tarkovsky* 9). From the beginning of the discussion of *Andrei Roublev* in the Soviet Union, the focus was on its sociopolitical and historical content and only secondarily on its broader artistic concerns: Roublev was seen as the incarnation of the humanistic and nationalistic yearnings of the Russian culture of the times. The fame of the film had thus begun to spread before a single frame had been shot.

While Turovskaya states that the preparation for filming began in September of 1964 and shooting went on for more than a year, until November 1965 (48), the film's producer, Tamara Ogorodnikova, gives different dates, stating that filming did not start until April 1965, a full year after approval was given. Tatyana Vinokurova (the head of the Mosfilm archive) also gives April 1965 as the date when the Goskino order was received for the film to go into production (Vinokurova 63). The long preproduction period may reflect the cinema administration's ambiguous, half-hearted support for the film. The film's budget was cut several times from the original 1.6 million rubles down to 1 million (Ogorodnikova Interview). The opening scene of the Kulikovo Field battle, the first major Russian victory over the Tartars, which alone would have cost 200,000 rubles, was the first of many to be cut. Shooting went on until November 1965, when it was interrupted by snow, forcing a return to the location in April and May 1966 and resulting in a budget overrun of 300,000 rubles.

Considering the technical difficulties of shooting in six different locations, the weather problems, and the complex costuming and mise-en-scène, Tarkovsky should have been congratulated. Instead, as Ogorodnikova points out, she, Tarkovsky, and Yusov all received official letters of reprimand for this modest overrun on what was to become one of the greatest Russian films, while Sergei Bondarchuk, a more powerful and influential figure, was allowed to spend 8 million on his eight-hour extravaganza of Tolstoy's *War and Peace*. The only reason that *Andrei Roublev* came in even close to its budget was that during filming, several major scenes were cut out and others shortened. One of the problems of *Andrei Roublev* would be that it ended up being a very different film from the script that had been approved, published, and widely discussed. The first cut of the film was ready at the end of July 1966 (Ogorodnikova). It was called *The Passion According to Andrei* and ran approximately 3 hours and 20 minutes. Vinokurova records that the film was accepted "with high marks" as a "talented and significant work of art," and on August 25, 1966, the permission (*akt*) for its release was written.

The film's five-year journey to the screen turned out to be even more convoluted and frustrating than the shooting. It is almost impossible to reconcile the often conflicting information provided by participants and observers about events more than twenty years in the past, yet comparison of a number of sources allows us to put together a basically consistent account of what took place. When *Andrei Roublev* was submitted for approval, it was immediately criticized for its length and graphic depiction of cruelty, and, predictably, suggestions were made for cuts. The artistic council of Tarkovsky's working group (headed by the well-known team of Alov and Naumov) noted that at 5,642 meters the film was too long and too violent. In a November 1966 letter to Alexei Romanov, the chairman of Goskino, Tarkovsky reported that thirty-seven changes had been made, representing a cut of 390 meters, or some fifteen minutes. He also complained that the endless requests for changes on an already accepted film had made the final editing process extremely difficult and insisted that further cuts would seriously damage the film's artistic integrity (Vinokurova 65). Yet some of the most controversial scenes remained: the on-screen slitting of a man's neck, a horse falling to its death, blindings, and torture.

Complaints about "naturalism" were to dog the film, which was further pronounced "anti-historical and anti-Russian, cruel and harmful" (Yermash

10) after the appearance of a highly inflammatory article falsely accusing Tarkovsky of burning a live cow for the scene of the Tartar raid (*Vechernyaya Moskva*, December 24, 1966). A number of Tarkovsky intimates see this article and the resulting "scandal" as part of a concerted effort to discredit the film. Clearly trying to forestall further attacks, Tarkovsky agreed in a letter to Romanov of December 27, 1966, to make a few more minor cuts in the "naturalistic" scenes: primarily the on-screen killing of a horse (Vinokurova 65). Maya Turovskaya posits that there were three variants of the film: the original 5,642 meters, a second of 5,250 meters, and a final, release print of 5,076 meters (48).

A premiere was held for the film industry at Dom Kino (either at the end of 1966 [Turovskaya] or the beginning of 1967 [Ogorodnikova]), with the audience "in ecstasy" (Akimov), "stunned" (Turovskaya), but also critical, especially of the film's "naturalism." In February 1967 Tarkovsky complained to Romanov that he still did not have the signed *akt* of the film's acceptance, even though Romanov had agreed on the final cut (Vinokurova 67–68). Tarkovsky refused to make any more of the newly requested "primitive" cuts, and the film existed in a kind of administrative limbo for almost five years, discussed at the highest levels of Mosfilm and Goskino, and even at a large gathering of the Central Committee of the Communist Party.

During these years *Andrei Roublev* was to become probably the most famous film *not* released in the Soviet Union, and much of its fame was to come from abroad. In 1967 the film was requested for the Cannes festival, where a Soviet film retrospective was planned in conjunction with the fiftieth anniversary of the Russian Revolution. The official response was that the film was not edited, and it was not sent. Instead of being the year of *Andrei Roublev*, 1967 became the year of Bondarchuk's more conventionally patriotic *War and Peace*. No wonder that Tarkovsky resented Bondarchuk and hated everything he and his film stood for.

As the fiftieth anniversary of the Soviet film industry approached in 1969, P. N. Demichev, the Communist Party *apparatchik* for culture, met with Romanov and Lev Kulidzhanov, the head of the Filmmakers' Union. The outcome of this meeting was a positive answer to their request to release the film, both in domestic general distribution and for sale abroad (Yermash 10). There was a "second premiere" for the film industry at Dom Kino in 1969, the film was sold to a company representing Columbia for foreign distribution, and it seemed that *Andrei Roublev* would finally open. It was requested once more for Cannes, and after the festival organizers had rejected all the other Soviet films offered them, an out-of-competition, unofficial screening was permitted. The film was greeted with great enthusiasm and was awarded the prestigious International Critics' Prize, much to the discomfiture of the Soviet authorities, who then made strenuous efforts to prevent its planned opening in Paris and refused to screen it at the 1969 Moscow Film Festival. Resisting the pressure brought to bear on him, the distributor who had—perfectly legally—obtained the French rights eventually opened the film in Paris, where it was much debated and discussed.[3] According to Yermash, its success abroad created problems at home, and renewed notoriety kept the film shelved for another two years.

Tarkovsky's film, however, had a number of influential admirers, such as the director Grigory Kozintsev, the composer Dmitry Shostakovich, and Evgeny Surkov, the powerful editor of *Iskusstvo kino*, who worked behind the scenes for the film's release. Both Tarkovsky and his second wife, Larissa continually wrote letters to powerful people in an attempt to gain their support; she even went to Alexei Kosygin, the official head of the government with the film (*TWT* 24). This "campaign" may, in fact, have been successful. Moreover, Tarkovsky's firm resolve not to compromise may paradoxically have been responsible both for holding up the film—more cuts were still the prerequisite for release (diary entries for 1970 and '71)—and then for bringing about the film's eventual release when he stood firm and the cinema administration "gave in."

Andrei Roublev was to have its third and final "premiere" at the very end of 1971. The London *Times* (December 21, 1971) reported that *Andrei Roublev* opened for general release on December 20 to "large but subdued crowds" and was ignored by the newspapers.[4] Tarkovsky complains in his diary that there was not a single poster in the whole city (*TWT* 46), yet says all screenings were sold out anyway. Widespread publicity and controversy for almost ten years had already made the film so notorious that by the time it reached the Soviet audience, it needed no introduction and enjoyed a *succès de scandale* unmatched by any other Soviet film of the time.

What was it that had created such a furor and so many vicious attacks on the film in the Soviet Union? While the name Andrei Roublev may have meant nothing to all but the most educated Western viewers, all but the most ignorant Russian viewers immediately recognized in the film's title the name of the greatest medieval Russian icon painter. Each critic and viewer came to the film with preconceived ideas about both the subject matter and the genre of such a film, and *Andrei Roublev* clearly did not meet these expectations. Lev Anninsky remarks that the film was primarily described by the use of negated expressions—by critics, supporters, and even the scriptwriters themselves—who had openly stated that this was *not* to be a historical or biographical film, nor would it have a traditional narrative structure (Anninsky 191). Anninsky ascribes this use of negatives primarily to the lack of historical data on the life of Andrei Roublev; but two other major factors played a role: the "failure" to live up to the genre expectation for an audience nurtured on rousing patriotic epics glorifying Russia, and the questioning of such films' underlying cultural myths of Russia's historical greatness.

Soviet criticism which appeared immediately after the release generally recorded a disappointment in the film. Besides the obvious failure to provide an active, positive socialist realist hero, the film was unfavorably compared to the previously published script. As mentioned earlier, major cuts were necessitated by the tight budget, and these significantly altered the narrative and thematic content of the film: instead of twelve episodes and two prologues (one for each part of a two-series film), the final film had eight episodes and one prologue.⁵ The cutting of the Kulikovo Field battle caused the film to be criticized for not showing the heroism and the sacrifice of the victorious Russian people, as well as omitting a positive image of a leader—Dmitry Donskoi—who fought alongside his men. As the first major victory of the Russians against the Tartars, the Kulikovo Field battle has become part of the Russian cultural mythology, with an importance far beyond its real historical significance.⁶ The prologue to Part II, the Icarus-like flight of the Russian peasant which deals with humanity's creative aspirations, became the prologue for the whole film, thus bringing the theme of the artist to the forefront. Other major episodes to be cut were "The Hunt" (a cruel destruction of beautiful swans by the Grand Duke's younger brother and his retinue—a fragment of this survives in the episode called "The Passion According to Andrei"), and most of an episode titled "Indian Summer" (in which hungry runaway peasants in search of food help the pregnant Holy Fool give birth to her Tartar-Russian baby).

A number of scenes were cut within episodes, including Roublev's memories of a happy childhood and the seasons that are perhaps also Tarkovsky's own and might have linked the autobiographical elements of *Ivan's Childhood*, *Solaris*, and *Mirror* to this film. Theophanes the Greek's vision of Christ's crucifixion—full of hate and betrayal in an alien, hot, dusty setting—was meant to contrast sharply with Roublev's much more humane, loving, and mundane vision of Christ as a peasant dying in a familiar snow-covered Russian countryside. Finally, Tarkovsky's avowed long-hair fetish would have been shared by his hero, whose imagination was captured by a tale of patriotic Russian women who sacrifice their hair in order to ransom Moscow from the Tartars.

It is also clear that several episodes were combined and altered because of Tarkovsky's evolving ideas about the film. Characters, places, and events which acted to connect the disparate parts of this epic gave way to an elliptical composition, in which past and present, reality and memory, were mixed without notice, and people and places were often left inadequately identified. By cutting out narrative connections between episodes, by making Roublev himself more a passive observer than an actor in the unfolding historical drama, and by eliminating "heroic" elements, Tarkovsky seemed to have significantly departed from the original script, as he was so often to do in the future.

The cumulative effect of these changes was to create a very different film from the script that had originally been so highly commended by the film's official historical consultant, V. G. Pashuto, for focusing on "the people"— the bearers of the ideas of "national liberation" and "social protest," and "the source of Roublev's creativity and humanism" (Afterword, *Andrei Rublyov* 159). When, however, the film's producer, Tamara Ogorodnikova, asked this same Pashuto to defend the film against blistering attacks in 1967, he complained that Tarkovsky had played down the social and historical significance of "the people" and their stoic heroism, and emphasized the "naturalistic" elements in added scenes of meaningless violence and cruelty. His proposed cuts, changes, and restorations were a litany of the official criticisms levied at the film.[7] By 1967 and afterwards, aesthetic issues were all but ignored in the rigorous historical and political examination of the film. Unlike Western criticism which, while often misunderstanding the historical/cultural context of the film, saw it only as an allegory of the repressed artist in the Soviet Union, Soviet criticism became mired in debates as to whether the film deviated from or challenged the generic pattern of the standard biographical or historical film, together with endless checking of Tarkovsky's use or misuse of historical facts. Since there were so few verifiable facts about Roublev's life, what the critics were dealing with, in fact, were the powerful political and cultural myths (such as the Russian "people") which Tarkovsky initially seems to have shared. Or was he just publicly being more conformist in order to get the film made?

Tarkovsky's own description of the film, from interviews of the time, presents good socialist realist terminology and reasoning: he wanted to show "Andrei Roublev's art as a protest against the ruling order of the times, against blood, treachery, oppression. . . . Andrei Roublev is not so much the main hero, but the basis and reason to tell about the spiritual, moral force of the Russian people. . . . Andrei Roublev himself, the builders, and Boriska are all proof of this." And then: "Boriska is a man from the people, embodying its creative principle" ("Strasti po Andreyu" 75–76). In *Sculpting in Time*, Tarkovsky adds: "The film was to show how the national yearning for brotherhood, at a time of vicious internecine fighting and the Tartar yoke, gave birth to Rublyov's inspired 'Trinity'—epitomising the ideal of brotherhood, love and quiet sanctity" (34). The original script was much clearer in showing the combined forces of oppression, the Tartars, the rulers, and the Church, all acceptable Marxist "enemies" against which the "people" were fighting. Roublev was a hero because he accepted his inspiration not from the church but from the "people."

It now seems particularly ridiculous that hostile critics spent so much time attacking Tarkovsky for historical "inaccuracy" when he clearly freely combined "generic" events from different periods to illustrate his premise. His "Grand and Little Dukes" go unnamed;[8] Roublev's vow of silence may in reality have been taken by his abbot, Nikon, at the Holy Trinity Monastery; the blinding of the masons was a well-known folk motif; and, though the various tortures and cruelties abounded in the Russian chronicles, they took place mostly at a somewhat later period, during the real consolidation of power by the Moscow rulers. The "internecine fighting" identified by film critics and historians alike as historical fact was more typical of an earlier period of Russian history, whereas the late fourteenth and early fifteenth centuries saw the struggles of Moscow with the neighboring principalities of Tver and Lithuania. The only case of an intrafamilial struggle in Moscow was between the Grand Duke Vasily's brother Yuri (here presumably the Little Duke) and Vasily's son—not the Grand Duke himself (Vernadsky 294).[9] Tarkovsky passes all the historical and ethnographic information through the prism of his poetic imagination, and even picks Roublev as his hero for two reasons: he was a genius—the first great Russian artist—and little was known about him. Tarkovsky was therefore free to create his own vision of the character (A. T., *Ekran 65: Sbornik* 156).

When the conventional image of Andrei Roublev and his times, presented in the script, gave way to Tarkovsky's more original conception in the film, the director soon found himself under attack. While admitting that *Andrei Roublev* had both critics and supporters, and that even the members of each group differed among themselves in their opinions of the film, V. Solovyov complains about the hero's "absence," is "disgusted by the physiological naturalism" and upset with the "unconnectedness of its poetics" ("Zamysel, poetika, film" 194). Writing only a few years later, Neya Zorkaya recalls that the film that had at first been called "complex," "difficult," and "too naturalistic" now offered few problems to a typical film club audience: "Where were the problems, where was the lack of clarity?" she asks. The film was not "difficult, but serious, not dark, but truthful" ("Zametki" 150–51).

Zorkaya's reaction is typical of the more positive and more perceptive criticism which appeared in the later 1970s and 1980s, which stopped berating Tarkovsky for what he had "failed" to do and focused instead on the greatness of his vision and the beauty of his imagery. Of all critics writing in the former Soviet Union, only Tatyana Elmanovits has to date attempted an analysis of the film's structure and motifs in more than just a cursory fashion, but her book has yet to be published in Russian. *The Mirror of Time: The Films of Andrei Tarkovsky* appeared in Estonian in 1980 and as a result had almost no impact on the Russian criticism. With the recent appearance of Maya Turovskaya's book in Russian and Lev Anninsky's *Shestidesyatniki i my*, critics have given *Andrei Roublev* a new life. With the widespread screening of *The Passion According to Andrei*, the film itself is becoming the focus of the Russian religious revival and unfulfilled nationalistic yearnings.

Critical response to *Andrei Roublev* in the West was very different. The "scandal" around the long-delayed release of the film, together with the circumstances of its screening at Cannes and the subsequent Soviet reaction, led to its initial interpretation—especially in France—as a "transparent allegory" (Michel Ciment in *Dossier Positif* 79) of Tarkovsky's own situation as an artist in the Soviet Union, struggling to tell his own truth in the face of official disapproval and harassment and in explicit rejection of official ideologies. Jacques Demeure also took the complete identification of Tarkovsky with Roublev for granted as part of "a serene allegory with no apparent connection to historical reality" (*Dossier Positif* 81), and Barthélemy Amengual saw the film as an "allegory" of Stalinism and a defense of intellectual, political, and religious freedom (*Dossier Positif* 83–84).

British and American critics tended, on the other hand, simply to be puzzled by the film—perhaps because most of them saw it initially in a truncated version that accentuated the problems of the unfamiliar historical setting and the confusing chronology, and also because of their lack of knowledge of Roublev himself and his importance in the history of Russian culture.[10] Vincent Canby, in the *New York Times* (October 10, 1973), found it heavy-handed and thought Tarkovsky's "movie lyricism" clichéd. William Paul, while admitting that it was impossible to judge this cut version fairly, objected to Tarkovsky's "clumsy 'Scope camera style" (*The Village Voice*, November 1, 1973). British critics, though more sympathetic to the visual qualities of the film, gave it, on the whole, a tentative and guarded welcome.[11] Nevertheless, a decade later, the 1982 *Sight & Sound* poll for the ten best films of all time placed *Andrei Roublev* as one of the runners-up.

Among later commentators, the most thoughtful analysis of the film is probably that by the Hungarian critics Kovács and Szilágyi, who have a better perspective than most Western writers on the historical and cultural issues that it raises. They comment on the ethical and artistic differences between Roublev and Theophanes, as well as the variations played by Tarkovsky on the overall theme of the relations between the artist and authority. They examine Tarkovsky's concept of history as a backdrop of unchanging violence against which he presents universal ethical problems, and see the structure of the film as dependent less on plot than on theme. They show awareness of the aspect of the icon that is most difficult for the Western mind to grasp: the fact that it represents the true nature of the object it depicts (Christ is literally present in the icon that portrays him) and link this suggestively to Tarkovsky's concept of the transcendental nature of art. They place the director's sense of Russia's historical and cultural mission in the context of the thinking of Pushkin and Chaadayev (a theme that recurs in *Mirror*) and suggest that his solution to the problems of the destructive qualities of Russian history lies not in Pan-Slavism but in maintaining the best qualities of the spiritual tradition through the individual conscience. Tarkovsky wishes to retain a belief in the purity of soul of the Russian people and their communal traditions: there is a basic difference between the people (who are religious, spiritual, moral, and permanent) and power (which is brutal, exploitative, and temporary). Roublev hopes to create a new relationship with the community based on love, beauty, and sensing the divine in the human, to replace the Byzantine tradition with its emphasis on fear and humiliation (chapter IV). In perhaps a similar vein, Anninsky sees the world of *Andrei Roublev* revolving in three spheres—in relation to power (and thus history), to the flesh (the human), and to God (the divine) (196).

All these themes are certainly central to the film and far more relevant than attempts to read it primarily as some kind of political or personal allegory, although certain aspects of the film could indeed apply as well to the Stalin and Brezhnev periods as to the fifteenth century. The nature of the artist and his responsibility toward the community is perhaps the theme that most pervades and unites the film, and almost every episode presents at least one variant on it. The balloonist in the Prologue takes the risks every true artist must take in stepping beyond the boundaries of the known and the familiar, and challenging not just authority but the fear and conformism of the people he wishes to benefit. The buffoon embodies the anarchic creative spirit of the people, their earthiness, and their instinctive resistance to hypocrisy and the arrogance of power: church and state combine to suppress him.

Those more traditionally recognized as "artists"—Kirill, Daniil, Theophanes, the stonemasons, and Roublev himself—are carefully distinguished from one another. Kirill, as his conversation with Theophanes makes clear, represents the untalented artist, conscious of his own inadequacy and jealous of those he knows to be superior to him: he denigrates Roublev's work, accusing it falsely of lacking faith and simplicity. He is proud and arrogant and, unlike Roublev, has fear of God, not love of man. Untalented and jealous, he is aware, to some degree, of what art should be and yet is too egotistical and materialistic to be a genuine creator. He is, however, redeemed by suffering to some extent by the end, as his plea to Roublev to resume his vocation makes clear.

Daniil is conformist: more talented than Kirill, he is locked into a traditional pattern of both style and subject matter that he sees no reason to alter, as is shown in his conversation with Roublev about painting the Last Judgment. For him art should go on forever doing what it has always done (or at least what it is now doing), making no response to changing circumstances or new ideas. In both aesthetics and morality he wishes only to follow the letter of the law, and he is as incapable of comprehending the idea of a "happy" Last Judgment as he is of recognizing that the Holy Fool is not a "sinner" just because she innocently entered a church with her head uncovered.

Although Theophanes, to begin with, seems almost as much businessman as artist, turning out a "product" that can be diverted to other uses (pressing cabbage) if it fails in its intended effect, he is revealed to be a genuine artist, with a sense of vocation. The problem is that—as is the case with Daniil—his main concern is to remind people of their inevitable and inescapable destiny as incorrigible sinners: his art is not intended to improve or change the world around him. His own paintings, his conversation with Roublev, and—in the script at least—his vision of Calvary all place him as the antithesis of Roublev's gentle, loving, humanistic vision. Yet, tamed perhaps by his experience of Heaven—"It's not as you imagine it"—his ghost is capable of consoling the distraught Roublev in the Vladimir cathedral and reminding him that his earlier ideals are still valid and art is still beautiful.

Roublev, in contrast to all three fellow painters, has genuine love, humility, and self-effacement, putting himself at the service of something higher than himself, of both man and God. For much of the film, however, he is confused and uncertain, as his growing awareness of evil seems more and more to contradict his instinctive faith in human goodness. He is also—unlike

The three monk-artists of *Andrei Roublev*. *From left to right:* Daniil (Nikolai Grinko), Roublev (Anatoly Solonitsyn), and Kirill (Ivan Lapikov). Artificial Eye.

Roublev welcomes the "Holy Fool" (Irma Rausch), while Daniil looks on disapprovingly. Artificial Eye.

Daniil and Theophanes, who are both limited by the values of their time—attempting to move away from the idea that the function of art is to expose and condemn human weakness, and that artists should unquestioningly support the teachings of the church and the state. Roublev is trying to forge a style that allows him to express his love of humanity. It is not too far-fetched to compare the medieval conformists (Theophanes, Kirill, and Daniil) to Tarkovsky's all too numerous contemporaries: professional artists/bureaucrats fearful for their own positions and terrified of unorthodox ideas and real talent.

For Tarkovsky Roublev is the first true *Russian* artist and his "Trinity" the first original Russian work of art, born of the hopes, struggles, and suffering of the times. All the episodes and all the events in the film are connected by "the poetic logic of the need for Rublyov to paint his celebrated 'Trinity' " (*Sculpting* 35). The film's composition is circular: Roublev leaves the Holy Trinity Monastery as a young man, to witness and share the suffering of the Russian people and lose and regain his faith, in order to return to that same monastery and paint the "Trinity" icon in honor of his spiritual guide, St. Sergius of Radonezh, whose ideals of "brotherhood, love and quiet sanctity" the icon embodies (34). He may also have been attracted to an icon painter as his hero in the light of his frequently stated view that *all* great art is at the service of something beyond itself and does not exist (as he felt too much modern art did) "to affirm the value of the individual for its own sake." For "in artistic creation the personality does not assert itself, it serves another, higher and communal idea" (*Sculpting* 38). The creation of an icon, as such critics as Kovács and Gauthier point out, had traditionally been seen not as an act of individual artistic aggrandizement, but as a "window on the absolute" (Gauthier 34) that literally contained the divine within it. Its beauty derived from the beauty of the eternal archetype that it recreated, and its inner essence could be understood only if there was a corresponding inner enlightenment within the person contemplating it (37). This idea relates suggestively to Tarkovsky's concern with what the viewer/reader/listener contributes to the "joint creation" of meaning in a work of art.

Without pushing this comparison too far—Tarkovsky, after all, saw the "divine" as being present not just in specifically religious or Christian works but in Leonardo, Dostoyevsky, Bach, Bresson, and Japanese *haiku*—his admiration for Roublev (at least as he puts him on the screen) seems to derive to a large extent from his self-effacement, his refusal to paint unless he is convinced that people will benefit from the existence of his work. People must "need" his art, and he in turn has no desire to paint simply to "express himself." He serves both a higher ideal (God) and a communal one (Man) by bringing the two into a truer relationship than had existed in the art of his predecessors and showing that the concept of a loving and kindly God both satisfies and expresses the highest spiritual aspirations of the people. Roublev's need to reject the orthodox view of art in his time, both in content and in style, is, of course, a challenge to *all* official dogmas on art, whether laid down by the Church or the State, and awareness of this may be one of the reasons for the hostility toward the film on a bureaucratic level. Like the Soviet film director, Roublev acknowledges that he has to work at the behest and under the control of an official power structure, and that he does not enjoy absolute freedom to create. But where Daniil and Theophanes accept, in effect, the socialist realist position that the "truth" has been discovered for all time and the artist's task is merely to illustrate and express this in a stylistically acceptable manner, Roublev (like Tarkovsky) insists that innovation and questioning are central to the purpose of art, and that without these it will stagnate and die. Whether he is working for a Grand Duke, the Church, or Goskino, the artist has a responsibility both to himself and to his audience and has a duty not to betray this.

This responsibility, however, brings its dangers, and the most chilling reminder of the vulnerability of the artist in relation to the official power structure is the scene of the blinding of the stonemasons. Their "offense" has been to assert their independence and to attempt to offer their services freely to the person most willing to appreciate and reward them; for Stepan (the steward) and the Grand Duke, however, the only proper use for their skills is to glorify their political master. Although this graphic and brutal scene was one of those singled out for attack for its "excessive violence" (and Tarkovsky did cut some of the more gruesome images), the real cause for dismay is more likely to have been its unacknowledged subtext. A generation that had seen many of its best artists killed, imprisoned, exiled, or silenced was likely to have little difficulty in understanding Tarkovsky's depiction of the essence of the relationship between the artist and the political power structure whenever the former dared to become too outspoken or independent.

Roublev's faith in himself and in his art is finally restored, of course, when he witnesses the struggles, frustrations, sufferings, and final accomplishment of another artist—Boriska—in his casting of the bell. The fact that Boriska is a true artist is underscored in the published Russian script by the description of his finding of the clay: "There it was. . . . He didn't know that it looked precisely like that, he could not have described it to anyone, because he had never seen it, but now he knew for certain—this was exactly the clay that he needed" (*Andrei Rublyov* 149). But Boriska's art is communal rather than individual, comparable, indeed, at almost every stage, with the task of the film director, who is dependent on financing from an outside source and on the talent, technical expertise, and cooperation of others, and who must constantly coordinate, cajole, bully, persuade, and flatter if he is to realize his vision.

Although Boriska has been somewhat unkindly compared to the ideal Komsomol leader in arousing the enthusiasm and devotion of his fellow workers and guiding them toward triumphant achievement of their goal (*Andrej Tarkowskij* 108; Turovskaya 45)—which may partly account for the fact that this episode was the most popular with Russian critics—he also represents a complex assessment of the nature of artistic achievement. His faith and self-confidence are combined with moments of self-doubt and frustration; he is driven, committed, and sometimes ruthless (as when he orders an apprentice to be whipped as a warning to the more powerful foreman), yet he knows when to step back, swallow his pride, and make the necessary compromise; he works others and himself into exhaustion and takes immense risks on every level (like the balloonist, he could well be risking not just his prestige but his life if he fails). He has literally to "get his hands dirty" and is usually shown as disheveled, ragged, and streaked with mud or clay (a portrait of the artist that outraged many Soviet critics). Yet all this is based on bluff and guesswork—or, to put it more kindly, intuition—for his father's "secret" does not exist.

Given Tarkovsky's acknowledgment that his own art of film direction is both a communal effort, drawing on the talents of many different people, *and* (in its highest expressions at least) the product of a distinctive personal vision, it is perhaps not too fanciful to see Boriska and Roublev as representing these two different facets of his own work and of the artistic personality itself— Roublev, after all, suggests at the end of the film that they should work together: "You will cast bells and I will paint." Although Roublev too (like all medieval painters) is dependent on patronage and works and travels with a crew of students and assistants, his reliance on the latter for *creative* purposes is significantly downplayed. Unlike Boriska, he is gentle and kind to his apprentices, even when rebuking them (it is Theophanes who tweaks Foma's ear), and the final product of their work is unambiguously attributed to the inspiration and ethical outlook of Roublev himself. We see him at work only briefly, in the "Last Judgment" episode, and though he too has streaks of paint on his clothing there and—like Theophanes—is linked to earth and water in "The Passion According to Andrei,"[12] the effect produced is much more that of the creator whose spiritual vision recognizes and experiences, but also assimilates and transcends, the sufferings and frustrations of everyday existence: the ideal *auteur*. Roublev is perhaps the artist as Tarkovsky would like to imagine and present himself, Boriska the artist that he recognized from his own working experience; and, as he saw well enough, the two need to complement each other.

Although the film is concerned primarily with Roublev's inner, spiritual journey, the sense of physical reality pervades it throughout and is one of its strongest accomplishments. The Prologue is an almost aggressive display of technical virtuosity, in both its camerawork and its determination to make us share with the balloonist the exhilaration, terror, and danger of flight. His adventure begins with an overhead shot straight down the facade of the church as the balloon leaves, and then a series of helicopter shots that alternate between the aeronaut's point of view as he gazes triumphantly down at the waterlogged earth he is leaving behind, and huge swooping movements toward him as he dangles in his harness, half-chuckling, half-sobbing in mingled delight and fear. Ecstasy and terror are powerfully combined, accentu-

The artist triumphant: Boriska (Nikolai Burlyaev) and his fellow workers. Artificial Eye.

Roublev consoles Boriska as he reveals his "secret." Artificial Eye.

The balloonist from the Prologue to *Andrei Roublev*. Artificial Eye.

ated by the rapid cutting throughout the sequence, the music that is by turns tense, suspenseful, excited, and ominous, and a careful choice of sound that moves during the flight from the calm creaking of the ropes to the terrifying rush and hiss of escaping air as the balloon collapses. Finally, and again from the balloonist's point of view, his vehicle plunges remorselessly back to earth to end in a shuddering impact and a freeze-frame of dramatic finality.

As in this scene, Nature and the Russian landscape—its vastness accentuated by the Cinemascope photography—are a constant backdrop to the actions of the characters. Roublev, Theophanes, and Daniil spend much of their time trudging around the countryside looking for work and a patron, at the mercy of the elements and dependent on others for shelter and the basic necessities of life. Boriska too has to contend with the power of Nature—in the seemingly endless root that he follows to its source in a huge tree, towering invincibly against the sky, his own insignificance stressed by a high-angle crane shot that pulls away from him lying spread-eagled at the edge of the pit. And he too has to trudge endlessly through the pouring rain in search of the right material to complete his task.

The casting of the bell itself strongly emphasizes the sheer physical effort and hardship involved in creating art. Much of this is conveyed in lengthy, complex camera movements that show the men working together but at their separate tasks, culminating in the spectacular high-angle shot of workers arranging ropes that stretch for hundreds of yards from the far side of the river to the bell area, as crowds begin to gather for the raising of the bell itself. The camera then pans to an overhead shot of the work area, full of bustling activity. The earlier scenes, too, of the workmen feeding the furnaces convey a strong sense of physical strain, discomfort, tension, and danger as the camera explores the garishly lit inferno in which they are laboring.

Here Tarkovsky perhaps has learned from Dziga Vertov as well as from

The panic-stricken townspeople flee from the Tartars. Artificial Eye.

Eisenstein—influences that he was never very happy to acknowledge.[13] In the raid on Vladimir, as in the bell-casting, he combines the intimate with the expansive, a sense of exact detail and individual activity with a comprehensive overview that seems to take as its model the "Odessa Steps" sequence of *Potemkin* or the attack on Kazan in *Ivan the Terrible, Part 1:* here we focus on the horror through following the fate of helpless individual victims, some of them familiar from Roublev's entourage. Although the cutting is fairly rapid, the use of the moving camera serves to slow down and prolong the action within each shot, stretching out time and intensifying the agony of the participants. Overall continuity is maintained more through sound and music than by presenting a logical progression in time and space. The more striking (and horrific) incidents emphasize the cold-blooded enjoyment of wielding total power over defenseless victims. The Little Duke on horseback pursues and slashes down an unarmed youth (recognized as one of Roublev's apprentices); the dying boy rolls over a saw propped against a log, his body twitching in macabre rhythm to the blade undulating gently beside him. The apprentice Foma, armed only with a stick, backs away from a Russian soldier who stalks him with measured enjoyment, sadistically delaying his assault and ignoring Foma's appeals to him as a Russian and a brother. A woman collapses with a spear protruding from her stomach; a different woman breaks free from one soldier trying to carry her off to rape her, only to be seized by another and dragged screaming along the battlements.

The sense of helplessness is encapsulated most strongly in one of the most controversial and shocking images in the film: of a horse losing its balance at the top of a staircase and sliding down the steps and over the railing to land, clearly badly injured, on the ground. (In the original version it was then killed on screen by a spearsman; Tarkovsky agreed to cut this, along with a shot of a cow—protected by asbestos—engulfed in flames.) After the Tartars

break into the cathedral and begin an orgy of indiscriminate killing and loot-
ing, the perspective switches to an objective bird's-eye view of the panic-
stricken townspeople milling confusedly in slow motion, their vulnerability
accentuated by geese that enter the frame from above, flapping clumsily and
awkwardly downwards.[14]

Stylistically brilliant, the Tartar raid, along with the blinding of the masons,
is emotionally one of the most powerful scenes in the film. For Tarkovsky the
violence was justified as part of his attempt to present history as truthfully and
realistically as possible—an intention that governed the deliberate choice of
shabby, everyday clothing, unglamorous and ordinary-looking actors, and
bare, stark sets that emphasized the poverty and hardship of the time. The
violence is necessary on a plot level—as the cause of Roublev's despair and
loss of faith in human goodness—and as part of one of the film's major
themes—an examination of power and how easily it can be abused.

In such episodes as the arrest and casual mistreatment of the buffoon and
the torture of the sacristan at Vladimir, Tarkovsky stresses the cold, detached,
businesslike manner in which the authorities and their servants go about
their task of intimidating and brutalizing defenseless victims. As the bound
sacristan is carefully maneuvered into place, the Little Duke watches impassively, and the Tartar leader—in rather heavy-handed manner—gloatingly
surveys the devastation for which he has been responsible. During the blinding scene, Stepan is more concerned with recovering his lost whip than with
the suffering of the moaning victims around him—and orders one of his men
to "help" one of them by simply dragging him out of the way.

Throughout much of this Roublev remains a detached and passive observer rather than a participant—different in this respect from the Roublev of
the script, who intervenes in the combat between the peasants, gets into a
fight with a Tartar, and tries to stop the Duke's men from leaving to attack the
stonemasons. It is chronologically after the blinding scene—on his way to
paint the Last Judgment at the Vladimir cathedral and in his encounter with
the pagans—that his passivity begins to be seen as culpable in the sense that
it involves compromise with the brutal exercise of religious or political authority. Here again the physical texture of the filming is of vital importance in
conveying the moral theme, with the smoke and flames of the fires, the shimmering water of the river, the flickering torches, the dark outlines of the trees
and bushes, and birds fluttering past to create brief patches of white against
the gathering twilight—as well as the hypnotic, pulsating rhythms of the
music. Here Roublev in his monk's robe appears out of place: an intrusive
and rigid figure in a setting where music, naked bodies, fire, water, light, and
nature combine to create something disturbingly and attractively sensual that
he is unable to come to terms with and yet cannot fully reject either. He is
tempted and almost certainly falls, and his passivity at the end as he turns his
face away from the woman fleeing from her persecutors is, for the first time,
presented as reprehensible: shamefaced and even cowardly and hypocritical.
(In the published Russian script this woman is the one who was dragged into

the bushes by the man, and Roublev recognizes her as "his shame, his sin.") Yet his "fall" is a necessary part of his humanization and eventual redemption: he has to recognize his own fallibility and capacity for sinning—culminating in his killing of the Russian soldier at Vladimir—before his art can truly serve the needs of ordinary, similarly sinful people.

For much of the film the stark black and white images, the careful composition, and the unhurried pacing create a distancing effect that encourages detached observation rather than the emotional involvement and subjective identification of *Ivan's Childhood*. Sven Nykvist, who told us that he recognized Tarkovsky's greatness immediately on seeing this film, pointed to the fact that almost every shot has the characters centrally positioned, yet there is never any sense of visual monotony because of the constant movement of the camera. Many shots in the film last more than two and occasionally three minutes—brief by Tarkovsky's later standards, yet long enough to impose a measured and studied rhythm on the film that contributes, along with the grandeur of the imagery, to its genuinely—rather than, as with Bondarchuk's *War and Peace*, spuriously—monumental effect.

Compositional devices that he was to explore further in later films include a consistent pattern in which conversations between characters expressing opposing viewpoints are shot so that they rarely make direct eye contact: either each speaker is visually isolated in close-up or, if they share the same screen space, they look in different directions, one toward the camera and the other away, or to opposite sides of the screen, or one addresses the back of the other's head. This is particularly evident in the conversations between Roublev and Theophanes and between Roublev and Daniil. In the scene in the Vladimir cathedral with Theophanes' stolidly realistic ghost, a sense of strangeness is created through a favorite device by which the moving camera shows Theophanes in an area of the screen that is incompatible with his position earlier in the same shot. Occasionally, however, the composition and framing seem merely perverse, as in the shots that introduce Boriska at the beginning of the final episode.

Another apparently perverse aspect of the film—the refusal to situate many of the episodes clearly in time and space or to account logically for some of the action—can be seen either as a deliberate aesthetic choice or as the result of cutting that left certain incidents in the film obscure. (In subtitled prints, these problems are sometimes accentuated by inadequate translation of information provided in the dialogue.) Whatever the reason, it is significant that Tarkovsky chose not to correct obscurities and apparent contradictions within the film—when someone pointed out that the unexplained reappearance of the Holy Fool leading a horse near the end of the film simply confuses the audience, his response was simply, "Let them make of it what they will" (Rausch Interview, 1989). If this sounds unnecessarily cavalier, it can be more sympathetically interpreted as part of a consistent aesthetic strategy that ignored conventional narrative explication and threw much of the burden of interpreting the film onto the audience.[5] The film's structure isolates key incidents in Roublev's life that show us the kind of world he lives in, his reaction to this, and his movement toward discovering his mission and his identity as an artist; compared with this nothing else matters—and this "nothing else" would include almost everything a more conventional director would consider important.

Tarkovsky and his cameraman, Yusov, deliberately chose black and white for the film to avoid the prettiness and false exoticism that color often brings to historical films. The use of color at the end of the film, he told Michel Ciment, was intended to link Roublev's life with his art: to show this life transformed through the conventions of artistic expression. Roublev's work was shown in fragments rather than as a whole because the perception of a painting follows a totally different temporal and spatial logic than the viewing of a film, and this experience would be distorted if he had shown the whole painting for a few brief seconds. Instead he allowed the viewer to recreate the sense of the total painting by accumulating a succession of details, guided by a "color dramaturgy" that created a flow of impressions (*Dossier Positif* 90–91).

The "transformation" he speaks of can come only through the experience—our own and that of the characters—of the "real," the hardship, the cruelty, the suffering and despair of everyday life, and also its moments of joy and fulfillment. The true work of art assimilates and transcends these: Roublev's paintings, like Tarkovsky's film, respect and incorporate both the human and the natural worlds, and it is fitting that the film should end not on the work of art but on the world of nature (the horses standing in the rain), without which art would have no meaning.

S I X

Solaris

Upon completing *Andrei Roublev* in 1966, Tarkovsky was to embark on an exhausting five-year struggle to get the film released. The surprising choice for his next project, an adaptation of *Solaris*, a science fiction novel by the Polish writer Stanislav Lem, can best be understood within the context of Tarkovsky's ongoing problems with the cinema administration. One by one all his film proposals were turned down by Goskino, including his favorite, an autobiographical film about his mother. Tarkovsky intimates suggest that science fiction was a relatively safe choice, as it was considered a light genre aimed primarily at the youth market, and therefore was not taken so seriously by Goskino (Mikhail Romadin, in *O Tarkovskom* 166). Moreover, the bureaucrats may have felt that they had "reined in" Tarkovsky (Akimov Interview 1989), and, perhaps for that reason too, *Solaris* turned out to be, at least in retrospect, Tarkovsky's least favorite film. At the very beginning of 1968 Tarkovsky quickly wrote a script for the autobiographical film *Bright, Bright Day*. When it was soundly rejected by colleagues and administrators alike, Tarkovsky went ahead with *Solaris*, an idea he had held in reserve (Akimov and Rausch interviews, 1989). By October 1968 he had already proposed *Solaris* to the studio (Turovskaya 51), and he had finished the script by June 1969 (June 26 letter to G. Kozintsev, "Ya chasto dumayu . . ." 94).

The beginning of 1970 found him waiting for V. Baskakov (Deputy Chief of Goskino USSR) and I. Kokoreva (head editor of the Script-Editorial Board of Goskino) to read and approve the script ("Ya chasto dumayu . . ." 99). By May he was already casting *Solaris*, and in June he was seriously considering the Swedish actress Bibi Andersson for the lead (*TWT* 4–5), but as usual, the actual preparation and shooting were plagued by administratively created difficulties. Diary entries for October reveal that the original approved budget of 1,850,000 rubles was reduced to 1,250,000, then to 1,000,000, and cut back even further to 900,000.[1] At this point Tarkovsky complained that the whole production was threatened: he had no leading lady, no Japanese scenes, no costumes, not enough money, and no production manager. Yet by March 1971 he had begun shooting the exteriors at the dacha (the opening sequence) and selected Natalia Bondarchuk for the lead. The film was finished rather quickly and received its official screening at Mosfilm on December 30, 1971 (*TWT* 45).

The published diary entries do not explain how this turnaround occurred, but the unlikely help may, in fact, have come from the notorious Filip

Yermash, Tarkovsky's nemesis throughout much of his career. Can one believe Yermash when he says that he was an "avid fan" of the project and that he helped the studio and the film group solve all problems: financing, the trip to Japan, Kodak film stock, and so on (Yermash 10)? Yermash seems to have genuinely liked Tarkovsky's project. At least this was a film he "understood": it is about a scientist who manages to rid himself of all the "internal nastiness which prevented him from reaching a new moral level." Yermash almost lyrically describes a film about love for a woman, and man's love for his father, his home, his Earth with its traditions, roots, and history (10). Recognizing the generally self-serving intent of Yermash's "memoir" of Tarkovsky, we take more seriously Larissa Tarkovskaya's suggestion that help may instead have come from Sizov, the head of Mosfilm (Interview).

As always, Tarkovsky's problems did not end with the film's completion. The official response after the Mosfilm screening was generally favorable, but thirty-five changes were requested. In his diary entry for January 12, 1972, Tarkovsky mockingly enumerates them: the science fiction elements were to be strengthened and ambiguities in motives and relationships clarified; he needed to say whether the hero, Kris Kelvin, comes from a Communist, socialist, or capitalist society; the Earth scenes were too long; religious references were to be deleted; the ending should make clear that Kris has fulfilled his mission; Hari should not become human; the scene with the mother should be deleted; "the bed scene" should be shortened and Kris shouldn't be shown without trousers . . . (*TWT* 49–50). All these requested changes demonstrate the ideological conservatism of the Soviet film bureaucracy at the time, but the last two ludicrous requests may reflect the puritanical bent of the head of Goskino himself, Alexei Romanov: "Even a wrinkled bed sheet or blanket was enough to get him upset" (Golovskoy 13).

Tarkovsky saw these demands as a "provocation," but he was prepared to, and did, make minor changes which he felt would not destroy the film's structure (*TWT* 51). While Sizov thought the film—though long—was now much better, Romanov insisted on more major cuts such as the city of the future and Hari's suicide. Tarkovsky typically refused further changes, and Romanov surprisingly agreed to accept the film, as is, only a month after his request. Offering no clues to this final riddle, Yermash in his memoir records that *Solaris* was finished in 1972 and represented Soviet cinema at Cannes, winning a Special Jury Prize there (10). Tarkovsky himself was clearly pleased with the film, seeing it in some respects as better than *Andrei Roublev*, "more harmonious . . . less cryptic" (*TWT* 53). While he tended to be least critical of his most recent film (Romadin Interview), Natalia Bondarchuk (Hari) makes the point in interview that *Solaris*, more than any other film, was released with few changes and in the form Tarkovsky had envisaged. It must have pleased him that the film had a normal debut in the Soviet Union and was relatively successful with viewers (Yermash 10).

In later years he clearly changed his mind about *Solaris*, ignoring it almost completely in *Sculpting in Time*, except to observe that the science fiction element was too prominent and a distraction from the film's ideas. In interviews and conversations he let it be known that it was his least favorite and least successful film.[2] Yet Tarkovsky's own retrospective view, which, incidentally, does not do justice to the film, cannot change the fact that in 1968 he was genuinely drawn to the thematics of Lem's novel. Thus the choice of *Solaris* should not just be seen as an act of compromise or simple expediency on Tarkovsky's part, as has sometimes been assumed. The film aroused considerable advance interest in the Soviet Union and in interviews both during shooting and after the film's opening, Tarkovsky explained that he was attracted by the novel's moral implications and psychological insights rather than its fantastic events, and by the story of a man who regrets the past and wants to relive it in order to change it. He saw the idea of man's inescapable responsibility for his every action and his potential moral transformation as the cornerstone of the novel (A. T., "Zachem proshloe . . ." 97–98; Abramov 163).

Nevertheless, although Tarkovsky retained the basic outline of Lem's story and even much of the dialogue, his interpretation of it was very different from Lem's own, and it is little wonder that the novelist indignantly rejected Tarkovsky's first draft of the script, which placed two-thirds of the action on Earth and added a new character, Kris's wife Maria, to whom he would return after his meeting with Hari at the space station. Lem's vehement hostility to this first adaptation led to a rewrite which excised the new character but kept the Earth story line, albeit in much-reduced form (Turovskaya 53; Romadin, *O Tarkovskom* 166). The sequences on Earth, and the Earth-space conflict that permeates the whole film, shift the film radically away from Lem's primarily philosophical and technological approach to something far more congenial to Tarkovsky himself—an exploration of family relationships, themes of guilt and betrayal, and a celebration of the natural beauty of Earth and humanity's inescapable links with it.

Tarkovsky's distaste for Lem's style of "hard" science fiction was confirmed, just as he began work on the film, when he, Romadin, and Yusov saw Stanley Kubrick's *2001*, which all three viewed as an unnatural, sterile demonstration of future man's technological achievements (*O Tarkovskom* 165; A. T., "Zachem proshloye . . ." 101). As a result, they decided to make their film an exact opposite: the perfunctory attention paid to the journey through space, the run-down space station, the messy rooms and elegant library—overflowing with an extremely odd assortment of earthly objects—were designed to counter the futuristic technology of Kubrick's film (Romadin Interview). All the work on the film turned into a struggle with the genre, an attempt to bind Lem's novel to Earth (*O Tarkovskom* 166). In doing so, however—in giving Earth preeminence over the cosmos, and privileging nature over technology—Tarkovsky created considerable confusion both for the cinema administration and for Soviet film critics, who were concerned largely with the degree to which Tarkovsky had or had not adhered to the conventions of the familiar science fiction genre and what he had or should have contributed to it. The philosophical, moral, and ideological stands attributed to him in the film were tediously and turgidly discussed with the utmost seriousness, and it was of little use for Tarkovsky to insist in interviews that this was not his main concern: that he needed Earth in the film not only as a contrast to the cosmos but because he wanted the viewer to feel its beauty, and the "redemptive bitterness of nostalgia." Fortunately, many viewers and some of the more perceptive critics (M. Turovskaya, N. Zorkaya, Yu. Hanyutin, T. Elmanovits) were able to understand and to share Tarkovsky's emotional, spiritual, and moral, but very much earthbound, space odyssey.

Solaris was quite well received in Britain, winning the annual BFI award for best film of the year, but American critics (reviewing it, of course, on the basis of a dubbed and badly cut print—see synopsis) tended to find it both confusing and pretentious. Jay Cocks, in *Time*, was flippantly dismissive, claiming that "the effects are scanty, the drama gloomy, the philosophy . . . thick as a cloud of ozone" (December 13, 1976: 100). Even the relatively sympathetic review in the *New York Times* commented mysteriously on the film's "visual poverty" (October 7, 1976), though a more perceptive review by Jack Kroll in *Newsweek* acclaimed it as "an extraordinary film of great sensitivity and lyrical power" and praised it as "engrossing and gravely beautiful," noting that the planet provided "a giant cosmic mirror of [the scientists'] own fractured consciousness." Like several other British and American critics, Kroll attempted to read the film as at least partly an allegory of contemporary Soviet society, comparing what he saw as its attack on a "strictly materialistic" Soviet society to the writings of Solzhenitsyn. Peter Kenez, reviewing the film for *Film Quarterly* (Winter 1972/73), also saw a condemnation of allegedly "scientific" Marxism and an attempt to come to terms with the memories of Stalinist crimes (58–59)—a theme that is rather more appropriate to *Mirror*. Few reviewers at the time went into much greater depth than this, the main exception being a thoughtful and sensitive review by Timothy Hyman, also for *Film Quarterly* (Spring 1976), that, despite one or two dubious interpretations, provides a good analysis of the film's major themes, stylistic patterns, and cultural references (54–58).

Tarkovsky's film follows the basic outline of Lem's novel quite closely, including the elements of Kris's mission to the planet, the strange behavior of the scientists, their—somewhat different—"visitors," the reappearance of the dead Hari (Rheya in the novel), Kris's failed attempts to rid himself of her, their rediscovered love, and her final disappearance—leaving Kris to hope, against all reason and evidence, that "the time of cruel miracles was not past" (195) and that she might yet return. Yet, while doing this, Tarkovsky alters the meaning of Lem's novel almost beyond recognition, and some consideration of the way in which this happens will illuminate what is particularly "Tarkovskian" about the film. The book, which is set totally on the space station, is—like much of Lem's other work—essentially a critique of anthropocentric thinking, focusing on the limitations of human knowledge and the human intellect (75–76). For Lem the love story is basically a means

Snaut (Yuri Yarvet, *on left*) and Sartorius (Anatoly Solonitsyn) in the latter's laboratory in *Solaris*. Contemporary Films.

by which he can explore what happens when—inevitably and inescapably—we "try to stay human in an inhuman situation" (147). Despite the glimpse of hope in the reference to "cruel miracles" which ends the book, the main theme is Kris's realization that the human values we cherish, such as love, have no significance or meaning in a universe that is probably organized along principles that we can never even begin to understand. These philosophical and moral ideas are explored within a solid and scientifically convincing speculative framework.

Tarkovsky's film, by contrast, is a *celebration* of human values and of the power of love in an indifferent or hostile universe, and it is little wonder that Lem took such exception to the results. Almost the first third of the film is taken up with a lovingly detailed presentation of the natural beauty of the Earth that Kris may be leaving behind forever, and family and personal relationships have a central significance totally absent from the novel. Although this section provides background information about Kris's mission, what really matters is our sense of the tense and yet loving bond between him and his father, the importance of friendship and loyalty, and the contrast between the fragile beauty of the landscape around the father's dacha and the aural and visual ugliness of the city to which the visiting ex-astronaut Berton returns.

Although the events that follow Kris's arrival on the space station parallel, with some changes of detail, those in the book, the emphasis here too is altered. Tarkovsky works within a humanist/scientist dichotomy that is characteristic of his work as a whole, and shows virtually nothing of the respect for scientific thinking that is evident in Lem. Of the two scientists on *Solaris*, Sartorius becomes much more of a coldly impersonal, almost antihuman figure than in the book, while Snaut is a well-meaning intermediary between the increasingly antagonistic viewpoints of Kris and Sartorius. Kris, who had been reproached both by Berton and by his father for his readiness to separate "pure" scientific investigation from its potential moral consequences, learns by being forced to confront his past behavior, and from Hari herself, that, as Berton had told him, "knowledge is valid only when it is based on morality"—a concept that has no place within Lem's novel. Hari herself embodies the idea, familiar elsewhere in Tarkovsky's work, that love finds its fullest expression in sacrifice (*Sculpting* 40), and as the film proceeds, the basic divergence between Lem's concerns and Tarkovsky's becomes virtually irreconcilable.

The conversation in the library between the three men, and Hari's interventions, perhaps provides the clearest indication of these thematic differences. When Sartorius proposes a toast to science, Snaut responds with a speech taken directly from Lem (76—though in a different context there) to the effect that man goes into space wrongly seeking for a mirror of himself rather than facing up to his own problems on Earth. We are searching only for "Man," for an ideal image of our own world, and so don't know how to handle the truly alien when we encounter it. In the context of Lem's work, this speech makes complete thematic sense, but since these issues have barely even been raised in the film, Snaut's words here are more obscure than enlightening, and when he proclaims that "man needs man," the ironic connotations of the original are completely reversed.[3] For Lem, humanity's need to understand everything in terms of human values is a weakness, but for Tarkovsky it is a virtue, as the next exchange makes clear.

When Sartorius accuses Kris of neglecting his scientific duty by fooling around with his former wife, Hari protests that Kris is at least attempting "to stay human in an inhuman situation," while they treat their visitors as inconvenient aliens. Although the quoted phrase is taken directly from Lem (147) where it is applied by Snaut to Kris, its meaning is once again totally reversed: anthropocentric thinking of this kind may be "noble," but it is also "idiotic" and even destructive in their present circumstances, for "we are in a situation that is beyond morality" (148). When Hari then goes on to tell the men that the visitors are "yourselves, your conscience," and announces defiantly that Kris loves her and that she loves him, Tarkovsky is giving a positive, humanitarian gloss to a situation that, for Lem, is morally and philosophically absurd.

Tarkovsky has thus—perfectly legitimately—reinterpreted the original material to bring out one of his own major themes: what it means to be truly human. Hari, who shows the capacity to love, is perhaps more fully a human being than the coldly detached Sartorius, who tells her cruelly that she is just a mechanical copy of the "real" Hari. The library scene is a crucial element in this reworking and in directing the film toward a moral and intellectual statement that is diametrically opposed to that of the book.

In both book and film Kris experiences hallucinations as the stress of his apparently insoluble situation overwhelms him, but in the novel Rheya is not part of these, "nor was there any echo of past or recent events" (172). In the film, however, his dreams center around Hari and his mother, whose identities (in anticipation of *Mirror*) fuse and merge and from both of whom he seeks absolution and forgiveness. Kris's need to achieve reconciliation with all those he has failed or neglected in the past becomes the film's climactic moment, when he kneels before his father on the steps of the dacha—an ending that has no equivalent in the book (where neither mother nor father appears) and which stresses exactly the opposite themes of alienation and separation. Reacting to the devotion and self-sacrifice of Hari, Kris has undergone a profound moral transformation. For Lem, however, all of this is irrelevant: his hero comes to the conclusion that "the age-old faith of lovers and poets in the power of love, stronger than death . . . is a lie, useless and not even funny" (194). Mankind is merely a "speck of dust" within the cosmos, "the tragedy of two human beings" irrelevant within its wider purposes—which we can probably never understand—and Lem asks us to face this harsh fact with courage and dignity.

Although Lem ends his novel with Kris voicing what appears to be a hopeless "faith that the time of cruel miracles was not past" (195)—and that Rheya may even yet return—he is concerned with the process and limitations of human knowledge in almost exclusively scientific terms. Tarkovsky, as later films such as *Stalker* and *The Sacrifice* were to make abundantly clear, had rather more trust in "faith" and "miracles" than he had in science, and the main characters of the film are reinterpreted in ways that are often at variance with their presentation in the book. Although Kris is presented as being emotionally cold at the beginning of the film, he is also intimately associated with the sights and sounds of nature—the pond, the trees, the horse, and the dog, his enjoyment of the rain, even the "still lifes" that combine elements of the natural world with beautiful artifacts of civilization. All these suggest a reluctance to leave Earth and its wonders behind, and he even takes with him into space a box containing some earth and a plant. In the space station he finds that the scientists—even the cynical Sartorius—need to remind themselves of Earth in their sterile, man-made environment.

In his personal relationships, however, Kris remains remote and expressionless for much of the first half of the film and seems a worthy partner for Sartorius in his pursuit of abstract, scientific truth at all costs. Yet, on his first meeting, he finds Sartorius "horrible," and if his immediate impulse on encountering the reincarnated Hari is to attempt to get rid of her, he seems to welcome her reappearance—the bed on which he lies asleep has the sheet beside him turned down as if, subliminally, he is expecting company—and shows himself for the first time to be gentle, considerate, and loving. He then introduces her to the others as his "wife," though he delays telling her the truth about how their life together on Earth had ended until she begins to discover this for herself. Lem provides this explanation at an earlier stage of the story, after Kris sends the first apparition off in the spacecraft, and Tarkovsky's postponement of it suits his concept of Kris as someone emotionally dead who slowly and painfully comes back to moral life and learns to face the truth about himself. Despite this, however, Kris remains puzzlingly willing to cooperate in the experiments designed to rid the station of the visitors (including Hari): perhaps Tarkovsky wished to suggest that he has not yet fully committed himself to her, or perhaps the obscurity results from undue compression of the complex interior argument that Kris conducts with himself at this stage (151–52) of Lem's novel.

By contrast, Hari now seems the more fully human of the two—more responsive to pain as well as to love, and more active in attempting to find a solution to their dilemma. By the time he is ready to respond on her level, it is too late: given the "miraculous" opportunity to relive and change his past, he has merely repeated it, and once again his lover has killed herself on his account. Yet, on this second occasion, the motivation and thus the meaning of the suicide are different: the new Hari's sacrifice is a redemptive one from which Kris is able to learn and to benefit, rather than a gesture of despair that drives him further into self-absorption and self-pity.

It is not until the scenes of Kris's hallucinations that we are offered any real explanation for his emotional deadness apart from the fact that he is a "scientist," and here, as in *Mirror*, an ambiguous relationship with a beautiful and remote mother seems to be at the root of the hero's problems. In Kris's video the contrast between the unsmiling, almost immobile figure of the mother and the laughing, waving father is striking.[4] Hari and the mother are clearly associated through the shared clothing of slip and shawl in the first hallucination and then, when the image switches to black and white, the dream presents a strong and reproachful mother who rebukes her (adult) son for "neglecting and offending" her. Kris's sense of guilty inadequacy seems to extend to both women: the hallucinations begin with his mouthing "Mama!" as Hari strokes his forehead and end with his saying "Mama!" and then "Hari!" as he returns to consciousness. Although he can make no amends to Hari, who has succeeded in destroying herself, or to his dead mother, at least the reconciliation with the father that follows remains possible.

The ending itself (which presents the dacha as now apparently part of the Solaris Ocean) is, however, extremely enigmatic and open to multiple interpretations. Has Kris really physically returned home, or is he still on Solaris, with the ocean compensating for his loss of Hari by giving him a different kind of emotional fulfillment? (The use of the electronic music associated with Solaris and Snaut's mention of islands forming in the ocean might support this.) Or is the scene largely metaphorical, providing the kind of imaginative reconciliation found so often at the end of Tarkovsky's films, suggesting that Kris has at last learned to express, and accept, love and forgiveness? Another possibility—picking up on the burning fire, the dangling balloon, and the metal box (seen in the last scene on Solaris and then already within the house as Kris supposedly returns), and on the existence of the edition of *Don Quixote* and the Greek bust both on the station and in the dacha—is to see his whole journey as purely subjective and interior. Things on Earth are almost exactly as he left them because he never *did* leave; no

Kris (Donatis Banionis) returns "home" at the end of *Solaris*.
Contemporary Films.

time has passed because no physical journey took place. Yet the pond is now
frozen—though this was apparently not intended and resulted from shooting
at two different seasons—and the warm "interior rain" is falling inside the
house. As in the ending of other films, Tarkovsky—no doubt purposely—
mixes the clues that he provides for interpretation.[5]

Whether or not one accepts the literal reality of the ending, it is clear that
Kris has undergone a spiritual transformation as a result of his experiences on
Solaris. Although Hari tells Snaut and Sartorius that their visitors also act as
their consciences, we never really learn enough about them to judge this:
Snaut's "visitor" is not identified, though their relationship seems to be both
frightening and violent; and Sartorius's mysterious dwarf is altered from the
book, where his visitors appear to be children (an idea retained in the child's
ball and the photos of the babies on the wall of his lab). Both men, however,
seem somewhat at a loss, and even regretful, when their visitors finally disappear. Gibarian's visitor is also changed from the book—from a gigantic black
woman to a pubescent girl—and the motives for his suicide are never given:
Sartorius attributes it to cowardice, and Kris first to "hopelessness" and then
to "shame." All this, however, is secondary to Tarkovsky's main concern in
his presentation of these characters, which is to show Sartorius as the coldly
rational searcher for scientific truth whose certainties are finally unsettled by
the events of the film, while Snaut is now a somewhat sad and ironic mediator between the other two rather than the almost demonic figure of the book
who delights in making Kris face up to the absurdity of his situation and the
inadequacy of his responses to it.

In the process of transforming the characters and events of Lem's novel
into something more appropriate to his own private universe, Tarkovsky displayed a characteristic impatience with the logic of the book's plot and its

Kris in a corridor of the space station. Contemporary Films.

concern for scientific credibility. One such example occurs with Hari's first appearance to Kris on the space station, where she comments that he is tense, like Snaut (a remark that does not appear in the book). Although each person's "visitors" can be seen by others, and even seem to survive the death of the person to whom they are attached (as is the case, in both book and film, with Gibarian), no reason is ever given as to how Hari could have encountered Snaut before Kris's appearance at the station "created" her.

Lem's use of a first-person narrator allows him to explain some of the more bizarre elements of the plot in a naturalistic manner (Kris recognizes Rheya/Hari on her first appearance but assumes at first that he is dreaming), while Tarkovsky prefers to make the audience do the work of piecing together the fragmentary information that he chooses to impart. As a result he often has to tread a fine line between the authentically strange and the potentially comic or grotesque: because we are not privy to Kris's thoughts when he shuts Hari up in the rocket ship, his behavior may at first appear incomprehensible. Snaut's ironic commentary on his actions in the following scene allows the audience to react to the submerged comedy of the situation, but later on, when Hari returns to life after swallowing liquid oxygen, Snaut's remark that he can never get used to these resurrections (though taken directly from the book) tends to undermine the pathos of the situation.

Some of these problems can be attributed—as they were by Tarkovsky himself and by critics such as Kovács and Szilágyi (chapter V)—to an attempt to observe the science fiction conventions of the novel even as the director was simultaneously struggling to disengage himself from these. For the most part, however, Tarkovsky succeeds in reinterpreting the material of the novel in terms of his own moral and stylistic universe, creating, at its best, a work of strange and evocative beauty. Sets, clothing, color, sound, and music are all integrated into a pattern that mirrors the film's moral and philosophical conflicts. The Bach music of the credits returns in the space station during the showing of the video and the levitation scene and is associated with Earth and its values—nature, art, love—while the alien and dehumanized setting of the station itself is filled with strange electronic sounds and rhythms. Yet, in space, the Bach music is gradually given subtle electronic enhancement, especially toward the end, as the settings of the dacha and the station seem to fuse, and when it occurs on Kris's (apparent) return to Earth it has become virtually a new, yet still recognizable, piece—just as Kris himself is still the "same" person, yet utterly altered.

Sets and costumes similarly reflect the conflict between the values of Earth and those of space. As, under Hari's influence, Kris becomes more "human," he begins to wear a grey sweater and slacks instead of the white uniform that he wore for the first few scenes after his arrival. The white initially associates him with the coldly geometric layout (circular on the outside, rectangular within) of the station itself and with the lab coat worn by Sartorius in all his appearances except the scene in the library—where he displays genuine emotion for the first time in the film—and provides a contrast with the rumpled and disheveled Snaut. Especially within the station, the film observes a very restricted color scheme, predominantly white, grey, blue, and black, with warmth associated with Hari (the intense red before her first appearance and the rich golden backlighting on her hair) and with the browns of the library. On Earth, of course, green predominates. The Estonian critic Tatyana Elmanovits has suggested that the colors are even associated with different spiritual states, with brown (Snaut's jacket, Hari's dress, the father's leather vest) representing the values of Earth, and blue those of suffering (the shirt Hari wears in her attempted suicide, the bed sheets in Kris's room, the shirt and tie Kris wears in the library).

Although Kris's room is relatively featureless—except for a reproduction of Roublev's Trinity icon, seen while a fragment of the choral music from Tarkovsky's film is heard on the soundtrack—both Snaut and Gibarian have tried to bring something of Earth with them into space: Snaut has a butterfly collection among his scientific apparatus, and Gibarian's room is filled with prints, photos, statuettes, and rugs. The interior of Sartorius's room is never shown. It is in the library, however, with its paintings and other art objects, its fine furniture, china, and glassware, and its books, that Earth becomes most inescapable and Tarkovsky makes it clear that, for truly "human" values, we must look to the past (Brueghel, Cervantes, Bach) rather than to a soulless future. In the levitation scene in particular, Tarkovsky brings poignantly together the timelessness of art (painting and music), memory, and love as the camera explores in extreme close-up isolated areas of Brueghel's *Hunters in the Snow,* and the reunited lovers are seen embracing to the sound of the Bach Prelude.

In his exploration of the painting, Tarkovsky adopts the method he had used at the end of *Andrei Roublev,* but with a subtle matching of off-screen sound to the details selected. Visual continuity is provided by a combination

The dead Gibarian (Sos Sarkissian) delivers a video message to Kris.
Contemporary Films.

of straight cuts and pans plus dissolves: from a snow-covered landscape to
dogs to people skating (voices heard off-screen), more landscape, a bell-tower
(sound of bell tolling), a bird in flight (bird sounds), a tree (now electronic
music accompanies the bell and the birds), hunters (a dog barking), and then
dogs. The sequence, however, ends with a cut to a similar image in a different
medium: the video of the young Kris, dressed in red, standing in the snow
beside the swing, as the bell continues to toll. Here Tarkovsky may be putting
forward the claims of a more technological art (film/video) alongside more
traditional ones, and an interesting subtheme of the film is the manner in
which technology can, in its own way, create the "timelessness" and the
"immortality" longed for by artists. Through the medium of video the older
Berton can watch his younger self, the dead Gibarian can speak to Kris, and
Kris can call up at will his younger self, his (presumably) dead but eternally
youthful mother, and the dead Hari whose reincarnated version sits beside
him, watching.

As the film proceeds, time and space become increasingly problematic. On
the one hand, Tarkovsky develops a systematic pattern of using extended sequence shots to create a sense of "real time": these rarely last more than two or
three minutes (Kris's first conversation with Sartorius and his second with
Snaut, his confession to Hari about how her previous life had ended, the conversation that follows Snaut's arrival in the library) but are frequent enough to
impose a certain measured and rhythmic pattern on the film. On the other
hand, it soon becomes impossible to judge the progress of time on the space
station: scenes follow one another without any indication of elapsed time, yet
often with crucial stages of the plot having occurred—Hari's conversation with
Sartorius that makes her suspect Kris's account of her past, or Kris sending an
encephalogram to the Solaris Ocean. (The frequent shots of the ocean itself or

the ominously black portholes have nothing to do with establishing time; rather they create a sense of pervasive strangeness and unease.) By the time Kris falls ill and begins to hallucinate, time appears to have become totally subjective—just as the events of the film may have.

The first lengthy hallucination, with its multiple, simultaneously coexisting Haris, seems primarily intended to create a dreamlike condensation of the problems Kris has encountered on the station; the introduction of the mother, however, and the association made with Hari through the clothing suggest that other unresolved conflicts continue to torment him. The setting appears to be the dacha, with the furniture and plants covered in transparent plastic, yet Kris's bed from the space station is there too; later we see a large TV screen that seems to contain the Brueghel *Hunters* within it. Meanwhile the pajama-clad Kris attempts to appease his enigmatic mother as she wanders around distractedly or sits munching an apple and tells him that he lives a strange life. As in the final sequence, he appears to have come "home" (even bringing his metal box and its plant with him) and, although the black and white and the obviously odd setting signal this scene clearly as a dream, its strategies seep over into the ending in a manner that suggests that the two are intended to parallel each other—one providing a failed reconciliation, the other an apparently successful one—but both equally subjective.

When interviewers at the time of the film's release expressed surprise that Tarkovsky was turning away from Russia, its history and culture, to a futuristic, seemingly non-Russian environment, he responded that *Solaris* shared the basic concept of his previous two films: all his heroes are united by the same passion and need to overcome all of life's tribulations. Knowledge of life comes at a colossal spiritual cost, and they all go through intense "spheres of contemplation, searching, and achievement" ("Zachem proshloye . . ." 98). Although this moral theme is clearly conveyed, *Solaris* is not without its flaws, deriving partly from an attempt to incorporate material from the book that seems out of place in the radically different moral universe that Tarkovsky is creating, and partly from a certain woodenness in the acting, especially that of Donatas Banionis as Kris. Yet the result is unmistakably "Tarkovskian" in its creation of a vein of visionary, often hallucinatory imagery, based on the real world yet simultaneously transforming it, and in its respect and love for the natural world. In Hari's first two appearances, the gravity and serenity of her behavior, combined with lighting that bathes her in a golden glow and frames her, shawl outspread, against the brightness of the porthole, barely needs support from words or actions in establishing the essence of what she represents within the film. Kris's dreams present his personality and his problems far more strongly than any dialogue could. But it is perhaps the matching and yet very different opening and closing sequences that show the two sides of the director—the realist and the visionary—most strongly: the first with its scrupulous respect for even the humblest aspects of the natural world, the second taking that world as its basis but transforming it into something no longer "real" yet containing its own inner, spiritual truth.

SEVEN

Mirror

Mirror (*Zerkalo*, 1975), the fourth of Tarkovsky's seven films, is "central" both numerically and aesthetically to his *oeuvre*. By his own account his most openly autobiographical, daring, and self-revealing film, it had a long and tangled history from conception to finished work, including some twenty rough cuts. Tarkovsky's eventual coauthor, Alexander Misharin, relates in interview that Tarkovsky wrote the earring episode (which in somewhat altered form would constitute one of the main sequences in the film) during the filming of *Andrei Roublev* with only the vaguest idea that the film would be about his mother, his family, the Stalinist thirties, and World War II. At the very beginning of 1968 an intense creative collaboration between Tarkovsky and his "brilliant co-author" (*Sculpting* 131) resulted in a twenty-eight-episode script (A. T., *Zerkalo* 124). Three streams emerged in this: (1) documentary-style interviews with his mother, to be held in their old apartment and filmed by a hidden camera; (2) acted sequences of childhood reminiscences; and (3) a documentary, historical level, presumably consisting of newsreels (Misharin Interview).

Although the original title of the film Tarkovsky proposed to the Mosfilm studio was *Confession*, the first scripted version was called *Bright, Bright Day* (Misharin Interview; in *Sculpting* [129] translated literally as *A White, White Day*). This title, significantly, is a line from one of Arseny Tarkovsky's poems about childhood happiness:

> A stone lies by the jasmine.
> Under the stone, a treasure.
> Father stands on the road.
> A bright, bright day. . . . (*Arseny Tarkovsky* 90)

Although Tarkovsky talked about making a film about his mother, it is clear that from the beginning the film was as much about his father. By March 1974 it was being referred to by its final title: *Mirror* (*TWT* 92).

In *Sculpting in Time* Tarkovsky gives a somewhat different, though not necessarily contradictory, account of the film's creative history, one without dates. While a vague first script was simply a childhood recollection, in the second he wanted to juxtapose the narrator's and the mother's—two different generations'—ideas of the past by interspersing childhood episodes with documentary interviews with his mother. But Tarkovsky subsequently abandoned the interviews, giving a purely aesthetic reason for discarding them—

they were too "direct and unsubtle," with the "acted" and documentary elements not coming together dynamically (129). He was clearly also concerned about the ethics of using a hidden camera as well as his mother's potentially angry reaction to the ruse. In *Sculpting in Time* Tarkovsky does not explicitly state when the idea of using newsreel footage came into being, although Misharin intimates that it was already present in the 1968 script.

A director's script for *Bright, Bright Day*, published by Mosfilm in 1973, contains three story levels: interviews with the mother, childhood events, and newsreel footage, but in different proportions than would be found in the final version of the film. There is less documentary footage here and more childhood reminiscences and dialogue. The world-weary narrator, identified as "the author" (and not married in this script), walks past a cemetery where a funeral is in progress, as he thinks about love and death. He quotes Pushkin's "The Prophet," while in *Mirror* only Tarkovsky's father's poetry is read and the theme of the artist's calling—so central to "The Prophet"—is not treated so openly. The interview questions to his mother range from the mundane—"Are you afraid of the dark?" "When did you begin smoking?"—to her tastes in art and her attitude to her work, her wartime experiences, and her thoughts on important issues such as nuclear war. In this script, the mother's name in the "acted" sequences is Tarkovsky's mother's real name, Maria Ivanovna,' but it has already been crossed out by hand and changed to Maria Nikolayevna, her name in the film. Perhaps uncomfortable with the openly autobiographical nature of the original script, and afraid of the interviews, Tarkovsky begins to move away from a blatant identification of himself as the narrator and his own mother as the heroine of his film.

The longest and most narrative episodes of *Mirror* are already present in *Bright, Bright Day:* the printing press, the stuttering scene, the barn fire, and the wartime episodes (going to sell earrings with mother, father's return from the war, the shooting range). This version of the script also contains a lengthy, strange narrative, the father's description of wartime casualties on a battlefield—possibly an alternative to the Kulikovo Field battle scene Tarkovsky so reluctantly cut out of *Andrei Roublev*. This whole scene was excised as well as the opening in the cemetery, the mother selling flowers during the war, the destruction of a church cupola, a hippodrome scene with mother and sister, and odds and ends of dialogue in the country house. The sequence with Spanish émigrés is different, yet expresses the same idea as in *Mirror:* nostalgia for one's homeland. In *Bright, Bright Day* the arrival of Spanish refugee children in Odessa is shown with the accompanying celebration. Not the mother but the narrator himself sees his own double—a man with his face. The analysis of the narrator's problematic relationship with his mother is here voiced by a friend, while in *Mirror* it is given to the mother's double, the narrator's wife Natalia. The documentary footage listed in *Bright, Bright Day* includes the balloon flight into the stratosphere, the May Day parade in 1939, U.S. intervention in Vietnam, a hospital in Hiroshima, and the Spanish Civil War. The crucial newsreel footage in *Mirror* of the Red Army crossing

Lake Sivash in 1943 was apparently not yet discovered by Tarkovsky. The end of the film was already present here with its mixing of time frames: the aged mother with the narrator as a young boy. *Bright, Bright Day* ends with a description of the narrator's thoughts: that he is finally at peace and understands that his mother is immortal.

Unfortunately the published script of *Mirror* (*Zerkalo*) is a composite which includes both material excised sometime in 1973 and thus not present in the finished film—the original opening cemetery sequence and the interviews with the mother—and a major unscripted addition made only during the actual filming, introducing the narrator's wife into the contemporary time frame. According to Tarkovsky, Margarita Terekhova's talent inspired him to write additional scenes for her, but he also seems to have used the new character to portray some of the residual conflict and guilt from his first marriage. Finally the idea of interspersing the episodes from the author's past and present came about during editing (*Sculpting* 131). Both in *Sculpting* and in his *Lektsii po kinorezhissure* Tarkovsky used the example of *Mirror* to point out his deliberate principle of not using a "fixed" script, calling it rather "a fragile, living, ever-changing structure" which "dies in the film" (*Sculpting* 131).

The path from script to the actual shooting, however, was a long one. Misharin writes that, in February 1968, Tarkovsky offered a finished script to the experimental Mosfilm group, known for quick productions and headed by the established director Grigory Chukhrai. Despite Mosfilm's support, the script was turned down categorically by Romanov at Goskino (*Zerkalo* 126). To Misharin's great dismay, instead of fighting back as usual, Tarkovsky began working on another film, *Solaris*, and did not keep pushing for *Bright, Bright Day*, as in the case of *Andrei Roublev*. However, Tarkovsky's diary entries for 1970–1972 demonstrate his continuing efforts on behalf of the film and his eagerness to finish *Solaris* (October 23, 1971, *TWT* 44). By the beginning of 1972 he writes that Chukhrai is "double-dealing" over *Bright, Bright Day* and he will have to make the film on his own, hoping to begin shooting in August (*TWT* 51–52). But Tarkovsky still did not have official permission and support for the film.

Filip Yermash, who replaced Romanov as Goskino chairman in 1972, writes about his own attempts to "help" Tarkovsky (4, 10). He states that in September 1972 Tarkovsky turned to him with a highly unusual request: to approve his script with its three levels (acted episodes, interviews with the mother, and historical newsreels), but to allow him to keep working on the script during preparation for filming. Yermash notes that this kind of request went against all principles of film production, but, nevertheless, Tarkovsky received permission and the financial backing to proceed. A diary entry for September 17, 1972, confirms that he indeed approached Yermash, but that "they" wanted him to make a totally different kind of film, on the progress of science and technology, and that instead he agreed to rework his script and resubmit it, with a length of 1 hour 50 minutes (*TWT* 60–61). Yet Misharin relates that Yermash behaved "extremely democratically," telling Tarkovsky to shoot whatever he wanted (*Zerkalo* 126). As both Tarkovsky and Misharin acknowledge Tarkovsky's worry about the interviews and filming his mother with a hidden camera, his agreement to rework the script may have been more personal than administratively imposed. Yermash writes that the filming preparation began in February 1973, with Tarkovsky noting in the diary on July 11 that 622,000 rubles and 7,500 meters of Kodak stock were allocated for *Bright, Bright Day* (*TWT* 77). Filming began in September 1973, and *Mirror* (as it was now called) was completed in March 1974 (*TWT* 92). But *Mirror*'s real problems were just beginning.

Considering the miserly sum allotted, it is understandable that Tarkovsky had to work fast. But that he produced a masterpiece in such a short time is truly remarkable, and is due, to a large degree, to the collaborative efforts of the extremely talented people he gathered on the set: Alexander Misharin (coauthor), Georgy Rerberg (cameraman), Nikolai Dvigubsky (set designer), Eduard Artemyev (composer), and the actress Margarita Terekhova. In their interviews with us they *all* remembered the marvelous creative atmosphere on the set: they were like a family, living out their life on the screen, creating a common autobiography, and Tarkovsky confirms this (*Sculpting* 137). With daily rewrites, the film really took shape on the set, but refused to come together in editing and went through some twenty variants (see "Editors" in chapter 3).

Mirror had a working screening in July 1974 with much negative feedback, not the least of which was from Yermash himself, who reportedly said: "We have freedom of creativity in cinema, but not to this degree" (*Zerkalo* 127). On August 1, 1974, Tarkovsky writes that, as Yermash refused to accept *Mirror*, he was planning a letter-writing campaign and screening of the film for prominent figures (*TWT* 97). As always he was asked to make cuts, but except for minor changes, he would not shorten the levitation or the stuttering scenes because—as he wrote to Yermash—this "would destroy the artistic structure of the film." Yermash makes the point that Tarkovsky later *did* shorten the levitation scene, yet allows that he "did not compromise if something did not conform to his ideas" (10). Tarkovsky and Misharin blame Yermash for holding back the film and not sending it to Cannes as requested. He, in turn, defends himself publicly by pointing to dissatisfaction both among Tarkovsky's fellow filmmakers and in the distribution systems of the republics (10). Misharin in interview confirms that some of the film's biggest opponents were in Mosfilm itself. Within the Soviet Union, however, the film was released in early 1975, albeit at first in the very limited third, and later second, category of distribution (*TWT* 107). Despite being relegated to a few small theaters and only seventy-three copies overall (107), according to both Misharin and Tarkovsky's wife, the film ran for several months to full houses from 6:00 A.M. to midnight.

Tarkovsky was always particularly conscious of *Mirror*'s central importance for him as an artist: "a film is not merely the next item in your career, it is an action which will affect the whole of your life. For I had made up my mind that in this film, for the first time, I would use the means of cinema to talk of all that was most precious to me, and do so directly, without playing any kind of tricks" (*Sculpting* 133). He went to extraordinary lengths in order to repeat "literally what was imprinted in my memory" (A. T., "Vstat na put" 110). The summer house of his childhood was reconstructed from photographs in its exact location, on the remains of the original foundation. The field in front of the house, which the local collective farm had been sowing with clover and oats, was rented and planted with the white-flowering buckwheat he remembered so fondly (*Sculpting* 132). Photographs of his mother were used to recreate costumes, hairstyles, and even individual poses, such as the mother sitting on the fence in the film's opening postcredits shot. Margarita Terekhova, the wife and mother in the film, bears a strong resemblance to Tarkovsky's own mother, as did his first wife, whom Tarkovsky had even wanted for the role, though understandably she refused. In interview, Irma Rausch said she "cried from beginning to end" upon seeing the film, feeling that the mother and wife story lines were very autobiographical.

The film ended up a family affair, with Tarkovsky's mother playing the mother as an old woman, his father reading his own poetry, his second wife, Larissa, in a telling cameo role as a shallow, well-to-do doctor's wife, and his stepdaughter as the wartime love interest of the teenage hero. According to Tarkovsky's sister, Marina, several episodes in the film have a heavily autobiographical content: the earring episode, the father's brief return from the war, as well as the narrator following in his father's footsteps by leaving his family. She also admits, however, that the central image of the mother is disputable, and not very much like their real mother, who had a more complex personality. To what extent Tarkovsky tried to be or succeeded in being "truthful" is another matter entirely. In an earlier, unpublished version of her article on Tarkovsky's autobiographical motifs, Olga Surkova, a former collaborator and friend, calls *Mirror* a "pseudo-autobiography," pointing out that Tarkovsky tellingly ignored his second family in the film.

Tarkovsky himself later attempted to generalize the film's autobiographical nature, calling *Mirror* "the remembrances of a man who recalls the most important moments in his life, a man dying and acquiring a conscience" (*Sculpting* 110), and then, with a significant switch from first to third person, stating: "The film aimed at reconstructing the lives of people whom *I* loved dearly and knew well. *I* wanted to tell the story of the pain suffered by one man because *he* feels he cannot repay his family for all they have given him. He feels he hasn't loved them enough, and this idea torments him" (*Sculpting* 133–34—our emphasis).

Mirror is, with some justification, regarded as the most "difficult" of Tarkovsky's films—though, with fifteen years' hindsight, many of its supposed obscurities seem largely illusory. It has suffered at the hands of Western critics in particular, many of whom show little understanding of its historical and cultural context and have compounded this with insufficient attention to what actually happens—is seen and heard—on the screen. Supposed "analyses" of the film in English, French, and German abound with elementary factual mistakes whose cumulative effect is either to make the film appear virtually incomprehensible or to distort the meaning of specific, often crucial scenes. Even worse, these inaccuracies are often then used as the basis for accusations that the film is needlessly "baffling" or "incoherent." While incidentally correcting some of the more egregious and widespread misreadings, we will demonstrate, through a close, almost shot-by-shot analysis, that *Mirror* is a highly complex and surprisingly coherent film: an autobiography of the artist, and a biography of two Soviet generations (Tarkovsky's and his parents') within a wide-ranging context of Russian, European, and world history, but linked subjectively by dreams, memory, time, and art itself.

The film's prologue, a brief television documentary about the curing of a young man's stutter, has no narrative significance as he never reappears in the film; but for a Russian audience, the doctor's instruction as she brings him out of a hypnotic trance—"You will speak loudly and clearly, freely and easily, unafraid of your voice and your speech"—is clearly metaphorical and unmistakably voices an artist's and a whole society's need for unfettered expression.[2] The young man's forceful pronouncement, "I can speak," is an optimistic guide to the narrator's and Tarkovsky's own attempts to come to terms with the past in the film that follows.

In the opening shot as the camera tracks in slowly to a young woman sitting on a fence against a lush green landscape, an adult male voice explains that this was "our" summer place before "the war"—for Russians, World War II, of course. The peaceful scenery, the woman's willowy shape, her white embroidered dress and comfortable black cardigan, the silky blond hair pulled loosely into a braided bun—everything is radiant with the golden glow of the setting sun and clearly imbued with a nostalgia for the past. Turovskaya notes that all this holds "an elusive charm of recognition" for the generation born in the thirties who lived this summertime "semi-urban, semi-rural existence" outside of Moscow in the "fragile pre-war days" (65). (From the very beginning the film speaks differently to Russians and non-Russians.) But the lovely childhood memory is mitigated by a sense of loss as the narrator wonders if the man walking up the path is his father—and if his father will ever return. During the bantering conversation which follows between the woman and the passerby, a local doctor, a cutaway shows two small children—a boy and a girl—sleeping in a hammock.

Although this scene is presented in voice-over by the adult narrator, it cannot be a direct memory, as he was both too young to understand it and asleep while it took place. Even if this paradox is not fully assimilated on a first viewing, it gives the film an unusual viewpoint, for the past which we are being shown is built up not simply out of direct experience but as a mosaic of what the narrator knew firsthand, what he was told, what he dreamed or imagined, and what happened around him as part of a historical process that he shared with millions of other people. For the viewer, this first scene shows

The young mother (Masha—Margarita Terekhova) and the doctor
(Anatoly Solonitsyn) at the beginning of *Mirror*. Artificial Eye.

the mother as a somewhat ambiguous figure, beautiful and yet remote, displaying her loyalty to her absent husband in a coolly detached fashion.

After the doctor leaves, the mother walks toward the house and a different male voice (Arseny Tarkovsky) is heard reciting his poem "First Meetings," about the joys and the transforming power of love and sexual passion. As the poem continues, the small boy and then the girl are again seen, first outside, and then inside a dark but warm house which the camera explores, eventually returning to focus on the lonely and vulnerable figure of the mother. In the poem, the lovers celebrate their meeting and the woman leads the man (the lyrical "I") into her "domain, on the other side of the mirror." Mirrors and glossy reflecting surfaces will abound in this film, where the whole world, the physical objects and human relationships, is always somehow distorted, refracted, doubled up, seen in a new, more truthful way. Not only will the poetic images provide thematic threads throughout the film, but at times they will be literally visualized. As the camera tracks past the mother to the open window to show the garden, a table, rain falling, the voice explains: "everything in the world was transfigured, even simple things like a basin, a pitcher, when between us stood, like a guard, layered and solid water." Just as love transforms the everyday reality in the poem, so in this film memory bathes the basins, pitchers, vases, tables, the hard, "solid" rain (all frequent images in the film) in the warm, enticingly mysterious glow of another world on "the other side of the mirror," the world of childhood. The camera tilts up the trees as if following the poem's invisible lovers who are joined by all of nature in their celebration. But the love does not last, and the camera cuts to a close-up of the mother, gently wiping tears from her cheeks as the poem ends, perhaps with a comment on the violent historical setting of those past memories, "when destiny tracked us, like a madman with a razor in his hands."

The peacefulness of this moment is interrupted by excited off-screen voices and dogs barking. There is a fire and the children run after the mother, with the camera lagging behind to capture more of the shadowy, mysterious house interior, where for no apparent reason a bottle falls off the table and rolls loudly on the floor. The camera stops at an old mirror, focusing to reflect the boy and girl standing in a doorway brightly lit by the fire in the distance. One of the peasant boys appears from behind the mirror and walks outside, answering anxious off-screen calls, and the camera tracks through the door to capture in long shot a beautiful tableau of figures against a dewy green landscape and the raging orange fire in the background. Frequently in *Mirror* the camera will linger over such images, creating the effect of a painting—for one of the film's underlying themes is a visual dialogue with other arts, with poetry and painting, in an attempt to create not a "composite" art but rather an organically unified one.

Yet there is an eerie, unreal feel to this barn sequence, shortly to be explained as one of the narrator's childhood memories. The challenge for the viewer is rarely found in the incomprehensibility of the images themselves, but rather in the necessity to keep reevaluating what one has seen in the light of new information. This becomes apparent as a sudden cut to black and white introduces the first identifiable dream sequence: a small boy of around five is lying in bed in a dark room; as an owl hoots and a mysterious clattering is heard, he sits up; ominous electronic music—a recurring refrain—creates a sense of strangeness. The music continues over a brief cut to a shot of bushes swaying in the wind and then back to the child, now lying down again. He says, "Papa!", the owl hoots again, he sits up once more, and then climbs off the kind of ornate brass bed that appears in several of Tarkovsky's films. As he walks across the room to stand in the doorway to an adjoining room, a mysterious white object (identified for us by Margarita Terekhova as a shirt) is thrown across the top of the screen.

A cut shows the father pouring water from a pan with a gas stove burning in the background. As he turns away, moving in slow motion, the camera tracks left to reveal the mother washing her hair in a basin. Flames leap brightly from the burners of the stove as, to the accompaniment of the sound of dripping water, the mother straightens up and, in slow motion, her face concealed by long strands of wet hair, begins to make awkward flapping gestures with her arms, as if performing some ritualistic dance. The camera tracks back, with electronic music again, to show her in a large, crumbling room with the stove and its two burners reflected in a full-length mirror to the left; she is barefoot and dressed in a white shift.

Then we see a virtually identical view of the room, but without the mother and with only one gas flame reflected in the mirror; lumps of wet plaster fall slowly from the ceiling and crash onto the flooded floor. In medium close-up, the mother adjusts her hair, still in slow motion, with electronic music and the owl hooting. The camera tracks past her to reveal her reflected in the mirror; water is streaming down its surface and down the walls as the camera moves away to pick up the mother again, now wrapping herself in a knitted shawl like an old woman, and tracks in to close-up. Another cut takes us back to the mirror, now with a landscape superimposed on it; the gas burner is reflected within the frame, and also an old woman wearing a shawl and in a similar pose to the mother. Water drips in the foreground, and the total effect is one of multiple reflections in several different mirrors as the old woman appears to walk out of the mirror and the camera tracks in toward her. She stretches out her hand and this is met, as if in reflection, by another hand entering the frame from the left which begins to wipe the mirror with a squeaking sound, its movements matched by the hand of the old woman. (This image will be echoed—or mirrored—several years later in *Nostalghia*.) The scene concludes with a cut to full color and an almost translucent hand outlined against a fire whose significance can be recognized only in retrospect, when it recurs in the earring scene as part of the teenage Alexei's fantasizing.

This dream has been explored in some detail as it introduces us to some of the characteristic patterns of the film. Dreams are generally signaled either by a change in visual texture (though not always by a neat black and white/color contrast) or by voice-over. Slow motion is frequently used, and the child's vision is haunted by a sense of loss or exclusion (here he is cut off from the sexual partnership of his parents). In this case, the viewpoint then becomes that of the adult narrator, remembering his mother as she was and as she is now—for the old woman in the mirror (played by Tarkovsky's own mother) is later identified as the aged mother of the present-day scenes. Confusing as they may be for a first-time viewer, the dreams also have the genuine oneiric sense of half-recognition, of creating a half-understood meaning whose full significance is grasped only in retrospect.

In color, the camera now explores a present-day apartment (identified partly by a French poster for Tarkovsky's own *Andrei Roublev*) as an off-screen phone conversation is heard between the never-seen narrator—addressed as Alexei[3]—and his mother. The black and white dream sequence as well as the color sequences in the countryside are now all "placed" for us as Alexei tells his mother he has just dreamt about her, asking if father left in '36 or '37—leading a Soviet viewer to think he may have been arrested in the Stalinist purges—and when was it the barn burned down. She tells him 1935 for both, thus situating the events for the viewer, and creating the "early childhood" time frame when the narrator was a small (five-year-old) boy.

Alexei is not very interested to hear that Lisa, the mother's coworker in the printing shop, has died, and the conversation ends with the mother hanging up as Alexei asks why they fight all the time and begs her to forgive him.

Just before the scene ends, a metallic, scraping sound leads into the next black and white sequence, and a streetcar conductor's voice announces the stop for the printing works. The frightened young mother runs along the street and into a large, harshly lit office. An ominously suspenseful mood is created by her obvious but unexplained distress, the pouring rain and the dull grey streets, and the prisonlike imagery of fences, security guards, glaring lightbulbs, and a solitary black car parked in the street—a powerful visualization of Stalinist terror in the late thirties. In the office, the disheveled mother looks for the proofs she had been checking the day before, alarming her coworkers, including the Lisa mentioned in the previous scene—an efficient, unflappable, middle-aged woman who quickly realizes that the situation is serious. An almost subliminal sense of strangeness is added to the situation by the use of barely perceptible slow motion as Lisa and the mother hurry through the harshly lit, paper-strewn rooms and corridors, their speech drowned out by the clatter of printing presses.

Triggered by the mention of Lisa and the mother's job in the 1930s, this scene is clearly a flashback, and, as with the earlier scene with the doctor, the perspective is that of the mother and not the narrator, who plays no part in it and can know of it only by hearsay. It forms, however, part of the context of fear and suspicion that has shaped his own and his mother's lives and the lives of their contemporaries, and so mediates between public and private memories in the overall pattern of the film.

The mother finds the proofs and begins flipping nervously through them, first denying and then admitting to her boss that she might have made a mistake, and demanding to know if he thinks she is afraid. "Let some work and let others be afraid," he reassures her enigmatically. After she silently finishes looking through the proofs, she walks back to her office as another poem by Arseny Tarkovsky is heard in voice-over, about a disappointing belated meeting on a gloomy, rainy day, ending with the words: "Words cannot soothe, nor handkerchief wipe away"—reflecting both on the mother's unhappy marriage and perhaps even on the frightening situation she has just experienced. As the poem ends, Lisa is seen following her along the corridor.

Hunched over her desk, apparently weeping, then laughing, Masha (a common diminutive for Maria) confides to Lisa—but not to the audience—the "word" that she thought had been set by mistake, and both women giggle conspiratorially. Suddenly and unexpectedly the good-humored mood changes as Lisa remarks that Masha reminds her of "Maria Timofeyevna," the half-witted sister of Captain Lebyadkin in Dostoyevsky's *The Devils*. She then becomes openly hostile, accusing Masha of being that Dostoyevskian character, expecting all to be at her beck and call; as the bewildered Masha begins to weep, Lisa continues her tirade, telling her that "her senseless

Masha whispers to Lisa (Alla Demidova) the word she thought she had misprinted. Artificial Eye.

emancipated ways" are to blame for her marital unhappiness. Finally Masha escapes into the privacy of the shower room, with the now-remorseful Lisa following and pleading for her to wait. The scene ends rather ambiguously as Masha's sense of relief gives way to almost comic frustration as—typical for Soviet plumbing—the water supply fails. The atmosphere of Stalinist suspicion, terror, mistrust, and repression is brilliantly conveyed throughout this episode, both in the overall situation and in its depiction of the psychological strains imposed on individuals (surely accounting for the sudden switch of mood in Masha and Lisa's conversation).

A quick cut to a color long shot with reverberating electronic sound shows green fields with trees in the background and a large fire burning in the distance. The different setting makes it clear that this is *not* another view of the barn burning, though it is often interpreted as such; it probably is meant to be another, purely dreamlike, memory of the fire. The shot may also be a transition between past and present, as it is followed by a cut, still in color, to a young woman looking into a mirror with a room reflected behind her. Though she appears at first to be the mother, visual clues identify her as a different person: her hair is down and her facial expression is harder and less vulnerable than the mother's. The off-screen narrator/husband immediately identifies her as someone else by saying that she always did *look* like his mother. She responds coolly that this is the reason they separated. Their hostile conversation—with her noting in horror that their son, Ignat, is becoming more like his father—continues over a cut to a childhood scene showing the young mother, and a woman carrying the young girl to the dacha, as the narrator comments that his mother in his memories always has his wife's face, and that he is equally sorry for both of them. Throughout the film so far, the dialogue has been a guide through the seemingly confusing visual imagery, with the narrator explaining what we either are seeing or have seen.

With a cut back to the apartment, all relationships are clarified as the narrator, Alexei, tells a twelve-year-old boy, Ignat, to stop fooling around. The son is a passive observer of his estranged parents' quietly antagonistic conversation, in which it becomes clear that Alexei has equally strained relations with his ex-wife and his mother; he openly blames his self-centeredness on his upbringing by women, urging his ex-wife to remarry lest Ignat suffer the same fate. As in Tarkovsky's own life, this unhappy family drama clearly repeats the unexplained broken marriage of the narrator's parents. For Alexei, and perhaps for Tarkovsky himself, the sense of longing and loss associated with the past is transformed in the present into feelings of anger, guilt, and responsibility, which can be exorcised only by recreating the past through dreams, memories, and projections.

Once he has set up these personal links between past and present and provided the motivation for the film's complex visual structure, Tarkovsky expands an individual family drama into a history of two Soviet generations, his own and his parents', pre- and postwar, within the context of major world events. It is only within this context that the next scene can be understood: seemingly in the same apartment, Spanish is heard off-screen, and as Alexei and his wife finish their conversation, there is a cut to black and white newsreel footage of a bullfight followed immediately by a Spaniard (in color) acting out the part of a matador with the sound of the bullring in the background. A group of Spaniards—usually identified by Soviet critics as guests of the narrator—are joined by the narrator's wife, now identified as "Natalia." Black and white newsreel footage of the Spanish Civil War is intercut with the first Spaniard's account of his life as a child refugee, and in particular his sad parting from his father. The continuing conversations in the apartment reveal people nostalgic for their country, but with no way back. The visual and verbal accounts of broken families and disrupted childhoods link this scene to the narrator's own experiences.

The newsreel images continue with shots emphasizing the effects of bombing raids on children and their families, then cut unexpectedly to different historical footage—of a huge balloon surrounded by smaller ones, with seated soldiers dangling from them. Classical music begins quietly over the haunting images of this record-breaking Soviet ascent into the stratosphere in the 1930s, ending with another event from the thirties, the May Day parade of 1939. The visual beauty of the newsreel footage chosen by Tarkovsky is underscored by the delicate classical music and can be appreciated even without

"This seems to have happened before." Ignat (Ignat Daniltsev) and his mother (Natalia—Margarita Terekhova). Artificial Eye.

understanding how emblematic it is of the childhood of the narrator and of Tarkovsky's whole generation. The fact that this documentary material is presented in chronological order (here the Spanish Civil War and the 1930s, later World War II and the Sino-Russian conflict) helps to give a logical and factual time frame within the film that counterpoints the a-chronological pattern of the overall structure.

Choral music continues over a return to color and a close-up of a drawing of an old man with a beard—a Leonardo da Vinci self-portrait. Other Leonardo drawings, mostly portraits, are seen as a hand (quickly identified as Ignat's) turns the pages of the book. When his mother drops her purse on the floor, Ignat notes that all this seems to have happened before. Ignat, we will shortly discover, looks identical to the young Alexei, his father (both roles are played by the same boy). Perhaps they even share a common memory, as will be seen shortly when Alexei as a child also helps his mother pick up things she has dropped. Leaving the apartment, Natalia reminds Ignat to tell Maria Nikolayevna to wait when she comes (the name indicates this must be the narrator's mother and thus the boy's grandmother).

The camera now follows the lone Ignat around the apartment (as ominous electronic music portends the occurrence of something unusual or even "fantastic") in an unbroken shot that finally pans to an older woman dressed in greenish-black sitting at a table, being served tea by a maid. The woman asks him to read from a notebook, but when he begins to read Rousseau's ideas on the negative effects of science and art on ethics (a belief Tarkovsky shared with respect to science and explored in *Solaris*), she interrupts him, directing him to another text. Ignat now reads a passage about Russia's isolation from Europe because of its unique role as a buffer between the East (the Mongols) and the West (Christendom)—a predominant Russian cultural and historical "myth." As the reading ends, the writer is identified as Pushkin. The extract is from his famous letter to Chaadayev in 1836, which was a key text in the Slavophile-Westernizer controversy raging in the second quarter of the nineteenth century: should Russia adopt the West as its cultural and political model or look to its own indigenous religious and historical traditions? Recognizing Russia's significance, Pushkin states that he would not, for any reason, change his country or choose a different history. It is not surprising that some Soviet critics have praised *Mirror*, like *Andrei Roublev* before it, for being a thoroughly nationalist, Russian film.

As Ignat finishes reading, a large picture of Tarkovsky's own mother as a young woman is seen directly behind him, one of many reminders to the careful viewer of the autobiographical nature of the film, but a lead-in to the next scene as well. Eerie electronic music is heard once again as Ignat opens the door to the old woman earlier seen reflected in the mirror in the first dream sequence; as Natalia had warned Ignat that Maria Nikolayevna was expected, the viewer should recognize her as his grandmother. Yet neither the boy nor the grandmother recognizes the other and the woman leaves, saying she has made a mistake! Is it possible, as some Soviet critics suggest, that the family situation was so bad that grandmother and grandson didn't really even know each other? Clearly, realistic motivation fails here, as so often in this film. Tarkovsky himself admitted that this scene is weak from a narrative viewpoint, but that he needed to portray the feelings of shyness and confusion of the old mother, as a kind of parallel to the young mother later in the earring scene (A. T., "Vstat na put" 111). As always, emotional rather than rational plausibility is Tarkovsky's goal.

Ignat closes the door and walks back, to find that the woman and her maid have disappeared. Electronic music and the camera movements accentuate the strangeness of this whole episode: the camera first tracks briefly out to a long shot of the empty room and then cuts to a close-up of the polished table surface. The electronic music rises to a crescendo and suddenly stops just before the heat mark from the now-absent teacup shrinks and vanishes, underscoring the "reality" of this rationally inexplicable event.

Alexei phones, asking if Maria Nikolayevna came, telling Ignat to amuse himself and invite friends over, a girl perhaps. Trying to find a common language with his clearly estranged son, Alexei tells Ignat about a redhead both he and their shell-shocked military training officer were in love with during the war. Once again, the dialogue explains the images, for as the father talks, the camera cuts in for a close-up of a teenage redhead walking on a snow-covered landscape. It's wartime and her clothes are too short and tight. A gently nostalgic mood is created by classical music as we see what we first assume to be Ignat and then realize is the teenage Alexei (usually addressed as "Alyosha"), dressed for winter and looking as if into the camera and away.

Although the scene that follows is one of Alexei's childhood memories, he is not the main character in it and is glimpsed only intermittently—presumably the intention here, as elsewhere, is to present the experience of a whole generation as well as that of an individual. The focus is on the shooting instructor, a wounded veteran, and a recalcitrant small boy, an orphan from Leningrad, whose obtuse behavior tests the instructor's patience to its extreme. The other boys are almost equally uncooperative, including Alexei, but the world-weary instructor bears with them until Afasyev (the Leningrad orphan) retaliates by throwing what we are led to believe is a live hand grenade onto the shooting range. The sequence is rapidly cut, mostly in close-up, and slightly disorienting: a series of different hands take and pass on the grenade and remove the firing pin, but the cries of "Afasyev, don't do it!" signal that it is he who actually throws the weapon. The instructor immediately hurls himself on top of the grenade; we hear the loud sound of his heartbeat and the camera moves in to show the war wound pulsating on his scalp. Finally a voice calls out that it was only a "dummy" grenade; the instructor rises slowly and disgustedly to his feet and sits down exhausted on a stool.

A brief cut shows the redheaded girl again, smiling and fingering a sore on her lip. She says something that we cannot hear, and a faint sound of drumbeats anticipates a cut to the next newsreel sequence, in black and white: exhausted naked or partially clothed soldiers are carrying supplies and equipment in shallow, muddy water (the Soviet crossing of Lake Sivash in 1943). There is a brief cut to the shooting range as Afasyev trudges up the steps and an almost immediate cut back to the lake to show the endless trudging of worn-out ragged soldiers. Visually this lengthy and intense sequence (lasting around four minutes) deglorifies war, virtually pulling the viewer down into its shallow, swampy water.

Sounds of footsteps in the water, intermittent drumbeats, and choral music introduce another reading of a poem: "On earth there is no death. All are immortal. All is immortal. . . ." By blending his father's poem "Life, Life" with these images of "suffering," which "spoke of immortality," Tarkovsky gives meaning to the men's "heroic sacrifice" (*Sculpting* 130). The poem continues over an extreme long shot (in color) of a snow-covered, Brueghel-like landscape with children sledding, and Afasyev walking slowly up the hill toward the camera and into close-up, whistling but with tears on his cheeks. Here the poem ends. But there are other important themes connected with immortality in this conjunction of poem and image: the meaning of time itself, and the role of the poet/filmmaker as a unifier of past and present, of personal/subjective and historical/objective time. In this film Tarkovsky calls up different time frames and makes them all "real," creating a visual correlation for his father's words: "I will call up any century, go into it and build myself a house."

More black and white newsreels follow, now of victory, but disturbingly intercut with its accompanying costs: the liberation of Prague in 1945, explosions, the dead Hitler, fireworks (Moscow, 1945), civilians on crutches in a trench, the atomic bomb exploding over Hiroshima, another mushroom cloud accompanied by reverberating electronic music, and finally back to color and Afasyev being "blessed" as a bird flies and lands on his head and he reaches for it, taking it into his hand. Then a final newsreel sequence of another kind of threat to the Soviet Union, this time from the East: huge crowds carrying portraits of Mao and waving the Red Book, endless busts of Mao, drumbeats as Soviet soldiers try to physically contain a Chinese demonstration (Damansk Island, 1959). Here the Russians are a visual projection of that buffer Pushkin wrote about, still pursuing their special destiny—literally keeping the Asiatic peoples out of Europe.

Two family scenes, both in color, follow in rapid succession, both demonstrating the tension between the parents in the past, and between the narrator and his ex-wife in the present time frame. A young woman (identified as the mother, for her hair is up and an off-screen male voice calls her "Marusya") is cutting and stacking kindling. The father is briefly glimpsed in army uniform before we cut to outdoors and the teenage Alexei quarreling with his sister over a book (the same Leonardo reproductions that Ignat had been looking at in a previous scene—like so many things, the book will pass from father to son). When the father summons the girl, "Marina," they both run off to the house. A brief cut to the mother, looking sad and exasperated, is followed by the father, embracing the children and trying to restrain his emotion. The electronic music gives way to a burst of organ music and a Bach chorale on the Resurrection, and we cut back to the Leonardo book and the portrait of Ginevra Benci that Tarkovsky, in *Sculpting in Time* (108), compares explicitly to Margarita Terekhova, the actress playing Maria/Natalia.

This is followed by what is virtually a match-cut to the wife's (Natalia's) face, identified by her wearing her hair down and by an almost immediate mention of Ignat. The camera tracks in slowly to close-up as she rebukes her off-screen husband for neglecting the boy, and the two proceed once again to bicker—which of them should Ignat live with, why are his school grades so poor, why is Alexei so dependent on his mother, should Natalia marry her lover . . . ? During the conversation Natalia examines some photos, including one of Alexei's aged mother (seen in the first dream sequence and in the "Pushkin" scene) and then a mysterious picture of Natalia and the old woman together, with *Natalia* wearing the dress that the mother had worn as a young woman almost forty years previously. Here Tarkovsky has made use of "found material" (according to Margarita Terekhova, a photo taken on set with the women wearing the clothes they happened to have on at the time) to reinforce the similarity between mother and wife that Natalia immediately comments on and the husband strangely denies. The scene takes place in a oom with several mirrors, in which Natalia is reflected as she walks around during the conversation; the predominant color tone is brown, almost mono-chrome, and the lighting is harsh, making Natalia look tired and unattractive. The use of real time here (at 3 minutes 55 seconds the film's longest shot), the mirrors, the restricted color scheme, and the camera's almost exclusive focus on Natalia in close-up or medium shot create a powerful sense of claustro-phobia, echoing the dreariness and repetitiveness of their arguments, marked by Alexei's empty sarcasm and Natalia's weary helplessness.

A brief shot, in sepia, of bushes rustling gently in the wind provides a transition to what a voice-over describes as a recurring dream, though, as if to avoid cluing us in too obviously, Tarkovsky presents the sequence in color rather than in black and white.[4] The dream, the narrator says, takes him back to those treasured places where grandfather's house used to be and where he was born forty years previously. The camera follows the mother through the dacha as we hear only the narrator's lament—he cannot enter the house in his dream and must wake up. As he expresses his longing for the childhood dream to return, the camera tracks into a patch of complete darkness which is sud-denly illuminated by a striking match held by the now five-year-old Alexei; he is happy again, the narrator tells us, because everything is still ahead, and all is possible. The placing of this quietly lyrical and tender scene, ending on a note of hope, immediately after we have seen (or rather heard) the adult Alexei at his most bitter and disillusioned, makes its own ironic point.

The lifelike, happy color dream now gives way to an ominously disorient-ing black and white one, beginning with an extreme close-up of a vase with a clock mechanism immersed in water—a visual metaphor for time standing still. The viewpoint is apparently from within the dacha of the previous se-quence, looking through a window as the five-year-old Alexei walks past outside, to the accompaniment of the familiar ominous electronic music. The camera follows him as he walks past a cloth-covered table, and then zooms slowly in on what seems to be *also* the dacha, the same building we are watching from, but now looking empty and deserted—a spatial paradox fa-miliar enough in dreams. A series of cuts show the boy approaching a door that (through reverse motion) creaks open of its own accord, then a rooster flies through a window pane in slow motion, breaking the glass. Leaves rustle loudly in the wind, and the camera tracks toward the table where the still-life composition of bread, apples, a spoon, and what is either a lamp or a can-dleholder is disrupted by the last of these being toppled off by the wind.

The boy is seen approaching the house again, in slow motion, moving past sheets flapping in the wind; he goes out of sight behind the house, and we see a well and bucket and a brief shower of rain. Almost all these images—the object falling off the table, the well and the creaking of the bucket, the rain—turn this scene into a distortion of the fire scene, and the mother too has changed: for when the boy reaches another door, which also opens of its own accord, and a dog trots out, she is revealed squatting on the floor of a shed, picking up potatoes, with rain visible through the window behind her and a look of intense melancholy on her face. Once again the dream deals with exclusion and loss rather than with the happiness or contentment of childhood memories.

A cut returns to color and the somewhat similar setting of a farmstead at dusk. The scene that follows is set during the war and involves the teenage Alexei, his mother, and the owner of the farm, a well-to-do doctor's wife. The mother has come to try to sell some earrings in order to buy food, and the action takes its meaning from the contrast between the well-dressed, obviously prosperous doctor's wife and the shabbily clothed Masha and her barefooted son. Inside the embarrassed mother drops the jewelry she is holding (providing a visual and aural duplication of Natalia's spilled purse earlier) and, once she has gathered it up, the two women move into another room, leaving Alexei behind.

As he sits down in the elaborately furnished room, the camera concentrates on another "still life" of milk spilt on a dresser and dripping from one shelf to another. Classical music begins as the boy studies his reflection in an oval mirror on the wall, and the camera tracks in very slowly on the mirror until his reflected, impassive face fills the screen. The angle then switches to an examination of the boy himself, followed, as if in the same setting, by what must be his imagining of the aftermath of an encounter between the redheaded girl and the military instructor, the man departing to leave the girl squatting beside a stove and warming her hands over a burning stick in an identical image to the mysterious intercut shot that ended the first dream sequence. As in that sequence, Alexei is excluded from a sexual encounter, in this case one that he had perhaps hoped to achieve for himself.

The music gives way to the sputtering sound of a dying oil lamp and then dripping water, as the doctor's wife adjusts her newly purchased earrings. She relights the lamp and offers to show them her child, proudly leading the way to an ornate baby bed with dazzling white sheets in which an obviously healthy and well-fed child is sleeping. Throughout this whole scene the warm interior lighting and the opulent furnishings create a sense of luxury that contrasts sharply with the mother's miserable state. As the doctor's wife gushes on about her precocious child, we see Masha stroking her own undernourished boy's hair protectively and then making a gesture as if she is about to vomit. She leaves the room, followed by the woman, and says she doesn't feel well.

The woman, who admires her new acquisition in every mirror she passes, offers to give them something to eat and suggests that they should kill a rooster: as she is pregnant, she would like either Masha or Alexei to do it for her. Masha reluctantly agrees and the bird is killed off-screen, some of its feathers fluttering into view; this is followed by a shot of Masha that Tarkovsky later felt was too explicit and contrived: harsh lighting from below combined with a disgusted, cynical smile makes her look evil, almost satanic. Rain streams down the wall behind her. Soft organ music heralds a cut to black and white and a medium close-up of her husband facing the camera.

Masha is seen levitating above their brass bed as he asks in concern if she is ill and she assures him that she loves him. Here the fantasy seems to be as much hers as the narrator's and is cued in from her experiences rather than from his.

Masha and Alexei virtually flee from the farmstead as the astonished woman asks if they won't wait for her husband's return so that Masha can be paid. As they walk along a riverbank a poem is read about the relationship between the soul and the body and the former's futile attempt to escape and exist on its own—creating an ironic parallel to the scene we have just witnessed, in which the mother fails to feed her child's hungry body. This continues over a cut to sepia and bushes blowing in the wind and another shot of the table with the lamp falling off it. The previous dream seems to continue in black and white as the five-year-old Alexei now enters the dacha, into a room full of billowing lace curtains. The whole house is filled with these and with sheets hanging out to dry, and the camera tracks through them to a mirror reflecting the boy as he holds a large jug filled with vigorously swirling milk. A dog barks and there is the sound of a train whistle. Then a cut to color shows the boy swimming clumsily across a pond to where the mother is rinsing laundry on the other bank (the sheets, perhaps, that appear in his dreams?). Here dream and memory seem to overlap and intermingle, sharing the same visual and auditory imagery.

The camera moves, in color, through the dacha and then to the window, through which we see the boy walking toward two distant figures—his sister as a little girl, and his mother as the old woman. He calls to the latter as if she is the young mother of his childhood, and she turns to look at him with a puzzled expression. Until now time frames have been kept separate, with dreams and memories from the thirties and from World War II contrasted with the present-day reality, presumably of the seventies. But now there is a merging of time frames, with characters belonging to past and present appearing together.

A cut takes us to a previously unseen location, a room with white walls, one of them covered with mirrors. A doctor and two women—the mysterious visitors in the "Pushkin" scene—are discussing the narrator's health and whether his illness is physical or caused by guilt. Alexei, off-screen, asks to be left in peace, and the camera then shows him, but only from the neck down, moving to his hand, which lies next to a seemingly dead bird on a sheet covered with bird droppings.[5] As he says that he wanted only to be happy and that everything will work out, he picks up the bird and releases it into the air, where it flies off in slow motion and we hear a sigh that, for many critics, signals the narrator's death.

In these last few scenes the tenuous barriers between dream and memory, past and present, real and imagined characters, that have held for most of the film have begun to crumble, and this process culminates in the final scene, which, as in *Ivan's Childhood* and *Solaris*, provides a vision of reconciliation of the conflicting forces in the hero's life. We are back in the sunlit landscape

The old mother (Maria Tarkovskaya) and the two children at the end of *Mirror*. Artificial Eye.

and the dacha of the past, with the young mother and father lying in the grass. "Would you rather have a boy or a girl?" he asks her. She smiles, not replying, then sighs and looks away. Joyful choral music swells on the sound-track as the camera cuts to the mother as an old woman, followed by Alexei as a small boy, then tracks in extreme close-up over natural and domestic debris in a silted-up well: the dacha seems simultaneously to be inhabited and to have been abandoned years before. The old woman leads the little girl by the hand as the boy follows, and the young mother is seen, choking back tears and then smiling, as if watching them. The old woman and the two children walk rapidly across a field in long shot; as the boy leaves the frame the young mother is seen standing in the middle of the field looking at her future self, perhaps in deliberate visualization of the Russian proverb and last line of Boris Pasternak's famous *Doctor Zhivago* poem "Hamlet": "Living life is not like crossing a field."

The tracking camera picks up the boy, and the music stops as he utters a loud yodeling sound, then hurries to catch up with the old woman. The camera tracks away from them behind some trees, moving alternately closer and then farther away as the three figures are glimpsed through the branches receding into the distance. As the camera continues to retreat and the figures become smaller and smaller, obscured by the branches and trees, the silence s broken by bird calls and finally the sound of an owl as the image fades to dark. The absence of the joyful music at the very end, the slow fading of the final image to black (rather than the pure white of *Solaris* and later *The Sacrifice*) perhaps qualifies the possibility of total reconciliation even if it is imaginary. And if the narrator has in fact died, does that mean that only *after* death can we achieve the kind of peace Tarkovsky is searching for?

The first serious review of *Mirror* in English (in the Spring 1976 issue of *Sight & Sound*), written by the well-known Soviet film specialist Herbert Marshall, immediately demonstrated the danger of writing about this film upon a single viewing (for which he does apologize). While Marshall's depiction of the unfriendly reception *Mirror* received in the official cinema circles is informative, his description of the film misses crucial autobiographical markers— the poems are *not* read by the actor Smoktunovsky (93) but by their author, Tarkovsky's father; moreover, in his description of a scene between Natalia and her off-screen narrator/husband (94), he confuses the all-important contrast between the present (wife) and past (mother) time frames.

In the Fall 1981 issue of *Film Quarterly*, also basing his analysis on a single viewing (15), Michael Dempsey describes the film as "enigmatic," "intractable," and "ineffable" (13) and ends by attributing to it "a pervasive sense of chaos" and "a beautiful bewilderment" (15). Although some of the many mistakes in describing individual scenes can be excused by the single viewing, the "chaos" and "bewilderment" result largely from an apparent unawareness of the double time structure that mediates between past and present: for example, Dempsey sees only one boy, whom he calls "Ignat" throughout, and makes no mention of any of the present-day characters and events.

Mark Le Fanu presumably saw the film more than once before writing his 1987 book on Tarkovsky, but he too misrepresents a good deal of what happens. Although he gets the general pattern of the film right, his account of it is riddled with niggling factual errors and misinterpretations that combine to create a strangely off-key account of the film as a whole. His description of what he calls the "indoor storm" (72) in the first dream sequence conflates several different images in a seriously misleading manner, as does his account of the throwing of the hand grenade in the military training scene (compare our own accounts of these scenes above). Discussing the printing-house scene (86), he identifies the mother's misprint as "Sralin" (based on the verb "to shit") for "Stalin,"[6] and implies that the audience learns this: "It emerges that. . . ." The word is in fact *whispered* to Lisa and the audience never hears it—though many in the Soviet audience might have known the reputed incident on which this episode is based (Terekhova Interview). The fact that, even in the seventies, the verbal slip could not be openly identified is part of the meaning of the scene. Other errors abound, and the cumulative effect— especially in a book-length study—is unsettling.

French critics, however, fare little better. The magazine *Positif* paid particular attention to Tarkovsky from the late 1960s onwards, and the essays and interviews appearing there have recently been collected into a volume, *Dossier Positif*. It is unfortunate, however, that no one saw fit to correct some of the more obvious original errors when certain of the articles were reprinted.[7] In "La maison en feu," for example, Petr Kral refers to the "earring" scene as if it were a cozy conspiracy between the two women, reinforcing this by mistakenly describing them as "trying on [the earrings] together" (*Dossier Positif* 43)—when the whole point of the scene is the *difference* between the women and the psychological tensions resulting from this. Even more astonishing, he tells us that, in the final scene, "leaving the narrator's mother and her little boys [*sic*] in a field in the background of the image, we pick up, in the foreground, a nurse [*sic*] with some other children [*sic*]" (49).[8]

In the German volume of essays entitled *Andrej Tarkowskij* a detailed and generally accurate synopsis of *Mirror* is provided (122–36). The attempt here to rationalize the color scheme by dividing it into the following "exact" categories—black and white for the documentary sequences; sepia-brown for scenes from early childhood; and color for the present and for flashbacks (126)—is, however, extremely misleading and fails to account for, in particular, the printing-house scene, which is both a flashback and in black and white, and early childhood sequences which can be color, black and white, or sepia.[9]

In comparison with Western critics of *Mirror*, Soviet critics describe more accurately what is occurring in the film, even if they occasionally misinterpret both its intention and its meaning. However, there are occasional factual mistakes, such as V. Dyomin's noting that Pushkin's letter to Chaadayev was written to Vyazemsky (270). More surprising is V. I. Mikhalkovich's statement that the mother in the earring sequence can't kill the rooster even though she and her son are hungry, "because she cannot raise her hand against a living being" (38). Maria *does* kill the rooster, as a protective gesture so that her son will not have to, but this act clearly takes a psychic toll on her. Several critics state with some certainty that the hero dies in the film, when in fact this is not shown, although it could be one of the possible interpretations.

What is it that has produced such a baffling array of misstatements and errors in the description, not to mention interpretation, of *Mirror* by both Western and Soviet critics? Unquestionably this stems from the film's challenging complexity on both the thematic and stylistic levels. Western critics and viewers were exhilarated by the visual beauty of Tarkovsky's images and intrigued by the film's convoluted narrative: his jumps from past to present, dream to reality, "fictionalized" events to newsreel documentaries. But they were often baffled by the many autobiographical and historical references only some of which were easily recognizable. In the interpolated newsreel footage, World War II scenes and the mushroom cloud over Hiroshima were obvious, but the sending of children to the Soviet Union during the Spanish Civil War, Soviet balloon flights into the stratosphere, and the border clashes between the Soviets and Chinese were not. The two scenes which Soviet critics understood and praised—the printing-press episode with its evocation of Stalinism and the atmosphere of fear in the late thirties, and the wartime scene of the narrator's mother trying to sell her earrings in order to feed her hungry children—puzzle the Western viewer who does not have the correct context or shared experience. The human suffering of World War II in particular was unforgotten and remained in the forefront of the Soviet cultural "mythology" in the 1970s to a much larger extent than in the West.

While Western critics had more trouble with the thematic elements and the plot, Soviet critics found it difficult to understand the openly subjective, experimental, and deliberately complex way in which the story was told. A "crossword puzzle" was the term most often used by critics. Marshall notes that this was an absolutely original film in Soviet cinema of the mid-1970s and very difficult for even sophisticated Soviet film professionals (95). Instead of a linear "objective" narrative structure, *Mirror* offered a confessional interior monologue, and in place of a positive hero or even any hero, it presented the disembodied voice of the world-weary narrator who is seen only once, from chest down, on his sickbed. Thus it is not surprising that the film came under heavy criticism from the cinema industry, film critics, and the average Soviet filmgoer. The most philistine critics saw the film as useless confessional drivel, but their predictable criticism did not bother Tarkovsky. He was, however, deeply hurt by the rejection of his own colleagues in the film industry. In its March 1975 issue *Iskusstvo kino* published an official discussion of *Mirror* and other new films, held jointly by the Secretariat of the Filmmakers' Union and the collegium of Goskino. *Mirror* was criticized for being an inaccessible "elite" film which "lacks precision in connecting the personality of the hero with his epoch" ("Glavnaya tema—sovremennost" 10). What comes through in this discussion is not simply the inability of these members of the establishment to rid themselves of old clichés or of their habit of contrasting "elite" films against those made for the masses. While recognizing Tarkovsky as a "master," respected senior colleagues such as the veteran directors Yuli Raizman and Marlen Khutsiev were honestly struggling with the form of Tarkovsky's new film. The thoughtful Khutsiev, while acknowledging Tarkovsky's ability to express feelings and give beautiful visual form to nature, nevertheless criticized this self-referential "monologue" (13), failing to recognize that Tarkovsky was in fact challenging the viewer to a higher level of *dialogue* than had been demanded before in Soviet film. At least one participant, V. I. Solovyov, did rise to the challenge at this very meeting, saying that the first viewing brought back his own unsettling memories, but after the second "I looked at the heroes and understood that these were not film images but *my* thoughts, *my* memories" (11, original emphasis). Solovyov's identification with *Mirror* is shared in particular by critics of Tarkovsky's own generation—Maya Turovskaya, Tatyana Elmanovits, and Leonid Batkin—whose perceptive multilayered analyses simply cannot be compared to anything published in the West. Batkin, a philosopher and cultural historian, astutely observes that much of the power of the film comes from its mystery and difficulty, even its inaccessibility: "As we reach to grab phrases

and shots which seem to openly give us the key to the whole, we come to
understand that one cannot exhaust the whole, that we must, like the hero
who exists behind the mirror, go over memories, strain our conscience and
impressionability over Alexei's life and our own" (Batkin 79).

Under siege from bureaucrats and even fellow filmmakers, Tarkovsky was
extremely proud of favorable viewer responses and quoted many in the introduction to *Sculpting in Time:* "A woman wrote from Gorky: 'Thank you for
Mirror. My childhood was like that. . . . Only how did you know about it?
There was that wind, and the thunderstorm. . . . It was dark in the room. . .
And the paraffin lamp went out, too, and the feeling of waiting for my
mother to come back filled my entire soul" (10). A factory worker in Leningrad expressed the film's impact most succinctly: "My reason for writing is
Mirror, a film I can't even talk about because I am living it" (10).

If at least some Soviet viewers of the mid-1970s felt more comfortable
with the autobiographical, historical, and cultural aspects of *Mirror* than
Western audiences, the latter should have felt more at home with its unconventional time structure and its switches between dream and reality. The late
1960s and early 1970s saw a stream of works by Resnais, Fellini, Bergman,
Bunuel, and Godard, among many others, that are at least as challenging to
conventional habits of movie viewing as *Mirror* is, and yet most Western
critics seemed to find Tarkovsky's film far more "baffling" than *Belle de Jour,
Providence, Last Year in Marienbad,* or *The Passion of Anna.* Certainly it presents several major obstacles to immediate comprehension, at least on a first
viewing: one is the problem of translation which, at least in the American
print, ignores the characters' names, thus making instant identification of
characters (Maria or Natalia? Ignat or Alyosha?) and therefore time frames
(past or present?) impossible. Even more important is the lack of a consistent
and easily identifiable point of view, and the pattern of "retrospective understanding" in which many images, episodes, and even characters make sense
and can be fitted into place only well after their first appearance, and perhaps
not fully satisfactorily so until a second or third viewing of the film. Tarkovsky would certainly have agreed that we rarely expect to receive everything
that *any* serious work of art has to offer after only one reading, viewing, or
hearing, and that his films are no exception to this.

The narrator's consciousness provides an overall framework for the film,
even if not all the episodes reflect his own direct experience, in much the
same way that Godard's musing voice-over for *2 or 3 Things I Know about Her*
provides a structure into which can be slotted meditations on history, culture,
politics, contemporary society, and personal relationships. Tarkovsky's film,
however, also obeys the logic of a dream, especially toward the end, in which
images and events merge, glide, and overlap, are mirrored and subtly distorted, to create a sense of half-recognition, forcing the viewer to conduct his
or her own reordering, filling in the gaps and constructing meaning on the
basis of the clues that the director offers. This effort is worth making, of
course, only if the images—as in this film—have the hallucinatory and rever-

)erative impact of a true dream. It might even be argued, as Herbert Eagle
ias suggested to us, that the profusion of errors made in describing the film
tre "legitimate" and could reflect something of its dreamlike quality, which
:ncourages the blurring of identities and the sense of "half-understood" ap-
)rehension of certain scenes. It is certainly a film that demands to be seen
nore than once—perhaps first in a "dream" (but not *written* about at that
tage!) and then in a "waking" state, for there is also much coherence and
·larity in the film.

Despite the film's overall oneiric nature, it is possible to delineate with
·ome certainty three time planes in the film, all united by the unseen but all-
mportant presence of the narrator: 1935, when the narrator is a five-year-old
)oy, presented mostly in the adult Alexei's dreams; the World War II period,
vhen Alexei is a teenager, seems to be recalled more than dreamt; and finally,
·here is an unidentified present (doubtless the 1970s), the vantage point from
vhich the narrator moves freely backwards through time. The newsreel se-
juences have a definite chronological development from the 1930s through
he 1950s.

Yet what gives the film its true oneiric power is its eventual disintegration
)f all such self-sufficient categories, so that the reading of the Pushkin text
ind the appearance of the grandmother can occur in the middle of an other-
vise perfectly commonplace scene, and can be stylistically integrated into it
)y means of the camerawork and the haunting image of the fading heat mark
)n the table that persists even after the "fantastic" element of the scene is
)ver. By the end—say, after the earring scene—it is impossible (as in *Persona*)
·o say with any confidence whether a particular scene really "happened" or
1ot; and yet, as with Bergman's film, this strengthens rather than lessens its
1rtistic impact. In *Persona* the harsh physical texture of sea, rocks, and sky,
.he vivid, almost tactile presence of the faces, the starkness of the sound
·ffects, convince us on a basic level of reality that allows us to "believe" what
s happening at each stage of the film. Tarkovsky's images, whether softly
1ostalgic (as with the mother on the fence) or conveying terror and panic (as
n the printing house), have a similar inner reality that compels belief. They
1re combined with a soundtrack that emphasizes the textures of real life: bird
;ong, the rattling of a streetcar and the clatter of a printing press, footsteps
:runching in the snow, the dripping of water, wind rustling through a clump
)f bushes. Even those dreams that are clearly identified as such have nothing
:onventionally vague or "dreamlike" about them. Their power comes not
`rom weird or outlandish imagery but from their ability to create a convincing
·isual equivalent for feelings of loss, separation, awe, longing, and wonder
:hat recognizably derives from the events and characters of waking life—
;heets hung out to dry, a woman washing her hair—and gives them their
nysterious resonance.[10]

The Hungarian critics Kovács and Szilágyi have written convincingly
1bout *Mirror* as a dialogue between past and present in which the narrator

uses the memories and experiences of others, as well as his own, to enlarge
his personal consciousness and free himself from his stifling egoism and self
centeredness. Whereas Kris Kelvin in *Solaris* wants to relive his past in order
to change it, the hero of *Mirror* cannot change the past, though he can learn
from it and so change the present. This can be done partly by recovering the
lost innocence of childhood, and partly by understanding his own place in
the context of his nation's culture and history (chapter VI: 107–28). Tarkov
sky's own comment, quoted earlier, that the film is about "a man dying and
acquiring a conscience" (*Sculpting* 110) might seem to support this and also to
link the film thematically to a work like Bergman's *Wild Strawberries*—yet
with the significant difference that, unlike Isak Borg, Tarkovsky's hero is
not shown attempting to make amends to any of the people he has hurt,
neglected, or mistreated during his life. If the final scene suggests a reconcilia
tion, it is with the past, not the present (his wife and son are noticeably ab
sent), and if he has freed himself from the "guilt" that the doctor attributes to
him in the preceding scene, it is once again toward the family of the past—
"people whom I *loved* dearly and *knew* well" (*Sculpting* 133—our emphasis)—
not that of the present.

Even the supposed happiness, or "lost innocence," of the childhood
scenes—always presented from the adult narrator's perspective—is, in fact,
qualified, primarily through the portrayal of the film's pivotal figure of the
mother. Though she is obviously admired and adored, she is puzzlingly remote
and aloof most of the time—not just to strangers like the doctor but even to her
own small children, whom she never even touches (she is more protective and
solicitous of the teenage Alexei). Only as an old woman, in the clearly unreal
dream/projection which merges past and present, does she firmly grasp the
girl's hand, the boy still significantly running behind to catch up with them.

The change of title from *Bright, Bright Day* (emphasizing childhood happi
ness) to the more ambiguous *Mirror* (suggesting that the problems of the past
are reflected and repeated in the present) may be relevant here, and the film's
catharsis may belong not so much to the narrator as to the viewer, who must
share Tarkovsky's belief in the possibility of reconciliation—outside of space
and time—by responding to the sheer visual beauty and power of images
which clearly transcend rational categories. Remembering Proust, Tarkovsky
describes the effect of finishing *Mirror*: "Childhood memories which for years
had given me no peace suddenly vanished, as if they had melted away, and
at last I stopped dreaming about the house where I had lived so many years
before" (128). Through this highly personal catharsis, he has tapped a vein of
imagery and emotions to which we can all respond: loss, love, regret, hope,
fear, and longing. If we are condemned, on one level, to repeat the mistakes
and unhappiness of the past, on the other, as his father's poem expresses it,
"Everything is immortal," and nothing that we have experienced is ever truly
lost.

EIGHT

Stalker

When he wrote in his diary for January 26, 1973 (*TWT* 66), that a "tremendous" script could be made out of Arkady and Boris Strugatsky's recently published story *Roadside Picnic*, Tarkovsky was still preoccupied with *Mirror*. But two years later, expecting that Yermash would reject his proposal for Dostoyevsky's *The Idiot*, he was prepared to suggest instead Tolstoy's "The Death of Ivan Ilyich" and *Roadside Picnic* (*Martyrolog*, January 6, 1975: 151). By March 27, 1975, he had an agreement to work together on the script with the Strugatsky brothers (*TWT* 108), and on November 20 he still expected the project to go ahead (117), with shooting the following summer. For almost a year there is no mention in his diary of the film, but Filip Yermash notes that by June 1976 work had begun on the script (Yermash 4). An entry for August 22, 1976, finds Tarkovsky hoping to get started with exteriors on *Stalker* (the film's new title) in the fall and, if that was not possible, to work in the studio over winter and shoot exteriors in April 1977 (129). After more delays, shooting had finally begun by February 24, 1977, with the interiors of Stalker's house (143).

Yermash (4) records that the film was included in the studio plan for 1977 for 650,000 rubles, at 2,700 meters, in a "wide format" (the Russian version of Cinemascope), but that the director soon changed to the regular format. May 1977 found the crew shooting in Tallinn, Estonia, for approximately three or three and a half months (Kaidanovsky and Fomina interviews). That spring and summer Tarkovsky was beset by a number of problems which almost shut down the film, including difficulties with his set designer (Boym) and director of photography (Rerberg), and, most important, a shortage of funds and 1,400 meters of useless film shot thus far (*TWT* 145: May 28 and July 21, 1977). He complained that everything shot in Tallinn had to be scrapped *twice*, once because of bad processing of the Kodak film, and then because of the poor condition of the equipment (146).

From published statements as well as interviews it is possible to piece together what may actually have occurred. There is general agreement that a technical problem with the film stock was discovered in the summer of 1977, when more than half the film had been shot and two-thirds of the money spent (*O Tarkovskom* 254). Strugatsky explains that Tarkovsky didn't see a single frame of the processed film until July because he was waiting his turn at the studio, and that the film was damaged at this stage. But the story of the defective film is more complex. The editor, Lyudmila Feiginova—present at the shooting and most closely concerned with this aspect of the film—related in interview that after the first day of shooting, Tarkovsky sensed something wrong with the apparently out-of-date film stock. He kept asking the lab to check carefully each batch of film sent for processing and even flew to Moscow to try to convince the lab that there was a problem (264). She also added that Soviet labs could not work well on Kodak and the rushes did not improve. No one wanted to take the blame for the damaged film, and by the time the defect in the film stock was confirmed, Tarkovsky had shot all the outdoor scenes (264).

But Tarkovsky was not the only film director with this problem. Other directors had been allocated the same expensive, foreign-bought Kodak stock and, on experiencing problems with it, had quietly reshot the damaged footage (264; Feiginova Interview). Tarkovsky, on the other hand, seemed to find the problem a godsend: relations with Rerberg had seriously deteriorated (*TWT* 146), and he was unhappy with the script and what had been shot so far. The actor Nikolai Grinko quotes him as saying at this stage: "This film isn't mine. I can't release such a film. I must reshoot it all" ("Talisman" 23).

Yermash records that an investigation was begun and, not surprisingly, Goskino officially refused to cover the losses. Arkady Strugatsky states that, on the sly, however, Goskino offered to consider the lost film as normally processed—i.e., to cover up—and to continue shooting; when Tarkovsky refused (was it a moral stand, or an expedient way of scuttling his production?), they let him know they would write off everything as a creative "accident" if he would drop the film (*O Tarkovskom* 255). Yet, by August 26, the "catastrophe" was over and shooting had resumed with a *new* cameraman (Kalashnikov), a *new* set designer (Abdusalamov), and a *new* script (*TWT* 147). Tarkovsky offers no explanation as to how he got permission to reshoot the same film, and in one month's time at that!

Both Yermash and Arkady Strugatsky confirm that Tarkovsky's solution had been to ask permission to make a two-part film, which meant new deadlines and additional stock and funds. He sent Arkady to Leningrad to produce a script with his brother Boris in ten days, and a diary entry is ecstatic: "The Strugatskys are writing a new Stalker . . . now a believing slave and apostle of the Zone" (*Martyrolog* 194).[2] But this "thin" script (a synopsis consisting only of dialogue and short summaries) was to serve merely as a basis for the eventual film, with continuous rewrites on the set and even during dubbing—Kaidanovsky (Stalker) and Grinko (Professor) cited at least ten scripts for *Stalker* overall. Grinko even quotes the Strugatskys at the *Stalker* premiere telling the audience not to believe the credits: "We are not the scriptwriters, he did it all—alone" ("Talisman" 23).

The film began its second life when approval was given to transfer it officially into the 1978 production year. Yermash confirms that time was given for a rewrite, expansion to a two-part film, and change of genre: instead of science fiction, the film was becoming a moral-philosophical parable. Very unusually—but only after Tarkovsky and his coworkers had petitioned Goskino (i.e., Yermash)—they were allowed to start shooting before a final script had been completed (Yermash 4). The director's script was ready in February 1978 and completion deadlines were moved, first to May 1978, and then even later. Yet the problem of how to write off the losses still seems to have remained. Yermash states that he had to ask permission of the Council of Ministers of the USSR to establish a new deadline (up to 29 months) because a significant change of creative conception had occurred. A new total of around 1 million rubles was allotted for the continuing production of a practically nonexistent film, with a third cameraman, Knyazhinsky, hired for the job. As Yermash himself says, "It was an unprecedented case!" Although Yermash's claims of unflinching support for the film should be treated with the usual skepticism, Nikolai Grinko confirms that another 300,000 rubles was found (making the total around 1 million) and that Yermash did support the new production ("Talisman" 22).

Tarkovsky's wife, Larissa, however, states in interview that it was *she* who kept the film alive by getting the whole team to sign a letter to Zemyanin, Brezhnev's deputy on production problems (implying they went over Goskino's head to the government itself), protesting the refusal by Goskino to accept the film stock problem and its intention to shut down the production. Everyone except Kalashnikov (the second cameraman) and Abdusalamov (the second set designer) signed it; thus it is not surprising that shortly both of these men would no longer be part of the team.[3] Knyazhinsky was hired to be the director of photography, and Tarkovsky himself became the set designer, although in fact only a few of the final sets were his.

The Tarkovsky diary is curiously silent on all the maneuvering that kept *Stalker* alive, perhaps because neither he himself nor his wife, who edited the diaries, wanted to give any credit to Tarkovsky's "enemies" in the film bureaucracy, especially Yermash and Goskino. After complaining in April (*TWT* 54) that he had no money for the second part of the film, at the end of June 1978 Tarkovsky was in Tallinn, shooting for the second time (155)! By December 23 he was working on the sound, calling the film a success and something new for him: "[It] is about the existence of God in man, and about the death of spirituality as a result of our possessing false knowledge" (159). Ever leery, he hoped there wouldn't be a scandal over this film, expected Yermash probably to "make a fool of himself" again (159), and on January 5, 1979, worried that he would be asked to make changes, which he would refuse to do (165). By February 6 he already knew that the film was not going to Cannes, and Sizov (the head of Mosfilm) was asking for changes, which, unlike most requested of his other films, turned out to be quite minor (172).

Yermash records that the film was accepted in May 1979, but there were angry letters and phone calls, with military leaders especially upset: "Where is it taking place? What are these people, whose helmets are they wearing? What is this zone?" It stretches the imagination to see Yermash, along with Sizov, defending the film, assuring the critics it was not "anti-Soviet" but "highly creative" and "should not be banned" (4). Lest one is tempted to laugh when Yermash—who had caused so many problems in the past—com plains of his "travails" on Tarkovsky's behalf, one should remember that Goskino and Yermash did have to answer to a higher authority—the Com munist Party itself! The Byzantine nature of Soviet bureaucracy could easily have made Yermash into both accuser and defender of Tarkovsky and hi film. Yermash also takes credit for getting approval in 1980 for the title o People's Artist of the RSFSR [Russian Republic] for Tarkovsky, a sign of offi cial recognition for his creative work (4).

Stalker was the first of Tarkovsky's films for which no significant cuts wer requested. Despite bureaucratic rumblings it had a successful premiere a Dom Kino in mid-May 1979 and a general release a few days later. Distribu tion was another matter. Arkady Strugatsky describes the negative reactio of a group of distributors from all over the Soviet Union and complains tha only 196 prints were made for the whole country, and only 3 for Moscow. Ye he adds that some 2 million people saw the film in its relatively short first rur in Moscow (O Tarkovskom 259). Official disapproval was exhibited in the al most complete absence of reviews in major Moscow newspapers and jour nals. What attention it received was either perfunctory or negative: it wa mentioned in passing in an article on science fiction films in Literaturnay gazeta (June 25), reported in Pravda to be on the program at the Pesaro Festi val, and, predictably, condemned for straying from the literary text in Sovet skaya Rossiya (July 12). At the 1979 Moscow Film Festival it was denied public screening and shown only to foreign journalists. Meetings were "se up" with well-rehearsed attacks by factory workers: Tarkovsky was accuse of wasting public funds for films he made "for himself and his friends" (Gershkovich 5). Yet, even if Stalker did not immediately get the wide distri bution at home and abroad that it deserved, it never came under the kind o vicious attack that Andrei Roublev and Mirror were subjected to.

Positive reviews and articles began to appear in the Soviet Union aroun 1981, after the film's 1980 screening at Cannes thanks to its French distributo (TWT 247), which resulted in wider acclaim abroad. Serious criticism gen erally took a cue from Tarkovsky himself, who was quoted in interview discussing the "non–science fiction" nature of the film and the change to moral-philosophical parable. He stressed the humanistic themes (comparing it to Solaris), its stylistic innovations, and the differences between the origina story, the various scripts, and the final film. Recent articles have begun t focus on the film's spiritual and religious thematics, and, especially since th Chernobyl nuclear disaster, it has been elevated to cult status and treated a prophetic of an ecological apocalypse.

Although Tarkovsky attempted—as with Solaris—to downplay the sci ence fiction element of Stalker, it has much more in common with the Stru gatskys' Roadside Picnic than the convoluted history of its script migh suggest. Roadside Picnic is set in what seems to be a not-too-distant fu ture—as is Stalker—but, apart from the brief written explanation at th eginning, Tarkovsky chooses virtually to ignore the speculations as to ⸜hat might have caused the Zone (or Zones—there are actually several in ⸜e book)⁴ and also eliminates the elaborately physical descriptions of the ⸜otic dangers to be encountered there. In *Roadside Picnic* the Zones are robably the result of an incursion from outer space that has left behind ⸜ysterious debris of great scientific and economic value: "stalkers" are li⸜ensed to lead expeditions into the Zone to retrieve this, but many choose ⸜so to use their knowledge privately and for their own enrichment; if ⸜aught, they are punished with imprisonment. The story follows, over a ⸜eriod of several years, four stages of the career of "Red," a far more ⸜own-to-earth and ruthless figure than the Stalker of the film, whose ⸜aughter "Monkey" suffers from progressive physical deterioration as a ⸜esult of genetic mutations caused by her father's activities inside the Zone. ⸜ather than merely being crippled, as in the film, she becomes increasingly ⸜onhuman both physically and intellectually. In a desperate attempt to ⸜ave her, Red enters the Zone illegally, accompanied by Arthur, the son of ⸜n older and rival stalker, in search of the "Golden Ball" which is reputed ⸜ grant wishes: his own wish will be for his daughter's recovery. To reach ⸜e Ball, they have to cross a dangerous stretch of open ground called the Meatgrinder": Red sends Arthur first, as a "minesweeper," knowing he ⸜ill likely be killed and he himself will then be able to pass safely. His ⸜tratagem succeeds, and the story ends with Red on the verge of reaching ⸜is goal but too tormented by the memory of Arthur's exultant words just ⸜efore his death—he wishes "Happiness for everybody!"—to be able to ⸜ake his own wish.

Apart from changing characters and events almost unrecognizably, ⸜arkovsky, as he did with *Solaris*, shifts the philosophic implications of the ⸜tory in more congenial directions. Rather like Lem, the Strugatskys are con⸜erned with the problem of knowledge and understanding (if the Zones *are* ⸜e result of some alien visitation, what was its motive? Is the debris intended ⸜ be beneficial or destructive to humans, or is that a purely irrelevant specu⸜ation?). These issues, debated at some length in chapter 3 (and especially ⸜ages 106–107), are virtually ignored by Tarkovsky, who likewise raises very ⸜ifferent moral issues from those examined in Red's sacrifice of the young ⸜an in order to save his own daughter.

Yet a surprising number of details remain, especially from chapters 1 and ⸜, and are incorporated at various stages into the film: the "Plague Quarter" ⸜f abandoned houses on the border of the Zone; mention of railways and ⸜atcars; ruined vehicles inside the Zone; the throwing of nuts and bolts to test ⸜he terrain;⁵ Red throwing a bolt at Arthur when he becomes overconfident; a ⸜omment that it is faster to take detours than to go in a straight line; Arthur's ⸜ringing a gun with him that Red makes him throw away. More significant ⸜erhaps are comments such as "The Golden Ball only grants your deepest ⸜nnermost wishes" (132) or "there really is no time in the Zone" (30); Red's ⸜ecognition that "the only thing he had left in the world, the only thing he lived for in the last few months was the hope of a miracle" (131–32); and his final inability to formulate a wish of his own after undergoing great hard ships. Even his relationship with his wife, who constantly threatens to leave him yet remains loyal and devoted, is echoed in the film, and, though the context is different, her words about her mother's hostility to Red (47) are almost identical to those in the film. While fully recognizing that Tarkovsky turned the original story into something very different and deeply personal, I should also be acknowledged that something more than the bare minimum of a Zone, a very different kind of Stalker, and a power that can (perhaps grant wishes survives from the Strugatskys' book. Working closely with the story's creators (who remain officially credited with the script), he absorbed rather more of the original and was less cavalier in the process of adaptation than he liked to assert for public consumption.

The links between *Solaris* and *Stalker* go rather deeper than their common origin in works of science fiction, in which Tarkovsky professed to find little interest for their own sake. In both films the characters are given the opportu nity to have their wishes granted—only to find that this involves a painful and searching self-examination, leading to the discovery that what they think they want is not quite what they really do want: "You dream of one thing and get something quite different," as Writer observes in the scene in the "tele phone room." Both films explore the conflict between science, rationalism and technology on the one hand and love, humanism, and faith on the other Sartorius of *Solaris* is close to Professor in *Stalker* in his belief that rational analysis can resolve all human dilemmas, and both are forced to acknowl edge a mystery (hope, faith, or love) that their world view cannot encompass

From another perspective *Stalker* can be seen as forming a trilogy with *Nostalghia* and *The Sacrifice* in presenting a society apparently bent on self destruction because it has lost all links with nature, its own past, and any sense of a spiritual or moral dimension to its behavior. Stalker leads on to Domenico in *Nostalghia* and Alexander in *The Sacrifice* as a "holy fool" whose words are greeted with scorn or incomprehension by those they are intended to save, while Writer's aimlessness, self-contempt, and sense of entrapment are echoed, to at least some extent, by Andrei and Victor in the later films.

The initial critical response to *Stalker* in the West was concerned less with its philosophical implications than with attempting—as with *Andrei Rublev* and, to some extent, *Solaris*—to see it as some kind of political allegory or parable, picking up in particular on such "clues" as Stalker's shaven head, his early comment to his wife that he is "imprisoned everywhere," and the fact that the term "Zone" had been used for Stalin's system of prison camps These perfectly valid points were, however, often accompanied by far fetched attempts to explain what the Zone "stood for."[6] Coming from the Eastern bloc, the Hungarian critics Kovács and Szilágyi give the most con vincing "political" interpretation of the film, though they deny that it is in tended as an explicit allegory of Socialism or Stalinism. For them the Zone is

the "Secret" that any society needs in order to exist and maintain its authority; it is the taboo area of memory and the past that is closed off for investigation and has constantly to be entered or "probed" by misfits or doubters if the
moral health of society is to survive (129–33).

Although Tarkovsky steadfastly refused to be drawn into any kind of political controversy when discussing this film (or his work in general) with
Western critics, and resisted in particular being identified as a "dissident,"[7] an
almost mythic aura was beginning to gather around his personality, while his
well-publicized problems in the Soviet Union encouraged speculation about
him as a remote, ascetic, oppositional Solzhenitsyn-like figure. By now he
was widely regarded in Britain and Western Europe as "the Soviet Union's
greatest living film-maker" (the London *Times*, February 6, 1981), and each
new film was automatically assessed as a stage in the development of a continuing and increasingly important *oeuvre*; in the United States, however—
with a few exceptions such as Jim Hoberman in the *Village Voice* (October 26,
1982: 60–61) and Ronald Holloway in *Variety* (September 19, 1979)—each
Tarkovsky film still tended to be greeted as an isolated and baffling phenomenon. Two separate reviews in the *New York Times*, by Vincent Canby (May 25,
1980—report from Cannes) and by Janet Maslin (October 20, 1982—on the
film's opening in New York), agreed in finding it obscure, tedious, and, for
Maslin, "stupefyingly slow and drab." Canby at least found the sets "extremely handsome and the camerawork . . . beautiful," but Maslin thought
it offered little to the eye and used "the most impoverished materials imagin-
able."

Recent criticism, especially in France, has tended to move away from political readings of the film to those that stress its religious and ethical dimensions. Too often, however, these are based on careless or even completely
mistaken accounts of what actually happens on screen, ranging from far-
fetched attempts by Gérard Pangon (in *Etudes cinématographiques*) and Antoine de Baecque to find crosslike camera movements throughout the film, to
serious and ultimately irresponsible misreadings of the film's enigmatic final
shot. As much of any interpretation of the film depends on understanding
what in fact happens here, it is worth examining it closely.

The final shot begins, in color, with a close-up of Stalker's daughter
"Monkey," wearing her headscarf, sitting reading a book. As dandelion fluff
drifts through the air—signaling something extraordinary about to begin—
the camera tracks slowly back to reveal a table with three glass vessels on it: a
half-full glass of tea, a jar containing a broken eggshell and some other un-
identifiable objects, and a tall, thick glass smeared with milk. The child puts
down the book and looks off-screen as we hear her recite, in voice-over, with
the occasional sound of the foghorn in the distance, a love poem by the nineteenth-century writer Fyodor Tyuchev. Her concentrated, serious reading of
this implies a precocious understanding which may be one of her "magical"
powers. As the poem ends, the camera too stops, with the surface of the table
filling more than half the screen and a window visible in the background

Stalker's daughter (Natasha Abramova) and the three glass vessels at the end of the film. Contemporary Films.

with some green bottles on the ledge. The girl looks toward the window, then back to the table; she inclines her head and stares intently at the nearest glass (the one containing the tea), which begins to move jerkily away from her as the dog whimpers off-screen. The glass moves toward the left-hand corner of the table and stops near the edge. Now the jar starts to move toward the right-hand corner, stops halfway, and the tall glass begins to move. The fog-horn sounds outside as the child lays her head on the table, her eyes obscured by the tall glass and the jar. The glass continues its movement and topples off the edge of the table; we hear it bounce but not smash on the floor. The child remains with her cheek resting on the table as the sound of a train is heard outside and the table begins to shake; the camera tracks in toward her as the train noise becomes louder and the whole surface of the table quivers violently. A fragmentary and disrupted version of Beethoven's "Ode to Joy" mingles briefly with the rattle of the train as the camera moves closer to the child's face and the fluff continues to fall; although she blinks, her face is blank and expressionless, and a slow fade begins as the music dies away and only the rumbling of the train is heard.

A prominent French critic, Barthélemy Amengual (*Dossier Positif* 33), attempting to force the shot into a specifically Christian framework, sees it very differently. First of all, for him, the child is "in all likelihood" reading the Bible. (There is no evidence for this, and it is more likely to be the volume of poems that she then quotes from.) The glasses, he claims, move as follows: "the beautiful glass" moves to the edge of the table and stops; the jar and another glass move and stop; "the beautiful glass" moves again, falls over the edge, and breaks. (In fact the glass that falls does so in one continuous movement, is far from "beautiful," and is so thick and clumsily made that it does not even break.) Amengual then launches into a paragraph of rhapsodic Christian imagery ("innocence is crucified but the Holy Spirit keeps watch within her and illuminates everything around her") that specifically associates the paralyzed child with "the 'miraculous' glass, the beautiful glass which breaks"; the three glasses become symbols of "faith" and "hope" in a world of "violence" and "ugliness"; and within twelve lines they have even come to represent the Trinity. But how valid is any of this if one of its key arguments (the "beauty" of the glass and its "breakage") is demonstrably wrong?[8]

Although attempts such as these, based on obviously mistaken analysis, to force "late" Tarkovsky into an explicitly Christian straitjacket must surely be rejected, it remains true that *Stalker*, like all his later films in particular, does operate within an overall system of Christian iconography and Biblical reference. This is most evident in the scene often referred to as "Stalker's dream," as the men rest after the "waterfall" scene and before they enter the "Meatgrinder." They are seen in a series of individual shots, with Writer lying prone on a mossy patch of earth projecting into a stream; Professor half sitting, half lying on a slope; and Stalker lying full-face, facing in the opposite screen direction to Writer, almost entirely surrounded by water, with a waterfall visible behind him.[9] After a brief cut—to what looks like quicksand and a background of trees, with windspouts and the unmotivated fluff that usually signals "strangeness"—an off-screen woman's voice (probably Stalker's wife) begins to whisper the passage from Revelation 6:12–17 about the opening of the sixth seal, the destruction of Heaven and Earth, and the vain attempts by the survivors to hide themselves from "the wrath of the Lamb." A brief shot of Stalker in close-up is followed by a cut to black and white and another extreme close-up of his sleeve and then his face before the camera tracks away, as in the "waterfall" scene, over a collection of debris lying in shallow water: a syringe, a bowl, a glass dish with a goldfish swimming inside,[10] rocks, a mirror, a metal box containing coins and a plunger, a fragment of Jan Van Eyck's Ghent altarpiece with coins lying on it, a rusting pistol, a coiled spring, paper, a torn calendar, a clockwork mechanism, and other detritus. The voice-over, which is occasionally spoken in a tone of uneasy laughter, gives way toward the end of the shot to the softly pulsating Indian-like electronic melody that had accompanied the opening credits.

Clearly enough this sequence, like some to follow in *Nostalghia*, makes its own comment on a world dominated by transitory material concerns, in which faith and spirituality have been forgotten or discarded. At this point in the film only Stalker has shown any real inclination toward faith (in his comments on the nature of the Zone and his prayer for his companions to be granted a childlike capacity for belief); Professor remains an enigma, characterized so far mainly by his pragmatism; and Writer, though expressing scorn for himself and his profession, has just been musing unexpectedly on the redemptive power of art. Stalker now goes on to offer a Biblical quotation of his own, that describing the meeting on the road to Emmaus between the resurrected Christ and two of his apostles who fail to recognize him (Luke 24:13–18), stopping with the words of Cleopas. (This crucial reading is translated in the subtitles of the British print, but not in the American one. It is, however, translated in the video available in the U.S., which may have been taken from the British print.) As he speaks there is a cut to Professor lying down, with his eyes closed, and the camera then tracks slowly along his body to show Writer resting his head against Professor, also with his eyes closed. The camera stops on Writer's face with the words "But their eyes were holden that they should not know him"—at which point Writer opens his eyes. The camera then tracks back to Professor's face and stops there on the words of Cleopas, as he speaks to, but does not recognize, Jesus. Although Professor's eyes are now open, the very specific matching of camera movement and words here suggests clearly that Writer has the capacity for redemption (opening his eyes) while the more pragmatic Professor has the capacity to see but does not yet use it.

Yet, though there is much explicit Christian reference here, the overall pattern of the film tends more toward a general framework in which faith, spirituality, and art (none of them seen as exclusively Christian attributes) are set against materialism, cynicism, and disbelief, with the oppositions clearly demarcated in the relationship between Stalker and his two companions. In the interviews that he gave around the time of making this film, Tarkovsky seemed more concerned with attacking the spiritual emptiness of contemporary society in general than with proposing specifically Christian remedies, and he even told Marcel Martin, "For me the sky [heaven] is empty," and that he did not have the "organ" that would enable him to experience God." Meanwhile, in his diary entries at the time, he was beginning to record the interest in Rudolf Steiner and Eastern philosophy (*TWT* 156, September 6, 1978) that was to coexist with traditional Christian doctrines throughout the remainder of his work.

For Tarkovsky himself, in *Sculpting in Time*, the main theme of the film was "human dignity; and . . . how a man suffers if he has no self-respect" (194). He also saw it as being about the redemptive power of love, embodied specifically in the figure of Stalker's wife, and how "her love and her devotion are that final miracle which can be set against the unbelief, cynicism, moral vacuum poisoning the modern world, of which both the Writer and the Scientist are victims" (198).[12] These ideas are clearly enough expressed in the film and are elaborated on by most critics—one problem with *Stalker*, in fact, which is in most other respects one of Tarkovsky's finest works, is that it is so explicit about what it is saying and articulates so many of its basic thematic conflicts in its dialogue.

Critics as varied as Maya Turovskaya, Peter Green, and Gilbert Adair all suggest that Writer and Professor learn little from their experience. For Adair, Writer "contemptuously declines even to formulate a wish" (63), while for Turovskaya the two men recognize only their own "poverty of spirit" (113), and for Green they realize little more than their inability to "subject themselves to a possible revelation" (53). Although Tarkovsky himself seems to support this negative assessment of Writer and Professor[13] ("They had summoned the strength to look into themselves—and had been horrified; but in the end they lack the spiritual courage to believe in themselves" [*Sculpting* 198]), he somewhat contradictorily asserts that "even though outwardly their journey seems to end in fiasco, in fact each of the protagonists acquires something of inestimable value: faith" (199). Kovács and Szilágyi seem to agree with this somewhat more positive view when they suggest that the silence of the two intellectuals (in contrast to their previous bickering and verbal assertiveness) as they look into the Room suggests a degree of respect and acceptance that is perhaps a form of prayer (137–38).

Tarkovsky told Aldo Tassone that he felt closest to Stalker, who represented "the best part of me, that which is also the least real"; that he also felt very close to Writer, who had gone astray but was capable of finding a spiritual outlet; but that Professor was too limited to be sympathetic—though he immediately went on to concede that Professor was capable of going beyond these limits and was in reality quite open-minded (*Dossier Positif* 129). It does in fact seem to be the case that both Writer and Professor learn a good deal about themselves during their journey and that both change as a result. Professor listens to Stalker's pleas not to use his bomb and finally throws it away and, though Writer accuses him of being a time-serving careerist, Professor tells his boss on the phone that he is no longer afraid of him, and acts accordingly. His refusal to enter the Room (which he had, of course, originally come to destroy) perhaps suggests a degree of humility and an acceptance that it is not up to him to save humanity from itself.

Writer is a rather more complex figure who appears to despise not art itself (he appears to speak directly for Tarkovsky in this respect) but himself as an unworthy practitioner of it. Though he knows what art *should* be, he is also aware that his own motives for writing are suspect and egotistical. It is the nonintellectual Stalker who becomes the spokesman for the "unselfish" nature of art in his comments on music and his heartfelt recital of the poem supposedly by Porcupine's brother. (The walls of his home are also lined from floor to ceiling with books.) Writer's self-disgust is projected outward in his cynicism and sarcasm toward his companions, his readers, and the world in general (his caustic humor is inadequately rendered in the subtitles). His ostensible reason for going to the Zone is to ask for inspiration, yet his attitude even toward that seems both half-hearted and flippant; his motives for the journey seem to derive from boredom and curiosity rather than from any real desire to change. It is perhaps his awareness of this that prevents him from entering the Room: in *The Wish Machine* (*Mashina zhelaniy*), an earlier

Stalker (Alexander Kaidanovsky) . . .
and his two companions, Professor (Nikolai Grinko) and Writer (Anatoly
Solonitsyn). The setting here is the tiled wall. Contemporary Films.

version of the script, he admits that "we haven't matured to this place"—a line not in the finished film, but implicit in his behavior on the threshold. It is not contempt or even fear that prevents him from entering, but a realization that he is not yet worthy to encounter what the Room has to offer. Though he has *said* this before, he perhaps *feels* it for the first time. His theatrical bravado gives way to the simple gesture of putting his arm protectively around Stalker—whom he had unmercifully ridiculed and even beaten—while the thoughtful expression on his face on their return to the bar suggests that a genuine transformation has at least begun within him.[14]

Stalker himself ("one of the last idealists," as Tarkovsky called him in the Tassone interview) is clearly both the most sympathetic and the most tormented of the three. In *The Wish Machine* script he is a much cruder and more down-to-earth figure, whose motive in going to the Room is to ask for his daughter's cure (as in the original story). Here he asks nothing for himself: recognizing his own wretchedness, cowardice, and inadequacy, he wants genuinely to help those in a worse state than he is because they have lost the last vestiges of hope and faith. The fact that he is weak and despised, even a bit mad, yet spiritually and morally strong, relates him both to the Russian tradition of the *yurodivy* and to the characters of Dostoyevsky, who often possess the same seemingly incompatible character traits. "Weakness" and "flexibility" are explicitly favored over "hardness" and "strength" in the lines[15] he speaks in voice-over as he edges his way toward his companions, whose intellectual and spiritual hardness has to be broken and who have to "become helpless like children" (Tarkovsky said this to his actors!) if they are to embrace "life" rather than "death." Though this "breaking" does seem to happen, at least to some extent, by the end of their journey, he appears—surprisingly—not to accept or recognize this. His expressions of despair to his wife on his return home, and his sense of failure as he condemns his companions for their lack of belief and their materialism and complains that no one needs him or the Room, have the effect of undercutting this sense of possible change for the viewer and help to give the film a bleaker and more despairing tone than Tarkovsky seems to have intended. When asked by Aldo Tassone if *Stalker* was a despairing film, he replied that if it was, it would not be a work of art, for art should create a sense of hope and faith (*Dossier Positif* 128). One could, however, interpret this scene as further emphasizing the nature of Stalker's character and his general perception of the world rather than as a statement about the unredeemable nature of Writer and Professor.

The Wish Machine script ended with the return to the bar, and after the wife has told Writer and Professor the story of her life with him, Stalker introduces the others to her as "my friends." The later *Stalker* script (1978) ended with the family walking off and Monkey chattering away about goodies she would like to eat or buy. Both Stalker's lament and the girl's "miracle" are later additions. The film's editor told us that three different endings were shot and tried out, all of them finally being incorporated in one way or another into the film. By including Stalker's lament and then following it with the wife's monologue (originally intended to be delivered in the bar), Tarkovsky may have chosen to throw another important theme into relief: the consoling and healing power of love as embodied in Stalker's wife, who clearsightedly sees her own situation for exactly what it is and yet chooses to accept it. The addition of the miracle shows that some good may result from Stalker's tortuous trips into the Zone.

Kovács and Szilágyi suggest that the wife represents the ethical principle in the film, Stalker the spiritual, and their daughter the mystical. As most critics point out, the three men likewise embody different philosophical principles: Stalker—faith; Professor—rationalistic, scientific materialism; and Writer—an artistic principle that has degenerated into skepticism, cynicism, and egotism. After the apparent but false "miracle" of the child appearing to walk at the end of the film, Tarkovsky gives us a typically double-edged sense of transcendence and hope through the daughter's telekinetic powers. Though the "miracle" in *Stalker* is trivial enough in itself, it is presented with such beautiful gravity and intensity that it offers a convincing alternative to the squalor, misery, and ugliness of the world outside the Zone and the ambivalent and remote promise of the Room itself.

The endings of Tarkovsky's films have two things in common: while offering reconciliation, they are essentially open-ended with a number of possible meanings and interpretations that cannot be fully rationally or "objectively" explained and require "a leap of faith" on the viewer's part. How else are we to accept the "reality" of Ivan's dream after his death or the mixing of past and present with the mother as both a young and old woman at the end of *Mirror*? Both of these films ask us to share the hero's own subjective perceptions and visions, which call into question the film's objective narrative plane. The ending of *Solaris* can be taken to suggest that the apparently physical, outward journey undertaken by the hero has been an inner, psychological one all along. In the final shot of *Nostalghia* the hero appears to be simultaneously in Italy and in Russia—an image that, as Tarkovsky recognized, could be interpreted either positively or negatively (*Sculpting* 213). And in *The Sacrifice* we are offered both the possibility that the hero's prayers have been answered *and* the sense that the mysterious events of the night could equally well have been a dream.

Stalker too creates its own ambivalences at the end: the child's moving of the glasses deliberately parallels the earlier scene in Stalker's bedroom in which we see the objects on the bedside table quivering and shifting position in response to the vibrations of a passing train. In the final scene the train is heard and its effects are seen only *after* the child has exerted her own powers on the objects, and it can hardly therefore be said to have "caused" the movements;[16] yet it might still be possible for a pure rationalist (like the Professor of the first half of the film or the Writer who lamented the lack of "mystery" in modern life) to claim that the vibrations of the oncoming train made their effects felt before the engine itself was heard. The rendering of the

The three men in the bar at the beginning of the film. *From left to right:* Professor, Stalker, and Writer. Contemporary Films.

"Ode to Joy" that struggles to make itself heard—briefly and discordantly—before being overwhelmed by the rattle of the train is likewise deliberately ambiguous: the final triumph of the ideals expressed by the music still seems a long way off.

The scenes in the bar also parallel one another, with the men standing in almost identical postures round the table, but, in contrast to the lengthy portrayal of their outward journey to the Zone, the return journey appears almost instantaneous. Most critics agree that the significance of the film lies in the fact that the men's quest is essentially an internal rather than an external one, and several (among them Adair, Dempsey, and Hoberman) have pointed to the similarities between Stalker's home and what they refer to as "the Room"—meaning presumably what we have called "the telephone room"—where the similarities in the floorboards, the defective lighting, and the presence of the sleeping pills have been noted in our synopsis. (The floorboards of the bar also resemble those in the other two settings, and a potentially defective light flickers overhead.)

Once the men reach the Zone it becomes impossible to measure the length of their journey, for the clues that would allow us to judge time are simply lacking;[17] and it would be equally impossible to draw a map of their travels, for the relationship between the various locations is purposefully obscured throughout, and few indications are given as to how they move from one setting to another. The real problems begin after the "*Stalker*, 2nd part" title, with Stalker mysteriously separated from his companions, the metal pipe from which they, equally mysteriously, emerge, and the threefold visit to the area with the tiled wall. Even within the various settings, the spatial clues are often contradictory and misleading, most notably in the complex and crucial sequence as the men rest at the swampy area near the tiled wall. The conversation here—first between Writer and Stalker on the motives of those who wish to visit the Room, followed by some musings by Writer on himself and his art and then an inventive exchange of insults between Writer and Professor—is virtually continuous, yet the physical positioning of the characters, in relationship to each other, their surroundings, and even within the film frame, changes, apparently arbitrarily, from one shot to the next. Stalker, for example, is sometimes shown totally surrounded by water, sometimes only partially so; he is lying on his back, on his side, and face down; sometimes he has his head to the left of the screen, sometimes to the right—all over what the dialogue indicates is a continuous period of time. Color alternates randomly with black and white or sepia, and a dog appears from nowhere and settles down beside Stalker. The sequence also includes the quotations from Revelation and Luke discussed earlier. Although the first of these, with its mysterious nondiegetic source, may be what Tarkovsky refers to as "the *dream*" in his diary (*TWT* 156), everything in this sequence is so totally dreamlike that it is invidious to single out any part of it as being especially so: we are clearly now following an interior, spiritual journey in which time and space operate in an oneiric rather than a naturalistic fashion. In this respect the Zone obeys laws of its own that differ from those of everyday reality, which is, after all, one of the premises of both the original story and the film itself.

Another curious and paradoxical feature of the Zone is that, for all Stalker's dire warnings of what will happen if his companions disobey his instructions, they ignore him with apparent impunity and no harmful consequences result: Professor safely retrieves his knapsack, and although Writer is turned back from the house, he is not punished for his transgression. Even the dreaded "Meatgrinder" appears frightening only because of Stalker's evident terror of it and the unease that he transmits to Writer. Certainly strange and inexplicable things happen within the Zone, but the sense of real danger, once they have broken through the barrier, is curiously absent. Perhaps what matters here is not the physical peril (which is much more evident in the original story) but the fact that Stalker understands and respects the special powers of the Zone, in contrast to the matter-of-fact Professor and the frivolous Writer.

With an average shot length of almost one minute (142 shots in 161 minutes, with many 4 minutes or longer),[18] *Stalker* also marks a decisive shift toward Tarkovsky's later style. The director's own desire to give the impression that the film had been made in a single shot is reflected in miniature in the scene which many viewers consider to be one of the most hypnotic and compelling in all Tarkovsky's work—the ride to the Zone on the flatcar—and which, significantly, is often misremembered as consisting of a single shot rather than the actual five. More even than in *Mirror* (where the leaps backwards and forwards in time are more evident), Tarkovsky succeeds in this film in creating a world governed by its own dream logic: on the one hand is the slow, inexorable pacing of individual shots (often with the camera virtually motionless or tracking forward so imperceptibly that it is only toward the end of the shot that we realize how much our spatial perspective has changed); on the other, the fusion of these shots into a whole whose seeming inevitability counteracts the spatial and temporal discontinuities of the individual segments. Within this framework the everyday world in all its commonplace and often sordid reality is authentically transformed and made strange, so that for two hours and forty-one minutes we live inside it and accept its laws.

In a good print, the arrival at the Zone becomes genuinely magical, the grass a pulsating green that contrasts with the shabbiness and dinginess (yet, in a good print, intensely tactile detail) of the preceding sepia images and allows us to share with the characters the belief that here things are really going to be different. The green is an obvious presence for most of the first half of their journey, before giving way (as the men's energies also ebb away into quarrels, doubts, and fears) to interiors and man-made constructions with their darker tones. As usual Tarkovsky works with a very restricted color scheme, centered around brown, black, and grey, until we reach the telephone room and the Room itself, where subtle shades of gold and red, rising and falling in intensity, suggest the magic and the wonder that the men can glimpse but cannot fully seize—colors that are echoed in the rich golden texture of the daughter's headscarf. Here, as later in *Nostalghia* and *The Sacrifice*, lighting takes on a quality of its own that helps to define and shape the spiritual state of the characters. The electronic music, with its haunting, pulsating rhythms that reappear in various permutations throughout the film, also creates its own sense of strangeness while providing almost subliminal links between the Zone and the everyday world of Stalker and his family: its main theme accompanies the opening credit sequence, parts of the scene in the swamp, and the scene in which Monkey is carried on her father's shoulders.

Maya Turovskaya, though writing with more favorable second thoughts about a film she seems initially to have disliked, characterizes its style as "minimal" (109), apparently intending this to convey a pejorative implication. Though this is true of obvious elements such as plot, sets, and number of characters, and the film as a whole certainly has a simple, stripped-down quality to it, "minimal" is hardly the right word to describe what is, in many respects, one of the most visually and aurally complex of all Tarkovsky's films. The film's virtues are perhaps best epitomized in the flatcar sequence,

The men arrive at the Zone. Contemporary Films.

Stalker carries his daughter on his shoulders across a polluted landscape. Contemporary Films.

where Tarkovsky perhaps comes closest to creating the "pure cinema"— working solely in terms of time, sound, and images—that he dreamed of in *Sculpting in Time*. This three-and-a-half-minute sequence is made up of five shots focusing on close-ups of the three men seen from the back or in profile as they look cautiously and curiously around against a blurred and out-of-focus background that occasionally sharpens to reveal a landscape scarred by industrial debris or dotted with piles of lumber. The monotonous clicking of the flatcar along the rails is slowly joined by whirring electronic music that gradually takes on a whipping, twanging, rhythmical intensity of its own that merges with and then drowns out the sound of the wheels.[19] Although the sound and music are an essential factor in creating the mesmerizing effect of this scene, Tarkovsky, like Bergman, also creates a whole landscape out of the human face and body and is not afraid to let his camera linger and explore it. The slowdown in the film's pace from the relatively action-filled (for Tarkovsky) sequences that precede this one helps to prepare us for the more reflective scenes that follow with their alien time/space continuum.

But there is much else, too: the faces, especially that of Stalker himself, lined, haunted, stark, and tormented; the scenes set around the tiled wall and the roaring waterfall and those in the swamp that follow; the lighting and the movement of the characters in the telephone room; the men sitting, staring into the Room as rain falls and trickles to a halt; the wife speaking of her hopeless devotion to her husband; Stalker carrying his daughter across a poisonous wasteland, with nuclear power stations in the background; and the final sequence—all these rank among the finest images in the whole of contemporary cinema.

NINE

Nostalghia

The first clear indication that Tarkovsky was interested in making a film in Italy occurs in a diary entry for July 30, 1976, in which Sizov and the inevitable Yermash are suddenly accused of sabotaging an invitation for him to work there (*TWT* 126). At the time he was still smarting from the official treatment of *Mirror*, struggling to get *Stalker* off the ground, preparing his stage production of *Hamlet*, and toying with the thought of setting up his own theater company with some of his favorite actors. The idea of an Italian film seems to have arisen out of his long-standing friendship with Tonino Guerra (Antonioni's regular scriptwriter) and was encouraged by Antonioni himself, who had attended the 1975 Moscow Film Festival and had forced a reluctant bureaucracy to show him *Mirror* (*TWT* 115). Tarkovsky had visited Italy several times already, liked the country, and was eager to work there.

By October 20, 1976, he and Guerra had almost finished the script of *Italian Journey*, essentially a collection of personal impressions to be produced for Italian TV (*TWT* 133). Guerra was to arrange an invitation for Tarkovsky to spend two months in Italy, to get to know the country better, between the end of the projected run of *Hamlet* and the start of filming *Stalker*. Nothing further came of this, however, and most of 1977 and 1978 were taken up with the much-postponed and poorly received *Hamlet* and the two-stage filming of *Stalker*.

Meanwhile, however, some of the details of what was to become *Nostalghia* were germinating in Tarkovsky's mind. As early as September 1970, in the midst of a lengthy meditation on the spiritual and moral decay of contemporary society (much of which could have been uttered by the film's Domenico), he comments: "Thank God for people who burn themselves alive in front of an impassive, wordless crowd," prefiguring that character's fate (*TWT* 17). In April 1978 he amused himself by writing a little scenario, "Crying in the Wilderness" (*TWT* 152), which was incorporated into the scene in the film in which a male and female voice discuss whether God should make his presence known to Andrei (see synopsis).

In April 1979, after a visit to Italy in which the main business was still *Italian Journey*, he records that he and Guerra had an idea for a fiction film about a man who locks himself and his family away for forty years to await the end of the world. When they are finally removed by the authorities, his little son asks him: "Is this the end of the world?" (*TWT* 180).

In mid-July he returned to Italy for two months, extensively recording his impressions in his diary.¹ Although the filming and editing of what was to become a sixty-three-minute television film called *Tempo di Viaggio* (*A Time of Travel*) were his primary concern, many of the basic themes and episodes of *Nostalghia*—the title was decided on almost immediately upon his arrival on July 17 (*TWT* 188)—were simultaneously being worked out with Guerra, as were the primary locations of Bagno Vignoni and St. Catherine's Pool, and the use of Piero della Francesca's *Madonna of Childbirth*. The script of *Nostalghia* at various stages included the following elements: at the beginning the hero dreams of a discussion with his wife; he is morose and apathetic, refusing to look at beautiful sights; he meets the father and son from *The End of the World*; he is a writer whose hobby is architecture; he dies accidentally from a terrorist's bullet; his female translator is beautiful but hysterical; there is "a scene with a psychiatrist" and an (unspecified) "Dostoyevsky scene" (188–202). A schedule of three months preproduction, two months shooting, and two months editing was agreed on with a potential producer, though Tarkovsky hoped to extend this by another couple of months.

Tempo di Viaggio itself emerged as a kind of preliminary sketch for *Nostalghia* as it records Tarkovsky examining potential locations, including St. Catherine's Pool and Andrei's hotel room, but usually rejecting them as "too beautiful," and discussing with Guerra his ideas on art, literature, and film in terms familiar from *Sculpting in Time*. He claims to be more interested in ordinary Italians and their lives than in works of art, and is seen rather self-consciously eating a simple Italian meal with Italian peasants. The most impressive sequence explores the landscape around the church at Arezzo containing Piero's *Madonna of Childbirth*, in images reminiscent of Dovzhenko's *Earth*, before examining the painting itself, while *Nostalghia*'s fluctuations between Italy and Russia are anticipated in the closing shots with their photos of the Russian countryside and a Russian folk song on the soundtrack.

Back in Moscow, however, Tarkovsky found himself bogged down in the usual bureaucratic quagmire. He had hoped to obtain permission to live abroad for a year, taking his wife and young son (Andrei) with him, but—doubtless anticipating and fearing his defection—the authorities insisted that the boy must remain in the Soviet Union (*TWT* 220–21). In March 1980 Tarkovsky was given a two-month exit visa, and he arrived in Rome on April 2, hoping at least to sign a draft contract with his Italian producers (RAI, the Italian television network). Despite illness, he continued to work on the script of *Nostalghia* with Guerra, deciding that Gorchakov should die of a heart attack rather than being randomly killed in the street. A preliminary contract was finally signed with the Italians on May 13 (247), but final approval still had to be received from the Soviet side. He began working on a budget and had to reassure the Italians that the film wouldn't need dubbing or subtitles for any dialogue spoken in Russian (252). Additional frustration was provided by the defection of his chosen cameraman (Tovoli) from *Tempo di Viaggio* and also his set designer, both of whom were claimed by Antonioni for his new film (253); but Tovoli was quickly replaced by Giuseppe Lanci after Tarkovsky had admired his work on Marco Bellocchio's *Leap into the Void*. A more serious problem was RAI's requested reduction of the projected budget: as he wrote on June 11, the film once again hung by a thread, and only a miracle could save it (257–58). He felt lonely and homesick in Italy ("It really is not possible for a Russian to live here," 259) but was consoled by the prestigious Visconti Prize at the Taormina Festival.

His return to Moscow brought little relief, and the project languished for over a year, even though RAI finally approved a budget in March 1981 (273). In the meantime he lectured in the Advanced Courses for Scriptwriters and Directors at Goskino, and visited London in February and Stockholm in April. During the latter visit he seems to have seriously considered defecting; the diary entries for April 15–16 (276–77) are obscure, but point in that direction, and Olga Surkova has confirmed this in conversation. The fact that rumors concerning his motives for visiting Italy were circulating in Moscow a year later (312) may help to explain the authorities' excessive caution in allowing him a lengthy stay abroad.

Things began to move again in July 1981 with a visit by RAI representatives to Moscow, the Soviet authorities having finally "found" the telexes confirming RAI's continued interest in the project (285). Nevertheless they treated the Italians shabbily (privately calling them "crooks") and offered none of the amenities—official cars, translators, daily allowance, reception—that, Tarkovsky sourly observed, would have been lavished upon them had they been coming to sign up Bondarchuk (287). He agreed to all of RAI's conditions, including filming on location without specially constructed sets and cutting the overall working time from thirteen months to twelve (286), and hoped to begin filming in October. Needless to say, this did not come about.

The diary entries for the remainder of 1981 are, unfortunately, sparse, and those for early 1982 say nothing about subsequent negotiations concerning the film. By March 1982, however, he was finally in Italy again, finding an ideal location for Domenico's house in a "strange, half-ruined factory" and being offered, to his amazement, far more film stock than he could ever hope to use—150,000 meters, ten times the amount he had needed for *Stalker*. The planned length of the film was 2 hours 20 minutes (*Martyrolog* 347).[2] Yermash, meanwhile, was refusing to allow Larissa to leave Moscow to join him,[3] and Anatoly Solonitsyn, whom he had planned to use in the main role, was in poor health (*TWT* 310). Solonitsyn was to die shortly afterwards—like Tarkovsky, from lung cancer.

Oleg Yankovsky, who had played the father in *Mirror* but had been offended at not being offered the title role in *Hamlet* (which went to Solonitsyn), agreed to a reconciliation. The other main actors were Domiziana Giordano (a film student) as Eugenia, the interpreter, and Erland Josephson, well known for his work with Ingmar Bergman, as the madman Domenico. Giuseppe Lanci was the cinematographer, and the film was ultimately financed by RAI, Gaumont/Italy, and Sovinfilm. Although the initial plans had called for the Russian scenes to be shot in the Soviet Union, this proved to be too complicated, and they were eventually filmed in an appropriate setting near Rome.[4]

Tarkovsky spoke little Italian at this stage (though, according to Yankovsky, he had improved considerably by the end of filming), and had to communicate with most of the actors and crew through an interpreter. For someone used to filming with a "family" of coworkers in mutual trust and understanding, this must have been initially very frustrating, and although the early stages of filming were quite tense, relations with the crew soon improved. Moreover, Daniel Toscan du Plantier pointed out another problem: the totally unfamiliar working conditions imposed by a "commercial" production, even though *Nostalghia* was essentially considered a low-budget "prestige" enterprise.[5] Although the film did not go significantly over budget, Tarkovsky worked very slowly and was reluctant to observe a strict shooting schedule and to accept that he could no longer—as in the Soviet Union—suspend production for several days to resolve creative difficulties.

According to his wife, the editing was rushed to get the film ready—at Yermash's request—for the 1983 Cannes festival; yet a repeated complaint on Tarkovsky's part afterwards, and a significant factor in his decision to stay in the West, was his belief that the Soviet authorities conspired, through jury member Sergei Bondarchuk, to deny *Nostalghia* the Grand Prix (*TWT* 327).[6] Nevertheless, he was awarded a special prize for creative achievement, *ex aequo* with his hero Robert Bresson. In Cannes he signed a contract with Anna-Lena Wibom to make a film for the Swedish Film Institute based on *The Witch*, a script he had been working on—initially with Arkady Strugatsky—since at least 1981 (327).

Tarkovsky went to considerable pains, in both interviews and written statements, to establish the correct, Russian meaning of the word "nostalgia" as "a complex sentiment, one that mixes the love for your homeland and the melancholy that arises from being far away."[7] "I wanted to make a film about Russian nostalgia—about the particular state of mind which assails Russians who are far from their native land. I wanted the film to be about the fatal attachment of Russians to their national roots, their past, their culture, their native places, their families and friends" (*Sculpting* 202—the wording is different in the 1986 edition).

Given the similarity between his own situation at the time and that of his hero (also called "Andrei"), it is hardly surprising that Andrei he stressed the deeply personal nature of the film: "The protagonist . . . [is] a mirror image of me. I have never made a film which mirrors my own states of mind with so much violence, and liberates my inner world in such depth. When I saw the finished product I felt uneasy, as when one sees oneself in a mirror" (Mitchell, "Andrei Tarkovsky and *Nostalghia*" 5, quoting interview in *Corriere della Sera*). In *Sculpting in Time* he talks of how the "unrelieved gloom" of the film

Andrei (Oleg Yankovsky) at "home" in both Russia and Italy at the end of
Nostalghia. Artificial Eye.

surprised him, until he realized that he had unconsciously recreated his own
"inner state" during filming (203).

If this is so, it is perhaps surprising that Andrei Gorchakov emerges as an
even less sympathetic figure than the adult Alexei in the equally personal
Mirror, unable—or unwilling—to overcome his understandable loneliness
and homesickness to the extent of making meaningful contact with other
human beings. His dreams and memories are self-enclosed, circular, and repetitive, and seem to be used as an excuse for avoiding any commitment to
his existing reality rather than as a force for emotional and psychic liberation
and self-understanding—as happens, at least to some extent, in *Mirror.* Even
his identification with Domenico is double-edged, for Domenico, too, shuns
normal human contact, and the latter's various "sacrifices," first for the sake
of his family and then for the sake of humanity as a whole, have distinctly
ambiguous effects on those for whom they are ostensibly made. (The same
could be said of the protagonist of Tarkovsky's next and final film, who is
unmistakably an extension of Domenico.) Although Andrei carries out the
task entrusted to him—carrying a candle across St. Catherine's Pool—he
does so with little enthusiasm, and it is only Eugenia's implausible phone call
(why should she be in contact with Domenico, in whom she has shown no
interest previously?) that prevents him from leaving Italy without even attempting to accomplish it.

Although the film's final shot (the Russian dacha inside the ruins of an
Italian cathedral) seems to fall into the "reconciliation of opposites" pattern
that concludes most of Tarkovsky's other films, and can be seen as implying

that Andrei has finally—if only in death—resolved his inner conflicts, the director himself preferred to leave it open to either positive or negative interpretation: for him either it could suggest the insuperable division within Gorchakov that eventually destroys him, or it could signify "his new wholeness in which the Tuscan hills and the Russian countryside come together indissolubly" (*Sculpting* 213). He admits, however, that "it is a constructed image which smacks of literariness" (216), and it can be questioned whether Andrei has earned this "wholeness" through suffering or a painful growth in self-knowledge—as Ivan, Roublev, Kris Kelvin, and Stalker can be said to have earned theirs. He is perhaps closer to Alexei of *Mirror*, whose catharsis is less the result of his own actions than the product of something within his creator that was released through the process of making the film. Andrei is continually associated with enclosed spaces (the hotel room, the foyer, the pool, Domenico's house, the flooded building, the ruined abbey) and endlessly repeated actions (lying down, standing up, flicking a lighter, jingling his keys, looking in mirrors, switching lights on and off, moving aimlessly to and fro). Even outdoors he either refuses to explore his environment (as in the opening, postcredits scene) or is confined by highly formalized camera movements (outside Domenico's house) or by the setting itself (the flooded building and St. Catherine's Pool). The most conspicuous sounds in the film—the buzz-saw, Eugenia's hair dryer, a ringing telephone, running, dripping, or draining water, a barking dog—are likewise deliberately repetitive and monotonous. All of this suggests his inability to escape from his basic egotism as well as—on another level—his reluctance to make the leap of faith that might release him from his self-imprisonment ("I do make My presence known to him, but he is not aware of it").

Domenico, as Andrei realizes, has faith—but he is also obviously mad. This perhaps enables him to escape the prison of rationalistic, materialistic thinking against which he rails in his speech and to attack the sickness of contemporary society from a new and possibly higher perspective; yet Domenico convinces *none* of his listeners (except his own, equally mad,[8] companions), and there is no evidence that Andrei's carrying out of his mission has changed anything in the outside world (a possibility that at least exists in *The Sacrifice*). Like Stalker, Domenico has many of the characteristics of the Russian *yurodivy*—somewhat mad, mocked and humiliated, poorly dressed, living outside accepted social conventions, insulting and insulted by others. If he does succeed in "saving" Andrei, it is in a somewhat problematical manner, for the final image seems to relate less to Andrei's salvation through faith than to a (possible) resolution of his psychological conflicts, and Tarkovsky has provided no necessary or inevitable link that connects one to the other.

Caught between his love for his homeland and his sense that—as with Sosnovsky, the Russian expatriate he is studying—he could never be totally free there, Andrei becomes increasingly unable to separate dream from reality and to relate meaningfully to his actual existence in Italy. For a Western

Eugenia (Domiziana Giordano) attempts vainly to interest Andrei by baring her breast. Artificial Eye.

viewer his most problematic relationship is with Eugenia: he appears coldly indifferent to her feelings and makes no serious attempt to communicate with her. To understand this, she should be seen not just as a beautiful and available woman but as part of the film's dialogue between past and present and between spirituality and materialism. For the critic Neya Zorkaya (Interview) she clearly represents the beauty of the past devoid of its spirituality (her physical resemblance to figures from Renaissance paintings has often been pointed out), just as we see little beyond ruins to remind us of Italy's glorious artistic and spiritual heritage. Andrei's rejection of her, from this viewpoint, is not simply indifference to, or fear of, the sexuality that she so vividly embodies, but stems from his search for spiritual fulfillment which he associates with his wife in the past at home in Russia and with Domenico here in the present. Realizing that she cannot compete with both these rivals, Eugenia finally leaves and returns to a more suitable lover in the sinister Vittorio, confirming Andrei's wisdom in rejecting someone who, for all her beauty, is inescapably linked with the materialism and corruption of modern society.

This, in turn, however, raises a basic problem with the film that is perhaps more damaging than the overexplicitness for which it has sometimes been condemned (Turovskaya, rather too glibly, refers to it as a "Sermon" in her chapter heading). At times Tarkovsky seems to be attempting to force too many themes together within the same general framework and to make the main characters carry the burden of too much meaning. Eugenia, as a result, has to represent rather too many concepts—Andrei's inability to escape from his own mental prison; his unwillingness to respond to the beauty around him (whether it is of a person or a culture); the problems of secularism and lack of faith; the materialism of the contemporary world; and the inevitable emotional sterility (and threatening sexuality) of a woman who has neglected her "natural destiny" of motherhood and submissiveness[9]—and it is little wonder that the credibility of the character finally collapses under the strain.

Similarly, although the theme of cultural alienation is of central importance and clearly mirrors Tarkovsky's own ambivalent feelings at the time, it is not always fully integrated into the other aspects of the film. Tarkovsky felt that he had made a "profoundly Russian" (*Sculpting* 202) and deeply patriotic film, and that he was in the tradition of other prominent Russian exiles in criticizing aspects of Russian life while retaining a profound love and need for his homeland. The figure of Sosnovsky is clearly intended to reflect his own ambivalence, and he was deeply hurt by later accusations that he was unpatriotic and anti-Russian. Tarkovsky once again seems to revive the Slavophile-Westernizer debate and places himself squarely in the camp of the modern-day Slavophile, Solzhenitsyn: Russia represents the eternal values of earth, maternity, family, home, patience, and spirituality; while Italy stands for a decaying and "sickeningly beautiful" culture whose superficial attractiveness masks a declining faith and a surrender to transient and destructive material values—Domenico, the exception to this, is only nominally Italian and is in essence a figure in the Russian spiritual tradition.

Whatever validity this analysis may have, it is unnecessarily complicated by Andrei's insistence that no one can "possess" or fully understand another culture, especially if the only means of entering it is by translation. Yet two of Arseny Tarkovsky's poems are read during the film, one in Russian and one in Italian translation—either or both of them requiring subtitles if a large proportion of the audience is (however imperfectly) to understand them. Is Tarkovsky reinforcing Andrei's point here or has he just forgotten it? Or is Andrei's assertion simply a rationalization of his refusal to open himself to what Italy has to offer? His solution—to "destroy the frontiers"—is both irrelevant and impractical and symptomatic of the intellectual confusion evident here.

What rescues *Nostalghia* from its overly determined thematics and its occasional overly explicit nudging is, as always, the reverberating and haunting splendor of its images and sounds, as well as those aspects of its theme that can be conveyed almost subliminally, by implication rather than explicit analysis. A central aspect of the film is the concept of doubling—and it is doubtless no accident that Tarkovsky used the word "mirror" three times in three sentences when discussing his own affinity with his hero Andrei Gorchakov in the interview quoted earlier. Apart from Tarkovsky/ Gorchakov, other doubles in the film are Tarkovsky/Sosnovsky, Gorchakov/ Sosnovsky, Gorchakov/Domenico, and even Tarkovsky/Domenico (in the sense that, in essence, Domenico is conveying his creator's own critique of the sickness of modern life).

Andrei more than once examines himself in a mirror in his hotel room and in Domenico's home, and Eugenia too studies herself in the mirror of his room. These shots may suggest the conventional ideas of narcissism and self-enclosure—though the fact that Eugenia breaks the mirror in the course of her tirade against Andrei[10] may imply that she can escape from the emotional trap she has set for herself with him. More interesting, however, are those shots in which Domenico's reflection is seen where we expect to see Andrei, which fall into the category defined as "the secret sharer" by Robert Rogers in his psychoanalytic study of the double and as "the second self as savior" by C. F. Keppler (who also uses the same Conrad story as a central example). Here the reflection is not that of a literal, physical double but of a psychological or metaphorical twin, whose presence—as Keppler convincingly argues—can have an influence for good and may even lead to the salvation of the character's soul: "the second self tends to be the possessor of secrets that the first self can never quite fathom, and thus in being the stranger is also the stronger, always tending to be in real control of the relationship" (11; see also chapter 6). Such psychological doubles also abound, of course, in Dostoyevsky, one of Tarkovsky's favorite novelists.

During the scene in Domenico's home, as Domenico entrusts Andrei with the mission of carrying the candle, both are seen in the same shot with the older man reflected in the mirror as if he were indeed Andrei's double. A more explicit mirroring of the first self by the second occurs, however, in Andrei's "wardrobe" dream. As he walks along the rubbish-strewn street, the camera tracks back to reveal a large mirrored wardrobe; he wanders past and then, as if recognizing it from his musings in the previous scene at the flooded cathedral ("I have a jacket in the wardrobe"), returns as the noise of the buzz-saw stops. He stands looking in the mirror as we hear in voice-over what are clearly Domenico's thoughts but are spoken by Andrei in Russian, as he reproaches himself for locking his family away for so long. The camera tracks in on Andrei and then to the handle of the mirrored door; a hand, reflected in the mirror, enters the frame and slowly pulls the door open, but the reflection revealed is that of Domenico, dressed identically to Andrei in coat and scarf. Andrei quickly slams the door shut and leans on it, and is now reflected in the mirror himself.

The (metaphorical) shared or common identity of the two men is reinforced by their possession of "the same" dog and even "the same" child, and by Andrei's substitution of himself for the other in carrying out his mission, with the parallel intensified by the preliminary striking of a lighter in each case. Throughout the film Andrei clearly feels that Domenico is "the possessor of secrets that [he] can never quite fathom," and he finally follows the older man's lead. Even if it is debatable whether Domenico succeeds in "saving" him, his existence has had the effect of stirring Andrei out of his state of lethargic self-pity and prompting him at least to act.

Andrei also identifies himself with Sosnovsky (as does Tarkovsky himself), but here the results are somewhat less positive, for he uses Sosnovsky's dilemma as an excuse for remaining in his own moral limbo, committing himself to neither one state of existence nor the other: it is impossible for him to stay in Italy and equally impossible to return home—Sosnovsky has proved that, so why should he (Andrei) make any effort? Tarkovsky at least managed to extricate himself from the dead-end conclusion reached by his fictional alter ego, in deciding to settle in Italy; thus one might even see Andrei as Tarkovsky's own "second self as savior."

"I am seeking a principle of montage," Tarkovsky said of *Nostalghia*, "which would permit me to show the subjective logic—the thought, the dream, the memory—instead of the logic of the subject. . . . To show things which are not necessarily linked logically. It is the movement of thoughts which makes them join together inwardly" (A. T., "Between Two Worlds" 76–77). The film goes even further than *Stalker* in this respect, to such an extent that it becomes difficult to decide whether certain scenes in the film really "happen" or not.

Andrei's dreams (or, perhaps more accurately, reveries, as he is not always asleep during them) of his family and homeland are signaled by a switch to black and white and the sounds of running or dripping water and/or a barking dog. They convey a largely static, timeless world of eternal values—love of family, home, nature, and country—but also an estrangement created by the virtual immobility of the figures, and by the music. One of the most powerful and complex of these comes after the reading of Sosnovsky's letter. As Andrei lies down on a bench, we hear dogs barking and whimpering and (in black and white) his wife rises from a large brass bed as his voice whispers, "Maria." She moves in slow motion to a window and draws the drapes; an apparently tethered bird is on the sill. She then moves over to the door. There is a cut to darkness before the door creaks open to show a small boy standing outside beside the dog; in the background are the horse, mist, and telephone pole of the credit sequence. The teenage girl enters, wrapping a shawl around her shoulders, and stands beside the boy; the older woman joins them. There is a cut to another angle of the horse and the dog, and then to the wife, facing the camera, as the noise of what might be Middle Eastern music is heard. The camera pans from her to the girl, then to the older woman, and then, without a break, to the wife and son with the dog and horse behind them, and on to the girl yet again and the older woman near her. The camera holds them all, as if frozen in a tableau, as a foghorn sounds and, one by one, all four turn slowly to look at the house behind them, with the sun rising behind it. The dog howls, and dripping and running water are heard."

Black and white (and the sound of the buzz-saw) similarly characterize Domenico's memories and also Andrei's "wardrobe" dream (introduced with dripping water). But other scenes are not so easy to identify. Although the

Bible, bottle, and comb in Andrei's hotel room. Artificial Eye.

first scene in Andrei's hotel bedroom is "real," it also establishes a pattern of "subjective logic" that Tarkovsky expands as the film proceeds. For 2 minutes 45 seconds Andrei "does" nothing except open and close shutters, switch lights on and off, drink some water from the tap, swallow a pill, open and close a closet door, and pick up a book lying on his dresser. As he puts down the open book and moves off-screen, the camera tracks in to show that it is a Bible with, as a bookmark, a comb wrapped around with long strands of hair. Here the audience is expected to respond not to plot or action or psychological analysis but to the subtle play of lighting, changing almost every moment; the textures of metal, plaster, water, paper, and hair; the subdued colors, moving from brown and bluish-grey to whitish-yellow and back again, as lights go on and off; and the sometimes explained, sometimes enigmatic sounds as Andrei constantly pauses as if listening for something. From these we assemble a mood, a sense of the character's inner distance from his exterior environment, as well as fragments of possibly useful information (the character has to take pills). We also pick up some details that are never rationally explained (the comb in the Bible) though, as the film proceeds, we come to realize that this is one of many signals relating to the spiritual debasement of the modern world.

When he returns to his room after his conversation with Eugenia in the hallway, subjective and objective worlds, dream and reality begin to merge in a manner prefigured in the swamp scene of *Stalker* and taken to even greater lengths in *The Sacrifice*. Once again the scene is impeccably composed, the camera at first holding an almost perfectly symmetrical composition with two

Andrei's wife (Patrizia Terreno) and Eugenia meet in his dream. Artificial Eye.

light sources, one on either side of the elaborately carved brass bed (similar to those in *Mirror* and *Stalker*), each reflecting onto the floor. Gradually, and without apparent cause, the room darkens and the camera tracks almost imperceptibly toward the bed, with the rain outside reflected on the wall to the left of the screen. Now the dog emerges from the bathroom and settles down beside the bed, and the lighting comes up to show Andrei apparently asleep. Here the move from outer to inner, from present to past, from waking reality to dream, takes place within a single, uninterrupted shot and is signaled not by sound or a switch to black and white, as before, but by changes of light. The dog—no longer a creature confined to memory and the past—has moved from one dimension of space and time to another and is as real and physical a presence as the pouring rain outside (the sound as it knocks over a glass is perhaps intended to confirm this). What we are witnessing is not wholly a dream, neither is it everyday reality: it hesitates on the border between the two. Having discovered a means of conveying this ambiguous state, Tarkovsky was to make it a key structural principle of *The Sacrifice*.

The black and white shots that follow (accompanied by the sound of dripping water) of Eugenia and Andrei's wife embracing and of the pregnant wife lying on the (differently positioned) bed are more conventionally dreamlike, both in structure and in significance. They create a wish-fulfillment solution to at least one of Andrei's dilemmas, as he subconsciously acknowledges an attraction toward Eugenia that he represses in waking life[12] but resolves this by having the wife and potential mistress lovingly accept each other. The tear visible on Eugenia's cheek at one point, however, suggests his awareness that, despite this, he will have to choose between them; and the pregnant, apparently levitating wife becomes a reminder of his inescapable role as husband and father as Eugenia's knock on the door brings him back to reality.

Although the scene in Domenico's house is "real," it is also extremely strange—partly because of the oddness of the setting and the objects it contains (external embodiments, perhaps, of Domenico's confused and tormented psyche) but also because Tarkovsky sends conflicting signals concerning time and space throughout it. It begins abruptly and illogically (Domenico having just refused to speak to Andrei) with a series of spatial paradoxes as Andrei enters the building and with the "dreamlike" black and white of the miniature—yet at first "real"—landscape that is never seen again. The dripping water and the buzz-saw (whose origin is never explained but which later accompanies scenes of dream and memory) also intensify the hallucinatory quality of what follows, as do the interior rain and the flooded floor, both reminiscent of the Room in *Stalker*. An early shot of Andrei inside the room is presented in one of the "impossible" camera movements, showing him in two incompatible spaces at once, familiar from the dream sequences of *Ivan's Childhood* and *Solaris* (and the "Russian" dream described above). The intention of all this seems to be to underline the interior, spiritual quality of the experience he is about to undergo, and in much of the remainder of the film, the logic of normal time and space is ignored in favor of a higher, transcendent inner reality experienced by the character.

The equally strange scene at the flooded cathedral with the significantly named "Angela" follows directly on Andrei's reverie after the reading of Sosnovsky's letter, and Tarkovsky makes no serious attempt to account for it logically in terms either of space or of time. It seems to end with the shot of the burning book and Andrei's face, followed by the obviously cued "wardrobe" dream and the bizarre scene in the ruined abbey—also in black and white but with the color insert of the falling feather—in which God and a saint discuss Andrei's spiritual state; but these are then "framed" by a return to Andrei's face and the book, and the sound of running water. Is the abbey scene, then, also a dream? And is it any more or less "real" than the scene in the flooded cathedral itself? As with the scene in the swamp in *Stalker* it would seem invidious to single out any one aspect of all this as being more or less "dreamlike" than any other, while—again as in *Stalker*—the normal coding of black and white vs. color seems no longer to apply as a guideline. The ambiguous distinction between dream and reality begun in *Mirror*, where the black and white vs. color distinction does not *always* apply, has now reached a stage where Tarkovsky seems to want to make it virtually impossible to distinguish between external and internal reality—a process carried even further in *The Sacrifice*.

Nostalghia is probably the most waterlogged of all Tarkovsky's films, with exterior and interior rain, thermal baths shrouded in steam, ponds, flooded buildings, and the sound of running or dripping water leading us into and out of Andrei's reveries. Ultimately it becomes impossible to assign any one con-

Domenico's (Erland Josephson) fiery death in *Nostalghia*. Artificial Eye.

sistent meaning to the use of water in this film, and there is not even the association of it with memory and the mother that provides a guiding thread in *Mirror*.[13] Often it is there for its own sake, its sound and texture and its interplay with other objects such as walls or bottles: if any one shot in the film can be used to characterize its aesthetic strategies, it is perhaps the long-held shot in Domenico's room of three bottles, two brown and one green, standing on the floor with the rain splashing around them and bouncing loudly from the glass as the camera tracks slowly toward them—a shot whose "meaning" is to be approached purely intuitively "on an emotional or even supra-emotional level" (*Sculpting* 40) rather than "interpreted" or "understood." (Here again Tarkovsky seems to be providing his own equivalent of the Formalists' "affectual signs": Eagle 10). Or water is used for atmosphere, adding to the sense of decay and dissolution that permeates much of the Italian setting. In the hotel room, Domenico's house, and the flooded building the water adds to the sense of unreality within these scenes, helping to place them on a borderline between real and imagined.

As in *Stalker* water covers the debris of past and present civilization, whether it is the submerged angel of the ruined cathedral or the bizarre collection of objects retrieved from the drained pool—its use as a deposit for trash both undermining its claims to be a source of renewed health and long life for the bathers, and emphasizing the decline since its original association with spiritual purity and the patronage of a saint. The fact that Andrei trudges across a drained and muddy surface rather than through the water (as Domenico had tried to do) reinforces the ambivalent and provisional nature of his achievement. Domenico in turn achieves his own, equally ambiguous purification by means of fire rather than water (again linking him to Alexander of *The Sacrifice*), where the physical horror of the manner of his death is intensified by yet another "double"—the mimic who simulates the agonies shrouded from us by the flames enveloping Domenico's body. The breakdown of the music as Domenico dies underlines the fact that what was intended as a solemn and triumphant affirmation of faith has degenerated into something uncomfortably and embarrassingly close to farce—an ambivalence found also in the simultaneously painful and absurd burning of the house in *The Sacrifice*. The clear links in theme and style between Tarkovsky's last two films—which in some respects even form a kind of diptych—have led many critics to see them as standing apart from the director's previous work and, for some, marking either a sad falling-off or, at best, a tired repetition of earlier themes and techniques.

Initial critical reaction to *Nostalghia*, in the West at least, was mixed and largely predictable.[14] Even at this late stage, Tarkovsky's work could be described as being "little known in America" (A. T., "Between Two Worlds" 14), and critics like Vincent Canby in the *New York Times*, who had found his earlier films boring and limited, dismissed *Nostalghia* as being more (or less) of the same: Tarkovsky is "a film poet with a tiny vocabulary" (October 5, 1983). Those, especially in France and Britain, who were already admirers of Tarkovsky's work attempted to situate the film as part of a continuing *oeuvre* and were generally respectful, though rarely unreservedly enthusiastic, and their ambivalence was shared by those few American critics who had followed Tarkovsky's career closely to date. Some, such as David Sterritt of the *Christian Science Monitor* and Yvette Biro and Jim Hoberman of the *Village Voice*, sought to make a distinction between the acknowledged splendor and beauty of the images and their disquiet at what they described variously as "a flawed plot . . . hazy symbolism . . . and heated melodrama" (Sterritt), "fractured scenes . . . overloaded metaphors . . . banal and lofty generalization" (Biro), and a lurch into "a kind of theater of gibberish" with Domenico's suicide (Hoberman). Among American reviewers, Kevin Thomas of the *Los Angeles Times* was almost alone in finding little to carp at in either theme or imagery and in welcoming the film as a successful and unified entity.[15]

Though some of these charges have some validity, it would be a mistake to see *Nostalghia* simply as a failure or as a film that adds little or nothing to what Tarkovsky had achieved previously. Certainly there are some problems: the continued experimentation with shot lengths, forcing the viewer to share—often with agonizing slowness—the experience of the characters, has mixed results. The opening, postcredits shot lasts almost four minutes, establishing a pattern right away, and many shots in Andrei's room, in Domenico's room, and at the pool last anywhere between two and a half and five minutes. In most cases—Andrei wandering disconsolately around his room, the real/unreal scene in which the dog appears, Eugenia's tirade—the length appears justified; but in the most extreme example—the eight-and-three-quarter-minute shot of Andrei carrying the candle across the pool—although the pain and intensity are acutely experienced, the prolongation of the shot, as will also be the case in *The Sacrifice*, carries its own dangers in foregrounding its own virtuosity and allowing the spectator to concentrate on that rather than on what the shot conveys. And, even more than in *Solaris*, the unrelieved gloom and self-absorption of the main character make it difficult to sympathize fully with him and his problems.

Yet there are also many compensations. While the film picks up on many of the director's earlier thematic and stylistic concerns, it also moves into new territory, especially in its concern with lighting as an expressive motif and its success in showing "the subjective logic . . . the movement of thoughts" that Tarkovsky spoke of. The subtlety of the lighting effects—especially in Andrei's room, the hotel foyer, and Domenico's room[16]—is not simply a source of legitimate aesthetic pleasure in its own right, but part of the thematic and psychological structure of the whole film. The darkness, while fully conveying Andrei's spiritual anomie, serves to force us to look and concentrate with unusual intensity and to respond on something other than a level of purely narrative interest. The unmotivated changes of level in the lighting, especially in Andrei's and Domenico's rooms, serve to question the "reality" of these scenes, working directly on our subconscious.

Exile, loneliness, and homesickness are themes that Tarkovsky had explored before, most notably in *Solaris* and *Mirror*. His own acknowledged personal unhappiness during the making of the film—spilling over into a remarkably jaundiced view of Italy, a country that, in other circumstances, he loved and in which he was making plans to settle—perhaps gives the film an intensity that transcends its purely "Russian" elements and allows it to speak on a universal level. In almost all his films his characters want to "go back" to a lost paradise—of childhood, moral innocence, unspoiled nature, or a loving family and home—even if this happiness is revealed to be illusory or unattainable. Here this perennial theme is combined with another that was to obsess him more and more in his final films, and however mad Domenico may be and however futile his sacrifice, his condemnation of a materialistic, selfish, and apathetic society receives chilling confirmation in the calm indifference with which the bystanders watch him die.

TEN

███████

The Sacrifice

The Sacrifice (*Offret*, 1986), Tarkovsky's second film abroad, and his fina
film, was made under the auspices of the Swedish Film Institute and produced by Anna-Lena Wibom.¹ Tarkovsky had visited Stockholm in 1981, anc
the original contact with the Swedish Film Institute came about as a result o
the friendship between Wibom and Olga Surkova, Tarkovsky's long-tim
collaborator. In a diary entry for May 22, 1983, Tarkovsky mentions that h
has signed a contract with Anna-Lena Wibom to make *The Witch* (TWT 327), ε
long-cherished project about a man terminally ill with cancer who is in
structed by a soothsayer to spend a night with a "witch." The man is miracu
lously cured, and then, at the witch's bidding, he leaves his "splendic
mansion and respected life happily and [goes] off with her, with nothing bu
the old coat on his back" (*Sculpting* 220).

For Tarkovsky the original story was both a "parable about sacrifice" anc
"a spiritual regeneration expressed in the image of a woman" (220). It wa
clearly during the shooting of *Nostalghia* that the apocalyptic story line wa
added to the film and the sacrificial aspect changed and expanded. Tarkovsky
rewrote the part of Alexander, originally intended for Anatoly Solonitsyn, tc
suit Erland Josephson, incorporating facets of Josephson's character in *Nostalghia*. The madman Domenico's futile attempt to protect his family from th
coming apocalypse and his suicide by self-immolation are transformed into ε
fiery sacrificial act in which a depressed Alexander "rescues" his family anc
humanity from an imagined or real nuclear catastrophe. Unfortunately, th
merging of the original and new story lines produces disharmony and confusion on the level of plot: an unexplained double sacrifice is created whe
Alexander *both* sleeps with the witch as encouraged by a new soothsayer, th
postman Otto, *and* burns down his house and becomes mute, thus fulfillinξ
his vow to God. This results in a frustrating absence of thematic and philo
sophical coherence that ultimately damages the film.

Although the setting of the film appears to be Sweden, it is obvious fron
the start that this is essentially a "Russian" film. Tarkovsky chose the settinξ
of Gotland because it was the closest to a Russian landscape that he coulc
find, and the characters (as actors like Erland Josephson and Susan Fleetwooc
were fully aware) are deeply Russian (both Chekhovian and Dostoyevskian
in their preoccupations and relationships). In *Nostalghia* the "Russian" ele
ment had been built into the plot and helped to shape it; here it is obviousl
of central importance for Tarkovsky himself, yet it is not motivated in th

ame way. Perhaps he was hoping to find a solution like that of *Stalker:* an apparently anonymous "small" country[2] that was nevertheless Russia in disguise, but here, of course, he had to work without the Russian actors who ould have made this fully convincing.[3]

Nostalghia had already clearly demonstrated that separation from his beloved homeland would not have any material impact on either the style or he theme of Tarkovsky's films: if anything, the imagery becomes even more personal, elliptical, and complex, especially in the interaction between the external and internal worlds of the hero, and between dream, memory, and reality. Though the themes and ideas follow naturally from those established earlier, they are now stated more directly, urgently, and long-windedly, as if he director no longer trusted his audience to absorb what he was saying without having it explicitly thrust upon them. In *The Sacrifice* the characters have a Dostoyevskian tendency to philosophize at the drop of a hat; the film's hero, Alexander, constantly reproaches himself for this, but neither he nor his creator seems able to stem the incessant flow of words. Where Tarkovsky still trusts his imagery, the best parts of *The Sacrifice* remain haunting and often extremely moving, but many of the conversations appear forced and unnatural, designed to explicate theme and even (in the best Russian tradition) to preach, rather than to illuminate character.

This tendency becomes evident right from the film's almost nine-and-a-half-minute-long opening shot, where Tarkovsky seems to be picking up from the "candle" scene in *Nostalghia* in testing the audience's patience, while simultaneously launching into lengthy abstract philosophical conversations and meditations. Although the ideas discussed—belief, hope, the purpose of existence—are both familiar and important, they are inserted so abruptly into what begins as a casual chat between Alexander and the local postman Otto (a retired teacher, resident philosopher, mystic, and perhaps "holy fool") that they appear almost forced and arbitrary. From the beginning Tarkovsky seems to be asking his audience to look for deeper meaning only (his friend Victor begins a conversation with Alexander by asking if he considers his life to be a failure), and we are faced with something that is explicitly a "parable" (*Sculpting* 218) rather than a work that allows its inner meaning to emerge from and coexist with a naturalistic surface.

This is true of much of the characterization, too: certain characters—Alexander's son "Little Man," Otto, and the servant/witch Maria in particular—are emblematic rather than realistic figures, and Alexander speaks far more directly for Tarkovsky, echoing ideas expressed in interviews and *Sculpting in Time*, than even Domenico or Andrei. When Alexander condemns modern civilization for its lack of faith and spirituality, its materialism and abuse of science and technology, and its reliance on power and fear, he is speaking not in "character" but from the perspective of an exile such as Solzhenitsyn or Tarkovsky himself who rejects Soviet totalitarianism ("power and fear") as well as Western materialism and has come to see them both as part of the same problem.

"Little Man" is primarily the focus of Alexander's thwarted affections, denied outlet in his marriage, and the repository of his faith and hope for the future. Just as Domenico's wishes are carried out by Andrei, Alexander's sacrifice may find its meaning and purpose through his son, and at the end the father's silence appears to have restored the power of speech to the child. (Even though Alexander—like the hero in *Mirror*—had complained about the ineffectiveness of words, for Tarkovsky the word remains all-important.) Although Tarkovsky certainly succeeds in making this love and faith meaningful—one of the most moving moments in the film occurs as the ambulance carries Alexander past his son and Maria, the only two figures in the film who have shown genuine affection and understanding of him—the child's role is not one that allows him to display any personality of his own. Otto is a deliberately enigmatic figure, whose sudden epileptic fall is very different from the stumbling that in other films precedes spiritual illumination (and is perhaps found in this film, too, when Alexander trips and falls just before he sets fire to the house). With his symbolic black hair and black clothing he somewhat confusingly combines the outward characteristics of tempter or "evil angel" and the role of helper and "holy fool."

Maria is explicitly identified as a nonnaturalistic, even supernatural figure, yet she displays qualities of humility, reticence, self-effacement, and (Biblical) charity that encourage us to see her also as a moral exemplar. In her encounter with Alexander after the plane has passed overhead, it is unclear whether we are witnessing a conversation between master and servant, the potential beginning of a love affair, or a meeting of kindred spirits. The strangeness of the setting, with the dreamlike washed-out color and the unexplained water lying in puddles around them (previous exterior shots had shown no sign of this), merely intensifies the sense of mystery.

If it is difficult—even impossible—to interpret many of the characters of the film in purely, or primarily, naturalistic terms, this is even more true of much of the film's "action," especially its central "events": the nuclear catastrophe and Alexander's sacrifice(s). Here Tarkovsky blurs even further than in previous films any distinction between dream and reality, actuality and hallucination, and the visual and aural coding that had earlier provided some clues for separating these out now becomes thoroughly ambiguous. Although some scenes (Alexander's visions of nuclear disaster, and his anxiety dream about losing his son) are clearly signaled as dreams by black and white and aural signals such as dripping water, Tarkovsky seems to want us to experience the central "action" of the film as simultaneously real *and* nonreal, just as the images themselves are simultaneously color *and* black and white.[4] In similar fashion, the shepherds' calls that accompany some obvious dreams occur also in what appear to be "real" situations and thus cannot be used to distinguish one from the other.

Although "clues" are provided—in narrative, visual imagery, sound, and dialogue—these are contradictory and perhaps even ultimately irreconcilable throughout. If there is a dream at the center of the film, where does it start? Does a nuclear war begin, or not? The ambiguity may have been a deliberate choice on Tarkovsky's part: writing about the film in *Sculpting in Time*, he acknowledged that "there will doubtless be others for whom all the events of the film are merely the fruits of a sick imagination—since no nuclear war is actually happening" (223); and Erland Josephson told us that when he asked Tarkovsky whether the visit to Maria and its apparent consequences really happened, the director turned very "populistic" and said it was up to the audience to decide.

The first sign that a nuclear war may be imminent comes with the sound of the plane overhead and the frightened reactions of Marta (Alexander's stepdaughter) and Julia (the housekeeper). Otto, however, remains unconcerned.[5] Alexander meets Maria outside; neither mentions the plane, and we hear the sound of flute music that is later given a "natural" source in Alexander's tape recorder. Alexander then talks to Otto in his study; again neither mentions the plane, yet both act as if they are afraid of something. Otto mysteriously leaves via the balcony rather than the stairs; Alexander overhears the broadcast, switches off the flute music, and goes downstairs to join the other characters listening to the broadcast, seeming almost to welcome what is happening: "I have waited my whole life for this." Yet the broadcast itself is very strange and seems—from the end leader—to be prerecorded (in the published treatment it is a live broadcast, the prime minister is shown on screen, and his speech is far more coherent). In an attempt to save humanity as well as his family and friends, Alexander makes his vow to God. He has a dream that expresses his fear of losing his son and wakes to find the preparations for war continuing. Otto arrives, somehow aware of the fact that Alexander can save humanity, and tells him that he can achieve this by sleeping with a "good witch." His advice thus parallels Alexander's vow (if you do this, things will be as they were before) but from a pagan rather than Christian perspective: Maria, he says, lives behind the church, which is now closed. Here the two story lines that Tarkovsky combined to create the script for this film (see the beginning of this chapter) begin to show signs of strain. How can a vow to God be fulfilled by a sexual encounter with a witch, even a "witch in the best sense"? In his description of *The Witch* in *Sculpting in Time*, Tarkovsky tries to blur the obvious contradiction by saying that the hero's cure occurs by "God's mercy" (220), and in the film he associates Maria with some blatant Christian symbolism—the egg on the table as Alexander leaves his room, the sheep outside her house, and the crucifix in her room.

Despite all this, there is no evidence to support Otto's claim that Maria possesses supernatural powers: when Alexander begs her to save the world by sleeping with him, she shows no understanding of what he is talking about and seems only a simple, pious person, who responds to Alexander's obvious personal unhappiness and does not even know that there is supposed to be a war on. Yet jets fly overhead as had happened in Alexander's house, with identical sound effects and similar consequences (breaking glass),

Alexander's vision of nuclear disaster in *The Sacrifice*. Artificial Eye.

Otto (Allan Edwall) and Alexander (Erland Josephson) in *The Sacrifice*. Artificial Eye.

and a purely naturalistic explanation of their encounter seems to be denied by the levitation scene that follows.[6] This is in turn unexpectedly followed by a reprise of Alexander's earlier vision of disaster (initially caused, perhaps, by the blow on the head when his son jumped on him?). Now the disaster is actually happening (earlier, he had seen its aftermath) and his son is still in danger. Why is this placed *after* he has done what Otto told him to do: is this some exorcism of the danger, or have both God and the witch failed him?

The shot following this, in which the identities of the wife and Maria merge, recalls *Nostalghia*, and seems to have little purpose[7] except to provide—along with dialogue and music—a bridge back to waking reality, which is introduced by the return to full color with the Leonardo painting (the Maria episode had begun after a shot of Alexander reflected in this painting) and the obviously dreamlike shot of the naked Marta.[8] Adelaide makes a brief, seemingly real appearance, then mysteriously vanishes and plays no part in the remainder of this sequence, despite her supposed concern for her husband, and is next seen, only a few minutes later in "real" time, sitting outside in the middle of a conversation with Marta and Victor.

The obscurity of these scenes (which, as they stand, seem intended as a transition, in aural and visual terms, between the world of the visit to Maria and the world in which Alexander's prayers seem to have been answered) is partially accounted for in *Directed by Andrej Tarkovskij*, where the whole sequence is shown as it was filmed. After his second vision of nuclear disaster, Adelaide is seen (in color) bending over her husband on the sofa, reassuring him that "it's just a bad dream." The camera tracks left from the couple in close-up to show them, apparently simultaneously, also in the far distance, with all the film's other characters, and some strangers, standing near the sofa; they all kneel. The camera continues to track left, picking up three more "Adelaides," one of whom walks behind a mirror showing the reflection of a young woman with very long hair, and past a door that swings open to show three men in dark suits in the distance, who then walk off-screen. Otto cycles from the foreground through the hallway, after which chickens then flutter to the ground from above and are chased away by the naked Marta.

By eliminating everything except this last image and a brief shot of Adelaide, Tarkovsky both gained and lost: much of the imagery in the dream is irrelevant and confusing (and repeats earlier effects from *Solaris*), and its essential function can be conveyed by the fragments he retained. Yet having Adelaide tell Alexander "It's only a dream," while obviously dreamlike actions continue, reproduces one of the most common features of the dreaming process, and could have added an extra dimension of complexity to what precedes and follows this scene.

The "dream" or "alternative reality" element of the film seems clearly to end here, with the restoration of full color, and Alexander waking on the sofa; yet it remains impossible to identify exactly when it began. From the first sound of the plane overhead,[9] the clues we are given, if used selectively, could place almost any scene as the starting point, yet taken together they cancel each other out. And even if everything now seems to have returned to normal—the electricity is on and no one mentions or seems to remember any crisis (unless the ambiguous comment made during the phone call is intended to hint at this)—problems still remain. Alexander had switched the tape recorder off *before* going downstairs to watch the TV broadcast, but now it is still on.[10] And, as with the introduction of the train *after* the glasses have moved at the end of *Stalker*, Tarkovsky allows us simultaneously to believe and not believe in the visit to Maria by showing Alexander bumping into the table and beginning to limp, thus giving a "naturalistic" equivalent of the injury he sustained when he fell off the bicycle.

Perhaps, however, this is the point: we have to believe and not believe simultaneously rather than attempt to place a logical structure on events which are ultimately, and perhaps deliberately, incompatible with one another and suit neither a "realistic" nor an "it was all—or mostly—a dream" explanation. From this standpoint, it is possible to interpret all the major "events" of the film—Otto's visit to Alexander's study, Alexander's visit to Maria, the miraculous reversal and elimination of the seemingly imminent nuclear catastrophe—as at one and the same time real *and* imaginary. If this is so, Tarkovsky has moved a step beyond his habitual tolerance for differing interpretations of his films by individual members of the audience (see *Sculpting* 168–69) and his consistent belief that audiences should *experience* rather than analyze his films and respond to them with dreamlike rather than rational logic. Interpretation is no longer a question of either A *or* B, but both A *and* B; and the already strongly oneiric qualities of *Mirror, Stalker*, and *Nostalghia* are pushed to an extreme that defies differentiation between one state of reality and another. In a dream, all explanations coexist, and perhaps this is the case here, too.[11]

Applied to the characters, this would suggest that Maria, for example, is *both* a humble, loving woman who can offer Alexander what Adelaide cannot—a total, self-abnegating, self-sacrificing love—*and* a "holy fool," a soothsayer (as Tarkovsky calls her in *Sculpting* [228]) and "witch" only in the Russian sense of that word, whose root means "to know." Thus she does not need any of the attributes normally associated with witches and can legitimately be linked to the Christian symbols and images noted above. This would in turn support Philip Strick's suggestion in his review of the film for the *Monthly Film Bulletin* that there is a dual sacrifice with a "double atonement" that solves dual problems: personal (Alexander's unhappy family and love life) and public (the threat to humanity). Tarkovsky, in this view, wants to find salvation both in the human love of a woman and in the divine love of God (8).

As well as pushing the dream/reality fusion even further than in his earlier experiments, Tarkovsky in this film carries the long take to greater extremes than previously. The film's opening, postcredits shot lasts 9 minutes 26 seconds, close to the maximum length possible, and shots of between 4

Don't touch him!

The burning house and the struggle for possession of Alexander at the end of the film. Artificial Eye.

and 8 minutes are common elsewhere in the film.[12] Although they are generally beautifully executed, there is sometimes a sense of strain, a feeling that the action exists for the sake of the shot, rather than the other way around. The incident with the rope in the opening shot is a case in point: it obviously does not work as it was intended to, for the rope comes loose from the bush and would not have caused enough tension to stop the bicycle, with the result that the actor has, rather unconvincingly, to fake his fall. As the action comes near the end of an elaborate shot lasting 9 minutes already, it was doubtless felt to be too expensive and time-consuming to redo the whole thing just to correct this small detail. Problems like this occur in other shots and have the paradoxical effect of undercutting the "reality" that Tarkovsky saw as the main virtue of this style of filming.[13]

The 6 minute 50 second "house-burning" shot has acquired almost mythical status because of the disaster that occurred in the original filming of it. Tarkovsky insisted on shooting it in one take, with only one camera carrying out the complicated tracking movements, despite Sven Nykvist's protests; a back-up camera was available but was not mounted on rails. Halfway through the shot the camera began to lose speed and had to be replaced by the back-up camera; though the shot was completed, it was no longer the single, continuous movement that Tarkovsky had his heart set on. His distress was so evident that the cast and crew arranged to have the exterior of the house rebuilt, and the scene was reshot two weeks later, now using two cameras running parallel to each other.[14] Daring and impressively executed as the shot is, it suggests once again that sustained camera movement was becoming an end in itself for Tarkovsky, rather than a means to an end, and it was certainly foolhardy to burn down his main set with only one camera to record the action as he wanted it.

This particular scene involves other problems besides its length. The action itself is simultaneously painful and ludicrous: when asked in interview about the almost slapstick quality of the entrances and exits around the ambulance, Erland Josephson made the perfectly reasonable point that the most distressing incidents in people's lives are not always performed with dignity and may seem comic to outsiders, yet it is still possible to think that there is just a little too much running back and forth within the scene. The sudden and totally improbable arrival of the ambulance is also disconcerting, for there is no way in which it could have been summoned in the time available (in the treatment there is a definite time lapse before it arrives). Otto turns up almost simultaneously with it[15]—has he mysteriously known what is about to happen and brought the ambulance with him? Or did Tarkovsky want to include everything in one virtuoso shot and choose to ignore dramatic plausibility to achieve this?

Other aspects of the visual style, however, are less problematic. Sven Nykvist's subtle and ambiguous color photography makes this perhaps the most visually beautiful of all Tarkovsky's films: the sharply metallic colors of the interiors and the shiny glistening floors create a coldness that echoes the characters' relationships with each other, as well as matching the deliberate formality of their movements, gestures, and poses. The natural world, despite its bleakness, provides a visual contrast in the intense green of the grass and the shimmer of sunlight on the sea. The stylized formality of the costumes and coiffures, especially with Adelaide and Marta, contrasts with the simplicity and hidden beauty of Maria, and matches the self-consciousness of their personalities and behavior. As with *Solaris*, there are some strikingly beautiful "still life" effects: the delicate cup and saucer and mirror beside Alexander's tape recorder; the glass, egg, and bundle of letters on the table beside his balcony; the almost symmetrical compositions, featuring a bottle, flowers, and fruit, on either side of the doorway as he builds his pyramid of chairs. Mirrors, as always, are strikingly evident and are given an unusual role in the reflections of the outside world, and sometimes Alexander himself, in the glass of the Leonardo painting: integrating the worlds of humanity, nature, and art, which are kept tragically separate elsewhere in the film.

Like Domenico, Alexander makes his statement and fulfills his vow through the destructive and purifying element of fire, but, as with Domenico, there are ambiguous elements to his sacrifice. His renunciation of worldly possessions affects his family as well as himself and, like the uncomprehending witnesses to Domenico's self-immolation, they will never understand his reasons: for them, he will simply be a pathetic madman rather than a prophet or martyr or "holy fool."[16] And, although Otto has told him earlier (when urging him to visit Maria) that they are all "very fond of him," this is self-evidently not the case; on a spiritual level this need not detract from the nobility of his sacrifice on their behalf, but it does—again as with Domen-ico—turn it into something of a gesture that exists for its own sake rather than really changing anything. Olga Surkova even argues that Alexander's act is not a true sacrifice because he destroys something which he no longer loves: except for Little Man, Alexander is alienated from his wife and family, and the house itself is only a cold reminder of their unhappiness (192).

Although *Nostalghia* may seem more openly autobiographical than any other film since *Mirror*, *The Sacrifice* combines intimate details of Tarkovsky's personal and family life with his spiritual, philosophical, and religious preoc-cupations. In *Mirror* a painful autobiography became cathartic in the context of Russian history, culture, and art, and through the exploration of memory and time. In *The Sacrifice* the personal elements are—less successfully in the eyes of some critics—combined with mystical, religious, and existential issues. Tarkovsky seems here to be somewhat desperately searching for answers he had previously been able to find in his own past and culture. Despite the foreign setting, the house which Alexander burns down is clearly another copy of the idyllic Russian dacha so prominent in *Solaris* and *Mirror:* one finds the same heavy wooden construction, the lacy white curtains, the substantial, shiny antique furniture, the lovely glasses and crockery. When Alexander tells Little Man the story of how he and Adelaide found the house by the sea, it is, in fact, Tarkovsky's own recollection of a happier past in Russia. While *Mirror* had looked back to Tarkovsky's childhood and first fam-ily, and to some degree had tried to make peace with them, *The Sacrifice* now looks at a more disturbing present, where, with the exception of the love of his son, there seems to be little harmony left either at home or in the world.

Until his last film, there had been little concrete autobiographical detail from more than twenty years with his second wife. Larissa is credited as assis-tant director on several films and played the very unsympathetic role of the rich doctor's wife in *Mirror*. She was also originally intended for the role of Stalker's wife. It is not until *The Sacrifice*, however, that Tarkovsky presents a character clearly modeled on her and recognizable as such to many who knew her both in Russia and abroad. Susan Fleetwood thought she was chosen for the role of Adelaide because of her physical resemblance.[17] Additional similari-ties can be found in Adelaide's soft, upswept hairdo, the flowing long multilay-ered "costumes," and the bouquets of wildflowers she carries, as well as her complex, highly emotional personality. Like Larissa, Adelaide has a grown daughter from a previous marriage who, in the film, is in sexual competition with her mother. Tarkovsky's reputed pathological possessiveness of his beau-tiful stepdaughter may give a rather disturbingly personal meaning to what might be seen as Alexander's possibly incestuous dream. In fact, the composi-tion of Alexander's family is the same as Tarkovsky's, with the "mute" Little Man representing a younger version of their absent son Andrei, whom they had been forced to leave behind in Russia. In a filmed interview the son con-firms that "the little boy is me" and that the house and characters are based on

Sexual competition for Victor (Sven Wolter) between mother and daughter.
Marta (Filippa Franzén) on the left; Adelaide (Susan Fleetwood) sitting at the
table. Artificial Eye.

real life. He remembers his father taking him for walks and conducting
lengthy, interesting conversations that he could not always understand (transcript published in *O Tarkovskom* 342–88; these remarks occur on p. 375).

Alexander himself, with his interest in Eastern music and philosophy and
his belief both in God and in all kinds of mystical phenomena, also reflects
Tarkovsky's eclectic preoccupations at the time. In his last years Tarkovsky
began attending church and studying the Bible more seriously than before.
But he was also fascinated by astrology, ESP, telekinesis, and any kind of
supernatural phenomena, as well as by such Eastern religions as Buddhism
and Daoism—though the latter are presented rather superficially in the film.
Alexander's kimono bears the yin and yang characters on its back—expressing the inseparable harmony of all opposites and of the male and female
principles. Yet this seems an almost impossible ideal, for what both Alexander and Tarkovsky see in the world is the *dis*harmony of the spiritual and the
material world, and on a personal level, of male and female. Alexander's
seemingly superfluous and rambling story about the forceful taming of his
mother's garden can perhaps be read within the Daoist precept that "to
do nothing is to do everything."[18] Alexander even exhibits Tarkovsky's taste
in art: he appreciates the beauty of Russian icons and Leonardo's paintings
and bemoans technology's destruction of culture and spirituality. One of the
film's problems may in fact arise from Tarkovsky's attempt to "burden" his
hero with all of his own philosophical and moral, as well as his personal,
concerns.

Like most of Tarkovsky's films, *The Sacrifice* was entered at the Cannes Film Festival, where it won the Special Jury Prize after receiving a somewhat mixed response from the audience. A Tarkovsky Memorial Retrospective in the spring of 1987 at Dom Kino (Turovskaya 150) allowed Soviet critics to see all of Tarkovsky's films, Soviet and Western, for the first time, and *The Sacrifice* was interpreted by many as a dying, martyred artist's final testament. At first, the paucity of accurate information about Tarkovsky's life and career in the West helped to fuel this myth. His defection and supposed continuing mistreatment by the Soviet authorities, his nostalgia for Russia and for a son forcibly kept from him, were all seen as causes for the fatal illness which then found its creative embodiment in the film. Even such a generally reliable critic as Maya Turovskaya states—incorrectly—in her book that Tarkovsky knew he was ill, and even that he alternated bouts in the hospital with the actual shooting (137, 159). As his diary makes clear (*TWT* 348–49, December 11–21), he was diagnosed with the cancer in December 1985, *after* the film's completion, but before the final cut had been completely edited. Turovskaya may have a point, however, when she states her belief that "the blind knowledge of the body is a powerful creative stimulant for a personality such as Tarkovsky's" (153). He was a highly intuitive man, and his general ill health that year (Larissa Tarkovskaya Interview) may have contributed an even more poignant personal tone to his final film, and it may well be legitimate to see it as a final testament, despite what his original intention may have been.

Although the myth of Tarkovsky's awareness of his fatal illness while shooting the film has also found its way into some Western criticism, the main focus has been on trying to resolve some of the puzzling structural and thematic problems that *The Sacrifice* poses. Much of the published reaction has been unsympathetic, citing the film as shallow and pretentious while often acknowledging its visual beauty and emotional power.[19] Philip Strick (*Monthly Film Bulletin*, January 1987), however, attempted to account for some of the multiplicity of possible interpretations by arguing for what he calls a message of "double atonement for a world of weaknesses": by sleeping with Maria, Alexander is resolving an intolerable family drama, just as in his vow to God he saves humanity. His main praise, however, is reserved for the film's composition and imagery: "In [Tarkovsky's] hallucinatory universe, catastrophe may be private or global or both, but it's no reason to ignore the essential, imaginably God-given texture of existence itself" (8).

Despite the convoluted, confusing dialogues and discussions—a weakness especially typical of the last films—and the often overt didacticism, *The Sacrifice* reaches conclusions that are both moving and simple: love, hope, and faith in God can rescue humanity from its rush toward self-destruction. Instead of attempting to dominate (and in the process destroy) the natural world, we should return to a spirit of reverence and harmony within it: only thus can potential or real catastrophes be averted and our life take its proper place within the unbroken cycle of the natural world. The film's final shot is an unashamed and unaffected affirmation of human potential when inspired by love and faith, embodied in the music of Bach and the dead tree which "Little Man" will lovingly nurture back to life. As the camera slowly moves through the dead branches with the sea glistening and shimmering in the background, the light creates its own miracle and the tree seems to come to life before our eyes.

PART THREE

ELEVEN

Imprinted Time:
The Development of a Style

Tarkovsky's last three films are so closely identified with such stylistic devices as the long, slowly paced sequence shot, sometimes six or seven minutes in length, the absence of conventional musical scoring, a minimal narrative in which theme takes precedence over plot, and a dreamlike atmosphere which blurs the borders between dream or fantasy and waking reality, that earlier works such as *Ivan's Childhood* and even *Mirror* that seemed puzzling and unconventional on their first appearance now appear relatively lucid and straightforward in retrospect. Nevertheless there is a striking continuity that links each film to its predecessor and points ahead to what is to come. Here we will discuss Tarkovsky's use of camera movement, composition, sound, music, color, and lighting as they developed over his career: the combination of these as "images" will be examined in the following chapter. We will also pay some attention to narrative structure and to Tarkovsky's concern with the presentation of "real time" in his films.

Although the diploma film *The Steamroller and the Violin* introduces some of the director's central images and thematic concerns, it is, from the point of view of technique, a compendium of devices that he would rarely use again. Much the same is true of *Ivan's Childhood* where, though the devices usually work well in their context, it is almost, with hindsight, as if the young prodigy were showing off what he *could* do—though the virtuoso, expressionistic camerawork, odd angles, moodily atmospheric lighting, and occasional heavy-handed symbolism are all discarded or modified later. What was to become his trademark—the lengthy uninterrupted tracking shot—is virtually nonexistent here, and the longest shot in the film, where Galtsev and Kholin select and launch a boat for their expedition, lasts a bare two minutes. Other elements, such as the alternately lyrical and ominous mood music and the editing—with its rediscovery of Eisensteinian montage—follow the conventions of the more experimental Soviet films of the "Thaw" period.

Although it would be unfair to suggest that the film's real virtues are limited to those aspects that foreshadow Tarkovsky's later style, it is nevertheless these hints of what is yet to come that provide much of what is most memorable about *Ivan's Childhood*. Opening, like Fellini's *8½*, with a dream that is not immediately signaled as such, it adopts from the very beginning his characteristic pattern of forcing the viewer to work to assimilate the fragmentary and elliptical information that the narrative—often only grudgingly and belatedly—provides. The imagery of the dreams, with their emphasis on the figure of the mother, water, hair, horses, fruit, and vegetation, is picked up again and again in later work, and is intensified by Tarkovsky's awareness that the truest film dreams are intensely real and physical rather than vaguely symbolic or abstract. Interesting use is made of nonsynchronous and subjective sound, both in the dreams and in the central narrative, while the controversial introduction of documentary footage testifies to a respect for the "real" within the overall fictional structure that he will demonstrate, in one form or another, in all his subsequent work—whether it is the use of his father's poetry or the historical Andrei Roublev's paintings, the long highway sequence in *Solaris*, the newsreels and the scene with the hypnotist in *Mirror*, the more ambiguous quasi-documentaries, home movies, and TV broadcasts in *Solaris* or *The Sacrifice*, or the newsreel-style filming of the flashbacks to Domenico's past in *Nostalghia*.

Black and white was still the norm for Soviet films in the early sixties, and, given the circumstances in which Tarkovsky came to direct *Ivan's Childhood*, he was doubtless not even given the option of filming it in color. From *Andrei Roublev* onwards, however, he had a much freer hand in making the initial creative decisions, and it is with his second feature that the characteristic and uncompromising Tarkovsky style begins to emerge, based to some extent on intuition as to what was "right" for him, but also on the aesthetic premises already outlined in chapter 2. One such premise concerned the use of black and white, which was deliberately chosen for *Andrei Roublev* in order to enhance the sense of reality (along with the costumes and settings) and to avoid anything that might seem falsely picturesque (Yusov Interview). The use of color at the end, as Tarkovsky explained to Michel Ciment, was intended to show the reality of Roublev's life transformed into, and by, his art (*Dossier Positif* 90–91). The apparent paradox here (for is not film, for Tarkovsky, also an art, and why then can it not, like painting, both express and transform reality through color?) is addressed, somewhat obliquely, in *Sculpting in Time*, where he makes a distinction between the *mechanical* reproduction of color in film, which is inevitably false, and "the touch of the artist's hand" in painting which permits conscious organization and selection (138–39). The equation of black and white in film with reality is extended in a lecture/discussion that he gave in Rome in 1982, where he argued that, though we perceive the real world in color, the reproduction of this reality *within a film frame* makes us *aware* of color in a disturbing and distracting fashion, while black and white seems both more normal and more expressive (*Dossier Positif* 60).

His argument here has been echoed, in practice, by a handful of contemporary directors who have chosen to make their more "realistic" films in black and white, as well as by the art critic Anne Hollander in her book *Moving Pictures*, where black and white is equated with "truthfulness" rather than "reality" (a more subtle distinction that seems to express what Tarkovsky really means). Discussing the use of black and white engravings in Western art, Hollander suggests that "photographs and movies in black and white are considered good because they are so true, not because they are so real. Their often brilliant beauty rests on this. 'Living color' may be more lifelike and more delicious, but, like life itself, it is also more distracting, entrancing and misleading" (33).

Tarkovsky's distinction between "mechanical" film color and the "personal" color of a painting is also reinforced by Hollander when she writes:

> All color in art is a code, as Gombrich has said, not an imitation. The colors in color photography and cinematography are no "realer" than those of paint, which have long adhered to artistic conventions independent of nature, and to the technical limitations of the medium. . . . The "reality" of color in photographic reproduction or in direct photography and cinematography is a fiction we all accept, because the relationship among the colors looks acceptably real, and the total result is often very beautiful. (48)

Tarkovsky's argument is very similar:

> You have to try to neutralise colour, to modify its impact on the audience. If colour becomes the dominant dramatic element of the shot, it means that the director and camera-man are using a painter's methods to affect the audience. That is why nowadays one very often finds that the average expertly made film will have the same sort of appeal as the luxuriously illustrated glossy magazine; the colour photography will be warring against the expressiveness of the image. (*Sculpting* 138)

Realizing, however, that, even for a Soviet director (especially one who wanted his work to be attended to abroad), color was now virtually a commercial necessity for most films, Tarkovsky adopted, both in theory and in the practice of all his subsequent films, the compromise offered in *Sculpting in Time:* "Perhaps the effect of colour should be neutralised by alternating color and monochrome sequences, so that the impression made by the complete spectrum is spaced out, toned down" (138). He seems also to have equated this monochrome effect, especially in his last three films, with particularly "spiritual" scenes (Hollander mentions Rembrandt's use of chiaroscuro "to invoke the soul"). His respect for "realism" in film presumably ruled out the alternative solution, suggested by Eisenstein and effected by Godard, Antonioni, and Fassbinder, among others, of employing color in a clearly nonrealistic and highly stylized fashion. And, though color is used to impressive effect from *Solaris* onwards, Tarkovsky works within a deliberately restricted range in each film, rarely moving beyond muted tones of brown, green, blue, yellow, and grey, while using black and white as colors in their own right.

In *Solaris, Mirror,* and *Stalker* the colors, though subdued, are basically naturalistic, with "thematic" contrasts centered around the "lifelike" (rather than—in Tarkovsky's terminology—"realistic") opposition between nature (sunlight and greenery) and indoors (the bland blues, whites, and browns of the space station or the dark browns of the apartment in which Alexei and

Natalia conduct their marital hostilities). Interiors, however, are not always forbidding or confining: even where the overall color scheme is neutral, a positive atmosphere can be created by means of indoor greenery, sunlight, or warm lighting (as in the dacha of *Solaris*). Black and white (often with sepia or blue tinting) normally suggests an alternative reality: that of dreams or memories or the historical past (in *Solaris* and *Mirror* and, on occasion, *Stalker*). The choice of black and white for dreams may reflect the conventional idea that most people dream in black and white, but more probably implies, in line with Tarkovsky's belief in the essential "reality" of black and white, that the inner truth of our experience is to be found within our dreams. In *Stalker* the basic pattern is reversed, with black and white creating the sordid reality of the everyday world of the future and color representing the potential escape from this offered by the Zone.

Yet the contrast is never mechanical or even consistent—though a shortage of good-quality color film stock may have had something to do with what sometimes seem random alternations. Kris's hallucinations in *Solaris* begin with a sequence in color before switching to black and white, and the long scene in the swamp in *Stalker* alternates color and monochrome even while the dialogue provides an apparent continuity in time and space. At the end of *Stalker* "reality" is shown both in black and white (or sepia) and in color, with the color of the final sequence suggesting some seepage of the powers of the Zone into the real world. In *Mirror* memories are presented both in color and in monochrome, and one sequence explicitly introduced by the narrator as a dream is in color.

In *Nostalghia* the ambiguous relationship between dream and reality hinted at in *Stalker* is conveyed largely through the lighting, which prepares us for the transition from one world to the other. Obtrusively artificial lighting had been used sparingly before (most notably on Masha's face after she has killed the chicken in *Mirror*), but in *Nostalghia* it becomes a major aesthetic device that, together with the browns of the interior of the hotel and Domenico's home and the refusal to show the (rarely seen) natural world as being particularly attractive—it is usually veiled in mist or coexists with manmade ruins and debris—helps to create the strange half-world, neither totally real nor totally illusory, in which Andrei lives. In contrast to the three preceding color films, the natural world makes its strongest impact in the black and white of Andrei's memories.

Color returns to its more usual function of celebrating—and perhaps even heightening—the beauty of nature in *The Sacrifice*, yet the main action of the film takes place in a world as ambiguous and hallucinatory as in much of *Nostalghia*. The restricted color range of the interior scenes (often virtually indistinguishable from black and white) conveys something of the artificiality of the relationships among the characters and merges easily into the black and white interior world of Alexander himself, where the events of the night could be either bizarre reality or hallucination induced by the terror of a nuclear catastrophe. As with *Stalker, Mirror, Solaris,* and even the otherwise black and white *Andrei Roublev*, the color of the closing sequence implies both transfiguration and harmony (the more ambiguous *Nostalghia* leaves its hero in the limbo of monochrome).

The reluctance to "help" the viewer by providing conventional or easily recognizable guidelines is characteristic of all Tarkovsky's films and accounts to a large extent for their notorious "difficulty" on a first—and often subsequent—viewing. This can take the form of an extraordinary laxness in providing basic narrative information even as to who the characters are and their relationship with one another, or in giving background details that would help the viewer situate the action in time and space (this is particularly true of *Andrei Roublev* and *Mirror* but applies to some extent to all the other films). Sometimes (especially in *Roublev*) this results from the omission or shortening of scenes during editing, or (as in *Mirror*) from the inadequacy of the English subtitling; but more often—as in cases where the information is provided in the script but not transferred into the finished film—it seems to reflect a genuine indifference on Tarkovsky's part to the importance of this level of understanding of the material.

Usually, however, the seeming confusion is purposeful and part of a deliberate narrative strategy by means of which Tarkovsky invites his audience to participate in creating the meaning of the film rather than passively consuming predigested images, character relationships, and patterns of plot. In this respect, of course, he is fully within the "art film" tradition of the past thirty years, whose formal devices have been exhaustively analyzed by David Bordwell in his *Narration in the Fiction Film,* and is consciously reacting against the "question and answer" format of the traditional linear narrative film in which various questions about action and motivation are posed throughout the story, and are then progressively answered or discarded until a satisfactory solution is reached at the end. As described by Noël Carroll in *Mystifying Movies* (206), this format works both on the overall ("erotetic") narrative scale of the whole film and within the structure of individual episodes or scenes, constantly guiding the audience toward perception of what is "relevant" for narrative understanding and ultimate clarity and intelligibility.

Ivan's Childhood conforms to this pattern by posing the "erotetic" question "What will happen to Ivan?" Internal narrative scenes offer possible solutions (he might go to military school; he might run away; he might be adopted by one of the officers; he might end up like the dead scouts whose bodies are displayed on the far side of the river), while the dream sequences provide a logical explanation for his fanatical hatred of the Germans. Finally the question is answered: Ivan dies.

This is the only Tarkovsky film, however, in which the structure is so simple. The narrative question of *Andrei Roublev* ("Will Roublev ever paint again?") is not even posed until halfway through the film, when the hero takes his vow of silence; up till then the events have no particular narrative logic, even if—as is to become characteristic of the later films—they have, in retrospect at least, a clear *thematic* unity. *Solaris* poses the question: "Will Kris find out what is wrong at the space station?" but by the end has largely diverged from this into an investigation of his inner spiritual development. If there is an overall question in *Mirror*, it is so vague as to be almost indecipherable (perhaps something like: "Will the narrator ever come to terms with his past?"), and the posing and answering of this question has little to do with the true meaning or structure of the film. The question in *Stalker* begins as "*Will* the three men enter the Room?" but ends as "*Why don't* they enter the Room?"—which is left to the viewers to decide for themselves.

In *Nostalghia* the question is once again purely interior ("Will Andrei resolve his inner tensions?") rather then exterior ("Will he go back to Russia or not?"), and this could have been presented, equally satisfactorily, within a totally different narrative framework. In *The Sacrifice* the question "Did Alexander's vow avert a nuclear holocaust?" is (a) once again subordinate to the more central theme of the character's spiritual development, and (b) impossible to answer given the deliberate ambiguity as to whether the events of the night really happened or not. In almost every case Tarkovsky either ignores or thwarts the narrative expectations that most viewers will apply to interpreting the film's structure: to make sense of the films, and to respond to their strong inner coherence, we have to learn to ask different questions and to tolerate an unusual amount of both narrative ambiguity and denial—or diversion into different channels—of what we consider to be legitimate narrative demands.

This pattern also applies on the smaller scale of individual scenes where, in accordance with narrative convention, each scene should introduce or develop some minor structural question that helps us to interpret and understand the overall question posed by the film. Carroll suggests a narrative "principle that the first thing the audience sees in a shot is that which is most relevant to posing, sustaining, or answering the questions of the ongoing story" (206). In *Mirror*, however, we are constantly left floundering at the beginning of each new scene, trying to orient ourselves in time and space and to relate to characters whose identity is often deliberately withheld from us until the scene is well advanced. As with the overall narrative, a coherence *does* exist, but it has to searched for and interpreted by means of visual and aural clues rather than revealed through explicit dialogue and action or "meaningful" camera placement.

We know, for example, from the preceding dialogue and the shift to black and white that the printing-house scene takes place in the past, and a powerful-atmosphere of fear (ultimately the "meaning" of the scene) is created through camerawork, lighting, acting, setting, and even weather. The actual time period of the late thirties has to be inferred, however (from visual clues such as a background portrait of Stalin), and the *reason* for Masha's distress is not revealed until the scene is well advanced, while the actual *cause* (the misspelling of Stalin's name) is whispered to Lisa and never even stated to the audience! Rather than ending at this point (the "solution" of the narrative problem), the scene then continues into the apparently unmotivated attack by Lisa on her friend and Masha's refusal to accept her belated apology. Moreover, none of this appears to have anything much to do with the "erotetic" structure of the film, which, in any case, has not been clearly established. Yet the scene *does* have meaning in itself and *does* contribute to the overall pattern of the film—though not in the ways that we might expect. Although *Mirror* perhaps takes this method to its extreme, much the same is true of the later films, where individual scenes contribute obliquely rather than directly to the film's meaning, and what is explicitly said and done within them is often of less significance than apparently peripheral or unmotivated details of setting, gesture, costume, sound, framing, and camerawork, and the effect created by imagery that has no specific "symbolic" meaning but shapes our deepest responses to the film nevertheless.

Something of this can be seen by tracing briefly the development of the dream sequences throughout the films. Although the unusual placing of dreams at the beginning and end of *Ivan's Childhood* is disruptive of normal narrative coherence, the dreams themselves follow a clear narrative pattern (Ivan remembers his lost childhood happiness and the death of his mother) that slots neatly into and "explains" his behavior in the rest of the film. There are no dreams as such in *Andrei Roublev*, but we have Roublev's dreamlike vision of a Russian peasant crucifixion and the hallucinatory scene at the end of the Tartar raid in which Roublev speaks to the dead Theophanes in a context that is fully integrated into the reality of the preceding and surrounding action and thus cannot be interpreted simply as "imagination." It is this "impossible" scene, incidentally, that provides the narrative motivation (Roublev's vow of silence) for the remaining action of the film.

Kris's dreams of his mother in *Solaris* relate to and are explained by the "inner" rather than the "exterior" plot of the film and have no relevance at all to his supposed mission to decide whether or not to shut down the space station. Their imagery of guilt and atonement relates to the "family" subtheme of the film, though the conflation of the settings of the dacha and the space station looks forward to the final shot of the film and suggests that the Solaris Ocean is performing some kind of healing function on Kris's psyche. In *Mirror*, however, neither the placing nor the content of the dreams can be accounted for so easily. It is not even always clear whether they represent the dreams the narrator had *as* a child or if they are the adult's dreams *of* himself as a child. Though the basic imagery of the dreams can be interpreted in standard Freudian terms, with the main themes a sense of loss and exclusion and the confusion of identity (as in *Solaris*) between wife and mother, much of the imagery remains deeply personal, even if it succeeds in setting off appropriate reverberations and resonances in the viewer. From the point of view of narrative structure, however, the placement of the dreams serves a rhythmic or poetic function rather than an explanatory one, and, though their content *reveals* a great deal, it *resolves* virtually nothing: the dreams do not, as they would in a Hollywood film (and, to a large extent, in *Ivan's Childhood*), provide an unambiguous reason for the narrator's problems, nor are they interpreted (by him or anyone else) in a way that would allow him to solve or come to terms with these problems. They simply *exist* and have to be related to by the audience in a way that transcends normal patterns of motivation or cause and effect.

The dreamlike sequence in the swamp in *Stalker* is not, as we have noted in the chapter on that film, significantly different from the formal strategies of much of the remainder of the film and cannot, in any case, be interpreted in any way that furthers conventional understanding of either plot or character. *Nostalghia*, on the other hand, though it too creates a dreamlike aura around apparently realistic events, returns to the methods of *Ivan's Childhood* with dreams (or reveries) that help to "explain" Andrei's waking behavior: he is unhappy because he is separated from his family and homeland; he has unacknowledged sexual feelings for Eugenia.

At first *The Sacrifice* appears to make a clear distinction between reality (color) and dream (Alexander's black and white vision of nuclear disaster), but as the color drains from the image, dream and reality fuse and become almost inseparable. All the formal devices of the film work to make it impossible to decide with certainty when (or if) Alexander's dream begins, though a return to everyday reality seems to be signaled by the eventual restoration of full color. Yet certain scenes in black and white seem somehow "more" dreamlike than the others: the snow scene in which Alexander envisions losing his son, and the reprise and expansion of his vision of disaster. None of this makes it possible to use the dreams to explain or account for the remainder of the story, as we would normally expect: the narrative has itself taken on the quality of a dream, and the guidelines that help us separate one world from the other no longer exist.

Despite all this, the dreams remain "realistic" in the sense that their imagery is drawn from everyday life and is presented in a way that eschews (with the exception of slow motion) special effects and optical tricks or distortions. The narrative structure of the films might equally be defended as being "realistic," in that, in real life, we rarely assimilate and process information with the neatness, coherence, and continuity of the conventional narrative film. What came to be Tarkovsky's trademark and perhaps his most extreme stylistic device—the long take—was likewise constantly justified by the director as a force for realism in its respect for the workings of "real time" within the shot.

The move toward films with average shot lengths of just over a minute in *Stalker* and *Nostalghia* or well over a minute in *The Sacrifice* was a gradual one. As mentioned earlier, only one shot in *Ivan's Childhood* lasts as long as 2 minutes, while shots lasting that length and up to more than 3 minutes occur with some frequency throughout *Andrei Roublev*. Two and 3 minutes, in turn, become relatively commonplace shot lengths in *Solaris*, with the longest take now lasting more than 4 minutes. *Mirror*, the shortest of the films at 106 minutes, contains almost exactly two hundred shots,[1] giving an average shot length of approximately 30 seconds, yet very few individual takes last more than 1, or at most 2, minutes, the chief exception being a shot during the conversation between Alexei and Natalia about Ignat that lasts just under 4 minutes.

Stalker marks a radical transition: here takes of two minutes are so frequent as to be almost unnoticeable, while several shots last more than 4 minutes and one (in the "telephone room") becomes, at 6 minutes 50 seconds, the longest in Tarkovsky's films to date. This is in turn surpassed by the shot of Andrei carrying the candle across the pool in *Nostalghia*, which lasts 8 minutes 45 seconds, while, as with *Stalker*, three or four other shots last well over 4 minutes. *The Sacrifice*, though more than 20 minutes longer than *Nostalghia*, has almost exactly the same number of shots (approximately 115) and thus a greater average shot length; the first postcredits shot, beginning with Alexander planting the tree, lasts 9 minutes 26 seconds and is the longest in all Tarkovsky's work. Several other takes last 4, 5, 6, or even 7 minutes (the conversation in which Otto advises Alexander to visit Maria is 7 minutes 12 seconds long).[2]

While many of the longest takes in each film (such as the house burning) are accompanied by elaborate camerawork, several are virtually static, with the camera either passively observing a lengthy conversation or monologue or moving very slowly with or toward the characters. In the latter instances (Writer's monologue in the dune room and the conversation in the telephone room in *Stalker*; Eugenia's diatribe about Andrei in *Nostalghia*; or Otto's second visit to Alexander's study in *The Sacrifice*) Tarkovsky relies heavily on the ability of his actors to create and sustain an emotional mood for what is—in cinematic terms—an unusually long period of uninterrupted time.

Within the overall structure of the camerawork, certain compositional devices recur with some regularity. One that is present in almost every film is the creation of a logically incompatible space within the compass of a single shot: the same character will be seen in a series of different spaces or positions that cannot be rationally accounted for. Usually this effect is used within a dream—Ivan's "apples" dream, Kris's hallucinations in *Solaris*, one of Andrei's dreams of his family and home in *Nostalghia*—or as the preliminary stage to one, as in *The Sacrifice*. A variant is the dream in *Mirror* that shows the child Alyosha moving from the inhabited dacha to the same building, now empty and abandoned. The device creates an effect that is dreamlike in *Nostalghia*, where Andrei is seen in Domenico's house examining himself in a mirror before the camera moves to show him also standing several feet away. A similarly unsettling and hallucinatory result is achieved by maintaining continuity of time by means of sound while editing creates strange spatial disjunctions, as in the conversation between Roublev and the dead Theophanes in the ransacked cathedral, or the "swamp" scene in *Stalker*.

A more conventional, but effective, technique is to suggest lack of com-

Overall caption: Images of noncommunication.

Ivan (Nikolai Burlyaev) and Galtsev (E. Zharikov) in *Ivan's Childhood*. Artificial Eye.

Theophanes (Nikolai Sergeyev) and Andrei Roublev. Artificial Eye.

Professor and Writer in *Stalker*. Contemporary Films.

The alienated family in *The Sacrifice*. Artificial Eye.

munication between characters by either showing one reflected in a mirror while the other is seen talking (or listening) with his or her back apparently turned, or having characters speak while their backs are turned to each other or they look in different directions. One or the other of these effects, and often both, can be found in each film, starting as early as *The Steamroller and the Violin*. A mysterious variant of this occurs especially in the last three films, where Tarkovsky will often begin a shot with a close-up of the character's head and shoulders from behind, against a blurred or out-of-focus background. The most striking example is during the flatcar sequence in *Stalker*, where the three men are seen only from behind or in profile, but similar shots are found elsewhere in that film, and also in *Nostalghia* and *The Sacrifice*. The effect is to create a sense of isolation and also perhaps of something strange and even threatening.

Almost all the stylistic elements described so far share a common function in forcing the viewer to constantly readjust his or her expectations about what will appear on the screen, in what order, and how it will be presented. Tarkovsky's use of music and sound is no exception to this. Once again *Ivan's Childhood* is relatively conventional in its use of "mood" music and recurring musical themes, and this is generally true also of *Andrei Roublev*. Both films also begin, in a somewhat tentative way in *Ivan* and with more assurance in *Roublev*, to experiment with sound leitmotifs and the use of music for more subtle atmospheric purposes than simply expressing the feelings of the characters or arousing the appropriate responses (happiness, fear, sadness) in the audience. The recurring sounds of the cuckoo and the dripping water that introduce Ivan's dreams become standard devices of Tarkovsky's later work; bird song is used (as in the blinding scene of *Roublev*) to create a peaceful counterpoint in sound to images of violence and warfare; subjective sound (German voices and marching feet) is used effectively both with Ivan himself and for Galtsev's discovery of Ivan's death.

In *Ivan's Childhood* most of the music and sound effects are still intended to further understanding of theme and character; though this is true for much of *Roublev*, sounds such as the tolling bells that are sometimes part of the natural sound of a scene and sometimes not, or the quiet and haunting song that follows the buffoon's performance (and recurs briefly before his later reappearance), serve a more independent function that was to culminate in the complex sound patterns of *Nostalghia* and *The Sacrifice*. Many scenes in *Roublev* dispense with music altogether and rely on tolling bells, barking dogs, and bird song (especially cuckoos and crows) to create the requisite mood; and another favorite device is introduced, of sound preceding and overlapping a cut to a new time or setting, that is used here particularly to introduce flashbacks.

The Chaliapin recording in *Ivan's Childhood* (like the Dürer prints) is employed mainly for emotional "patriotic" purposes; *Solaris*, however, introduces a more complex treatment of classical music. The Bach Prelude that accompanies the credits is used as a reminder of Earth, but is also subtly rescored throughout the film to suggest the effect that the Solaris Ocean is having on Kris; meanwhile the electronic music performs the more usual function of creating an atmosphere of strangeness, mystery, and suspense. In the scenes on Earth, bird song and barking dogs accentuate the feeling of melancholy preceding Kris's departure, while the chaotic traffic noise of the highway sequence offers an aural and thematic contrast to the peacefulness of nature. Just as a fragment of the music from *Ivan's Childhood* had been introduced into *Andrei Roublev*, so a sound quote from *Roublev* appears in *Solaris* (accompanied by a reproduction of Roublev's "Trinity").

Classical music from various sources (Bach, Purcell, and Pergolesi) appears in *Mirror*, both (in what was to become standard practice for all the later films except *Stalker*) over the credits and to accompany some of the more peaceful (or ecstatic) memories of the past, or newsreels. Electronic music generally emphasizes strangeness (in dreams or Ignat's encounter with the mysterious woman in his apartment) or the more disturbing and violent aspect of the newsreel footage. In this visually fragmented film, the music also performs an essential unifying function in providing aural continuity between past and present, dream and everyday reality, fiction and newsreel. Birds (most notably crows and an owl), dogs, and dripping water (to indicate dreams) all create mood but also begin to be used as a kind of rhythmic punctuation in the soundtrack that provides a subtextual pattern of associations throughout this film and carried over into others.

The total absence of conventional musical scoring in *Mirror* is an indication of Tarkovsky's growing dissatisfaction with the use of music and sound as a means of guiding the audience toward a predetermined response. Having dispensed with much of this assistance in the narrative structure and visual codes of the films, it was now time to do something more radical with the soundtrack. The principles which shaped his thinking in his last three films are laid out clearly in *Sculpting in Time* and match, almost word for word, what Noël Carroll has to say on this subject in *Mystifying Movies*. Carroll argues that music is a central force for clarity in the conventional film that "enhances the filmmaker's expressive control over the action" (222); "modifying music . . . assures that the untutored spectators of the mass movie audience will have access to the desired expressive quality and, in turn, will see the given scene under its aegis" (223).

Tarkovsky, writing in the context of his work on *Stalker* and *Nostalghia*, rejects what he calls a "mechanical and arbitrary" use of music that does little more "than intensify the impression of the visual image by providing a parallel illustration of the same idea," and suggests instead that music should be used "like a refrain" that creates "a *new*, transfigured impression" each time it recurs, or "to produce a necessary distortion of the visual material in the audience's perception" (*Sculpting* 155, 158). The result is not to remove the director's control entirely, but to loosen it "by widening the range of their perception of the visual image." Music "must be so completely one with the visual image that if it were to be removed from a particular episode, the visual image would not just be weaker in its idea and its impact, it would be qualitatively different" (158–59).

Nevertheless, he admits, "in my heart of hearts I don't believe films need music at all," and it could well "be replaced by sounds in which cinema constantly discovers new levels of meaning" (159). His models here are Bresson, Antonioni, and Bergman, though he would like to achieve something even "more accurate, more true to the inner world which we try to reproduce on screen" than even they had achieved. The result, in the last three films, is a sound texture built up from a mosaic of extracts (often deliberately distorted) from classical music, Chinese and Japanese instrumental music, folk songs, chants, and shepherds' calls, which is then combined with the kind of resonant, real, and yet nonnaturalistic sound effects that he particularly admired in Bergman, where "the sounds of the visible world, reflected by the screen, are removed from it, or that world is filled, for the sake of the image, with extraneous sounds that don't exist literally, or . . . the real sounds are distorted so that they no longer correspond with the image" (162). Here Tarkovsky, despite his professed antagonism toward Eisenstein, clearly echoes the argument for a "contrapuntal" use of sound from the famous Eisenstein/Pudovkin/Alexandrov "Statement" of 1928 (Eisenstein 257–59).

In the last three films, then, sound and music function in a very different way from providing what Tarkovsky calls "a kind of emotional aura around the objects shown" (159) and what Carroll describes as "a continuous channel of information about the emotional significance of the action" (223). Although classical music continues to be used, it operates to troubling and disturbing effect rather than to prompt the emotions usually associated with any particular selection (the main exception to this is the use of Bach's "Erbarme dich" at the end of The Sacrifice, where Tarkovsky intends an explicit and unambiguous sense of affirmation). The distorted fragments of Wagner, Ravel, and Beethoven that occur in Stalker (often drowned out by the rattle of passing trains) suggest the decayed spiritual condition of the society portrayed and the tentative nature of the film's resolution. Beethoven's "Ode to Joy" is heard again in Nostalghia, first in Domenico's house, where it is brusquely interrupted, and once more during the fiasco of his self-immolation, where the malfunctioning of the record helps to undermine the intended solemnity of the gesture. Yet the use, a few minutes later and without distortion, of another gravely beautiful extract from the same music, as Andrei succeeds in placing the candle on the far ledge of the pool, implies that this completes Domenico's action and compensates for his failure.

The Russian folk music heard in connection with Andrei's memories of his homeland intensifies his "Russian" nostalgia, yet, in the long sequence that follows the reading by Eugenia of Sosnovsky's letter, the strangely discordant "Turkish" music creates an unexpectedly exotic effect. The Chinese and Japanese music heard in Nostalghia and The Sacrifice is used partly for its "strangeness" to a Western ear (the hotel guests and the bathers in the former film, and Alexander's family in the latter, all demonstrate their narrow-mindedness by complaining about the music) and partly to suggest the reconciliation of Eastern and Western values that Tarkovsky intended to embody in Alexander himself. The electronic music in *Stalker* is sometimes ominous (as in *Solaris*) but also almost lyrical at times; the use of the same music both inside and outside the Zone serves, along with other elements in the film, to break down the apparent barriers between the Zone and the everyday world.

However original and powerful these effects are, they still remain to some extent emotional or interpretative "props." A device halfway between music and pure sound, the shepherds' calls in *The Sacrifice*, has something of the more ambiguous function of the alternations between color and black and white in Tarkovsky's work. Normally they are heard as a kind of premonition of something strange and ominous and occur before or during such scenes as Alexander's first vision, Otto's collapse, Alexander's taking of his vow, and his visit to Maria. Yet they also appear in less meaningful situations, as part of an overall sound tapestry, and as initial accompaniment to the peaceful closing scenes of Maria on her bicycle and Little Man watering the tree.

Many of the most distinctive sounds in these last films serve little or no naturalistic function and fall into the categories defined by Tarkovsky, where "the sounds of the visible world, reflected by the screen, are removed from it, or that world is filled, for the sake of the image, with extraneous sounds that don't exist literally" (*Sculpting* 162). An example of the first category is the scene of the release of Domenico's family in *Nostalghia*, where the eerie absence of natural sound is intensified by isolated fragments of speech, and of the second, from the same film, the unseen buzz-saw that accompanies both real and dreamlike events. Eugenia's hair-dryer, though real enough, functions as an aural irritant that prepares for the pent-up outburst of anger against Andrei that is to follow. In *The Sacrifice* the melancholy, hesitant, and almost incoherent voice that announces, on a crackling and malfunctioning TV receiver, the outbreak of a nuclear war gives the scene an almost dreamlike unreality, while the tinkling glasses and the roar of airplane engines make the threat of war only too vivid and tangible: as with the narrative structure and the visuals, Tarkovsky is able to say "yes" and "no" simultaneously.

Stalker, Nostalghia, and *The Sacrifice* are full of sounds like these that create a rhythm and atmosphere working in counterpoint with the images rather than simply reflecting or intensifying them: telephones that ring unanswered in the background of a scene; mournful foghorns; coins that fall and rattle on the floor; off-screen thunder; creaking doors and billowing curtains. As much as the images, they contribute to realizing Tarkovsky's aim of being "true to the inner world which we try to reproduce on screen; not just the author's inner world, but what lies within the world itself, what is essential to it and does not depend on us" (*Sculpting* 159). They form part of the defamiliarization, the "making strange" of conventional screen language that operates from almost the very beginning of his career and proceeds according to its own inherent logic and necessity.³ The "inner world" that results is shared between audience and filmmaker and is the joint creation of both; though no one element within it—as Tarkovsky would have been the first to admit—is without some parallel in the work of other "art film" directors, the combination of them is unique. Ingmar Bergman probably put it best when he credited Tarkovsky with the invention of "a new language which allows him to seize hold of life as appearance, life as a dream" (*Dossier Positif* 8).

TWELVE

The Image:
Indivisible and Elusive

Virtually all critics of Tarkovsky have commented on the recurrence of certain images throughout his work: those most frequently noted include water, fire, trees, horses, dogs, milk, and mirrors. This list, however, is far from exhaustive, and a careful examination of all the visual and aural motifs reveals a rich network of image clusters which permeate and unify Tarkovsky's films. Both the nature of these images and the contexts in which they appear can tell us a great deal about the sources on which Tarkovsky drew—either consciously or unconsciously—in creating what many viewers find to be most memorable about his work.

In attempting to define and analyze the most characteristic image clusters, we will be cognizant of the fact that they operate in various ways. Certainly one cannot deny the possibility that they may often be "innocent," reflecting Tarkovsky's personal preference for trees, horses, rain, red hair, and dogs, for example, and that he uses them to give visual density or texture to his images, or to create a particular mood—and no consideration of his films should ever ignore his obvious respect and love for the natural world and his ability to film it in such a way that we come to share his sense of wonder and awe. In *Sculpting in Time* Tarkovsky tries to give the impression that these images have no "meaning" beyond this and that it is useless to look for one: "Rain, fire, water, snow, dew, the driving ground wind—all are part of the material setting in which we dwell" (212); though he may use them "to create a particular aesthetic setting in which to steep the action of the film," it is pointless ("Heaven forbid!") to look for any further meaning.

This, however, is surely disingenuous, given the multiple and inescapable associations that the natural elements (and many of Tarkovsky's other motifs) have accumulated around them in myth, folklore, religion, literature, and art over the centuries—all of which the educated Tarkovsky was aware of—not to mention the various psychoanalytical and archetypal interpretations put forward in the course of this century. These are now an inextricable part of their "meaning," especially when they are forced on us as insistently and repeatedly as is the case, for example, with water in Tarkovsky's films, and, whether he is using them consciously or subconsciously, they inevitably shape the responses of the viewer and provide a guide to interpretation. In the chapter on *The Sacrifice* added to the book shortly before his death,

Tarkovsky himself is rather more honest in admitting that the dead tree—surely as much an "innocent" feature of nature as rain, snow, or fire—is "a symbol of faith" (223). Even as early as 1969, discussing *Andrei Roublev* with Michel Ciment, he let slip remarks to the effect that the sky *could* have "symbolic meaning" or that the horse is a "symbol of life" throughout the film (*Dossier Positif* 92, 91). His reluctance, however, to speak of his imagery in figurative terms justifiably stems from the critics' tendency—in both the East and the West—to overload his images with, at times, preposterous and far-fetched symbolism.

The "meanings" even for the most essential elements of the natural and human worlds can take on various forms in different contexts, with narrower or broader figurative associations. Trees, water, and fire seem to have much the same basic cluster of associations, both positive and negative, in a wide variety of religions, myths, and cultures; but fish and sheep, for example, have a specific meaning in Christian symbolism that is not found in other religions. There is widespread agreement that dogs are associated with loyalty; horses, on the other hand, may be a sexual symbol in some contexts but not in others. Although the concept of "house" usually calls up security, family, and childhood (also perhaps motherhood and the womb) to most people's minds, Tarkovsky's houses also draw on very personal memories and associations that are not always immediately evident; a Russian of Tarkovsky's generation will relate to the contents and furnishings of the dacha in *Mirror* with a "shock of recognition" that it is impossible for a foreigner to share. In addition, Tarkovsky imposes his own private, perhaps arbitrary significance on certain images (such as milk and dripping water) or interprets other concepts (such as falling) in a manner that diverges from the commonly accepted meaning: in these cases, we have to create our own interpretation from the overall context or learn, from film to film, what they seem to signify for the director.[1]

Our analysis of the major image clusters in the films will attempt to reveal both the metaphorical significance of Tarkovsky's images within an overall cultural context and their specific "intertextual" and "intratextual" significance within his own work. It is precisely these replicated combinations of visual and sound images and their accompanying themes that define what Alexander Zholkovsky in his *Themes and Texts* so systematically examines as an artist's "poetic world."[2]

The Natural World

THE FOUR ELEMENTS

Water in its various forms, heard as well as seen, is the most pervasive image, found, almost to surfeit, in every film. Ponds, rivers, oceans, swamps, pools, and puddles are everywhere; rain and snow fall both indoors and out; buildings are knee-deep in water; water drips incessantly from taps and

ther, less identifiable sources; it takes a secondary form as mist, clouds, and
mud; and the camera lovingly caresses plants and weeds that make their home
in water. Sometimes its use is purely naturalistic, but more often it is associated
with certain recurring concepts or functions to create a dreamlike aura around
particular scenes, characters, or incidents; often its resonances are mythical and
archetypal. *Ivan's Childhood* introduces many of these uses in a relatively un-
complicated way: the scenes in the swamp remind us, as do the documentary
shots of soldiers trudging through water in *Mirror*, that war is neither glamor-
ous nor pleasant; Ivan's crossing of the river may also recall the classical idea of
the River Styx and the approach of death. The sound of dripping water, often in
visual association with the fire in the stove, signals dreams, and in the dreams,
happiness and the figure of the mother are invariably associated with water,
rain, or sea. Here Tarkovsky is drawing on long-held concepts that link water
with the feminine (specifically motherhood), spiritual rebirth, and purification,
and he will return frequently to these in his future work.

    Andrei Roublev begins and ends with a river, and several episodes ("The
Passion According to Andrei," "The Celebration," "The Raid," and "The
Bell") take place on or near a river or stream. Here perhaps we have the river
of life, as we follow Andrei's journey of self-discovery—and also the river of
death for his apprentice Foma. Rain in Tarkovsky's films tends to begin and
end suddenly and almost unnaturalistically: it drives the civilized monks indoors, but the buffoon, who lacks their inhibitions, welcomes it (the pagan
revelers encountered later carry out their main rituals on water). Rain provides a structural bridge to the brief flashback during the casting of the bell,
when Andrei remembers happier times, and also leads from the shots of
Roublev's paintings to the final peaceful scene of the horses grazing by the
river. Water mixed with or lying on earth is regularly associated with creativity: the intrepid balloonist/artist flies over a flooded landscape; Boriska cannot mold his bell until he finds the right clay; Roublev resolves to resume his
career as an artist, in partnership with Boriska, as he cradles the boy, sitting
among the puddles on a muddy riverbank.[3] Another favorite device—rain
falling indoors—is prefigured in the snow that falls inside the ruined cathedral at the end of the Tartar raid: the effect, as befits a scene in which the hero
is talking to the dead Theophanes, is strange and eerie.

    Solaris opens with a shot of a pond and its vegetation: water (the pond in
which Kris dips his hand, the rain in which he allows himself to be soaked)
becomes the chief embodiment of the beauty of the natural world that the
astronaut hero may be leaving behind him forever, and also suggests his
potential for ultimate redemption. The indoor rain at the end also suggests
purification and cleansing. Although Kris is traveling to a planet whose surface is entirely covered with water, the Solaris Ocean—a morass of changing
colors and drifting clouds—offers nothing familiar and tangible to match the
water of Earth and remains alien and forbidding throughout. In the film that
he carries with him to Solaris, his mother is seen standing beside the pond,
and in his dreams she rather sternly washes his hands.

Overall caption: Water images in *Stalker* and *Nostalghia*.

Stalker in the swamp. Contemporary Films.

The three men outside the Room (*Stalker*). Contemporary Films.

The flooded interior of Domenico's house (*Nostalghia*). Artificial Eye.

Andrei in the flooded cathedral, talking to Angela (*Nostalghia*). Artificial Eye.

Gaston Bachelard has written eloquently about the role of water as a profoundly maternal and feminine element (170–71), and this archetypal association is carried over from *Solaris* to dominate *Mirror*, where the mother is in
fact wet for a good deal of the film! She is rained on in the scene where the
barn burns, at the beginning of the printing-house scene (and takes a shower
at the end of it), and at the start of the "earrings" scene. Less naturalistically,
when she reluctantly kills the chicken later in this scene, rain (which has been
absent from the previous shots) is seen falling on the wall behind her, creating—along with the lighting—a weird and hallucinatory effect. In the first
dream sequence she is seen washing her hair, and later indoor rain surrounds
her; in the dream of her sorting potatoes in a shed, rain is seen falling outside
the window behind her. Toward the end of the film, the child Alyosha swims
across a pond toward her as she rinses laundry on the far bank, and in the
final scene, the mother, now an old woman, leads the two children along a
muddy road dotted with puddles. The narrator's wife Natalia, by contrast, is
only once, and peripherally, associated with water (watching her son Ignat
standing in the rain in the courtyard), reflecting her husband's much colder,
even hostile, feelings toward her (even if he says at times that she reminds
him of his mother).[4]

In these first four films water generally has a positive significance, associated with happy memories of childhood and a loving (if sometimes rather
distant) mother, with the beauty of nature, and with purification and creativity. Here the water itself is "alive"—moving, often falling as rain or flowing
as a river. "Dead," stagnant water, however, appears prominently in the last
three films and is linked with decay, neglect, and pollution. In *Stalker* water
covers the rusting and disintegrating debris of human civilization, and the
men have to wade through a good deal of—often stagnant—water to reach
their goal. Nevertheless, the scene in the swamp restores something of the
previous links of water with creativity and spirituality, as Stalker lies on an
outcrop totally surrounded by water and the more pragmatic Writer and Professor remain on dry land, or Stalker talks feelingly about music as the camera examines the surface of a lake and the trees reflected in it. Writer is
discovered lying in a puddle in the dune room and proceeds to a searching
self-examination of his weakness and self-deception. As the three men sit
and look into the Room, rain starts to fall within it; the effect now is not
so much of another barrier between the men and their goal as to create a
mood of quiet acceptance as they come to terms with their weakness and
limitations.

Nostalghia continues the linkage of stagnant water with decay and ruins,
and also returns to the earlier use of running or dripping water to introduce
dreams or memories. The small pond in front of the Russian farmhouse
seems to be of particular importance to Andrei and is retrieved into the final
composite image in which Russia and Italy are united, while rain and snow
fall and mingle in the foreground. Rain from outside is reflected on the wall
of Andrei's hotel room as he plunges into reveries of his past, and the now-

familiar indoor rain inundates Domenico's strange dwelling, accentuating his unworldly—or otherworldly—nature. Like the men in *Stalker*, Andrei has to wade through a considerable amount of water to reach his spiritual goal, creating a somewhat strange effect in this rather more naturalistic world. St. Catherine's Pool no longer seems able to fulfill its healing function in an age of materialism and disbelief; those bathing in it jeer openly at the one man who still puts spiritual values ahead of worldly ones. The pool is drained when Andrei crosses it, perhaps suggesting the "draining" of spirituality from the modern world, though it is still wet and muddy, thus linking his achievement to the "creative" flooded earth of other films.

Water in *The Sacrifice* is found almost exclusively as sea and flooded ground. The sea appears mostly as a backdrop to the action, though, as a widely recognized symbol of motherhood and birth, it perhaps substitutes for the absent and unsatisfactory Adelaide in the opening scene between Alexander and the boy. In the film's last shot the sea, shimmering with light, seems to revivify the branches of the dead tree and to suggest the eternal cycle of nature that even man can never totally destroy. No rational explanation is offered for the partly flooded ground around the house, which is first noticeable during the scene between Alexander and Maria that is one candidate for the point at which the action of the film becomes a dream. The puddles are particularly obvious during the house burning, the water perhaps representing Alexander's hopes for spiritual rebirth while the fire simultaneously destroys and purifies his previous existence.

Fire, like water, traditionally has both negative and positive connotations (destruction and purification). It is also associated with domesticity (the hearth or, for Russians, the stove), religion (in the form of sacrifice or the burning away of the sinful and earthly), and the uncontrollable force of nature or of sex; even at its most destructive, it exerts an almost hypnotic fascination over human beings. Tarkovsky draws on most of these associations at one stage or another. Human misuse of fire for destructive purposes is seen in the war-ravaged landscape of *Ivan's Childhood* and in the Tartar raid of *Andrei Roublev*; it is used constructively, however, in the casting of the bell. The pagans in *Roublev* make fire a central element in their fertility rites, and Roublev himself is almost "set alight" as he watches and is tempted to join them. The wood stove is prominent in Ivan's temporary home in the military field station, and its flames are often seen as a prelude to his dreams, in conjunction with the sound of dripping water; it is also a central element in the comfortable home of the narrator's childhood in *Mirror*. In the first dream sequence in the latter film, however, the leaping flames from the gas burner contribute to the eeriness of the scene and also perhaps to its sexual subtext, and in Alyosha's later fantasy of the teenage redhead, the burning stick that she holds and the fiery stove behind her have clearly erotic significance. When the barn burns, both mother and children are drawn to watch and enjoy the spectacle. Ignat is also attracted to fire, lighting one in the courtyard and poking distractedly at it with a stick, to his father's obvious contempt (the adult having forgotten his own childish fascination).

Before setting out on his journey to the space station, Kris Kelvin burns relics of his past (though he spares Hari's photo), recognizing, perhaps subconsciously, that what he has learned on Earth will be of little use to him in his new environment (what appears to be the same fire is still burning on his return at the end of the film). Other memories of Earth are important to him, however, and he takes with him a tape of scenes from his childhood in which a burning fire is linked with the family happiness and unity that appear to have been lost as he grew up. Andrei in *Nostalghia* burns the Italian translation of Tarkovsky's father's poems—not a particularly filial act on the director's part, even if, as his hero argues, poetry is, in its essence, untranslatable.

Burning as spiritual purgation or purification involves three major characters. When Kris sends the first Hari off in the rocket ship, his clothes catch fire; this is the starting point for his slow development from what Berton has scornfully called "a bookkeeper" to someone capable once more of love and compassion, and when she reappears, he is now ready to welcome and respond to her. Domenico in *Nostalghia* burns himself alive in what seems a vain attempt to warn others of the moral and spiritual decay of contemporary society, and Alexander in *The Sacrifice* burns his house and possessions in fulfillment of his vow to God.

Air, in the form of sky, is relatively unimportant (several critics have noted that, though Tarkovsky favors horizontal compositions, the sky as such is rarely shown; *Ivan's Childhood* is the main exception·to this). Tarkovsky acknowledged indifference toward the sky when discussing *Andrei Roublev* with Michel Ciment, saying that he was much more interested in the earth and that the sky had no "symbolic meaning" for him in itself: "I love the earth, I love *my* earth" (*Dossier Positif* 92). Even in scenes of flying, as in the opening dream of *Ivan's Childhood* or the balloon sequence in *Roublev*, the camera looks downwards at the earth rather than at the sky. Objects belonging to the sky, like sun, moon, stars, and clouds, are rarely seen, and sounds associated with the sky, like thunder, occur—especially in *The Sacrifice*—only for portentous or ominous effect.

Wind, however, which has affinities both with the imagination and with the spiritual, plays a more significant role, especially in *Mirror* and *Stalker*. It usually springs up suddenly, as if from nowhere—as the doctor walks away across the field at the beginning of *Mirror* or as Writer approaches the house in *Stalker* and is warned to retreat—and it forms an integral part of the dream imagery in *Mirror*, either in the repeated shots of wind blowing through bushes or upsetting the objects on a table, or as the child Alyosha moves in slow motion toward the deserted dacha.

The living *earth*, the land itself, whether filmed in penetrating close-up or extreme long shot, almost always has positive associations. Many characters in Tarkovsky's films seem to feel a particular affection for the earth and are seen at crucial moments lying or sitting in close contact with it; wet earth, as mentioned above, is linked with creativity and the imagination.[5] Kris literally brings some earth with him (in his metal box) to the space station, and one of Stalker's first actions on arriving in the Zone is to stretch face downwards on the earth with his body in total contact with it. Andrei sits on the ground beside the pond in the final image of *Nostalghia*, and Little Man, after watering the tree, lies on his back looking up at it at the end of *The Sacrifice* (the image cluster in this shot—earth, water, sea, sky, and tree—is especially rich and affirmative). Earlier in the film Alexander sits on the ground with his back against a tree and meditates on the ills of the modern world. Roublev and Boriska sit together on the muddy ground as Roublev renounces his vow of silence and determines to paint again. Also in *Roublev*, earth teeming with life is seen in the close-up of Theophanes' feet and even becomes the source of food as Foma forages in the leaves. In the opening scene of his first film, Tarkovsky imbues it with almost magical, life-affirming qualities in Ivan's dream. Considering the close connections in the Russian folk tradition between earth, mother, and Russia itself (all feminine nouns in Russian and combined in such common expressions as "Mother Russia" and "mother earth"), it is hardly surprising to find the earth as a dominant positive image in Tarkovsky's films.

THE LANDSCAPE AND ITS INHABITANTS

The whole "live" physical landscape forms a highly positive cluster of imagery in Tarkovsky's films, and the absence of natural elements is always marked as negative. In *Ivan's Childhood*, the lush vegetation of Ivan's dreams is sharply contrasted to the dead trees in the swamp and the scorched and barren earth of wartime. Long shots and close-ups of the landscape in *Andrei Roublev* mark the relentless passing of seasons in which nature and humans are inextricably bound. Though always subservient to nature, man—notably the artist—always struggles and is occasionally victorious: Boris manages to cast the bell before winter has set in and scuttled the project. Life is literally renewed in nature, in a pagan ritual, when men and women sink into the thick summer vegetation for a night of love. In *Solaris*, *Mirror*, and *Stalker*, luxuriant, often undulating water weeds, grass, bushes, and trees fill the screen with rich tonalities of saturated, mostly green, color. Yet that beauty is increasingly threatened: in *Solaris* the dacha seems an oasis of tranquility in an otherwise ugly urban environment, and the future looks equally grim in *Stalker*, where the mysterious Zone is another oasis of greenery, dangerous, but alive, in a colorless polluted world almost devoid of vegetation. In *The Sacrifice* Alexander's dream reveals an inanimate, postapocalyptic landscape of glass, concrete, and garbage.

Trees are second only to water in Tarkovsky's landscapes. Like water, they often function simply as part of a natural setting, but they too are part of a subtextual language that calls up both private and universal associations from one film to the next: it is significant that a tree appears in the very first shot of his first feature film and is the last image of his final film.

We first see Ivan standing behind a tree (whose height we never see, just as we never see Ivan reach his full growth), and trees, with sunlight streaming through them, appear often in his dreams. A young birch forest is the site of the film's only romantic interlude, and the swaying trees through which Masha dances signal a happy, momentary respite from the realities of war. Yet the true reality of war—death—is embodied in the dead trees that permeate and finally end the film; for all Tarkovsky's rejection of "symbolism," he has made a clear parallel by moving from a live to a dead tree and from a live to a dead boy.

In *Andrei Roublev* trees are once again associated with both life and death. Trees are the mainstay of life itself, providing shelter (the log cabins) and warmth (logs). The huge stack of white birch logs which serves as the background for almost all the outdoor monastery scenes creates a beautiful visual pattern, but also is a reminder of life's hardships in these times and humanity's basic dependence on nature's bounty. Tarkovsky insisted on using birch logs here and shot a later scene in a birch forest to create a typically *Russian* landscape. As a national emblem full of emotional and spiritual connotations, the birch functions on both a realistic and a figurative level for Tarkovsky's Russian audience (Andrei, in *Nostalghia*, yearns for the birches of his childhood).

When Boriska is digging the pit for the bell, he pulls at a seemingly endless root which finally leads to a spectacularly beautiful tree reaching high into the sky. As in the beginning of *Ivan's Childhood* the tree acts as a traditional symbol of life, of the power, endurance, and beauty of nature, and a link between earth and sky, the material and the divine. But trees are associated with death as well. The white birch forest (the same one as in *Ivan's Childhood*) becomes the setting for the blinding of the stonemasons, and the Tartars use a huge log as a battering ram to smash the doors of the Assumption Cathedral; the consequences are fire, torture, and death. Trees take on Christian associations in Andrei's vision of the Last Judgment, as Christ drags a rough-hewn cross[6] over the snowy Russian landscape, and in the Tree of Life in a Roublev icon at the end.

In the films that follow, the tree becomes an overwhelmingly positive image, which operates on realistic, emotional, and symbolic levels and is repeatedly connected with Tarkovsky's most deeply felt memories and longings. In *Solaris* trees are part of the natural earthly landscape Kris leaves behind; on the space station they can appear only in the Brueghel painting and Kris's home video. But trees represent more than Earth: in this film, as in *Mirror* and *Nostalghia*, they are part of an autobiographical thematic cluster that links home, family (wife or mother), and childhood to a wooden dacha surrounded by trees. In *Nostalghia* trees are conspicuous by their absence in the Italian setting of the present and appear mainly in the dream/memories of Andrei's family back in Russia. The film's closing shot shows him sitting surrounded by his Russian dacha and its trees inside barren Italian ruins. The ending of this film and also that of *Mirror* connect the trees of a typically Russian landscape with the state of dream or memory in which past and present miraculously merge.

In *Stalker* trees are absent from the colorless, polluted "everyday" environment and are found only in the Zone, which has managed to preserve some of the natural beauty of the *past*, where *miracles* can still happen, and spiritual rebirth is still possible. In Tarkovsky's films people are often found next to trees in decisive moments in their lives: Masha hugs a tree when she realizes she is in love (*Ivan's Childhood*), Foma dies next to a tree (*Andrei Roublev*), and Alexander hangs onto one as he falls down and has his first apocalyptic vision (*The Sacrifice*).

In *The Sacrifice* trees come full circle, becoming even more openly symbolic than in *Ivan's Childhood* and extending the religious symbolism of *Andrei Roublev*. The film opens with a close-up of the Tree of Life in *The Adoration of the Magi* by Leonardo da Vinci, which will later seem to come to life when real trees are reflected in the glass covering the painting. The "miracle" will be paralleled by another one involving trees: the dead tree which Little Man is watering at the end does "come to life," in a shimmering vision of light, through Alexander's sacrifice and his son's belief. Tarkovsky's parable of the tree applies to his own work as well; film by film, he watered the dead tree of *Ivan's Childhood* with memory, faith, and love until it came to life in *The Sacrifice*.

Although most of Tarkovsky's natural world is undeniably "alive," we rarely—with the exception of *Andrei Roublev*—see many of its *inhabitants.* Goats, sheep, cows, chickens, cats, fish, birds, a butterfly, a spider's web appear occasionally—or even only once—either as part of a naturalistic setting or with more specific thematic or iconographic significance; a particular role is reserved for feathers, either drifting mysteriously from above or found lying on the ground, usually in situations of heightened spiritual awareness. Two animals have major significance for Tarkovsky: dogs and horses. Dogs, either seen or heard, are in every film except *Ivan's Childhood;* their barking is often used for—often subliminal—atmospheric effect. Horses are especially visible in *Andrei Roublev,* but appear also in *Ivan's Childhood, Solaris,* and *Nostalghia;* a still from a take not used in the finished film shows one in *The Sacrifice* as well.[7]

Birds (most notably the cuckoo) are heard in every film, but are rarely seen. As a disheveled Roublev leaves the pagan village, a cock crows. Is it simply dawn, or has Roublev succumbed to temptation and betrayed his faith: "before the cock crow, thou shalt deny me thrice" (Matthew 26:34)? The bird sounds can intensify the natural elements: the discordant cawing of crows underscores the harshness of life in the hunger sequence in *Andrei Roublev;* or, in the same film, they can provide an ironic counterpoint when lovely bird songs are heard in the blinding scene. From *Ivan's Childhood* onwards bird sounds, especially the cuckoo, are associated with memories/ dreams of childhood and the past, and in *Stalker*, where the cuckoo is heard at least seven times, it is a hopeful reminder that life still exists even in the Zone.

Birds flying rapidly or unnaturally across the screen create an oneiric effect in both dream and reality, like the barely identifiable bird flitting across the screen as Boriska contemplates the huge tree whose root he has just discovered, another in the levitation scene in *Mirror*, and the bird that mysteriously vanishes halfway across the room filled with sand dunes in *Stalker*. They are also used for more obviously symbolic purposes, as with the close-up of the dove in the Roublev Trinity icon or the sparrow that may represent the narrator's departing soul near the end of *Mirror*.

While animal sounds, primarily dogs barking, are heard much less often than bird sounds, animals, especially horses and dogs, *appear* much more frequently. In *Andrei Roublev* Tarkovsky uses them as part of the natural setting, to breathe life into a distant historical period and comment on human nature; but mainly they appear as part of an emotionally charged personal landscape linked most often with memory and childhood. In Ivan's dreams the natural world of the past is teeming with life: at first he marvels at a spider's web, a butterfly, and a goat; later a horse eats apples which have spilled profusely on the ground. Horses, when free and untethered, are always for Tarkovsky images of the grace, power, and beauty of nature: such is the horse which twice briefly trots past in the opening of *Solaris*. Restrained in the barn, however, and shot in disconcerting close-up, it becomes terrifying. Since no horses appear in the most autobiographical film, *Mirror* (and none as well in *Stalker* and *The Sacrifice*), one might deduce that horses, unlike dogs, were not animals Tarkovsky was particularly familiar with, and that he associated them with a somewhat traditional, though effective, pattern of symbolism.

Horses play a mainly functional role in *Andrei Roublev* where, broken and trained by man—especially the Tartars—they are part of a terrifying war machine. The Russian princes and their soldiers carry out much of their oppression of the defenseless populace on horseback, most notably in the blinding of the masons. In the most gruesome torture scene, the sacristan's body is dragged out of the church by a galloping horse. The animals themselves are not evil, however, but innocent victims of their association with man. One of the most haunting images in the film is the fall and death of a horse, made more horrifying for the audience because it is real, whereas the deaths of humans—no matter how gory—are still simulated.[8] At the end of *Andrei Roublev* horses become a reminder of nature's beauty, power, and endurance: the "miraculously cured" Fool, dressed in white, leads a beautiful white horse; horses then appear in Roublev's icons, and the very last shot of the film is of four horses standing in the rain, swishing their tails peacefully.

Like horses, dogs in *Andrei Roublev* share and act out the humans' fate:

fighting furiously over a piece of meat thrown by the Tartars, they give us a visceral feel for the hunger of the times. Like the humans, they too are tortured and killed: the angry Kirill beats his dog to death. More "civilized" than man in these primitive times, dogs show more loyalty, and the Little Duke's animal—in barking at the Tartar chief—is more "patriotic" than his master. A dog is identified with home, family, and childhood in *Solaris:* the puppy in the mother's arms in Kris's video of his childhood is the large puglike dog seen at the beginning of the film, which also runs to greet Kris on his return at the end. The dog is also part of Kris's dream and appears on the window sill in the space cabin along with Kris's mother and Hari. Dogs, like trees, wind, or landscape, can exist only in reproduction or substitute form in the space station: in the Brueghel painting, on a mysterious page torn out of an art book, and in Kris's hallucination. In *Mirror* dogs are heard rather than seen, their barking part of the childhood memory of a rural existence which opens the postcredits sequence of the film. A dog is seen briefly with the mother as she picks over potatoes in the barn, and a puppy is on the dresser inside the house—here simply part of the whole complex of positive childhood associations.

In both *Stalker* and *Nostalghia* a large German Shepherd makes its appearance—the same breed of dog that, according to Larissa, the Tarkovskys acquired at the time of the shooting of *Stalker.* The black dog which mysteriously appears in the Zone has been seen by a number of critics as Cerberus, the guardian of the Underworld. But he is not a proper guard; he joins the men and leaves the Zone with them to begin a new life with Stalker (and he has only one head!). It is his loyalty to man that is important for Tarkovsky here, as in *Nostalghia,* where another German Shepherd similarly crosses from one world to another to follow his chosen master. The dog Andrei left at home in Russia joins him in Italy, first in a dream (walking out of the bathroom of the Italian hotel) and then in "afterlife." But he is mysteriously and miraculously Domenico's dog, too, equally loyal to his master: while the humans look on impassively as Domenico sets fire to himself, the dog whimpers and howls in protest. The visual "doubling" of the two dogs further unites Domenico's and Andrei's fates and underscores that theme in the film. But the dog's role is not just thematic or symbolic. As in other films, his improbable appearances and the barking heard occasionally in the film also signal transitions between dream/memory and reality, and between past and present, tying in again to that very personal and positive cluster of images to which Tarkovsky finally gave a name: nostalgia.

PRODUCTS OF NATURE

Food—primarily in the form of milk, bread, fruit, eggs, and potatoes—plays a role in all the films, especially *Mirror,* yet meals as such are rarely shown. These particular items may have held significance for Tarkovsky, as his sister Marina suggested to us, because they are staples that were often in short supply during their childhood, and this certainly accounts for many of

Spilt milk in *Nostalghia* as Domenico's wife gives thanks for her rescue by the police. Artificial Eye.

their appearances in *Mirror*, where hunger is a recurring fact of life for Masha and her children. Milk, however, turns up again and again and not always in obvious contexts, taking on rather different associations each time. Usually it is spilt, or in danger of being spilt: the Duke's daughter sprays milk over Roublev, and in the blinding scene, milk from a flask carried by one of the masons slowly spills its contents into a stream; in the dacha in *Mirror* a cat licks milk spilt on a table, and in the doctor's house milk drips onto the surface of an elaborate piece of furniture; in one of the dreams in this film the child Alyosha holds a large jug of milk that seems in imminent danger of overflowing. Near the end of *Stalker* the dog noisily laps milk from a bowl, spilling some on the floor. In the flashback to the release of Domenico's family in *Nostalghia*, his grateful wife kisses a policeman's feet as milk flows from an overturned bottle nearby. And as the planes scream overhead in *The Sacrifice*, a jug of milk falls from the shelf of a cabinet and shatters on the floor. Less dramatic appearances are in *Solaris*, where Gibarian is offered a glass of milk by his "visitor" in the video recording, and in the final scene of *Stalker*, where the tall glass that falls to the ground appears to have recently held milk.

Why milk in all these cases? Milk once again is a symbol of maternity (it is certainly identified with childhood and mother in *Mirror*), but Tarkovsky seems also to be creating his own private meanings that relate to our awareness that milk is something "good" that should not be "wasted." Thus one might accept Eva J. Schmid's suggestion that the milk after the blinding substitutes for blood, and that in *Nostalghia* it signifies both gratitude (for the rescue) and betrayal (of her husband). Her idea that it is a revelation of Adelaide's infidelity in *The Sacrifice* (*Andrej Tarkowskij* 46–47) seems rather forced and makes sense only if one also attributes a sexual meaning to this precious fluid. The milk-semen parallel common in dreams can perhaps be seen in *Mirror* in connection with the hero's budding sexuality: in the earring scene images of dripping milk are followed closely by Alyosha's jealous speculations on a sexual encounter between the redhead and his competitor, the military instructor; or perhaps in the dream where the even younger Alyosha holds a large jug of milk very gingerly, clearly afraid that he might spill it. In both cases, however, the more obvious meaning is that the doctor's wife can afford to waste milk, even in a time of shortage, while for Alyosha it is something to be protected and cherished. However one interprets it in *The Sacrifice*, the spilt milk certainly marks a decisive turning point in the action of the film: nothing is quite the same after it, and perhaps even the "reality" of the film alters at this point.

Bread and apples are used as staple foods in many of the films, though they occasionally have other functions: Domenico offers Andrei bread and wine (in communion), and apples are used at various times to suggest happiness and abundance (one of Ivan's dreams), hardship (the rotten apples in the famine scene in *Roublev*), or self-absorption (the mother in Kris's hallucination indifferently munching an apple). In one context where an apple would be appropriate, Tarkovsky uses a pear instead, when Marta seductively places this fruit on Victor's knee (her mother has perhaps already offered the apple).

Fruit also often occurs as part of the "still lifes" that punctuate the action of many of the films as the camera surveys a grouping of household objects whose color, shape, texture, and positioning reveal the instinctive eye of a painter, as the objects seem to be used primarily for what Pudovkin and other 1920s directors would call their "plastic" qualities. These include, early in *Solaris*, a half-eaten apple, some small plums, a milk jug, and a beautifully patterned cup and saucer (with rain splashing into the cup),[9] another lovely cup and saucer during the Pushkin/Chaadayev reading in *Mirror*, and, once again, a cup and saucer and a mirror next to Alexander's tape recorder in *The Sacrifice*.

The Human World

THE HUMAN BODY

Tarkovsky often cast on the basis of physical similarities to the characters' prototypes in real life: the tall, thin Nikolai Grinko resembled his father, the blond, beautiful Terekhova his mother. The intense, angular, scrawny figure of Nikolai Burlyaev created a new kind of hero—not clean-cut and cute like most child heroes of the time. Obviously very attuned to external appearance and indulging in his own kind of "typage" (in the best Eisensteinian tradi-

"Still lifes" in *Solaris* . . . Contemporary Films.

. . . and *The Sacrifice*. Artificial Eye.

tion), Tarkovsky also sometimes gave his characters an emblematic physical attribute. Children and teenagers often have sores on their lips, suggesting perhaps their status as victims of a cruel, indifferent, or crazy adult world: Boriska and the Fool in *Andrei Roublev;* Alyosha's teenage love in *Mirror* and also Alyosha himself, during the "earring" scene; Domenico's son in *Nostalghia.* Noses bleed a lot, resulting from violent contact: Stalker after being hit by Writer, Andrei after being slapped by Eugenia, Little Man after jumping unexpectedly on his father's back. The motivation in each case is realistic enough, but the repetition of unusual physical characteristics or actions from film to film leads us to consider other "meanings"—perhaps these are modern-day "martyrs," bleeding/suffering for their faith?

Characters fall, stumble, and trip a great deal, usually as a prelude to some form of self-discovery, spiritual enlightenment, or change of circumstances; the fall may also imply that they need to learn the humility that most of them initially lack. Boriska stumbles as he searches for the right clay in *Andrei Roublev,* literally falls down the side of a cliff to discover it, and trips as he hovers around anxiously waiting for the bell to be tested. Kris trips and falls immediately on his arrival at the space station in *Solaris.* Writer trips on the threshold of the pub (the action is prescribed in the script) just after he has committed himself to the visit to the Zone. Andrei in *Nostalghia* stumbles in the hallway of the hotel (catching his sleeve on a door handle) before entering his room to receive some well-chosen home truths about himself from Eugenia ("You dress badly and you bore me"); and he trips and almost falls just before beginning his third, successful attempt to cross the pool carrying the candle. Eugenia herself falls as she tries to sprint up the stairs, a victim no doubt of her fashionable shoes and clothing, which also prevent her from kneeling in church. Alexander falls three times in *The Sacrifice:* when Little Man knocks him over, followed by his first vision; on his way to the encounter with Maria; and as he begins his preparations to burn down the house—all them crucial stages of his inner crisis. In the burning scene, Marta falls as the family run toward Alexander; this may have been accidental, but Adelaide's falling to her knees in a puddle as the house collapses in ruins is clearly planned and may suggest a belated humility and a moment of self-recognition on her part. Otto's dramatic and different fall in this film is more problematic, however.

Besides stumbling down toward the earth, characters may also fly above it—in imagery reminding us of human beings' perennial attempts to achieve physical as well as spiritual transcendence over this earth. Both *Ivan's Childhood* and *Andrei Roublev* open with scenes that involve flying; prints of early balloons adorn the walls of the dacha in *Solaris* (whose hero is an astronaut); and documentary footage of a balloon flight appears in *Mirror.* Levitation, of a couple in *Solaris* and *The Sacrifice* and of the woman alone in *Mirror* and *Nostalghia* (where it is an effect caused by lighting rather than a physical movement), is a crucial image throughout Tarkovsky's work.

Female characters are often defined by their long hair, which (especially

red) was virtually a fetish with Tarkovsky, as he acknowledged in his diary
(*TWT* 89); it is dwelt on most frequently in *Mirror* and *Nostalghia* but is prominent in all the other films. Tarkovsky clearly liked to explore hair's texture
and its purely filmic quality—dripping wet in *Mirror*, radiantly backlit in *Solaris*, wildly luxuriant in *Nostalghia*. Again his insistence on it must recall for
the viewer its legendary associations, this time with strength and power and
also with sexuality. In classical Hollywood cinema, loose, flowing hair implies
an (often dangerous) sexual availability, while a woman with short hair or
her hair pinned up is more suited to the role of wife and mother. In Russian
society long hair has always been "properly" worn braided or pinned up,
restrained. Tarkovsky most definitely identified loose, long hair (preferably
wet) with sexuality: the classic opposition between loose and pinned-up hair
is made in *Nostalghia*, where Eugenia's long, curly red hair is often seductively backlit, whereas Andrei's wife's hair is chastely gathered up in a bun.
In his dream of the two women embracing, Eugenia's hair too is pinned up,
suggesting his hope that she might take on some of the homely, maternal
qualities he values most deeply in a wife, but a moment later he is imagining
her leaning over him with her hair loose and dangling once more. He resists
manfully, however, even when she later lounges wantonly on his bed drying
her hair and then confronts him with heaving, naked breast and disheveled
hair, ending her tirade by telling of a patently and insultingly Freudian dream
in which "a soft worm" fell into her hair and she was unable to squash it.
Finally she gives up, concealing her hair from view with a cap before she
leaves.

Eugenia frequently performs a gesture characteristic of Tarkovsky's
women in either tossing her hair back or running her hands through it to
smooth it (this gesture becomes one of the distinguishing features of the
mother in *Mirror*, just as the hair up, hair down motif identifies which role
Margarita Terekhova is playing).[10] Though Masha wears her hair up as befits
her role as mother, she becomes dangerous and seductive (more so than the
wife Natalia ever is) when she washes it (in the first dream) and sways mysteriously, her arms flapping and her face draped in her long wet hair; she also
lets her hair down in the shower that ends the printing-house scene and is the
only (almost) nude scene in the film.

The little girl in Ivan's dream has long wet hair in the scene where they
ride in the wagon full of apples; Mary Magdalene in Roublev's *Passion* has
appropriately long, luxuriant, wavy hair; the woman who (perhaps) seduces
Roublev in the pagan rituals is long-haired (as are most of the other, mostly
nude, women in this episode); and in Hari's first appearance in *Solaris*, the
camera focuses on her gorgeously backlit golden hair (almost the only possession she has brought with her is a comb). The mother too in this film has long
hair, perhaps to facilitate the confusion of identity between her and Hari, and
to suggest the tension between her and her son. The loyal wife and mother in
Stalker, however, has short hair.

In *The Sacrifice* Adelaide wears her hair in an elaborate loose bun, yet she is neither a faithful wife nor a particularly loving mother (she gushes over the boy on her first appearance but neither talks to him nor touches him after that). Here Tarkovsky's desire to create a physical resemblance to his own wife Larissa may have been the decisive factor. The more overtly sexual daughter, Marta, has typically long, frizzy hair. Maria, who is both spiritual and sexual, at first keeps her long hair concealed beneath a scarf, but during Alexander's visit it is down. The story that Alexander tells during this scene about his sister, who cut off her "lovely golden hair" to their father's great distress, makes Tarkovsky's own ideas on this subject almost too transparent. In the original script of *Andrei Roublev*, there was to be a scene in which Russian women sacrifice their prized possession, their long hair, to pay tribute to the Tartars—an act which would have symbolized both their bravery and the powerlessness and emasculation of their men. A chilling variant of this motif is found after the Tartar raid, as the Fool plaits the hair of a dead woman. In general, these screen images and his own professed personal predilection for long hair say much about Tarkovsky's ideas of femininity.

HUMAN ARTIFACTS: FURNITURE, CLOTHES, AND HOUSES

Just as he carefully composed the many still lifes in his films, Tarkovsky scrupulously selected all the objects associated with his characters, again choosing many "real" objects from his own childhood and adult life. Even in the most haphazard of scenes, each detail has been thoroughly discussed, selected, and located within the mise-en-scène.

Recurring furnishings include elaborate lace curtains, oversized vases and jugs that are usually set on the floor, brass bedsteads, indoor plants, and musical instruments such as a piano or an organ. Bottles are both functional (to drink milk or vodka out of) and (empty, brown, and green) the occasion of some of Tarkovsky's most mysteriously beautiful and powerful images in his last three films. Candles, torches, and lamps serve both as physical and as spiritual illumination; sometimes, either as oil lamps or as electric bulbs, they threaten to malfunction or dramatically expire. Sheets, hanging out to dry (*Mirror*), spread on the ground (*Andrei Roublev*), or draped over furniture (*The Sacrifice*), are used in a context of strangeness rather than reassuring normality.

Clothing is both functional and a traditional source of information about the inner nature, social status, or self-image of the characters (see chapters 5, 6, and 8, and also chapter 3); in *Mirror* it is also an essential clue to time and place. Objects associated with characters can have both inter- and intratextual meaning: Kris, in *Solaris*, carries with him to the space station a metal box containing earth and a growing plant; Stalker's wife clutches what looks like a similar box as she pleads with her husband to stay at home and not to enter the Zone, but it is never explained: has it somehow migrated from the earlier film? During Kris's hallucinations, the box also contains coins, which appear in other dreams, in *Stalker*, *Nostalghia*, and *The Sacrifice*, usually with negative associations.

Overall caption: Mirror images.

Natalia examines herself in *Mirror*. Artificial Eye.

Kris and Hari (Natalia Bondarchuk) in *Solaris*. Contemporary Films.

The old mother in *Mirror*. Artificial Eye.

Domenico in *Nostalghia*. Artificial Eye.

Mirrors are probably the most obtrusive and emblematic of all objects, present in every film and rarely merely a normal element of the décor: the wall of a room in the narrator's "deathbed" scene in the film appropriately titled *Mirror* is covered with an impossible number, in a multitude of shapes and sizes. Although Tarkovsky often employs mirrors according to the standard visual language of both Hollywood and "art" cinema—as a convenient shorthand to express "vanity," "self-absorption," "loneliness," or "problems of identity," or to create interesting visual patterns and textures within an otherwise dull shot—he also uses them as part of a very personal network of images that is an integral element of his own distinctive film language.

The use of mirrors to suggest noncommunication between characters, seen as early as *The Steamroller and the Violin* when the boy tries vainly to persuade his mother to let him keep his appointment with the driver, is common throughout the films. It is found in the conversation between Galtsev and Ivan, as Galtsev tries vainly to persuade the boy to go to military school, and in the two lengthy conversations between Natalia and her off-screen husband, as she moves around the room coolly examining herself in a series of mirrors. Mirrors and vanity are perhaps also linked in these last two scenes, as they certainly are in the "earring" scene as the doctor's wife proudly admires her new acquisitions in not just one, but two separate mirrors.

Mirrors perhaps occur most frequently in situations where characters first become conscious of—or question—their own identity. Ivan is reflected in a mirror in the scene in which he reveals both his potential for violence and his paradoxical vulnerability as a young child, when he "plays" his bloodthirsty game of hunting and capturing Germans. Hari in *Solaris* has to undergo a painful process of acquiring and accepting an identity—not once but three times. When she first appears she studies both a photograph of herself and her reflection in the mirror, finally accepting that "it's me." She seems more sure of her identity on her next return, but after watching the video with Kris and seeing her "original" self, she becomes confused once more; looking into a mirror, she says she doesn't know herself at all: "I can't remember." This leads to a complex sequence of mirror shots, with both Kris and Hari and their reflections visible (implying that Kris too still has to discover his true identity), and then only their reflections left as both move off-screen. Kris's own identity crisis, as he slips into hallucinations later, was originally to be visualized through a room totally made up of mirrors, but only a fragment of this remains in the film.

The first black and white dream sequence of *Mirror* shows the mother as a young woman and then a mirrored image of herself as an old woman; this is less a discovery or confusion of her own identity, however, than a dreamlike distortion of the narrator's tendency to identify his mother and his wife. A similar scene occurs in *Nostalghia* when Andrei looks in a mirror and sees not his own reflection but that of his alter ego, Domenico—an image prefigured earlier in Domenico's house when Andrei is seen in the foreground with

Domenico reflected in a tarnished mirror behind him. Domenico at one point examines himself intently in this mirror, as if trying to discover who he really is, while Andrei (torn between his "Russian" and "Italian" identities) is also frequently seen reflected in mirrors. There are two moments in *Mirror* when Alexei seems to become fully aware of his identity: in the dream in which, as a child, he stands before a mirror holding a large jug of milk; and as a teenager, when he examines his reflection in the mirror in the doctor's house. In both cases some sort of sexual self-awareness seems to be implied as well. And in *The Sacrifice* Alexander is seen reflected either in a mirror (the small one beside his tape recorder or the full-length one in his room) or in the glass of the Leonardo *Adoration*, in a pattern that seems to accompany the various stages of his self-discovery. Mirrors have sometimes been thought to be able to reflect and even steal a person's soul; one of Tarkovsky's finest achievements was to rescue the image of the mirror from its pedestrian employment in most other films and restore something of its ancient magic, mystery, and even terror.

The *house* that shelters these objects, and one of the most enduring images, appears in four films—*Solaris, Mirror, Nostalghia,* and *The Sacrifice*—and is typically a wooden summer house in a rural, lightly forested setting, based on the dacha of Tarkovsky's childhood or the somewhat different one of his adult life. Although in each case the house exists in reality—whether past or present—it is most powerfully embodied in dreams, or dreamlike states. In *Solaris* it is both the real childhood home Kris takes leave of at the film's beginning and—thanks to the effect of the Solaris Ocean—his imaginary resting place, identical in almost every respect except that it is now raining inside and not outside the house. The house definitely exists in *The Sacrifice* both in the film's "normal" beginning and in the end, where we will see it burn. But depending on where one places the beginning of Alexander's "dream," much of its appearance may, in fact, not be "real": this would explain its strangely related spaces and Alexander's perplexing movements within it. In both *Mirror* and *Nostalghia* the dacha actually appears only in the narrator's dreams or memories, but so vividly as to convince us of its real existence.

In order to analyze the dacha's place and meaning in Tarkovsky's imagery, one might look to standard dream symbolism which, according to Charles Rycroft, identifies the house with "the dreamer's body, his mind, his mother's body in which he once lived, and more rarely his father's family" (91). In *Mirror*, the most autobiographical and oneiric of Tarkovsky's films, the interior of the dacha itself is very womblike: dark, but cozy, warmly lit by oil lamps and full of comfortable sturdy wooden furniture. Mother herself is closely identified with the dacha as she walks gracefully through its rooms. Lace curtains provide a nonthreatening, diaphanous transition to the outside world. (Mother's dress has lovely embroidery around the neck.) Indoor plants and oversized round vases can also be identified with her. There is a large,

Overall caption: Houses.

The dacha of *Solaris*. Contemporary Films.

The mother outside the dacha of *Mirror*. Artificial Eye.

The young Alexei tries to enter the dacha in a dream sequence in *Mirror*.
Artificial Eye.

The Russian house and family of Andrei's dreams in *Nostalghia*. Artificial Eye.

Andrei and Eugenia on the brass bed in *Nostalghia*. Artificial Eye.

ornate wrought-iron bed with fluffy pillows in which the boy sleeps and from which he dreams of a sexual encounter between the parents.

Many of these objects migrate into Tarkovsky's other films, often with similar emotional and symbolic connotations to those found here. A wrought-iron bed is shared by the whole family in *Stalker*, and is a desired conjugal bed in *Nostalghia*: when he is lying on it Andrei dreams of his wife and then imagines her floating above it. Although he dreams of Eugenia too, in waking life he resents her intrusion into this conjugal space and pointedly ignores the posture of sexual invitation in which he finds her later, ostensibly drying her hair. Lace curtains are seen in *Stalker, Solaris, Nostalghia,* and *The Sacrifice*, and the large round jugs or vases reappear in *Nostalghia*. Although we see little of the interior of the dacha in *Nostalghia*, this building, like the one in *Mirror*, is explicitly connected to the feminine and maternal: Andrei repeatedly dreams of, or imagines, his wife standing with their children outside the house, close to a pond.

In *Solaris* and *The Sacrifice*, however, one cannot so easily find the maternal/womblike associations of the other two films. The dachas themselves and the objects within them are, in fact, quite different, and the primary similarity is found only in the houses' wooden construction and rural landscape. The *Solaris* dacha is new (built as a *copy* of an older family house, as the father tells Berton) and, although it has lace curtains and indoor plants, it is also crammed with an eclectic collection of modernistic objects (such as the strange cowboy cut-out) presumably meant to portray the home of the future. Although there is a woman present (the self-effacing aunt), the home belongs to the father, and it is with his father and with himself that Kris must make his peace in the end. Nothing in this house, except the photograph, is connected to the mysterious, presumably dead mother—seen in the video in luxurious, feminine clothing and as a remote and somewhat inaccessible figure in Kris's dreams, which are set in a space that combines the dacha and the space station.

In its construction the two-story *Solaris* house is in fact similar to the dacha in *The Sacrifice*, and both are unlike the old, single-story dacha of Tarkovsky's childhood." For there is another dacha in Tarkovsky's life, the one he shared with his second wife at Myasnoye, near the city of Ryazan. In their interiors, the superficial similarities between the *Mirror* dacha and the one in *The Sacrifice* disappear upon close examination. The lace curtains are there (some hanging rather ludicrously outside), and so are the heavy furniture, pitchers of milk (which break), and bouquets of flowers (aggressively held by Adelaide). But the small, cozy, warmly lit rooms have been replaced by the large, cold room around which Adelaide strides imperiously. The floors and furniture are polished to a cool perfection. While in *Mirror* Tarkovsky's narrator, uneasy in his relationships with both wife and mother, could retreat in memory into the childhood comfort of the dacha, Alexander, his alter ego in *The Sacrifice*, unable to find solace in his nonmaternal setting, destroys it instead.

The house, in almost all these cases, is comfortable and welcoming mainly when seen in the perspective of dream or memory. The lived-in house or apartment of the present, as in *The Sacrifice* or *Mirror*, is an appropriately alien setting for the personal tensions and hostilities that take place within it. Andrei's unwillingness to adjust to the reality of the Italian world around him is reflected in the anonymity of the hotel in which he lives (its glistening floors presaging the coldly impersonal living room of *The Sacrifice*), while Stalker inhabits a run-down hovel in a world where most of the buildings are ruined or decayed (yet, paradoxically, he finds here the wifely devotion and support denied Alexander or the narrator of *Mirror*). Kris leaves home for the antiseptic space station, while Ivan has no home any longer and moves—like the peripatetic Andrei Roublev—through a landscape scarred by war and violence.

While thematic considerations account for many of the contrasts between the "good" home of the past and the "bad" or nonexistent home of the present, it is also true that Tarkovsky's imagination was powerfully drawn to ruins and debris, as much for their visual and tactile qualities as for their thematic significance. Some of the most memorable sequences in *Stalker* and *Nostalghia* languidly survey the discarded relics of modern civilization, stranded underwater, and a shot near the end of *Mirror* that exists simultaneously in the present and the past tracks slowly over the natural decay of rotting leaves and logs before settling on a silted-up well containing abandoned household goods. Ruined vehicles litter the landscapes of *Ivan's Childhood* and *Stalker* and provide a central focus for Alexander's vision of apocalypse. According to his first wife (Rausch Interview, 1989), Tarkovsky had a particular fondness for ruins, especially for the color and texture of old walls, and would point out choice specimens to her on their walks around Moscow: the results of his researches can be seen in all the films, perhaps most impressively in the rain-streaked wall at the close of the survey of Roublev's paintings and the tiled wall to which the characters inescapably return in *Stalker*.

As with all the other image clusters examined in this chapter, Tarkovsky works on multiple levels throughout: the ruins—like the houses, trees, mirrors, and rain—perform a narrative function, are visually fascinating in their own right, tell us something about the characters and the director himself, strike sympathetic chords in our own subconscious, and reinforce the thematic patterns of war, loss, cultural and spiritual decay, materialism, and memory that reverberate and interact from the beginning to the end of his career.

THIRTEEN

Life as Appearance, Life as a Dream

In much the same way that one can discern various "image clusters" and stylistic devices in Tarkovsky's work that recur from film to film, so certain basic themes established themselves early on that were to be reworked, often with significant variation, throughout his career. Kovács and Szilágyi argue that the overriding theme is a conflict between "two worlds": one external, materialistic, historical, violent, destructive, "real"; the other internal, spiritual, atemporal, peaceful, hopeful, and usually given a transcendent quality by means of dream, hallucination, or inner vision. The films are structured around this opposition between the outer world and personal consciousness, with a few individuals providing the only remaining link between the brutalized and fragmented present and the spiritual values of a largely forgotten communal past and a universal culture.

Mark Le Fanu likewise argues that, for Tarkovsky, personal, inner experience is more important than external political events, but his book misses much of the historical and cultural dimension that the Hungarian critics are better equipped to register in Tarkovsky's work. Antoine de Baecque's book covers a whole range of themes—the solitary hero; the wisdom of the child, madman, and "holy fool"; motherhood; the flaws of intellect and intellectuals; the spiritual quest; the role of dreams—but suffers from an attempt to force Tarkovsky into a far more orthodox (and even Catholic) religious framework than the films themselves ever justify. The only monograph on Tarkovsky published in the lifetime of the former Soviet Union was in Estonian, by Tatyana Elmanovits, and was little known by Russian-speaking critics. Maya Turovskaya's book, previously published in both German and English, consisting of articles written over a number of years, was published in Russia in 1992, but the bulk of Soviet (and now Russian) criticism is found mostly in reviews and relatively short articles which offer impressionistic, though often perceptive, evaluations rather than thorough comparative analyses of Tarkovsky's characters and thematics. Individual films have usually been analyzed within the artistic, social, and political contexts of the times. Heavily genre-oriented, the standard Soviet criticism tried to see *Ivan's Childhood* as a war film, *Andrei Roublev* as a historical film, *Solaris* and *Stalker* as science fiction films, and struggled with *Mirror*, which could hardly be forced into any of the existing genre categories or into the broader socialist realist mold.

Since three films (*Ivan's Childhood, Solaris,* and *Stalker*) were literary adaptations, they had to suffer interminable comparisons with the original as well—a traditional focus of Soviet film criticism. As a result, many critics ended up writing about what the films were *not* about—and what, in their opinion, they *should* have been about.

The more astute critics (Turovskaya, Zorkaya, Elmanovits, Batkin) recognized the futility of fitting Tarkovsky's films into preexisting categories and instead focused on their refreshing truthfulness and subjectivity, the originality of Tarkovsky's cinematic language, the complexity of his characters, and the films' powerful visual and emotional impact. They analyzed Tarkovsky's thematics from the point of view of insiders who belong to his generation and to his social and professional milieu. Thus they understand and explore the cultural, social, and even autobiographical thematics in his films, rather than his religious and philosophical preoccupations, which they seem to find less consistent than Western critics would like them to be.

Since we have already commented in some detail on major themes as they have appeared in individual films, here we shall identify significant "thematic clusters" (along the lines of the "image clusters" in the previous chapter) which are shared by several or all of Tarkovsky's films. We shall use them to clarify a central core of Tarkovsky's thinking and its evolution throughout his career as a whole. By "thinking" we mean here not only reasoned, independent thought but ideas shaped (whether consciously or not) by the cultural, social, and political context in which he lived, as well as by his family background, and by personal quirks, prejudices, and blind spots.

The Hero and the Quest

While some critics have recognized the repetition of visual devices and imagery, and the films' unifying philosophical concerns, others have postulated that Tarkovsky's *oeuvre* constitutes a single unified artistic whole, a "visual fugue" or a "meta-film." Dmitry Salynsky's article "Rezhissyor i mif" ("Director and Myth") is typical of the glasnost-era Soviet criticism which leaves behind sociopolitical interpretations in favor of more complex symbols and mythic archetypes. For Salynsky, Tarkovsky's films offer a "mythological model" in which the hero undertakes a journey to another world. There are four basic elements in this myth: (1) the journey itself; (2) the goal—saving the world, which he equates with immortality; (3) the hero's contact in the other world with the rulers of life and death; and (4) the offering of sacrifice and catharsis—the acceptance of sacrifice—as the path to salvation. While his construct does not hold equally well for all the films, Salynsky argues that the films themselves represent different stages in this progression: the journey predominates in the early films, *Ivan's Childhood* and *Andrei Roublev;* the "middle" group, *Solaris* and *Stalker,* focus on the contact with the nonhuman or otherworldly forces; and sacrifice is found in *Nostalghia* and *The Sacrifice.* Salynsky posits that the whole *oeuvre* thus has a complete inner plot which develops from beginning to end. It takes a great leap of Salynsky's imagination to fit *Mirror* into this construct: "the motif of sacrifice is broken up in the spiral composition of the film and embodied in the fire, each time noting the transition of heroes into a new moral state" (83). However, *Mirror* fits more easily into this structure if one sees "otherworldly forces" as the unseen evils of Stalinism, Nazism, and Maoism which haunt the hero's childhood and youth.

Salynsky's work does point to an overall theme in Tarkovsky's films: a journey or quest, which can be real and/or imagined, physical and/or spiritual. Ivan, Andrei Roublev, Kris Kelvin, Stalker, Professor, Writer, and Andrei (in *Nostalghia*) are all physically headed for some destination; all except Ivan undergo a spiritual journey as well. Ivan's tragedy (or is it his deliverance?) is that he dies unchanged. Alexei's passage is primarily through time and memory, while Alexander's spiritual journey ends physically in his running back and forth in front of the fire he has set and then in transportation to a mental asylum. Thus the journey can involve "real" space and time, as well as a passage through memory, hallucinations, or dreams. The "evil" which the hero encounters can be external and concrete (if not always actually present), especially in the early films: the Nazis in *Ivan's Childhood*, whose voices are more frightening than they themselves might have been; the brutal forces of oppression, both Russian and Tartar, in *Andrei Roublev*. But increasingly in Tarkovsky's films evil is not concrete, or personified in individuals; it is diffuse, the pervasive absence of faith and spirituality, in a world ruled and potentially destroyed by reason, science, and technology, as in *Solaris* and the last three films.

The "hero" who undertakes the quest is always a man (or a man-child) seeking an understanding of self or of his place in a wider social, spiritual, or metaphysical reality. But his journey is never just an individual personal one. The stakes in Tarkovsky's films are always high, as the hero also stands for his generation (Ivan and Alexei) or for his people (Roublev, Boriska, Andrei), or remains the last hope of humanity (Kris, Domenico, and Alexander). Yet Tarkovsky's protagonists are not active heroes who make great sacrifices to destroy evil by demolishing its perpetrators. The closest we come to this is in *Ivan's Childhood*, where the sacrifice of Ivan's (and Kholin's) lives is redeemed by Galtsev's new understanding and by the final victory of their cause; or with Boriska, who emerges victorious in his struggle against the forces of nature, the prejudices of his fellow artisans, and the threat of punishment by his rulers, and actually accomplishes something—a lasting work of beauty, the bell. Most important, he restores the faith of the "real hero," Andrei Roublev, allowing him to create even greater works of art. Roublev himself is a very passive "hero" in his own story, observing rather than acting, because, beginning with *Andrei Roublev*, the primary journey for Tarkovsky is to be an interior, spiritual one. Tarkovsky increasingly frustrates viewers who look for traditional active heroes and plots, and the transformations that take place in *Solaris* and *Stalker*, though real, are internal.

Heroes such as Roublev, Kris Kelvin, Andrei, and Alexei tend to be both passive and solitary: they retreat from, or cut themselves off from, the world around them, living in their dreams and memories and—under the stimulus of outside forces—achieving an often precarious degree of harmony and insight only at the very end of the film. Even that insight is made doubly ambiguous by often happening just before or even after their deaths (*Mirror*, *Nostalghia*) or outside their sphere of conscious knowledge or awareness (*Stalker*, *The Sacrifice*, perhaps *Solaris*) so that it is the audience, rather than the character, who benefits from it.

It is not surprising that the leading male characters are usually artists or intellectuals: Kris, Professor in *Stalker*, and Domenico are scientists or mathematicians; Roublev is a painter; Andrei in *Nostalghia* is a poet and musicologist; Alexander is a theater critic and former actor; Writer is given the name of his profession; and Stalker, though hostile to intellectuals, has a room filled with books and recites poetry with ecstatic fervor. Alexei's profession in *Mirror* is never defined, but he may well be a writer, and the poems frequently quoted in the film are central to his inner world. "Pure" science, as embodied in Kris and Professor, is assumed to be cold, arrogant, and unfeeling, and needs to be tempered by humility and compassion. Domenico has come to question the rigid formulas of his profession ("$1 + 1 = 1$"), and his speech to the indifferent crowd in Rome, however garbled and incoherent, is filled with poetic imagery, rhythms, and invocations.

The humanists and artists, however, have their own problems. Even if Roublev's retreat into silence and inactivity is understandable, it is an evasion of his responsibility to his fellow human beings and a denial of the gift granted him by God. In Writer, verbal facility has been so tainted by self-loathing that, instead of being used to enrich the experience of others, it has degenerated into barren (if witty) scorn and vituperation. Alexei, too, uses words as weapons to hurt and humiliate his wife, her lover, and even his son. Andrei denies the possibility that literature can speak across national boundaries and refuses even to look at the artistic heritage that surrounds him. His interest in Sosnovsky is largely solipsistic and seems to extend no further than in drawing parallels to justify his own melancholy and self-pity. Like Writer, Alexander despises his verbal fluency, seeing it in his case as an evasion of action, a means to avoid "doing something" about the problems that haunt his imagination. All of these characters seem, to some degree, to be descendants of the "superfluous man," the long-standing ineffectual "hero" of the nineteenth- as well as of the nonsocialist realist twentieth-century Russian literary tradition.

For Tarkovsky true art cannot exist without a moral foundation, without some higher belief or religious faith, which humanity seems to have lost, and which his heroes increasingly seek. Roublev finds his voice and becomes "active"—paints again—only after his faith in man and God has been restored.[1] The central "plot" of Tarkovsky's films was to be this search. Talking in interview about the recently released *Andrei Roublev* and the forthcoming *Solaris*, ıe showed himself eager to point out continuities in character and theme: ɔoth films dealt with "a man sustained by an idea [who] searches passionɪtely for the answer to a question and goes to the limit in his understanding ɔf reality" (*Dossier Positif* 94). In the earlier films, the end of the journey—the ɪttained understanding—is more humanist than religious: Roublev dedicates ɪis vow of silence to God, but his faith in people is restored by watching ɪuman energy, commitment, and artistic skill turned to constructive rather ·han destructive ends. The heroes of *Solaris* and *Mirror* seek atonement for ·heir earlier selfishness and egotism and realize—perhaps too late—the cenɪrality of altruistic, nonpossessive love in human experience.

Though all these characters may also suffer, as Tarkovsky puts it, from 'torment of soul" (*Sculpting* 208), it is not until *Stalker* that the issue of 'faith" as such is explicitly and insistently raised, and this becomes the domiɪating theme of the last three films. Stalker, Domenico, and Alexander all ɪesemble "holy fools," a specifically Russian cultural and literary phenomeɪon, in which spiritual insight, simple faith, and goodness are combined with ɪadness. Their seemingly insane actions—silence (Alexander) or incoherent ɪavings (Domenico)—and their destructive yet "purifying" rituals by fire are ɪttempts to stop mankind from hurtling to annihilation. We have pointed out ɪn the individual chapters on *Nostalghia* and *The Sacrifice* the problematic ɪature of these actions. Are they truly sacrifices? Is this how the journey ɪnds? It is only within the context of the characters' and Tarkovsky's own ɪaith and his increasingly apocalyptic vision of the world that these acts can ɪe seen as truly sacrificial and therefore redemptive.

Nevertheless, *Stalker*, *Nostalghia*, and *The Sacrifice* draw most of Tarkovɪky's basic ideas together in attributing the self-destructive elements in modern ɪivilization to materialism, blind reliance on technology, loss of respect for ɪature, loss of faith, and an abandonment of spiritual values that has infected ɪodern art and literature as well as daily life. The inevitable result will be the ɪhysical and moral wasteland brought about through nuclear war or (in *Stalker* ɪnd, by implication, *Solaris*) the mindless poisoning of the natural environment ɪn which we depend for our survival. War reverberates throughout Tarkovɪky's films: in *Ivan's Childhood* it is inescapable, treated in a rather orthodox ɪway as a just and necessary defense against brutal invaders, with Galtsev exɪpressing the pious hope at the end that no further wars of this kind will ever ɪccur. Patriotism is strong in *Andrei Roublev* too: the Tartars are ruthless, sadisɪtic intruders who profit from the disunity and mindless self-seeking of the Russians (both rulers and ruled). *Mirror* traces, without overt commentary, the ɪwars and conflicts of the director's own lifetime, with the unspoken warning ɪhat the hydrogen bomb has—or should have—made war redundant as a ɪmeans of solving problems between nations. This theme is made explicit in Alexander's anguished appeal to God to spare humanity the impending catasɪtrophe: "Because this war is the ultimate war. . . . And after it, there will be no victors and vanquished, no cities or towns, no birds in the sky or water in the ɪwells." Tarkovsky's own voice is clearly heard here.

Beginning with *Stalker* and increasingly in *Nostalghia* and *The Sacrifice* Tarkovsky moves toward the "tendentiousness" that he previously found objectionable in the work of an artist such as Raphael (*Sculpting* 109). Stalker Domenico, and Alexander all "preach" to a greater or lesser degree, even if like Alexander, they simultaneously reproach themselves for doing so. For the most part *Stalker,* where the journey is both real and allegorical, physical and spiritual, manages to maintain an overall unity between words and images; and even if the philosophical meditations may sometimes sound unconvincing, the accompanying powerful visual imagery rescues this film, and *Nostalghia* to a lesser degree, from occasionally sounding trite. This is less true of *The Sacrifice,* where Tarkovsky's apparent need to speak directly to the viewer through Alexander creates rather more imbalance between the visual and verbal texts, though the film's finest moments—visually splendid and largely silent—remain unforgettable. Especially in these films, it is the portrayal of the inner journey itself, rather than the increasingly pessimistic vision as to where it will end, that is most striking.

The Inner Journey through the Time-Space Continuum

The complex structure of *Mirror*—moving freely backwards and forwards in time over a period of some forty years and cutting unexpectedly between dream, memory, and waking reality—can be paralleled in much Western cinema of the 1960s and 1970s, perhaps most obviously in the work of Alain Resnais. Yet, while the overall structure is somewhat reminiscent of *Providence* (a bedridden narrator attempting to relive and make sense of his past life and his relationships with his family), Tarkovsky's use of memory is comparatively straightforward when set against the kind of experimentation carried out by Resnais and other Western directors. Tarkovsky does not use disorienting flash cuts that chop memories up into disconnected segments nor does he create "false" memories that offer different versions of past events or, consciously or unconsciously, distort them to suit the character's current wishes or preconceptions. Likewise, there are no "flash-forwards," as in Resnais' *La Guerre est Finie,* where a character speculates on, or imagines, what *might* happen to him in the future.[2]

The memories in the film (as opposed to the dreams) follow a linear pattern that corresponds to the chronological arrangement of the documentary material: the mother sitting on the fence and the printing-house sequence are set in the late 1930s; the shooting-range scene occurs during the war, as do the brief return of the father and the scene in which the mother tries to sell her earrings. Within each scene space and time operate in a coherent and logical fashion to create an understandable sequence of events; the only real "problem" is to identify who is "remembering" in the first two instances, where Alyosha is either asleep (the fence scene) or not present (the printing house). While Maya

Turovskaya is correct to identify an "individual stream of time" (87) in this film, it results less from the relatively conventional handling of the flashbacks than from the intermingling of memory, dream, and present and past historical reality in ways that begin to question the borderlines between them.

Although this use of "inner time" is most obvious in *Mirror*, it exists in at least potential form in most of the earlier films. The main action of *Ivan's Childhood* seems to take place over a couple of days, followed by a jump to the ending of the war, but it is subjectively lengthened by means of Ivan's dreams. The chronological action of *Andrei Roublev* spans twenty-three years, but, with the exception of "The Bell," each episode has a duration of only a few hours and occurs essentially within a single space, though "The Last Judgment" is subjectively extended by means of Andrei's memory/recreation of the blinding of the stonemasons. Each marks a stage in an inner journey rather than a progression through a clearly defined exterior landscape (the vagueness as to the location of many of the episodes serves only to heighten this subjectivity). *Solaris* takes place over one day and night on Earth and an undefined period on the space station that *seems* to be no longer than a few days; it also includes a doubtless lengthy journey through space that is compressed into a few moments of subjective time. We are given few time clues other than scenes of Kris asleep and one specific mention that it is nighttime; the frequent cuts to the Solaris Ocean do not, as they would in a conventional science fiction film, help us judge the passing of time and serve mainly to punctuate and accentuate Kris's inner anguish. Instead, the chronology of the film is divided up into blocks of *space* that we assume occur at unspecified intervals of time—i.e., shifts in time are signaled mainly by changes of location, with virtually no clues offered as to the elapsed time between each change—and at the end of the film, both time and space become meaningless as ways of judging how far, and where, Kris's internal voyage has taken him.

Mirror covers a historical chronology of some forty years within a subjective framework that could be a matter of days, hours, or even minutes, depending on whether one includes the present-day scenes with Natalia as being part of the external or the internal chronology: are we to see the phone call to the narrator's mother, the scene with the Spaniards, Ignat's reading of the Pushkin letter, and Natalia and Alexei's discussion of Ignat as a process that culminates in the narrator's illness and possible death? Or are these scenes also memories from a time perspective that is situated in the narrator's final moments? It is *Stalker*, however, in picking up and extending to its logical limit the use of space *as* time previously seen in *Solaris*—collapsing both of them into a continual and eternal present—that provides Tarkovsky's most original and provocative handling of time. In *Stalker* time exists only to the extent that it is coterminous with the space traversed by the characters; beyond that there is literally no means of judging or assessing it. The extensive use of the long take, which traps us within the protagonists' subjectivity, is particularly important in removing any external guidelines beyond their own immediate perception.[3]

Nostalghia combines the methods of the previous two films, taking us into Andrei's internal world where past and present, Russia and Italy, literally coexist and infringe on one another (his wife is "present" in his Italian hotel bedroom, as is his dog) and our only means of judging the passing of time is to see the characters in different spaces. Time and space are abolished as distinct entities, not only (as in *Solaris* and *Mirror*) in the final shot, but in the preceding sequence in which Andrei, in St. Catherine's Pool, "continues" and completes the action begun by Domenico miles away in Rome. *Stalker* and *Nostalghia* take us into a "dreamscape" as much as into a landscape, and much the same is true of *The Sacrifice*, despite the apparent precision of its setting (Alexander's house and its immediate environment and—perhaps—Maria's cottage) and its time scheme (a day, a night, and the following morning). If the major action of the film is no more than a dream, then time and space in the film are largely imagined, and if Alexander's vow has in fact been answered by God, then time and space have literally been obliterated and replaced by a new sequence of events—not just within the film's immediate location, but everywhere else in the world as well.

The Uses of Dreaming

In a diary entry for January 26, 1973 (*TWT* 66), Tarkovsky distinguishes between "two kinds of dreams. In the first, the dreamer can direct the events of the dream as if by magic. He is master of everything that happens or is going to happen. He is a demiurge. In the second, the dreamer has no say, he is passive, he suffers from the violence done him and from his inability to protect himself." He recorded several of his dreams in his diary (e.g., 95–96) and clearly believed that dreams have meaning ("We need . . . to see all the elements of reality which were refracted in that layer of the consciousness which kept vigil throughout the night": *Sculpting* 72) and that film could convey something of that meaning to a viewer.

The dreams in his films, as has been suggested earlier when discussing their place in the narrative structure, sometimes "explain" the character's waking behavior in a relatively straightforward manner (as in *Ivan's Childhood* and *Nostalghia*), sometimes suggest or hint at reasons for his dissatisfaction with his present state (as in *Mirror* or *Solaris*), and sometimes create an oneiric atmosphere that seeps into and pervades what would otherwise be waking reality, making it virtually impossible to distinguish one from the other (as in *Stalker* or *The Sacrifice*).

Tarkovsky's neat division of dreams into "two kinds," however, is rather simplistic and does not adequately account even for the various kinds of dreams within his own films. We are very seldom offered situations in which the dreamer is in control of events: almost the only examples are Ivan's dream of the little girl, the apples, and the horses (the only one of his dreams that does not end in death); the two color dreams in *Mirror* (of the child "happy" in the warm, comfortable house, yet knowing that he is dreaming and will have to wake up; and of him paddling across the pond toward his mother); and (possibly) some of Andrei's dreams in *Nostalghia* of his home, wife, and children. Yet not all of this last group are dreams, in the sense that they are preceded by the character going to sleep: the credit sequence, which introduces the imagery of all the other "dreams" of home, is never identified as a dream, and it may be more appropriate to talk of "reveries" or "waking dreams" to describe these (despite the coding of black and white and the sounds of trickling water and barking dogs), for they are mostly cut into the middle of everyday waking action and conversation. In any case none of these dreams/memories/reveries really suggests the controlling position of the dreamer: he is never present in them himself and they always take place *outside* the house, leaving him doubly alienated from the fulfillment and reunion he desires.

Almost all the dreams in the films fall into Tarkovsky's second category of passivity and suffering, and can be further subdivided into what both Charles Rycroft and Robert T. Eberwein call "traumatic" and "anxious" dreams. Ivan's dreams—of his mother's death—are clearly traumatic; Kris's dream in which he attempts to placate his mother in *Solaris* is an anxiety dream, as are most of the black and white dreams in *Mirror*, where the child is generally lost and alone, surrounded by emptiness and strangeness, and confronted by a melancholy or almost unrecognizable mother. The printing-house scene, though it is not identified as a dream and has a coherent narrative structure, nevertheless includes most of the characteristics of an anxiety dream, including Lisa's sudden and inexplicable hostility. The scene in *The Sacrifice* that is most obviously a dream—when Alexander, having made his vow, seems to fall asleep on the sofa and sees himself in a snowy landscape—is again an anxiety dream, as he tries vainly to find his barefooted child and the sounds signaling the approaching war are heard. His apocalyptic visions of nuclear disaster, however, are not preceded by sleep, though the first may occur in a state of semiconsciousness, and the second is *followed* by awakening.

One dream in *Nostalghia*—of Andrei seeing Domenico's reflection instead of his own in the wardrobe mirror—falls into the category that Eberwein calls "proleptic" or foreshadowing: Andrei will "become" Domenico and complete the other man's task for him. Yet again its status as "dream" is problematic, even though Andrei is seen lying down (at the edge of the flooded building) and may be assumed to be at least half-asleep; it is also preceded (the conversation with Angela) and followed (his walk through the ruined cathedral with voice-over courtesy of God and St. Catherine) by scenes that are clearly "dreamlike" and may even be considered—like Alexander's dream above—as a dream or reverie within a larger dream.

Three other dreams fall into the category popularly known as "wish-fulfillment": Andrei's dream of his wife and Eugenia embracing, and the closing scenes of *Mirror* and *Nostalghia*, in which the conflicts and oppositions shown throughout the films are temporarily reconciled. Yet these (like the last "dream" of *Ivan's Childhood*) occur after the presumed dreamer has (or—in *Mirror*—may have) died: who, then, is dreaming them? Ivan's "dream," in fact, even though it shares the imagery of the other dreams, is presented much more like a straightforward memory and has little specifically "dreamlike" about it apart from a couple of spatial or temporal ellipses involving a tree and the other children. Is it his last memory of happiness before he is hanged by the Germans, with the blackness that ends it representing his death? Is it "dreamed" by the audience on Ivan's behalf? Or is it, perhaps like the credit sequence and final shot of *Nostalghia* and the last scene of *Mirror*, less a dream than a means of bringing together or introducing, for narrative purposes, the main thematic material of the film—in which case its "logic" is irrelevant?

The more one investigates the dreams, in fact, the harder it becomes to distinguish between "dream," "reverie," "hallucination," and "dreamlike memory," especially in the later films, and even unambiguously to identify the dreamer. What is the status, for example, of the scenes showing the release of Domenico's family from the imprisonment he has imposed upon them, which simultaneously display characteristics of documentary realism and the dream? They are cued in by a close-up of Domenico's distraught face and thus seem to be his memories, yet they are also signaled as dreamlike by the buzz-saw, the nonnaturalistic sound, the alternations between black and white and color, and slow motion. They also step outside the narrative logic of the film, which is otherwise concerned exclusively with Andrei's mind (a feature they share with some of the dreams and memories of *Mirror*, which cannot always be attributed to the film's narrator).[4]

What matters, perhaps, is less to be able to rationalize these apparent contradictions than to recognize an "oneiric space" within the films that can be entered into by both characters and audience. It possesses certain recurring characteristics, in terms of both sound and image, and it has "meaning"; its boundaries, however, are flexible and porous and not always easy to distinguish. The most extensive attempt to define this "oneiric space" in Tarkovsky has been made by Vlada Petrić in his article "Tarkovsky's Dream Imagery" and, in a more general way, in his introduction to the collection of essays *Film and Dreams*.

In the latter work, Petrić lists "some of the most effective cinematic techniques which can enhance the oneiric impact of a film and stimulate the neural activities similar to those occurring during dreaming" (*Film and Dreams* 23). Several of these (dynamic montage and special photographic effects) are deliberately eschewed by Tarkovsky, but he resorts, at some time or another, to almost all the others: "camera movement through space [contributing to] a kinesthetic sensation"; "illogical and paradoxical combinations of objects, characters and settings"; "dissolution of spatial and temporal continuity"; "ontological authenticity of motion picture photography [which] compels the viewers to accept even the most illogical events . . . as real"; and "sight and sound counterpoint, including color juxtaposition [which] emphasizes the unusual appearance of dream imagery" (23–24). All of these effects have been illustrated and commented on in the analyses of individual films and in the chapter on style; the point to be made here is that, especially in Tarkovsky's later films, they are no longer coded exclusively as *dreams* and eventually serve to throw a dreamlike aura over virtually the whole film. Petrić's later article, concentrating on *Mirror* and *Stalker*, usefully applies some of these concepts to particular scenes in the films and should be consulted by readers who wish to look at some of our own analyses from a somewhat different perspective.[5]

If it is ultimately the fact that Tarkovsky creates "dream films" that is one of his finest achievements as a filmmaker, it is nevertheless worth looking briefly at the content of some of the dreams and the means by which it is conveyed. Charles Rycroft suggests that "by conjuring up evocative imagery and relating the particular images evoked to one another spatially as well as temporally . . . dreams tend to resemble moving pictures more than they resemble literary texts," but also points out that most dream imagery is intensely private and almost impossible to describe or convey successfully to another person (46). This need not worry dreamers, but it does present a problem for a film director who wishes *both* to convey an authentic dream atmosphere *and* to suggest that these dreams have meaning beyond the private experience of the dreamer. Most directors get around this problem by either employing the standard Freudian or Jungian variants of dream imagery and analysis (thus making them generally "understandable") or using dreams as psychoanalytic therapy for the characters and an "explanation" of their behavior.

Though Tarkovsky does resort to the use of transparently Freudian imagery at times and, especially in *Ivan's Childhood* and *Nostalghia*, uses dreams/memories/reveries to provide a narrative explanation for his characters' state of mind, his most original accomplishment in this respect is to use the dreams in his films in the way in which dreamers themselves use them: "to discover information about the dreamer [*and*, we would add, *the viewer*] of which he himself, by reason of repression or alienation, is unaware" (Rycroft 57). He uses both "transient, private images which derive their meaning from their relations within the total structure that constitutes the dream" (63) and "symbols which are part of the shared iconography of the culture of which [he] is a member, and which, therefore, carry a heavy charge of shared public associations and resonances" (165). Like certain poets and writers he displays "an exceptional sensitivity and receptivity to the symbolic, iconic network that constitutes the culture he inhabits, which makes it natural for him to express his private emotions in universal terms" (166).

Dreams are central to Tarkovsky's imaginative achievement because they bypass all that he felt was most inhibiting and destructive in the contemporary world—the scientific rationalism, the materialism, and the mindless faith in technology that he and his favored characters reject—and speak directly to what is both most private and most universal within us. His greatness, as Bergman recognized, was his ability to find the language through which we might "discover information" about ourselves and our truest needs, of which we might otherwise "by reason of repression or alienation" remain unaware.

All Unhappy Families Are Alike

Tarkovsky uses dreams or dreamlike states to trace an inner journey he often shares, to a greater or lesser degree, with his heroes. Identifiable autobiographical elements appear from his earliest work, though they are often used to create a kind of pseudo-autobiography, allowing the viewers to share only partially the complex and passionate world of his emotions. Having discovered an effective means of sharing his subjective, innermost feelings with the viewer (especially in *Mirror*), he may have been frightened of what he saw within himself through the camera's lens, and thus censored both the dreams and the reality. Nevertheless, it is to his credit that he persisted in exposing, if only partially, a tortuous web of family relations with which his viewers both at home and abroad could identify.

With the exception of *Andrei Roublev*, family relations (including, but not limited to, mother/son, father/son, husband/wife) create much of the narrative and psychological tension in Tarkovsky's films. The mother-son relationship is of particular significance in *The Steamroller and the Violin*, *Ivan's Childhood*, *Solaris*, and *Mirror* (where it is found in both Masha/Alyosha and Natalia/Ignat). In *Steamroller* the mother is a rather unemotional disciplinarian; she is not unkind or unloving, she just cannot enter her son's emotional world and, as Tarkovsky's own mother had done, sees it as her task to mold his interests and abilities. Only in *Ivan* is the mother totally idealized, her love freely and unreservedly given—but she appears solely in Ivan's dreams. In *Solaris* and *Mirror*, although she is loved, the mother is often inhibiting or remote, and the son (whether child or adult) seems to feel guilt and the need for absolution. The father is usually absent or dead (*Steamroller, Ivan, Mirror*): Ivan has no dreams about his father, and of the two fathers in *Mirror*, Alyosha's makes only a brief, though affectionate, appearance, and Alyosha himself, as the adult narrator Alexei, is alienated from his son, Ignat, who becomes a weapon in his battles with his wife. The father in *Solaris*, for once, is given equal importance with the mother, though here too the relationship is tense and difficult. In all these cases the parents tend to be seen from the viewpoint of the son (Tarkovsky?) and are judged according to the degree to which they satisfy his emotional needs; although at least two "sister" figures appear, in *Ivan's Childhood* and in *Mirror*, they are almost totally insignificant, and their relationship with the mother is nonexistent. (No wonder Tarkovsky and his sister had an extremely uncomfortable adult relationship!)

In *The Sacrifice* the situation is reversed, and the father (and also the director?) projects his own psychological malaise onto the child. Here, unusually, we see from the father's perspective rather than the son's, and on the surface, this is the most mutually affectionate family relationship in all the films (apart, perhaps, from Ivan's dreams of his mother); yet it is not until the very last scene that the boy gives any sign of having understood, or even listened to, all that his father has been telling him. It is noteworthy too that Adelaide's role as mother in this film is relatively insignificant, as she is too self-absorbed to give the child any attention. Considering the already noted obvious parallels with Tarkovsky's second wife, Larissa, this is not a very flattering family portrait.

The somewhat ambiguous evidence of *Mirror* to the contrary, childhood is rarely a time of unalloyed happiness for Tarkovsky: this is most obvious for Ivan, but the other children (and not just those at the center of attention—Domenico's, for example) are generally at the mercy of the arbitrary whims and decisions of their parents or of a violent and disordered world. Their lives are threatened by war, hunger, pollution, nuclear disaster, and technology gone berserk; their predominant characteristics are loneliness, frustration, deprivation, and grief. It is little wonder that so many of them are psychologically or physically crippled, wounded, or maimed—Ivan, the "Fool" in *Roublev* (who is mentally a child), Stalker's daughter, Little Man—or bear at least an emblematic sore on their lips. Again Tarkovsky's own childhood, defined psychologically (for the parents at least) by the Stalinist purges and followed by the physical hardships of World War II, must find its reflection here. Where was he to find the stability that every child needs?

Women, for Tarkovsky, are seen primarily in relationship to their families and to the men (husbands, lovers, sons) in their lives; they function mainly as mothers and as wives, and must meet certain criteria of loyal and dutiful subordination to the needs of their husbands and children in both capacities. Ivan's mother, being safely dead, and "frozen" in Ivan's memory, can stand as the embodiment of perfect maternal love and caring. Much the same is true of Andrei's wife in *Nostalghia*, who is seen only in idealized memory. Kris's loving wife (or mate) is probably the only totally positive "living" female, but the real-life Hari—hysterical and suicidal—is of course dead, and Kris falls in love with an ideal replica of his own making. No wonder she is so totally meek, loving, and devoted, and this—as a skeptic might observe—to a man who drove her to suicide! As this surrogate Hari learns to think and feel, i.e., becomes human, she rejects the original Hari in herself, denying her weak human side. One might say that Kris's (and Tarkovsky's?) misogynist thought projections have done their work all too well. Only an ideal replica of a woman is able to do what no earthly female could: to humanize Kris and his shipmates on the space station.

Provided they fulfill satisfactorily their destined wife/mother role, women offer, in most of the films, a stable moral or emotional center which the men have either lost or neglected, or toward which they finally move. This is particularly true of Ivan's mother, Hari, Stalker's wife, Andrei's wife (*Nostalghia*), and Maria, who, though in reality neither wife nor mother, is more of a "true"

Overall caption: A montage of mothers.

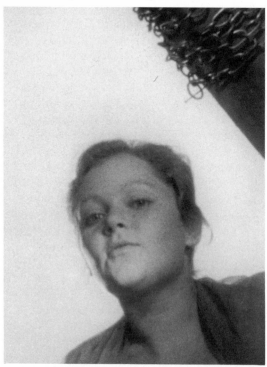

Ivan's mother (Irma Rausch) in *Ivan's Childhood*. Artificial Eye.

Kris's mother in *Solaris*. Contemporary Films.

The narrator's mother (Margarita Terekhova as Masha) in *Mirror*. Artificial Eye.

wife to Alexander than Adelaide and comforts him as if he were a child. Masha represents a lost stability in *Mirror*, and the Fool, in her final appearance at least—which coincides with Roublev's decision to resume his artistic calling—seems to have regained an emotional and psychological serenity that matches his renewed faith. (In the original script she was supposed to be transformed and become "normal" after giving birth.) The whole concept is crystallized most clearly in the calm and radiant beauty of Piero's *Madonna of Childbirth*, whose closest physical and moral analogue in *Nostalghia* is Andrei's "dream" wife—in sharp contrast to the worldly and sexually enticing Eugenia; or the sexually ambiguous angels of Roublev's *Trinity*, whose features seem more feminine than masculine.

Living or physically present women are problematic for Tarkovsky; as noted above, they are not always satisfactory mothers, and as wives they are sometimes in competition with their husbands for the affection of their children—Masha and Natalia in *Mirror*, and possibly Adelaide in *The Sacrifice*. Female sexuality—when its function is not procreative—seems to be a threat in Tarkovsky's world, and where it is shown positively it is generally displaced into the metaphoric form of levitation in *Solaris* and *Mirror* (where the body literally rises above its earthly self), in *Nostalghia* (where it is associated also with pregnancy), and in *The Sacrifice* (where Maria behaves more like a mother calming a frightened child than a lover). Negative sexuality takes the form of the ugly competition between Adelaide and her daughter for Victor's favors; Eugenia's purely physical and nonspiritual interest in Andrei; the Fool's desertion of Roublev to become a Tartar's wife; Natalia's cool detachment and sexual self-possession in *Mirror*; and the unseemly hysterical writhings of Hari, Adelaide, and Stalker's wife (though the last named emerges, nevertheless, as the most positive wife-mother figure in all the films).

By idealizing women and focusing on their special power to offer emotional and physical comfort to the distraught and suffering heroes (Ivan's mother, Hari, Stalker's wife, Maria, Alexei's wife in memory and dream) and on their miraculous child-bearing ability—both unattainable to men—Tarkovsky does not allow woman a normal range of thoughts and feelings. In his world (on the screen and off) women do not change, but are rather caught in an emotional and physiological time warp, playing out their biologically programmed roles. It is also precisely this openly subjective and personal (masculine?) vision which Tarkovsky projects on the screen that explains the almost total absence of women as equals and fellow travelers on the inner journeys of his heroes. Men alone occupy the world of ideas and higher spirituality. (As noted in connection with *Nostalghia*, Tarkovsky saw creativity as man's domain, and "subordination and humility for the sake of love" as woman's: *Martyrolog* 133.) In Tarkovsky's world the women are incapable of—or perhaps also do not need—the spiritual transformation which his men undergo. Theirs is a self-contained, at times mysterious, but basically unchanging physical and emotional universe which ideally should—but often fails to—provide a support system for the men.

Overall caption: "Hysterical" women.

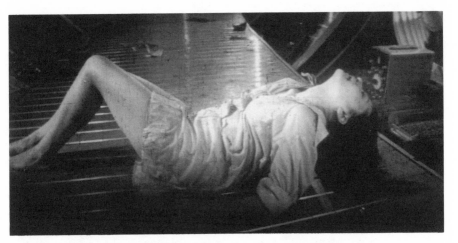

One of Hari's "resurrections" in *Solaris*. Contemporary Films.

Stalker's wife (Alyssa Freindlikh). Contemporary Films.

While in the mother/son or parent/child relationship emotional closeness is still possible for Tarkovsky, there is little real communication or affection between adult men and women. The only exceptions again are Hari (a non-human) and Kris, and Stalker and his wife—though the latter treats him like a child who needs comfort and protection and (with good justification) is somewhat hysterical in her wifely role. Although Stalker's wife is not even named in the film, her supportive role is imbued with genuine feeling, and she remains one of Tarkovsky's most positive creations. In the last two films "normal" male/female relationships seem no longer feasible, and woman's love and self-sacrificing devotion are either totally absent or, as with Alexander's nighttime encounter with Maria in *The Sacrifice*, presented metaphorically—though here the encounter is an unconvincing embodiment of Tarkovsky's statement concerning *Stalker* that "human love alone is—miraculously—proof against the blunt assertion that there is no hope for the world" (*Sculpting* 199).

From the very beginning in Tarkovsky's films, most of the intellectual and spiritual communion—and even affection—is between men: in *Ivan's Childhood*, *Andrei Roublev*, *Nostalghia*, *The Sacrifice*, and even *Stalker* and *Solaris*. (In *Mirror* the adult world is marked by an absence of and a longing for intimacy.) Is Tarkovsky just a product of a very patriarchal society, or do we find here more than just typical male bonding? With the doubling of the wife/mother in *Mirror* Tarkovsky seemed to have encouraged his viewers to make a simple Freudian analysis of his relations with women; was he trying, consciously or not, to distract the viewers from a psychological examination of a more complex sexual identity? While most of the other facts of his private life were well known to insiders, his apparent bisexuality is only now being quietly discussed. Was this the "deep, dark evil" that tormented him (Rerberg Interview), that he could not share with anyone in the extremely homophobic Soviet society? Or what, for example, are we to make of the voluptuous young girl with luxurious red hair who wanders enigmatically through *Solaris* and *Mirror*? While the sexuality of adult women is presented generally in a negative light (with the already noted exception of the nonhuman Hari), it is somewhat disturbing that the young girl's precocious sexuality is not similarly portrayed. Is it moreover significant that she is played by Tarkovsky's real-life stepdaughter (a redhead) and that Tarkovsky's favorite hair color was red? His friend and early collaborator Andrei Konchalovsky noted that Tarkovsky moved away from exploring their shared interest in "the emotional nature of cinema and its eroticism" (*O Tarkovskom* 229). Did he do so because of his increasingly intellectual and spiritual preoccupations or because of a deep personal discomfort with the confusing and dangerous world of his own sexuality?

It might be worth noting here a current, widely discussed topic both in the former Soviet Union and in the West—the "emasculation" of men by the Soviet system and the deformation of "normal" male-female relations. While we have shied away from interpreting Tarkovsky's films as political allegories, this deeper psycho-political undercurrent may in fact be present throughout Tarkovsky's films. Tarkovsky's adult male heroes tend to become increasingly asexual or even possess "feminine" characteristics: Roublev is sensitive, soft-spoken, and even if he does "fall" in the pagan scene, it is a "sin" that is never repeated. Stalker looks like an ex-convict, yet cries like a woman. Andrei's thin frame is hidden behind layers of clothing and protected by the warm coat he wears even indoors to shield him from the intrusion of real life and the beauty of a living woman. The helpless, cuckolded Alexander, who wears his wife's shawl, seems long ago to have lost any interest in her; when he begs a "witch" to sleep with him and thus save the world, their encounter is conspicuously devoid of sensuality. It is indeed ironic and even confusing for Tarkovsky's viewers that the sexual intimacy which he had previously avoided, ignored, or condemned in his films is now given a lofty, life-affirming role. But it is still devoid of all eroticism.

Yet, despite Konchalovsky's statement, Tarkovsky does explore the "erotic" nature of cinema, though not through the human relations which he seems to find so threatening; his heroes are instead surrounded by the tactile, even erotic beauty of a lush, fertile nature. Andrei Roublev watches helplessly as naked pagan couples sink into the welcoming tall grass, and he himself is so scratched by tree branches that his companions, and the viewer, suspect that he too succumbed. The water weeds in the opening of *Solaris* and the tall grass and bushes in *Mirror* undulate or sway sensuously. Perhaps the best example of the transference that takes place in Tarkovsky's films is found in *Stalker*. Stalker has no loving gesture for his wife, but instead has an intense sensual experience as he communes with the Zone: he falls to his knees and then lies prone, his face buried in the lush green grass. He speaks passionately of the Zone (a feminine noun in Russian) as if "she" were a woman—mysterious, life-giving, able to satisfy man's every wish. Tarkovsky's increasing asceticism in the last two films is reflected not only in his treatment of the male/female relationship, but also in his depiction of nature. He subtly strips it of its fecund beauty by draining it of color and polluting it with the debris of past and present civilizations, and he also increasingly drowns it in water—not the refreshing, life-giving rain of earlier films but muddy, stagnant, "dead" water. The dead tree which Alexander and later his son attempt to revive is likewise symbolic in the very absence of its leaves; its spare beauty is perhaps the best analogy for Tarkovsky's own strivings to reach a higher, more austere spirituality by denying the flesh and totally suppressing the life-giving forces around him. Thus paradoxically the barren tree—a metaphor for death in Tarkovsky's first film—has been transformed into a symbol of renewed life through faith alone (first the father's and then the son's) and outside the human and natural realms ruled by the feminine principle. In Tarkovsky's and his heroes' increasingly religious quest, there is no room for real, living women (Maria is a "witch," Andrei's wife is a "vision"), and Piero della Francesca's *Madonna of Childbirth* remains the unattainable ideal.

A Dialogue with Art

Although Tarkovsky argued in the first chapter of *Sculpting in Time* that "as it develops, the cinema will, I think, move further away not only from literature but also from other adjacent art forms, and thus become more and more autonomous" (22), his films are, of course, full of references to and quotations from literature, painting, and music—so much so that art itself becomes an underlying and unifying theme in Tarkovsky's work. Despite his expressed opposition in that same chapter to adaptations of literary "master-pieces," he spent much of his time during the 1970s vainly trying to film Dostoyevsky's *The Idiot,* and one of his last planned projects before his death was *Hamlet.* Besides this, his diary entries from 1970 onwards record, again and again, a desire to film, among many others, Thomas Mann's *Doctor Faustus, Joseph and his Brothers,* and *The Magic Mountain,* Tolstoy's *The Death of Ivan Ilyich,* Bulgakov's *The Master and Margarita,* and yet more Dostoyevsky, including *Crime and Punishment* and *The Devils* (see, for example, TWT 153 and 211). His readiness to test himself against such obvious "masters" suggests not only a change from his earlier position (this chapter of the book dates, in its essentials, from 1964) but a growing confidence in film as a self-sufficient art that can now begin to challenge the older art forms. His plans for *The Idiot* and *Hamlet* treated them as raw material for radical reshaping rather than already "perfect" works to be treated with slavish admiration and fidelity: the story of *The Idiot* was to be told twice, once from Myshkin's point of view and once from Rogozhin's, and *Hamlet* was to be virtually silent, with only a few lines of dialogue.

The relationship between Tarkovsky's films and the other arts is thus a complex one that goes far beyond the explicit "quotations" that we have drawn attention to in writing about specific films. In many cases there is a temperamental, stylistic, or intellectual affinity—with such favorites as Bach, Beethoven, Leonardo da Vinci, Pieter Brueghel the Elder, Dostoyevsky, Tolstoy, Ingmar Bergman, or Robert Bresson—that shapes his concept of film as an art and its (for him, still largely unrealized) potential. His tastes in literature, painting, and music (as in film) were largely limited to a handful of recognized European "classics," and on occasion these seem to be used mainly as a prop to give aesthetic and intellectual respectability to a still-"suspect" art form (the composer Eduard Artemyev suggested in interview that this may have been a major reason for his extensive use of classical music); or to contrast past and present, the human and the alien, the spiritual and the materialistic. Yet visual or verbal references to other arts also serve a thematic function as part of a continuing "dialogue" through which Tarkovsky attempted to examine the strengths and weaknesses of his chosen medium and to communicate the timeless beauty and mystery of art. Although he rejected the common view of film as a "synthesis" of the other arts, rather than excluding them from his work, he preferred to test himself against them, working from the assumption that the filmmaker was—or could be—a valid artist in his own right.

Tarkovsky and the Visual Arts

Tarkovsky writes at some length about his favorite painters in *Sculpting in Time*, and he "quotes" them frequently in his films. Leonardo da Vinci is most frequently referred to in both book and film, with Pieter Brueghel the Elder second in terms of visual allusion or influence, though Tarkovsky makes no attempt to analyze his work in *Sculpting*, as he does with Leonardo. His feelings about Brueghel, however, seem to be displaced into his enthusiastic discussion of Carpaccio (50), whose work is never actually shown in any of the films. The qualities Tarkovsky admired in Carpaccio—his use of space and composition—are largely found in Brueghel as well: "The point is that *each* of the characters in Carpaccio's crowded composition is a center. . . . As you gaze at Carpaccio's canvas your will follows, meekly and unwittingly, the logical channel of feeling intended by the artist, wandering first to one figure apparently lost in the crowd and then on to the next" (50). Art critics emphasize this type of composition in Brueghel's work, in such paintings as *The Conversion of St. Paul* and *The Procession to Calvary*: "In Bruegel there is no balletic framework, only the disparate motion of created things pursuing their own destiny" (Hollander 96); "as if to show that most people are unaware or don't care, Bruegel has filled the panel [of *Calvary*] with hundreds of humans engaged in manifold everyday actions and activities" (Klein and Klein 151).

Brueghel's paintings are shown at greatest length in *Solaris*, where the library is decorated with five almost full-size reproductions, mostly from the series of the *Seasons*, though *The Tower of Babel* is also there.' The landscapes of course "bring" Earth into the sterile environment of the space station, and one of the most famous, *Hunters in the Snow*, is explored in great detail during the levitation of Kris and Hari. Apart from containing many of Tarkovsky's own favorite images—trees, birds, dogs, and snow among them—the filming of this sequence demonstrates Tarkovsky's, perhaps instinctive, sensitivity to what Anne Hollander identifies as the specifically "movielike" quality of Brueghel's art: "These pictures have another unity, a sweep and coherence of motion that is like the movie camera's kind of scan" (97). Discussing the reasons for Brueghel's renewed and widespread popularity in our own century, she adds: "We are primed to respond to those breathing landscapes that offer the shifting, subjective view of central events that only movies now employ" (98).

The Brueghel-like "Russian Calvary" in *Andrei Roublev*. Artificial Eye.

Although Tarkovsky shunned imitation of actual paintings or painterly effects in his films, at least two sequences in his work have commonly been identified as "Brueghel-like": the children playing in the snow in *Mirror* (in the wartime scene with the orphan Afasyev) and the "Russian Calvary" in *Andrei Roublev*. In the *Roublev* scene Tarkovsky again shows himself to be inwardly tuned to what is most deeply original in the artist's work: Brueghel's religious and mythological paintings "obliterate the old format for the holy subjects and create a modern subject, the internalization of sacred themes in common experience" (Hollander 97). Another critic writes: "In Brueghel's imagination, Bible subjects become intensely real; he sees the events of the Bible as scenes of exuberant peasant life. . . . Only holy personages appear in a sort of idealized costume; the others wear contemporary dress" (Glück 5).

Brueghel's works are often accused of indulging in cruelty, as was Tarkovsky in *Andrei Roublev*, and (perhaps naturally given the medieval setting of the film) certain details such as torture wheels in an otherwise peaceful or everyday setting are found in the work of both. "Shocking things are taking place [in Brueghel's print of *Justice*]. Yet these were not 'cruel and unusual punishments' for the 1550s. There is no reason to suspect Bruegel of trying to be sadistic" (Klein and Klein 110). Nor is there reason to accuse Tarkovsky of sadism in his film: he too was trying to present a "great pictorial record of man's inhumanity to man" (Klein and Klein 110) and to universalize his record of one particular historical period from the past. And, much as Tarkovsky (rightly) valued Brueghel for his truthfulness and realism, it is possible to say of him, as of the earlier artist, that "much of his finest work remains veiled or even baffling in specific meanings. Its cryptic character reflects . . . the special symbols and insights that came to form his private world. Yet the power and beauty and intrinsic interest of even his most puzzling pictures are never in doubt" (Klein and Klein 178).

Most of Tarkovsky's other art "quotations" are more specific and localized in their effect. Dürer's *Four Horsemen of the Apocalypse* is used to intensify the horrors of war in *Ivan's Childhood* and to provide an outlet for the anti-Nazi sentiments still strong in Soviet war films of the sixties. A fragment of Jan van Eyck's Ghent Altarpiece serves in *Stalker* to suggest the decay or abandonment of cultural values in the world of the film (and, by implication, modern society generally). In *Nostalghia* the calm and serene beauty of Piero della Francesca's *Madonna of Childbirth* contrasts with Eugenia's dangerous seductiveness and represents an ideal of femininity associated above all with motherhood that Andrei returns to in his memories and dreams throughout the film.

In *The Sacrifice*, Piero della Francesca is explicitly set against Leonardo da Vinci, whose *Adoration of the Magi* is described as "sinister" by Otto. Leonardo is the painter most frequently referred to in Tarkovsky's work, both in this film and in *Mirror*, as well as in *Sculpting in Time*. In his book he discusses the portrait of Ginevra de' Benci (shown in *Mirror* as Ignat examines the reproductions in the Broghaus edition of the painter's work that was a familiar part of Tarkovsky's own childhood), calling it "at once attractive and repellent" (108), and finds the same qualities in Margarita Terekhova in the film. This ability to combine "an exalted idea" and "base passions" in a single image, giving "the beholder a simultaneous experience of the most complex, contradictory, sometimes even mutually exclusive feelings," was valued by Tarkovsky as an intrinsic element of a "true artistic image" (109).

His analysis is supported by Kenneth Clark, who finds several of Leonardo's most famous paintings (though not the *Adoration*) "sinister," "disturbing," and "terrifying." As with Brueghel, however, Tarkovsky does more than simply provide shrewd and accurate art criticism; much of what Clark says about the nature of Leonardo's imagination and his artistic ideals and development is echoed—no doubt unconsciously—in the characteristic features of Tarkovsky's own work. They share a common pattern of imagery: Clark comments on Leonardo's fondness for horses, long hair, trees, mirrors (146), "stains in walls" (82), and water (148); he points to his taste for chiaroscuro ("He had never used the bright colors of the *quattrocento*," 106) and the way in which his later paintings "were growing more and more shadowy, so that his last work, the equivocal St. John in the Louvre, only just emerges from the darkness" (135)—a description that could equally apply to scenes from *Nostalghia* and *The Sacrifice*. Even their theories of art share distinct similarities: Leonardo's *Tratatto* speaks, in Clark's paraphrase, of "painting as the science by which visible objects are recreated in permanent shape" (75) and of "the divine element in the science of painting" by which "the mind of the painter is transformed into the likeness of the mind of God" (74). Tarkovsky writes of "the capacity of [film] images to express a specific, unique, actual fact" (*Sculpting* 72) and of "*Time, captured in its factual forms and manifestations,"* as "the supreme idea of cinema as an art" (63). He ends his book with words that could well have been written by Leonardo: "Perhaps our capacity to create is evidence that we ourselves were created in the image and likeness of God?" (242).

Tarkovsky's art "quotations," then, function on different levels: they serve (like his use of classical music) to associate film with older, more established arts; they make specific allusions and contrasts that (as with similar effects in Godard's films of the 1960s) provide a moral and social commentary on past and present; and they also link the images of particular art works to individual characters or settings in the films, and connect the films to each other. With Brueghel and Leonardo in particular, however, the affinities run much deeper and shape—whether consciously or not—the very foundations of his aesthetic thinking.

Tarkovsky and Literature

As is made clear in his writings and interviews, despite Tarkovsky's respect for his pantheon of great film directors, his deepest affinities and influences were not so much with them as with the tradition of Russian art and literature that he felt he had inherited and was destined to perpetuate and consolidate in his own medium. The writers[2] most referred to in *Sculpting in Time*[2] and elsewhere are largely predictable, if select: Dostoyevsky, Tolstoy, Chekhov, Bunin, Gogol, and Herzen in prose, and in poetry Pushkin, Pasternak, Mandelshtam, Gumilyov, Blok, and Vyacheslav Ivanov. As an educated member of the Russian intelligentsia (which survived into the Soviet period) Tarkovsky would also have been expected to know the great works of Western literature, as witnessed by his references to Shakespeare (especially the perennial Russian favorite, *Hamlet*), Dante, Mann, Goethe, Hesse, Hegel, Kafka, Proust, Flaubert, Zola, Paul Valery, Hemingway, and others.

But for his "dialogue" with literature, Tarkovsky chose the great triumvirate of writers who embody the old Russian—and not the new Soviet—culture: in his self-administered diary questionnaire of January 3, 1974, he names Dostoyevsky's *Crime and Punishment* and Tolstoy's *Death of Ivan Ilyich* as his favorite Russian prose and Pushkin as his favorite poet (89). While Pushkin defined for Tarkovsky his role as a Russian artist—that of prophet and martyr—Dostoyevsky's writings provided the spiritual foundation for his films (see *Sculpting* 193, where he praises "their total incompatibility with materialism" and their presentation of "spiritual crisis").

Raised on and steeped in nineteenth-century Russian culture, Tarkovsky became, especially toward the end of his life, its champion, a modern-day Slavophile who believed in Russia's—and therefore his own—special destiny (see the Pushkin letter in *Mirror*) and who, like Dostoyevsky, saw the problem of faith as crucial in art and life.[3] One suspects that he also identified all too closely with Dostoyevsky's own spiritual struggles and the torments of the spirit and of the flesh that plagued his heroes. And what about Tolstoy, whose *War and Peace* he carried, as a talisman perhaps, in the crucial juncture of his life when he took his VGIK exam? Was he inspired by the breadth of his vision of Russia and its people to make *Andrei Roublev*? Tarkovsky astutely captures the secret of Tolstoy's greatness when he writes of how "the artistic image he has created as it were pushes aside its own ideological frontiers, refuses to fit into the framework imposed on it by its author. . . . And the masterpiece goes on living it by its own laws, and has a tremendous aesthetic and emotional impact even when we don't agree with the author's fundamental tenet" (*Sculpting* 41)—a comment that could perhaps apply equally to *Nostalghia* or *The Sacrifice*.

Tarkovsky's dialogue with primarily Russian literature and, through literature, with the "roots" of his culture, with its moral and religious foundations, lies at the heart of his artistic creativity: "In all my pictures the theme of roots was always of great importance: links with family house, childhood, country, Earth. I always felt it important to establish that I myself belong to a particular tradition, culture, circle of people or ideas" (*Sculpting* 193).

References to literature are found in all of Tarkovsky's feature films: Germans in *Ivan's Childhood* desecrate their cultural heritage by burning books; the Bible in *Andrei Roublev, Mirror, Stalker,* and *The Sacrifice; Don Quixote* (like *Hamlet,* a seminal work in the Russian nineteenth-century discussion of the "superfluous man") and Tolstoy in *Solaris;* Dostoyevsky in *Mirror* and again along with Shakespeare in *The Sacrifice;* Fyodor Tyuchev (after Pushkin and Lermontov arguably the greatest nineteenth-century Russian poet) in *Stalker*—and of course his father's poetry in *Mirror, Stalker,* and *Nostalghia.*

Mirror, however, is the film most "burdened" with literary baggage, from the opening reference to Chekhov's story, "Ward Number 6," to Pushkin's letter to Chaadayev, Dante's *Inferno,* and Dostoyevsky's *The Devils.* The literary references act as a kind of shorthand identification of the narrator's cultural and artistic "genealogy," helping to define the lofty company which he and the film's author would like to keep. After mocking his ex-wife's fiancé as a talentless "Dostoyevsky," the narrator superciliously points out that a book is "not a paycheck" but a "deed." (The powerful Russian word *podvig* would best be translated as "heroic deed.")

What at times seem to be tangential literary references and quotations function on a subtextual level: together they define to a high degree the scope of Tarkovsky's world view. We have earlier noted that Tarkovsky seems to move from a basically broadly humanistic to a more religious conception of the universe in the last three films. Perhaps one could also describe this transition as a movement from Tolstoy's to Dostoyevsky's influence, with Pushkin's role remaining primarily symbolic—that of the ideal Russian artist. In *Ivan's Childhood* and *Andrei Roublev,* as well as in *Solaris,* Tarkovsky raises the "Tolstoyan" question of the individual's role in society and history and defines good and evil as based primarily on external events and characters' actions. Kris's inner world in *Solaris* remains unsatisfactorily defined, while his emotional transformation and change in actions are well motivated by Hari's reappearance. Despite the recognizably subjective intrusions—Ivan's dreams, Roublev's "visions," and Kris's hallucinations (and dreamlike childhood videos)—the central consciousness which guides us through the first three films is basically "objective," although the very end of *Solaris* may cause us to reevaluate the "reality" we think we have been seeing. This "objective" narration is in the Russian literary tradition associated with the epic novels of Tolstoy, whose *War and Peace* certainly helped to shape *Andrei Roublev*.[4]

Mirror is the pivotal film which marks Tarkovsky's growing interest in the subjective point of view, attempting a kind of first-person narration which exposes the inner world of the hero. The narrator's mocking tone and desire to describe, even "expose," his contradictory interior and exterior reality, is broadly reminiscent of Dostoyevsky's narrators. The autobiographical "confession" Tarkovsky envisaged clearly has literary rather than cinematic roots. But in *Mirror* the documentary footage "objectivizes" and provides a foil for the inner reality, where a personal history becomes the story of a generation, of a people, and raises questions about the survival of humanity. The film could be seen as achieving an ingenious combination of the external Tolstoyan and the internal Dostoyevskian perspectives. Moreover, its richness derives, as Vladimir Solovyov points out, from the creative borrowing and organic union of different literary genres. He argues convincingly that in *Mirror*, Tarkovsky looks to literature not for the plot or psychological "nuancing" but to "borrow" what "literature has perfected and cinema has not": "He takes from the novel its penetrating look at human life as historical fate, from poetry its intoxicating freedom and sharp precision of associative imaging, and from the memoir a candid, unconcealed and insistent 'autobiographism' " ("Semeynaya khronika" 4).

In the last three films Tarkovsky moves more clearly into the spiritual/ religious realm of Dostoyevsky, with the primary goal of attainment of faith through suffering and sacrifice. Whereas human love and even passion could be a positive life force in *Solaris*, beginning with *Mirror* Tarkovsky seems to subscribe to Dostoyevsky's view in the major novels that sexual passion engenders only evil, and thus denies it completely in his own heroes. Dostoyevsky's antagonists are exploitative, even satanic sensualists (the worst being Stavrogin, the "hero" of *The Devils* and the husband of the very Maria Timofeyevna to whom Masha is compared in *Mirror*: he "seduces" [rapes] a child, driving her to suicide). Tarkovsky himself stated, however, that what drew him to Dostoyevsky was the heroes' *spiritual* crisis—something all of Tarkovsky's own protagonists (with the obvious exception of Ivan) undergo (*Sculpting* 193).

There are many similarities between the characters of writer and filmmaker: the spiritual, meek, asexual, childlike seekers of faith and goodness—Prince Myshkin (*The Idiot*) or the novice Alyosha (*The Brothers Karamazov*)—find their contemporary incarnations in Stalker, and also in Domenico and Alexander (who even played Myshkin).[5] Many of the protagonists in both

Dostoyevsky's and Tarkovsky's work possess some characteristics of the "holy fools": Stalker, Domenico, and even Alexander are all "touched," slightly mad or considered so, and like Prince Myshkin are "blessed" (*blazhennye*), as is Maria Timofeyevna, to whom Masha is compared by Lisa in *Mirror*. Men of pure reason, however, are equally condemned because they lack faith: Ivan in *The Brothers Karamazov* and Writer in *Stalker*. Among the women, the virtuous, inaccessible, and self-contained Aglaya in *The Idiot* is like Masha in *Mirror*, and her opposite, the hysterical, passionate, and fascinating Nastasia Filippovna, may be reflected perhaps in Eugenia and Adelaide. And even the self-sacrificing, humble Sonia who follows the hero into exile in *Crime and Punishment* may find a counterpart in Stalker's devoted wife, or Maria in *The Sacrifice*. It is not so far-fetched to suggest that in Tarkovsky's continued but futile attempts to film *The Idiot* throughout the seventies, some of Dostoyevsky's characters and thematics clearly spilled over into his other films.

A favorite Dostoyevskian theme of "the double" (which came into Russian literature through German Romanticism) is especially prominent in *Mirror*, *Nostalghia*, and *The Sacrifice*. Stigmatized, ill, or suffering children are found in the works of both artists. The climactic final scenes of *Nostalghia* (Domenico's self-immolation) and *The Sacrifice* (Alexander's house burning) are perhaps reminiscent of the grotesque scandals in Dostoyevsky's novels. Lisa, in her unexplained hysterical outburst in *Mirror*, herself acts more like a Dostoyevskian character than the innocent Masha she accuses.

Leaving aside possibly disputable specific comparisons of characters and themes, Dostoyevsky's influence is undeniable in the director's overall philosophical and religious conception. Like Dostoyevsky, Tarkovsky repudiates the materialistic, disbelieving world he lives in. Dostoyevsky had rejected the Crystal Palace, a symbol of nineteenth-century "progress" (*Notes from the Underground*), just as Tarkovsky rejects modern technological society, whose lack of faith and spirituality will lead it to ruin. Reason is always subordinated to faith in both. Domenico's taunting formula $1 + 1 = 1$ is unmistakably a quote from the Underground Man's challenge to reason in his $2 + 2 = 5$. Tarkovsky's last three films can justifiably be seen as an ongoing "dialogue" with Dostoyevsky. Unfortunately therein also lies their weakness: Tarkovsky was no match for Dostoyevsky on the verbal plane and, unfortunately, even some of the most profound ideas he attempts to express begin to sound trite, especially if one is concerned more with listening than with watching (despite his various scriptwriting collaborations, the final text is basically always Tarkovsky's own). His increasing reliance on the spoken word is demonstrated in alterations while dubbing *Stalker*—not just changing the dialogue, but adding the Biblical and philosophical readings in voice-over. Yet the film is rescued from pomposity by the sheer virtuosity of its visual imagery and a surprisingly good "fit" of voice-over and visuals. By *The Sacrifice*, however, there is an escalating tension, and at times confusion and conflict, between word and image, or put differently, between the film's "poetic" imagery and its "prose" content. The pull of Tarkovsky's literary roots may simply have been too strong to overcome as he increasingly saw himself in the role of moral guide and prophet—characteristic of the Russian literary but not its cinematic tradition, which until recently remained firmly grounded in social, political, and ideological concerns.

A final, and perhaps the most important, literary challenge was of course provided by Tarkovsky's father, the poet Arseny Tarkovsky, whose esoteric, at times strikingly beautiful imagery and archaic lexicon the son internalized and transformed on the screen. All other literary allusions pale before Tarkovsky's attempts to create visual equivalents to his father's poems, so prominent in *Mirror*, but already present in *Ivan's Childhood*—even though there is not a single textual reference in the film. The dream sequences, aptly cited by critics as a breakthrough in "poetic" cinematography, often resonate with images closely related to Arseny Tarkovsky's verse. Could the association of boy-water-tree-death at the end of the film be explained by a very short poem titled "Ivan's Willow" ("Ivanova iva") which tells about a boy who—before the war—walked by a brook with a willow tree over it and now has returned to lie beneath it (Arseny Tarkovsky 85)?[6] Is "the boy standing on golden sand, in his hands an apple and a dragonfly" (23) reminiscent of Ivan in happier times? Can the complex perspective of Ivan in the dream sequence in the well, where he looks from both below and above the water and reaches for a round ball of light, be related to the lines "and I lie on the river bottom and see out of the water a distant light" (37)? However, if one attempts to compare whole poems with Tarkovsky's visual imagery, these rather remarkable similarities become more tenuous, with the exception of only a handful of poems in *Mirror* where Tarkovsky tries to find literal visual equivalents to specific poems (see the discussion of "First Meetings" in the *Mirror* chapter).

In general, Tarkovsky's visual language is marked by the originality, precision, and concreteness of imagery found in his father's lyrics. The son occasionally borrows strikingly unusual images from the father, but, more important, he seems to have absorbed the elder Tarkovsky's natural universe: trees, earth, sand, grass, falling leaves, birds and butterflies (*Ivan's Childhood* again?), wet snow, and water—brooks, rivers, and especially rain—and "the road reflected in tearful eyes" (32). Does the "layered, solid water" ("sloistaya i tvyordaya voda") of "First Meetings" reappear as a downpour in *Andrei Roublev, Solaris,* and *Mirror* itself?

Much of the elder Tarkovsky's poetry is melancholy in tone, with a bittersweet awareness of the transitory beauty of nature and the human relationships reflected in it.[7] The importance of home and hearth, and a nostalgia for the fleeting happiness of childhood are shared in equal measure by father and son. Tarkovsky used with particular effect the poems his father wrote in the late 1930s in the rural setting where Andrei was born; while his mother may have *taught* him to love nature (for Tarkovsky credits her with having taught him everything else in life!), his father *inspired* in him the ability to perceive it emotionally and spiritually. In *Mirror* Tarkovsky also effectively uses his father's poetry to probe the emotional truth about his parents' relationship—something he could never do in real life.

The four poems Tarkovsky quotes in *Mirror* form a shared personal and artistic core between father and son. "First Meetings" celebrates the beauty of a nature organically linked with human existence, the transforming power of love and passion, and the inescapability of fate. "From morning on I waited yesterday . . ." ("S utra ya tebya dozhdalsya vchera . . ."), in which rain prefigures a deteriorating relationship where "words cannot soothe, nor handkerchief wipe away," is a very personal poem defining the inescapable nature of male/female relations. "Life, life" ("Zhizn, zhizn"), which Tarkovsky transposed onto dramatic newsreel footage of a debilitating, unglorified picture of war, demonstrates both father and son's awareness of history, of the poet's relationship with the past, and the ideas of immortality and a belief in the family of man. In the final poem, "Eurydice," Tarkovsky makes no effort to match his father's extremely unusual imagery and elliptical, difficult syntax, but shares the poem's idea of a soul imprisoned in a body it cannot live without; the poem's image of a "burning" soul traversing the earth is clearly connected with the frequent fire imagery in *Mirror* but seems especially pertinent to *Nostalghia* and *The Sacrifice*.

Through all the cycles Arseny Tarkovsky keeps returning to the role and fate of the poet himself. In the tradition of Pushkin's poem "The Prophet," the poet is a lonely "prophet" ("To verses" ["K stikham"], 52]), a suffering martyr, who sacrifices himself and literally "burns" for those he has lived for—"grass, and stars, and butterflies and children" (67). He also pays his dues to other martyrs who "burned," such as Joan of Arc in "Joan's Tree" ("Derevo Zhanny," 65). Once again the imagery of self-immolation and burning may have strongly influenced the last two films. But there is also another, very personal, aspect of Arseny Tarkovsky's depiction of the poet's role—an awareness that he has not played that role adequately. In "Manuscript" ("Rukopis," 152), dedicated significantly to Anna Akhmatova (one of the suffering poets of his generation), he admits to being "the one who lived in my time yet was not myself. I am the youngest in the family of men and birds, I sang with everyone in unison. . . ." In "Actor" ("Akter," 231), a response to Pasternak's famous "Hamlet," he compares himself to an actor:

> . . . I despised your art.
> What else can I compare life to,
>   tell me,
> If someone else played my role
> In the whirl of fateful events?
>
> Where are you, my happy double?
> You, it seems, took me away,
> Because a strange man is here
> Arguing by the mirror with fate.

Significantly in *Stalker* Tarkovsky quotes only one of his father's poems ("Now the summer is gone . . ." ["Vot i leto proshlo . . . ," 258]), whose refrain can be translated as "there has to be more" or "even that wasn't enough" ("tolko etogo malo"). The poem is one of regret for not having been tested by life. Although the poem is read by Stalker and attributed to Porcupine's brother, its thematic or narrative role in the film is insignificant. Rather the son here recognizes the father's torment for having escaped his destiny unscathed, unlike so many of his contemporaries:

> Life gathered me up
> Safe under its wing,
> My luck always held,
> But there has to be more.
>
> Not a leaf was *burnt* up,
> Not a twig ever snapped . . .
> Clean as glass is the day,
> But there has to be more.
> (Translated by Kitty Hunter-Blair, *Sculpting* 191; emphasis added)

Tarkovsky's insistent struggle with the authorities and his almost pathological conviction of being a martyred artist can perhaps best be understood as a reaction to a probably subconscious fear of repeating his father's artistic fate.

The complex artistic dialogue between father and son, poet and filmmaker, operates on two levels. It is a highly personal conversation of a son with a father whose perception of life, art, and the surrounding world he shares; more important, it is also a self-conscious exploration into the very nature and structure of "poetic" cinema. The language of lyric poetry, specifically his father's, seems to have shaped Tarkovsky's own cinematic language. He must have been attracted to the subjective point of view of the lyrical "I," the elliptical, nonlinear narrative of a poem's "story," its progression through associative leaps, the absence of rational motivation, the convoluted syntax, and probably, as well, the unabashedly emotional appeal and the confessional potential of this type of lyric poetry.

Tarkovsky clearly had a contradictory relationship with words, expressing his suspicion of verbal communication, yet time and again demonstrating his inability to wean himself from it. After all, he was raised on his father's poetry, with its firm grounding in the belief that "the last to die is the word" (Arseny Tarkovsky 55). One must not forget that Andrei Roublev, Tarkovsky's premier visual artist, could not paint until his faith and his ability to speak were restored. And these two functions are connected, as all of Tarkovsky's heroes—with the exception of Andrei in the final scene of *Nostalghia*—eventually express their faith verbally, as does Tarkovsky himself in the voice-over readings from the Bible. Although *Mirror*'s narrator complains about words being "inert" and unable to convey all his feelings, the film's opening scene in which a stuttering young man acquires the ability to "speak loudly and clearly, freely and easily" can be read as an affirmation of speech as well as a metaphor for freedom of artistic expression. Despite his anger at the ineffectiveness of words and the need "to do something," Alexander seems to have left the stage because the emotions he portrayed and—rather obviously—the words he spoke, transformed him into his characters and invaded his own identity. And Alexander's own vow of silence serves to transfer the power of speech to his son. "In the beginning was the Word. Why is that, Papa?" asks Little Man at the film's end. There is no answer, only the shimmering beauty of the tree which he will bring back to life with the faith passed down from father to son in life's unbroken continuum. Despite his increasing predilection for words in the later films, Tarkovsky nevertheless ends each and every film with powerful visual images which exploit and glorify the artistic potential of cinema. In the end Tarkovsky demonstrates the need for both word and image in the unique, organic combination that only the cinema can achieve.

Appendix: Film Synopses

Ivan's Childhood (Ivanovo detstvo, 1962)

[*N.B.*: The British title of the film, *Ivan's Childhood,* is a literal translation of the Russian *Ivanovo detstvo* and will be used throughout. The American title, *My Name Is Ivan,* misses the intentional irony of the original and loses the literary allusion to the well-established Russian "childhood" genre, best represented by Leo Tolstoy's *Childhood,* Maxim Gorky's *My Childhood,* and Alexei N. Tolstoy's *Nikita's Childhood.* (The original title of the novella on which the film is based is simply *Ivan.*) The American print also omits a few shots from the opening sequence and, more significantly, drastically shortens the newsreel sequences near the end. These omissions will be noted in this synopsis, which is based on the British print.]

The film opens with a sequence that is revealed, in retrospect, to be a dream: a boy of around twelve is seen wondering at the sights and sounds of nature and then apparently flying over a rural landscape. He approaches a woman whom he addresses as "Mother"; as he drinks from a bucket of water beside her, she is abruptly killed by off-screen gunfire. [The American print omits several shots here: a close-up of a goat's head and some shots of the boy and a butterfly. These shots, however, are included in the video of the film available in North America.]

The boy wakes up inside a deserted windmill and goes outdoors. Signal flares, abandoned army vehicles, and ominous music create a mood of wartime. The film's credits are shown over shots of the boy wading through a swamp. The wet and dirty boy (Ivan) is next seen in a local military post, where he is interrogated by a youthful lieutenant: he refuses to give any information until his presence is reported to a Colonel Gryaznov at headquarters. There is a curious reversal of roles as the child orders the man about. When the suspicious lieutenant (Galtsev) reluctantly telephones, he is ordered to take good care of the boy and let him write down "everything." Ivan, now revealed to be an army scout, indicates the German positions by means of seeds, nuts, and leaves. He bathes then tries to eat, but falls asleep exhausted.

Another dream follows, introduced by the sound of dripping water. The boy and his mother are looking down a well and talking; switches of angle show the well now full of water and now empty, while Ivan himself constantly changes position, now beside his mother at the top of the well, able to touch the water with his hand, now at the bottom, looking up at her through the empty shaft. Whispered voices, probably speaking German, are heard before a shot rings out and a bucket starts to hurtle toward Ivan at the bottom of the shaft. The mother is seen lying face down on the ground as water from an unidentified source spills over both her and the bucket in slow motion.

The boy wakes up and joyfully greets a newcomer, Captain Kholin. He tells Kholin what he has been doing and is then seen with him and another (adult) scout, Katasonych, reporting to the colonel at headquarters. The men want to send Ivan to military school, but he refuses and threatens to run away.

He is next seen on his own, outdoors, in a ruined landscape, where he meets a crazed old man who talks about his wife's death at the hands of the Germans. The officers arrive by car to retrieve Ivan and take him away despite his protests. An abrupt cut, with no indication of elapsed time, shows Galtsev reprimanding an attractive nurse at the field hospital for alleged slackness. Kholin enters and sardonically notices Galtsev's attraction to the young woman (Masha). A lyrical interlude in a birch wood follows, in which Kholin flirts aggressively with Masha, but tells her abruptly to go away when she is on the point of succumbing to him. Masha, apparently overwhelmed by the encounter, meets up with Galtsev, who has been looking for her and is uneasy about Kholin's influence over her.

In the bunker, Kholin and Katasonych discuss how to retrieve the bodies of two scouts who have been executed by the Germans. The bodies, each attached to a tree by a noose, have been left on display, with a placard reading "Welcome" in Russian. Galtsev is next seen with Kholin, who teases him about his interest in Masha; Masha herself is seen being greeted by a passing soldier (played by Andrei Konchalovsky) who recognizes her from school, but she shows no interest in him, for she is now besotted with Kholin, as another lyrical sequence in the woods makes clear; the mood is abruptly broken by the sound of gunfire and a dissolve to the battleground, followed by the dangling bodies and the jarring, discordant music that generally accompanies this image.

In Galtsev's post—a ruined church—Ivan looks through a book of Dürer reproductions and comments that the figure of Death in the *Four Horsemen of the Apocalypse* reminds him of a German he saw on a motorcycle; he also adds that the Germans can't have writers because they burn books. The men discuss again how to retrieve the bodies of the scouts, and Katasonych plays a Chaliapin recording of a folk song, "Masha Must Not Cross the River." At Ivan's request, Galtsev lends him his knife, and Katasonych says he will get him one of his own tomorrow. The three men talk about Ivan as they walk to the riverbank and select a boat for their expedition. His mother and sister had been killed by the Germans and his father, a frontier guard, died in action. They discuss which of them might adopt him, and Kholin comments that the boy is obsessed with war and the desire for revenge. Ivan, left alone in the church, acts out a fantasy in which he stalks and kills German soldiers; though this is not a dream, the atmosphere is hallucinatory and dreamlike and Ivan's mother appears to be present. The scene ends with the distraught and weeping Ivan ringing the church bell and an explosion that reveals a damaged icon of the Madonna and child.

Galtsev returns and talks to Ivan about attending military school. Ivan again rejects this suggestion and, as elsewhere in the film, seems much more "adult" than the man is; he also treats Kholin, when he returns, as if he were a child needing advice and protection. As the three eat a meal, Ivan wonders where Katasonych has gone to and Kholin, as usual, teases Galtsev, suggesting that he might not be allowed to join their—apparently unauthorized—expedition. As the camera focuses on Ivan's pensive face and the sound of dripping water is heard, another dream sequence begins. Ivan and an unidentified little girl (presumably the sister mentioned earlier) are sitting in a truck loaded with apples, as rain falls and they move against a background that is back-projected in negative. After Ivan offers the girl an apple on three occasions and is refused, the truck drives onto a beach, spilling apples; a horse appears and begins to eat them.

Ivan and the two men continue with their preparations for departure. Galtsev is sent outside to distract the sentry while the others slip past; he comes across the body of Katasonych and is told that he was killed when they brought back the boat. Kholin warns him to keep quiet about this and they set off with Ivan in the boat; when Ivan asks about the bodies hanging from the tree, he is told that they were the scouts sent out to find him earlier. They continue through the swamp to the point where Ivan is disembarked to set off on another mission. Galtsev and Kholin elude a German patrol and collect and bring back the bodies of the scouts.

Back in the church, Kholin puts on the Chaliapin record. Masha appears and Kholin teases her about the friend she was talking to earlier. Galtsev says he is sending her away and, while Kholin is attending to the record, Masha slips off unnoticed. As Kholin comments on how quiet it is, the loud ringing of bells provides a transition to newsreel footage of the victorious Soviet army in Berlin. In a sequence omitted from the American print and the American video, an elderly German shows Russian soldiers the bodies of Goebbels and his wife and six small daughters; brief scenes of officers signing the surrender agreement and of the dead bodies of more high-ranking Nazis and their families follow.

The fictional story resumes with scenes of Galtsev supervising Soviet soldiers as they sort through piles of German documents. Galtsev talks in his imagination to the now-dead Kholin as the soldiers read off the fate of executed Nazi prisoners. He discovers a file with Ivan's photo, and an impressionistic montage of sound and imagery conveys the fact of the boy's death, ending with a shot of his head and torso swirling and twisting upside down.

A cut to the now immediately recognizable music and visuals of the dreams shows Ivan's mother on the beach and Ivan playing with other children, who then disappear, leaving Ivan and his sister playing hide-and-seek. He chases her along the edge of the sea, passes her, and runs out into the water; as he stretches out his arm, there is a cut to a dead tree ahead, which fills the screen as the image goes black.

Andrei Roublev (Andrei Rublyov, 1966, 1971)

[N.B.: The version of *Andrei Roublev* released in the Soviet Union in 1971, incorporating the cuts to which Tarkovsky had agreed, ran 185 minutes, and this version played commercially in Paris. The version released by Columbia in the United States and Britain in 1973, however, was only 146 minutes long, omitting the whole of the balloon prologue and shortening or eliminating other scenes. During the 1980s this print was joined, but not universally replaced in circulation, by the 185–minute copy, and it is on the latter that our synopsis is based. Although Tarkovsky's "original cut," the 3 hour 20 minute *Passion According to Andrei*, was shown in the Soviet Union in 1989, Tarkovsky himself preferred the 185–minute version (as he confirmed in his interview with Michel Ciment: *Dossier Positif* 93), and his judgment is borne out by a viewing of the longer print. There are no totally "new" scenes in it, and the main difference, apart from the length of several sequences, is that it retains the graphic and controversial eye-gouging and animal-killing scenes.]

Andrei Roublev is a "two-part" film,' with the division coming after the episode titled "The Last Judgment." It begins with an (untitled and undated) prologue; this is followed by eight titled and dated but unnumbered episodes and then an (untitled and undated) epilogue in color. Apart from the unfamiliarity of the historical setting, one major problem, certainly for a Western viewer, comes from the fact that the locations of the various episodes are rarely clearly identified: some take place in the vicinity of Moscow, some at the Andronnikov monastery (at that time outside the Moscow city limits), and some at the city of Vladimir, where the Tartar raid occurs. Occasionally the location is suggested in the dialogue (though not always in the subtitles) or in the script, and we have provided this information wherever possible. A Western viewer is also unlikely to know much about Roublev's life or work, and the explanatory caption provided for the French print (Gauthier 45) does not appear in the American version.

The opening credits are shown to the accompaniment of an irregularly tolling bell (a leitmotif throughout the film), later joined by an atmospheric musical theme. This is followed by a *Prologue* in which a man arrives by boat at a church where several other men are inflating a primitive balloon; he is being pursued, also by boat, by a group who are attempting to stop the balloon from being launched. In the ensuing struggle (with the attackers screaming "Burn them alive!") he manages to set off from the top of the church and enjoys a few brief moments of sublime accomplishment ("I am flying!") before plunging back to earth and (presumably) death. The prologue ends with a shot of a horse rolling over in the grass in slow motion.[2]

Episode 1, "The Buffoon," set in 1400, is introduced by a tolling bell. Three monks walk through a hayfield discussing their prospects of finding work (the original script shows them leaving the Trinity monastery and makes it clear that they are looking for work in Moscow). A sudden rainstorm sends them running for shelter in a hut where a "buffoon" is entertaining an audience of peasants with energetic dancing and an obscene song (only partially translated in the English subtitles). The mood quiets as the monks enter and sit and talk, though the buffoon displays some hostility; a woman's voice singing a plaintive song off-screen is heard through most of the remainder of the scene. One monk (later identified as Kirill) remarks that "God made the priests but the devil made the buffoon"; this is followed by a slow, circular pan around the room, beginning with the peasants and implying that some time has elapsed by showing that one of the monks (Daniil the Black—traditionally thought to have been Roublev's teacher) is now asleep, while Roublev turns to look out the window as voices are heard outside. The camera follows his gaze, and the shot ends just before we can register that Kirill is no longer present. The studied ambiguity of this camera movement is not fully accounted for until almost the end of the film (and a lapse of 23 years in its time scheme).

The noise emanates from two drunken peasants brawling outside in the mud and pouring rain. Four horsemen (retainers of the local duke) arrive and summon the buffoon to join them; two of them take him by the arms and calmly hurl him headfirst against a tree. They load his unconscious body onto a horse, while their leader smashes the buffoon's lute on the ground. As the horsemen ride off, Kirill appears from outside, avoiding a direct answer to Roublev's question as to where he has been, and the monks prepare to leave. They walk along a riverbank in the rain while the horsemen move parallel to them on the far bank.

Episode 2, "Theophanes the Greek," dated 1405, begins with Kirill walking through a city crowd while, in the background, a man is dragged to be tortured on the wheel. Kirill pays no attention and enters a darkened room where an old man is lying on a bench as if on a sarcophagus and asks if he is Theophanes the Greek (the most famous icon painter before Roublev). Asked in turn if he is Andrei Roublev, Kirill says that he knows Roublev and is like a brother to him, yet, as the conversation continues, he subtly denigrates Roublev's merits as a painter while praising the work of Theophanes: Roublev, he says, has a delicate sense of color but lacks "fear and faith." Theophanes invites Kirill to help him paint the Annunciation Church in Moscow, and Kirill finally agrees, provided that Theophanes come to the Andronnikov monastery to invite him in the presence of Roublev and the other monks. Responding to the sound of shouting outside, Theophanes runs to the door and, over a medium close-up of a blood-soaked man being placed on the torture wheel,³ his voice is heard off-screen asking if this kind of thing will never end. Meanwhile Kirill, still indoors, studies one of Theophanes' somber and forbidding Byzantine-style icons of Christ.

At the Andronnikov monastery, a messenger from the Grand Duke summons not Kirill but Roublev to work with Theophanes on the Annunciation Church. (The Grand Duke referred to here had his seat in Moscow, though his title was Grand Duke of Vladimir.) Roublev accepts the invitation, but both Kirill and Daniil are clearly unhappy. Kirill is seen in his cell, examining some icons stacked against the wall, as an off-screen voice reads extracts from chapter XII of Ecclesiastes with its refrain of "Vanity of vanities, all is vanity" (in the version of this scene given in the published script he chops up his work with an axe). Roublev and Daniil, however, are tearfully reconciled.

Kirill prepares to leave the monastery, ignoring Roublev's attempts to reason with him and berating the other monks for condoning the corruption and materialism of the Church; he admits his own lack of artistic talent, but claims that this allows him to be honest. The abbot now appears and orders him to leave, and Kirill storms off, hurling some last insults at the monks; when his dog tries to join him, he beats it to death.

Episode 3, "The Passion According to Andrei," is set in 1406. Roublev and his apprentice Foma are walking in a wood beside a stream, with the master lamenting the boy's incorrigible habit of lying. Bird song is heard and the camera focuses as much on tree trunks, roots, mud, and the surface of the water as on the human figures. His criticism of Foma is echoed by Theophanes, who is discovered brushing a horde of ants from his legs. (Le Fanu [38] suggests unconvincingly that it is Theophanes' ghost that we see here.) A conversation between Roublev and Theophanes follows in which their contrasting intellectual and moral positions are revealed (as the English subtitles here are often printed white-on-white and are thus virtually illegible, our version of the dialogue is taken directly from the Russian text). While Roublev admits but attempts to excuse human frailty and ignorance, Theophanes is dismissive of earthly concerns, for it is the Last Judgment that really matters. Roublev asks indignantly how he can paint with such slight regard for people and their needs; Theophanes responds that everything is part of an eternally recurring cycle and nothing will ever change: Christ would be crucified once more if he reappeared on earth. When Roublev tries to argue that goodness still exists in human beings, Theophanes reminds him that Christ was betrayed by his own disciples, and the people clamored for his execution. Roublev stresses that they repented, if too late, but admits people do commit evil acts; as he speaks we hear a drumbeat and cut to a piece of cloth floating in the water.

Roublev continues to speak off-screen over the progress of a "Russian Calvary" across a snow-covered landscape, to the sound of muffled drumbeats, and then mournful female voices: a Christ figure painfully carries his cross to a hillside, followed by a procession of clearly Russian peasants including the two Marys. He collapses, rises to his feet, then positions himself carefully on the cross; a weeping Magdalene is ordered away; a radiantly smiling young girl watches. Finally the cross is raised into place. Meanwhile Roublev's voice-over speaks of the suffering of the ordinary Russian people under the Tartars, with hunger, plague, endless toil; their only hope is in their endurance and their trust in God. Perhaps, he speculates, Christ was born and crucified to make peace between God and man; the people who came to love him as a man should not have felt betrayed because he behaved cruelly in choosing to die and leave them. As we return to the present, Theophanes reminds Roublev that he could be exiled for such thoughts (emphasizing Christ's human rather than divine nature). When Roublev replies that Theophanes is never afraid to speak *his* mind, Theophanes responds that *he* is not a monk. The camera then follows the swirling paint as Foma rinses his brushes in the water.

Episode 4, "The Celebration," dated 1408, begins with Roublev traveling by boat with Foma and some other monks (including Daniil, whose reappearance is not explained); from snippets of dialogue we gather that they are on their way to paint a cathedral (in Vladimir—script) and hope to complete the job before winter. While Roublev and Foma gather wood for a fire, their attention is caught by strange sounds nearby and bonfires burning on the riverbank. As the pulsating rhythms of the music intensify, they see a naked figure carrying a torch, and then others running toward the water. Despite warning Foma that they are casting spells, Roublev begins to run after them, leaving the boy behind. He is accosted, and obviously tempted by one naked woman, but before he can respond, she is dragged down into the bushes by a male companion. He continues to gaze at them until he realizes that his monk's robe has caught fire and has to beat out the flames. A huge white-robed figure passes by; the music, chanting, and excited voices continue as he approaches a wooden building and watches through the window as a young woman, naked under a sheepskin coat, jumps repeatedly from the lower rungs of a ladder over a fire (a ritual to purify the home, according to the script).[4] He is seized suddenly from behind by some men who call him "a black snake" and threaten to drown him the next morning. They tie him to a post in a crucifix-like posture and leave him.

The woman in the sheepskin coat approaches and asks why he is threatening them. He tells her their kind of love is sinful and bestial and what matters is brotherly love; she is puzzled and asks if all love is not the same. She kisses him passionately on the lips; he asks her to untie him and then quickly leaves the hut. After a brief cut to another ritual in which a boat with a straw effigy is set adrift on the river, Roublev is seen running through the wood; he is disheveled and exhausted and has a scratch on his face. The young woman watches him, smiling enigmatically. The following morning, he leaves the village and rejoins his companions, ignoring Foma's questions about where he had been, saying that he had scratched his face on a branch. Daniil reproaches him for setting a bad example for his students. As they set off, they witness a struggle on the riverbank between some of the pagans (both men and women) and a group of the Duke's retainers; Kirill, in his monk's robes, is helping the latter. Roublev tells his youngest apprentice (Seryozha) not to look as the woman who had freed Roublev breaks away from her attackers, runs naked into the water, and starts to swim. Roublev averts his eyes as the woman passes very close to his boat and swims on toward the far bank.

Episode 5, "The Last Judgment," still in 1408, takes place in Vladimir (their destination from the previous scene), where Roublev has been hired by the Grand Duke to paint the interior of the cathedral. But Roublev himself has disappeared and his apprentices, preparing the dazzlingly white walls for him to start work, want to take time off. The fussy sacristan warns Foma (now the senior apprentice) that the bishop has sent a messenger to find out why the work is falling behind schedule.

Outdoors, against the background of a featureless plain with a road running through the fields into the foreground, Daniil echoes this complaint, while Roublev says he wants to abandon the commission but can't explain exactly why. Daniil says they should have started already on a Last Judgment full of gruesome torments that will "make sinners' flesh creep," but Roublev objects that his task is not to frighten people. Daniil replies that that is the whole point of a Last Judgment; Roublev remains unconvinced but agrees that, if Daniil feels that way, it is probably dishonest of him (Roublev) to accept the assignment. Meanwhile a horseman (identified by Daniil as the bishop's messenger), who has been steadily approaching, gallops noisily past.

Back in the cathedral, Foma announces that he is leaving as Roublev anxiously surveys the still-bare walls around him. He is heard in voice-over quoting the famous passage on charity from 1 Corinthians 13, and this leads into a flashback[5] in which the voice-over continues as we see what looks like a charred tree trunk or wooden pillar, and then the Duke walking around another blindingly white interior (his palace). Roublev completes the Biblical quotation on screen as he picks up the Duke's mischievous little daughter, reproaching her gently for throwing milk at him, and walks past the Duke, asking how he likes the house. Meanwhile the Duke's steward (Stepan) attempts to deal with another, more refractory child and tells one of the artisans that the walls must be repainted in brighter colors. The man replies that he knows his job and they won't repaint anything; in any case they are leaving to work for the Duke's brother, who offers more money and better materials. After muttering, "Then go to Zvenigorod," the Duke calls for Stepan.

The stonemasons eat and congratulate themselves on their move to a better job, as Roublev works on an icon in the background. Daniil comments on the rivalry between the Duke and his brother. Roublev is then seen sitting in a doorway working on an icon, watched by the Duke's daughter.[6] The Duke angrily calls for his steward and is told he has left for Zvenigorod (where his brother lives and where the workers are heading); he says that's all right and exchanges glances with Roublev as he leaves.

The masons are attacked by the Duke's horsemen as they travel through a forest. Stepan blinds one of the men with a knife, and his followers pursue and mutilate the others. The horsemen ride off, the sound of their victims' groans mingling with peaceful bird songs. The only unharmed survivor, the youngster (Seryozha) who had earlier brought the masons their food,[7] backs away in horror, and the scene ends on the hand of one of the victims dangling over the edge of a stream as a white liquid, probably milk, flows into the water from a flask.

A shock cut of paint being hurled against a white wall and spreading out in thick blotches ends the flashback and returns us to the present. Roublev smears the paint viciously with his hand and is then seen sobbing. Daniil tells Seryozha (see note 7) to read from the Bible. He reads a passage from St. Paul as a young woman dressed in rags enters the church; she is bareheaded, has a sore on her lip, and seems mentally subnormal.[8] The off-screen reading deals with the relationship between men and women and the due subordination of the latter to the former and of man to God, before going on to stipulate that women must always have their heads covered when entering a church. The woman rubs her hands excitedly over the smears of paint on the wall, then sniffs her fingertips and utters strange sobbing noises. As if struck by some revelation, Roublev tells Daniil that it is a joyous day: what kind of a sinner is this, even if she doesn't wear a headscarf? Overjoyed, he runs to the door and exits into the pouring rain as Daniil tells his puzzled companions to "let him go and repent" and the woman follows him outside. The point of this somewhat obscure scene is that Roublev, seeing this obviously innocent and harmless woman—who is nevertheless technically a sinner for entering a church with her head uncovered—realizes that his instinctive trust in human goodness is more valid than Daniil's punitive respect for the strict letter of the law (or the Bible). He is thus given the confidence to paint a "happy" Last Judgment rather than the scene of terror and torment envisaged by Daniil. This is made more explicit in the script, where he and his crew are shown working on such a painting.

Episode 6, "The Raid," begins Part II, still in 1408 and set in the city of Vladimir.[9] A Tartar army preparing to attack the undefended city joins up with Russian allies commanded by the Grand Duke's brother and rival (the two brothers are played by the same actor). We learn in flashback that the brothers had earlier been forced to make peace by the Church; the armies then begin their assault and force a surprise entry before the gates can be closed. In the massacre that follows, Tarkovsky focuses on helpless individual victims, some of them recognizable from Roublev's entourage. Every now and then the Tartar and Russian leaders meet to congratulate themselves on their easy victory, and watch calmly as the attackers prepare to break into the church where the surviving population has taken refuge. Inside the church Roublev drags the young woman (the "Fool") through the praying crowd and makes her kneel beside him. As horsemen surge into the building, Roublev and the woman are separated and she is carried off by a soldier. The Duke's brother walks through the screaming crowd, obviously satisfied with his work. Roublev, carrying an axe, follows the soldier up the stairs and kills him off-screen.

The invaders begin to loot the church and the city and prepare to torture the sacristan (seen at the beginning of the "Last Judgment" episode) in order to find out where the church's gold is hidden. The victim accuses the Duke's brother of being "a Tartar-faced Judas" who has betrayed his country. As a flaming torch is thrust into the sacristan's face, there is a flashback to the scene of the brothers' opportunistic reconciliation, accompanied by choral church music. They exchange the traditional three kisses as the camera tilts down to show that the Grand Duke has placed his feet over his brother's as a reminder of his seniority.

A flaming liquid is poured into the sacristan's mouth, and he is dragged out of the burning interior of the church by a horse. Dramatic orchestral music accompanies high-angle and slow-motion shots of people fleeing through the devastated city, intercut with shots of the brother's face as he appears to reflect on what he has done. On the verge of escape, Foma is shot in the back by a Tartar bowman. In the church, a bell tolls as an anguished Roublev kneels among the bodies on the floor, and the Fool plaits the long hair of a dead woman. He then talks to the long-dead yet visible Theophanes (a scene presented not as a hallucination but as everyday reality) about his despair at what is happening to the country, with Russians joining the Tartars to rape and murder their own people. Theophanes was right: they are not even human. He will no longer paint: no one needs his art and, worst of all, he has sinned by killing a man, a Russian. Theophanes tries to reassure him, saying that evil is part of human nature and God will forgive him, and reminds him of his own earlier ideals—to do good, to search for truth, to save the oppressed and defend the poor. Roublev's response is simply that he will take a vow of silence. He asks if "all this" will last for long; probably forever, Theophanes answers, but, pointing to the half-destroyed frescoes, he reminds Roublev that art is still beautiful, whatever happens. Snow begins to fall: "Nothing is more terrifying than snow inside a church," Roublev says. The Fool is now asleep, and a riderless horse clatters into the building as the bell continues to toll.

Episode 7, "The Silence," is set in 1412, at the Andronnikov monastery. Famine is widespread and the Tartars rove at will over the countryside, living in an uneasy truce with the population. The Fool searches, animal-like, for scraps of food in the snow-covered courtyard, watched by Roublev, who seems to have aged considerably. In-doors the monks talk of the people's suffering, and among the beggars and cripples who have taken refuge there is a maimed and almost unrecognizable Kirill. The men gossip suggestively about Roublev's relationship with the "Holy Fool" (*blazhennaya*) he has brought with him.[10]

Tartars arrive and begin to tease the starving dogs and then the hungry Fool. Indoors Kirill begs for forgiveness from the abbot (who had driven him away earlier) and is allowed to stay but is told to perform a virtually impossible penance. The Fool is fascinated by the Tartar leader's armor, and he laughingly offers to make her his eighth wife. When Roublev tries to intervene, she angrily resists him and rides off willingly with the Tartars. Kirill approaches Roublev and attempts to reassure him about the Fool's fate; Roublev ignores him.

Episode 8, "The Bell," is set in 1423 and draws together themes and characters from the previous twenty-three years. Horsemen (retainers of the Grand Duke) enter a deserted village looking for the bellmaker. His teenage son (Boriska) says that his father and everyone else have died of the plague, but that he can do the bell-casting for them as his father passed on the secret; though they are skeptical, the men take him with them.

Scenes of the preliminary work follow, with little indication of elapsed time be-tween them, as the youth attempts to impose his authority on the recalcitrant older workers. He begins a search for the right kind of clay for casting and finds it by accident as he loses his balance on a muddy clifftop and slides to the bottom; his ecstatic response is observed by Roublev, who is passing nearby and is then seen watching later stages of the work. His self-confidence restored by his discovery, Boriska takes full control of the work, ignoring warnings that he is proceeding with dangerous speed and dealing ruthlessly with any dissent—yet betraying a latent hys-teria and insecurity beneath the show of authority. When, at one point, he collapses from nervous exhaustion, as Roublev watches, an interlude follows that seems to represent Roublev's memories of a moment of past serenity: the haunting sounds of the woman's singing and the quiet lute music from the buffoon episode accompany shots of two monks walking along a road in the rain, a younger Kirill standing beside a tree holding a bird in his hand, and a younger Roublev gazing at leaves on a tree. The music gives way to the lyrical "dream music" from *Ivan's Childhood* as Roublev, now standing beside a tree with bare branches and falling snow, watches the sleeping Boriska being carried past on a stretcher.

Work begins on firing the clay, with Boriska almost childishly cocky and self-assured once more. The aged buffoon suddenly reappears and accuses Roublev of having betrayed him to the Duke's men twenty-three years previously; he is mutter-ing almost incoherently as half of his tongue had been cut out in punishment. He threatens Roublev with an axe, but when Kirill intervenes and offers himself as a victim instead, he calms down—though he repeats his accusation against Roublev. The casting of the bell continues and, as the hardened clay is chipped away, the metal is discovered to be sound. The exhausted Boriska falls asleep once more. At the An-dronnikov monastery Kirill admits to Roublev that *he* had betrayed the buffoon, ac-knowledging his jealousy but also accusing Roublev of sinning by wasting his God-given talent. He urges him to accept an offer to paint the Trinity monastery; Roublev makes no response but seems troubled by what he hears.

A crowd gathers to witness the raising of the bell, and the Duke and his entourage ride out from the city (identified in the script as Moscow). Boriska seems lost and bewildered, hovering on the fringes as priests bless the bell; he is thrust forward by the workmen to take credit for his achievement—the noblemen, however, show little interest and virtually ignore him." A workman sets the clapper ringing; we see the bystanders including the Fool, now well dressed and apparently normal, leading a horse and smiling. Boriska wanders over the desolate, muddy riverbank as the Duke and his entourage ride off, and then lies sobbing at the foot of a pole as Roublev approaches him. Boriska admits that his father died without telling him the bell-casting secret, and Roublev consoles him: they will go to the Trinity monastery together, where Roublev will paint and Boriska will cast bells; he shouldn't cry when he has created such joy for the people. As the camera pans down the boy's body and over to the glowing logs in a fire nearby, there is a cut to color and a different heap of logs as the epilogue begins.

Epilogue. To the sound of choral music the camera explores what appears to be a series of abstract colors, mainly red and blue. A series of dissolves, cuts, and panning shots gradually reveals identifiable but obviously damaged fragments of paintings, including a church, a horse, the apostles from Roublev's *Transfiguration,* the Christ child, the Magi, angels, Christ the Savior, and the Virgin, as the music rises steadily in intensity. The final group of fragments begins to cohere as the camera explores the different figures and then the full image of Roublev's most famous painting: the three angels of the Old Testament Trinity[12] (panning up, down, and across it, yet never showing the picture as a whole). The music stops as the camera reaches their faces; there is a cut to color fragments once more and the sound of thunder and rain as the image dissolves to the face of Christ and the camera tracks slowly away; another cut to what seems to be a crumbling painted wall with rain streaming over it; and a dissolve, still in color,[13] to a peaceful, intensely green landscape where four horses stand on a spit of land in the middle of a river as the rain falls.

Solaris (*Solaris,* 1972)

[N.B.: *Solaris* was heavily cut in the United States on its original release, and, unlike *Andrei Roublev,* also in France and Italy. The version shown at Cannes in 1972 seems to have been 2 hours 45 minutes long, though it was rumored that 30 minutes had been cut from a longer version (*Dossier Positif* 96). The French-release version was 2½ hours, prepared by Tarkovsky himself during a visit to Paris (*TWT* 61). In Italy the film was cut by 40 minutes, which Tarkovsky said "destroyed" it (Yermash 10). The release copy in Britain in 1973 ran 2 hours and 45 minutes, but in the United States and Canada the film was delayed until late 1976 and then shown in a dubbed version lasting 2 hours 12 minutes, for which Tarkovsky seems not to have been consulted. In 1990 this dubbed print was replaced by a subtitled version, identical in length to the British copy.

Our interviews with the film's editor, set designer, and leading actress indicate that Tarkovsky's original cut was indeed longer, at over 3 hours, but that the director himself shortened it before the film went to Cannes. According to the editor, Feiginova, the major scenes deleted were a conversation between Kris and his father that might have clarified the strained relationship between them, and a lengthy scene in the specially constructed "mirror room" that survives only as a fragment. The 2 hour 45 minute version, therefore, on which our synopsis is based, appears to be the definitive one, even if rumors still persist that an "original" version remains to be disinterred.

Some confusion reigns over the correct naming of the characters, which varies, often quite drastically, in the official British, American, French, and German credits and even in the subtitling of the various prints. Kris Kelvin is sometimes given as Chris; Hari as Harey or Kari; Snaut as Snauth, Snouth, or Snow; and Berton as Burton, with his first name either Henry or André. We give them here in what is the closest approximation to the Russian forms: Kris, Hari, Snaut, and Berton.]

The opening credits are accompanied by Bach's organ Prelude in F minor, re-placed, as the film begins, by natural sounds—wind, water, insects, birds—as the camera pans in extreme close-up over underwater plants, and then to the hand of a man (Kris Kelvin) holding a small metal container, and then up to his face. He moves off past a wooded landscape to stand at the edge of a pond; we hear a cuckoo and see a wooden dacha (country house) in the distance, with a yellow balloon caught in the branches of a tree. A horse trots past. Kris is seen dipping his hands in the pond and looks up as he hears the noise of a car off-screen.

The scene which follows introduces Kris's father; the newcomer, Berton, a former astronaut; a middle-aged woman called Anna whom the father refers to as Kris's aunt;[14] and two children, a boy who arrives with Berton and a girl whose presence is never explained. As Berton and the father talk indoors, the camera follows them in one of the uninterrupted sequence shots typical of the film; the walls are lined with prints of early balloon flights, and other elements of the décor include a birdcage and a Greek-style bust. A sudden rainstorm begins, and Kris deliberately allows himself to be soaked; the camera moves to a "still life" composition on the table of fruit and china. The rain stops as abruptly as it began, and Kris goes indoors to join his aunt and Berton in front of a large TV screen.

The scenes on TV, mostly in black and white but with color for Berton's "film within a film," alternate with color shots of the reactions of the three viewers. In a large room filled with huge portraits of (mostly Soviet) astronauts,[15] an official investi-gation is being conducted into a previous expedition to the planet Solaris during which some members of the crew had vanished. Berton as a much younger man is giving evidence: while flying over the Solaris Ocean (which covers the whole planet), he saw a "garden" on its surface; but when he shows the film that he shot, it reveals—to his own amazement—nothing but clouds and sky. He then describes seeing what he at first thought was a spacesuit belonging to Fechner, one of his missing compan-ions; to the obvious incredulity of all except a Dr. Messinger, he goes on to say that it was really a naked child, four meters high. Despite Messinger's objections, it is an-nounced that research into the nature of the planet is to be terminated.

Kris, watching all this, seems as disbelieving as the scientists, and Berton (who had brought the film) is apologetic and embarrassed. The father returns and Berton goes outside; a conversation between father and son reveals an uneasy relationship that both are aware of but neither is able to resolve. (As they talk, the camera cuts briefly to a black and white photograph of a young woman who is later identified as Kris's—presumably dead—mother.) Outdoors Kris has a tense conversation with Berton in which we discover that he is leaving for Solaris to decide whether the research station there should be closed down entirely. Their argument reveals totally opposite worldviews, with Kris claiming that science has to follow its own course, no matter where it leads, while Berton sees knowledge as valid "only when it is based on moral-ity." When Kris admits that he believes Berton had experienced hallucinations, the other man stalks off angrily. Kris's father reproaches him for his behavior, saying that it is dangerous to send people like him into space.

Back inside the house, Anna—joined by the father—is watching a TV program on Solaris: the planet may have a brain and be capable of thought, and only three people now operate the station there. Each (Sartorius, Snaut, and Gibarian) is briefly introduced, and then a video phone message from Berton interrupts. He tells Kris's father that, when he later saw Fechner's child, it was exactly like the one he had seen in the Solaris Ocean—except that the real child was not four meters tall.

A long (4 minutes 55 seconds) sequence now follows, mostly in black and white but interspersed with color, of Berton and the boy driving along a freeway and into a city. As they enter it, the initially naturalistic soundtrack merges with electronic noises and what could be the sound of a spaceship taking off to build to a deafening crescendo as the image switches to color shots of superimposed views of highways jammed with traffic against a background of garish, neon-lit buildings.

The cacophonous sound gives way immediately to silence and to a black and white night scene of Kris burning papers and photographs at a bonfire.[16] Anna watches sadly, and he tells his father that he no longer needs these but intends to take "the tape" with him. Among the material that Kris is sorting through is a photograph of a young woman wearing a shawl who is later identified as Hari.

Another "still life" follows, including Kris's metal box (from the opening scene) and a copy of a book—an illustrated *Don Quixote*—that is later seen in the library of the space station. The horse and the pond are also seen. This moment of quietness leads into Kris's journey to Solaris, filmed mostly in a close-up of his face, and accompanied by the electronic music that henceforth suggests the alien environment of space. On arrival at the station (in orbit above the ocean that covers the whole planet) Kris finds neglected, malfunctioning machinery and no sign of the scientists, though he hears strange sounds and a child's ball rolls along a corridor toward him. Finally he encounters Snaut, a frightened and disheveled man who tells him that Gibarian has killed himself from depression and asks him to come back later. He maneuvers Kris away from a hammock inside his room that seems to contain something (identified only by a huge close-up of an ear).

Kris selects an empty room but is immediately distracted by another sound and makes his way to Gibarian's room, which, while obviously belonging to a cultured person, is in complete disorder. He watches a video message Gibarian has left for him: Gibarian says he is not crazy and what happened to him could happen to any of them. More strange noises outside cause Kris to leave (taking a gun he finds here) as ominous rumbling music begins and the camera tracks rapidly toward a round window that fills the screen, showing only blackness outside. (Similar shots and music occur at intervals, emphasizing the planet's indifference and mystery, as do brief intercuts of the ocean's surface.)

Kris is seen in a circular external corridor, lined with round windows, and with large rectangular metal blocks tilted at odd angles on the floor, again suggesting neglect and disorder. He finally contacts the third scientist, Dr. Sartorius, who talks scornfully about Gibarian's "cowardice" and seems to share his room with a powerful male dwarf who forces his way out and has to be recaptured. The openly hostile Sartorius tells Kris to leave, saying that he is too impressionable. After a shot of the swirling Solaris Ocean, Kris glimpses in the corridor a young (barely teenage) girl dressed in a short aqua nightdress; he follows her to a room where he finds only Gibarian's plastic-covered frozen body, which he examines briefly before leaving.

He returns to Snaut's cluttered room, but Snaut still refuses to answer his questions, either about Sartorius or about the mysterious girl—again seen walking past the half-open door, accompanied by a soft tinkling sound heard previously. Snaut denies being mad, and again Kris leaves without any clear information. Back in his room he barricades his door, in a shot that begins in vivid color and then becomes black and white. He watches the remainder of Gibarian's video, where a frightened Gibarian tells him that it all has something to do with conscience, and the girl is also present.

Kris lies down on the bed with the gun beside him. As he sleeps, there is a switch from black and white back to color; an extreme close-up of a woman's hair in a golden glow fills the screen, and the camera tracks back to show her face as the rumbling associated with the Solaris Ocean intensifies. The woman is seated in a chair, wearing a fringed shawl; she approaches the bed, lies down beside Kris, and kisses him. He shows no emotion at first, then asks in bewilderment how she knew where he was. He reaches for the gun but she accidentally kicks it away.

Searching for her shoes in his suitcase, she finds the photo (of her) seen earlier at the bonfire and asks who it is, then, perplexed, says, "It's me," as she looks in the mirror and holds up the picture. Kris, obviously disturbed, says they have to leave and must put on spacesuits; as he cuts open the thongs at the back of her long leather dress, he notices a torn patch on her sleeve with the mark of a needle on her skin. The strangeness of the scene is confirmed when we see that the metal chests are still blocking the doorway.

In the arrival area, Kris tricks her into entering a small shuttle rocket and fires it off, but is himself trapped in the flame-filled room and saves himself only by rolling up in a blanket. He returns to his room to rest and is joined by Snaut, who asks cryptically if he has had "visitors" and offers some sardonic recommendations as to how to handle things next time. Kris tells him that the woman (Hari) died ten years ago, and Snaut explains that the phenomenon began after the ocean was illegally subjected to radiation; it appears to extract "islands of memory" from the human brain, and Hari will likely return in an infinity of replicas.[17] They discuss whether to close down the station, and Snaut leaves after attaching torn paper strips to a ventilator, saying their rustling reminds him of Earth and even Sartorius has this in his room. The scene ends with a close-up of Hari's shawl hanging on the chair as Kris prepares for bed.

When Kris wakes, Hari is with him once more, but this time he seems to expect her and greets her tenderly. She too is prepared, and has brought scissors to cut her dress open; she deposits her shawl on the chair beside the one already there and lies down beside him. When Kris later tries to leave the room, taking one dress and shawl with him, she displays superhuman strength in breaking through the metal door to join him, injuring herself badly; but when he tries to clean her wounds, he discovers that they have already begun to heal, leaving her skin undamaged.

Kris joins Snaut and Sartorius at the laboratory and introduces Hari to them as his wife.[18] Snaut seems willing to accept her as human, but Sartorius refuses to do so, trying to convince Kris that she is nothing more than a subject for scientific experimentation. Kris threatens Sartorius with violence if he attempts this, and Sartorius comments sarcastically that Kris has made contact on a "pointless" emotional level.

In Kris's room, he and Hari watch his tape from Earth, with the Bach music of the credits as accompaniment. The tape, covering several different seasons and time periods, shows Kris as a boy and his youthful father and mother, always in the setting of the dacha and the pond. At the end Hari is shown twice, near the dacha, wearing her now-familiar dress and shawl. After the tape ends, Hari looks in a mirror once more and says that she doesn't know herself at all and can't remember her face; Kris, reflected in the mirror as well, gives her what we later discover is a false account of their earlier relationship and their parting, trying to convince her that she had never met his mother who, she says, "hated me," and that they had separated by her own choice. (The "interior rain" that mysteriously falls at the end of this scene is, according to the script, water from a shower.)

As Hari lies asleep, Snaut tells Kris that the rate of regeneration appears to be slowing, and the visitors might be removed completely if Kris agrees to send an encephalogram of his waking thoughts to the ocean. Hari is shown, open-eyed, listening to them. Kris asks: "What if I want her to die, to disappear?" and Snaut tells him that Sartorius is working on an annihilator that destroys the neutrino system which creates the visitors, but that he has persuaded him to try the encephalogram first.

In a series of brief scenes that give no indication of elapsed time between them, Kris suddenly leaves Snaut in the corridor and runs back to his room, where he finds the apparently unconscious Hari and begs her forgiveness; he is then (after a cut to the ocean and clouds) seen asleep. In a further conversation Hari says that (thanks to Sartorius) she now knows she is not the real Hari, who poisoned herself; she needs to know who she is in order to help Kris. He admits that the original Hari killed herself after a quarrel, probably because she felt he didn't really love her, and he blames himself for not saving her. He tells this Hari that he loves her and she responds similarly.

The four characters meet in the library to celebrate Snaut's birthday; the room is elegantly furnished, full of books, statues, busts, and paintings, most notably five full-size illuminated reproductions of paintings by Brueghel on the far wall. Snaut arrives late, tired and disheveled; he talks about the need for sleep, whereas "they" always come at night. He asks Kris to read aloud a passage on sleep from *Don Quixote* (in the same illustrated edition seen earlier in the dacha). Snaut goes on to express skepticism about man's urge to explore alien worlds, but Sartorius, arguing that Man was created to learn about nature and is fated to acquire knowledge, reproaches Kris for neglecting his scientific duties. Hari defends Kris and tells Snaut and Sartorius that, instead of treating their visitors as inconvenient aliens, they should realize that they are "yourselves, your conscience." She proclaims her love for Kris and asserts that she is a woman; Sartorius tells her she is just a mechanical copy and the real Hari is dead. Weeping, she says she is becoming human and can feel the same emotions they can. In the corridor Snaut informs Kris that there will be thirty seconds of weightlessness while the station is repositioning, and Kris returns to Hari in the library.

After an examination, in extreme close-up, of details of one of the Brueghel reproductions (*Hunters in the Snow*), Kris and Hari, tenderly embracing as the Bach organ music begins, are seen floating in midair, along with objects such as a candelabrum and the copy of *Don Quixote*. The scene ends with the couple seated on the floor, as the organ music is given electronic enhancement; an ominously lengthy shot of the blue-grey Solaris Ocean ends with the sounds of an explosion and a crash, and the music stops abruptly.

Hari is seen lying, apparently dead, in a corridor, wearing only a light blue shirt which has frozen solid and crackles as Kris (wearing only underwear and a jacket) turns her body over and stares at her helplessly. He tells the approaching Snaut that Hari drank liquid oxygen out of despair; when he says he will await her return, Snaut warns him not to turn "a scientific problem into a bedroom farce." Meanwhile Hari begins to revive, jerking convulsively, her clearly erotic writhing accentuated as her garment melts and clings transparently to her naked body. Kris assures her that she is now the "real" Hari and dearer to him than any scientific truth; but she denies this and insists he must find her disgusting.

Time and space are now condensed over a series of brief scenes. In his room, Kris promises her that he will not return to Earth (where she could not exist) and they will live here on the station. Obviously ill, he wanders through the corridor; a strangely disturbing dissolve shows him in medium close-up, facing the camera, and then from the back, not in a conventional reverse angle, but with his surroundings unchanged. He joins Snaut, who is looking through a window at the ocean and tells Kris that his encephalogram has helped; Kris talks feverishly about compassion, suffering, and love as the camera focuses on the swirling ocean outside.

Supported by Snaut and Hari (now—in her third incarnation—once again wearing a completely undamaged dress), Kris walks along a corridor where bright lights at regular intervals flare into the camera lens: Gibarian died of shame, Kris says, and shame is what will save humanity. A sudden crescendo of organ music mingles with the electronic sound, and we see the interior of the dacha, orange-tinted, showing the birdcage, and then cut back to the station and Kris ill in bed, silently mouthing the word "Mama"; he is in a room whose totally mirrored walls and floor endlessly reflect him as Hari kneels beside him, stroking his forehead.

A hallucinatory sequence follows in which Tarkovsky revives a technique from *Ivan's Childhood*: the same character appears several times within one continuous shot, often in totally incompatible and "impossible" spatial juxtapositions. The setting is the space station, and several "Haris" appear, sometimes wearing a slip, sometimes her dress, and sometimes her shawl. Kris's mother as a young woman is also there, wearing a slip similar to Hari's and holding Hari's shawl; the dog from the dacha is present too. Electronic music is heard throughout.

Another complex dreamlike sequence follows (analyzed more fully in the chapter on *Solaris*), this time in black and white, set in an ambiguous space that is sometimes the dacha (but with its furniture covered in transparent plastic), sometimes the space station, and sometimes a strange fusion of the two. Kris, in pajamas and looking tired and ill, talks to his aloof and sadly reproachful mother (dressed as in the video), who accuses him of neglecting and offending her; she speaks to him as if he were a child and insists on washing his arm for him, then leaves as he looks after her, weeping, and sighs, "Mama!"

Back on the space station, in color, the revived Kris inquires about Hari. Snaut, who is looking after him, says she is "no more" and reads her letter: she has chosen extinction in Sartorius's annihilator, for this is better for both of them. Snaut reports that the visitors haven't returned since Kris's encephalogram was sent, but islands are beginning to form in the ocean. Sartorius, listening outside, walks off, looking depressed and bouncing the ball seen on Kris's arrival. In the library Kris and Snaut discuss happiness, death, and immortality; Kris's voice is heard over a shot of the clouds and ocean outside, musing on his future and whether he should stay here, hoping for the impossible, that Hari might return. Back in Kris's room, Snaut says it's time for him to return to Earth.

A brief transition shot, of the metal box containing a plant that Kris brought with him from Earth, leads to the water weeds that opened the film. Kris walks past bare trees and branches to the now-frozen pond, then toward the dacha, where a fire burns outside and the dog rushes to greet him. The electronically enhanced Bach music heard over the transition now stops and is replaced by the electronic rumbling associated with Solaris. He peers through a window; his metal box is on the sill and his father moves around the room arranging books, seemingly oblivious to the rain falling indoors; he turns and looks off-screen, as if surprised. Kris approaches the house and falls to his knees as his father opens the door and embraces him in almost the exact pose of Rembrandt's *Return of the Prodigal Son*.

The camera moves away in a helicopter shot to show the house gradually becoming obscured by clouds. A cut, with the camera still rising, reveals the yellow balloon from the opening scene still dangling from the trees by the house, and also the highway. Again clouds obscure the image until another cut shows the Solaris Ocean, and in the middle, an island containing the dacha, the pond and trees, and a cut-off portion of the highway. The music, gathering intensity throughout, reaches a crescendo as the camera continues to move away through the clouds and the screen goes white.

Stalker (Stalker, 1979)

[N.B.: Available *Stalker* prints vary greatly in visual quality. While in 16mm prints the opening sequence seems simply to be black and white, the more reliable 35mm prints have a definite sepia tone. Some later "black and white" sequences in the film also have (in 35mm) clearly discernible sepia or blue-grey tones. The film's cameraman, Alexander Knyazhinsky, told us that these variations were deliberate. As with *Nostalghia* and *The Sacrifice* in particular, the film's visual richness and subtlety are fully evident only in a good 35mm print and are lost almost completely on video.]

The credits appear over sepia images of a dingy bar, to the accompaniment of electronic music; the bartender enters, serves a customer, and exits. A crawl title follows, explaining, in the words of a "Professor Wallace," the appearance in an unnamed small country of "a miracle of miracles"—the Zone.

After a slow fade-in, two lengthy tracking shots (in sepia) move through a half-opened door and back and forth over an ornamental brass bed with three figures—a woman, a child, and a man—lying in it. During the second shot, the camera passes over a round table with various objects on it, including a box of pills and a glass of water which quivers and slides across the table as the rattling of a train is heard off-screen. A pair of crutches is propped against a wall, and the poverty-stricken interior suggests a life of misery. The man gets cautiously out of bed, dresses, and tiptoes out of the room; the woman sits up as he leaves.

He begins to wash himself in a primitively furnished kitchen with bare wooden floors. A light comes on, then immediately burns out, shattering the bulb. His wife berates him for going back to his old ways and warns he will land back in jail, for a ten-year term this time. He wearily begs her to let him go, for he is "imprisoned everywhere." Finally he pushes his way past her and leaves, the woman shouting that she curses the day she met him and that it is his fault they have "such a child." She gradually sinks writhing to the ground and begins to weep, as the rumbling of the train is heard, briefly interrupted by a fragment of Wagner's *Meistersinger*.

The man (shortly to be identified as a "stalker"—the English word is used in both the original story and the film) keeps a rendezvous in a dockyard with a client, a cynical intellectual accompanied by an elegantly dressed woman to whom he is lamenting the tedium and lack of "mystery" in modern life—even the Zone is a "boring" product of a supercivilization. Stalker, who has not expected to find the woman, orders her to leave and notes disgustedly that his client has been drinking.

Stalker and his companion enter the bar, where they join the customer from the credit sequence. Foghorns (from the docks) are heard intermittently as Stalker again forbids his client to drink and addresses the men as "Writer" (the drunk) and "Professor." In the conversation that follows, Writer presents himself as a total cynic with no belief even in the worth of his own vocation and begins the needling of the Professor (a physicist) that is to continue for most of their journey. Professor offers scientific curiosity as his motive for their expedition to the Zone, while Writer says he has lost his inspiration and is going to beg for some. Their conversation is shot in a single take lasting almost four and a half minutes, the camera tracking in almost imperceptibly from long shot to medium close-up.

Stalker, who has said little so far, now takes charge as a train whistle is heard outside, and says it is time to go. Writer tries to buy some cigarettes but is prevented by Professor from doing so. The men enter a jeep and drive through a wasteland of abandoned buildings and streets littered with rubbish, avoiding a sinister-looking policeman on a motorcycle, then sneak through one of the barriers to the Zone by following a train as it passes through the gate. This takes them not to the Zone itself but to another guarded area where they again have to conceal themselves to avoid detection. As Stalker plans their next move, Writer begins to lose his earlier bravado and voices some misgivings about the expedition. Professor, by contrast, remains calm.

By following a train they penetrate a fenced-off, floodlit area, coming under fire from the guards, and take refuge in a dilapidated building. Professor volunteers to look for a railway flatcar and comes under further fire. He finds one and they set off once more, after an altercation between the clearly frightened Writer and Professor, when the latter insists on bringing his knapsack.

Although this whole sequence is well-filmed and suspenseful, it is often illogical and confusing in its handling of space and time: the men follow no consistent directional pattern in their crossing of the two barriers, and the gatekeeper who runs to raise the alarm at the first gate has barely moved when he is next seen, even though two or three minutes of "real" time have elapsed. Tarkovsky may here be trying to prepare us for the non-Euclidean space and time encountered in the Zone itself.

The 3½-minute sequence of the journey to the Zone is discussed in more detail in the chapter on *Stalker*. A change from sepia to a color shot of the landscape signals their arrival at the Zone. This landscape combines lush greenery and a body of water visible in the distance with the kind of industrial debris encountered earlier in the film. Stalker announces that they are "home" and talks about Porcupine, his teacher, who had brought people to the Zone until something broke in him or he was "punished." He says he is going to take a walk and asks Professor to tie some bandages around metal nuts while he is away. Professor tells Writer about their guide (the script, but not the film, mentions that Stalker used to work in his lab): he was imprisoned and his daughter is reputed to be a mutant, with no legs. He also mentions Porcupine—he became incredibly rich and then hanged himself—and gives the history of the Zone itself: what might or might not have been a meteor fell there twenty years ago, after which strange things began to happen. When rumors circulated that there existed a place within the Zone (later identified as "the Room") where one's wishes could be fulfilled, the authorities started to guard the Zone like a treasure, for who knows what kind of desires people might have? When Writer asks what it was, if not a meteorite, Professor says it could have been a message to mankind, or a gift.

Stalker, who has been briefly seen lying full face on the earth, returns and they set off, with Professor going first and Stalker throwing the nuts attached to strips of cloth to indicate the way and warning that it is dangerous to deviate from his chosen path. Ruined military vehicles litter the landscape; Stalker says that he remembers an expedition being sent to the Zone when he was a child. Despite his initial apprehension, Writer shows himself increasingly reluctant to follow Stalker's warning that they cannot proceed directly toward the clearly visible building that is their destination; his defiance at one point leads to an angry confrontation between them: speaking of the Zone as if it were a living being, Stalker warns that it demands respect, otherwise it will punish them. When Writer insists on setting off on his own nevertheless, Stalker politely takes his flask of alcohol from him and empties it. As Writer apprehensively approaches the building, he is stopped on the threshold by a series of mysterious noises, culminating in the warning, "Stop, don't move!"

The others deny having spoken, and Professor suggests that Writer became frightened and told himself to go back. As they argue, Stalker, in an anguished speech, warns them that the Zone is a complex maze of traps, all of them fatal. It may seem capricious, but at each moment it's just as we have made it with our own minds; people have had to turn back, they have died on the threshold to the Room, but everything that happens depends not on the Zone but on us. When Writer asks if the Zone lets the good people through and destroys the evil ones, Stalker answers that he thinks it lets through the wretched ones, those who have lost all hope, but even they perish if they do not know how to behave here. Writer is lucky, for the Zone has warned him. Apparently impressed by this, Professor declares that he will wait here for them to come back, but Stalker says that it is impossible to return by the way they entered; he offers to abandon the journey and refund (some of) their money, but a taunting remark by Writer makes Professor change his mind and they continue on their way, as the call of a cuckoo (the only sound of life in the Zone, apart from the occasional howling of a wolf or dog) is heard.

"*Stalker.* 2nd part" begins with Stalker calling for the other two, and Professor and Writer are seen in front of a passageway in a wall covered with dilapidated tiles; one of Stalker's pieces of cloth and its metal nut hangs behind them, and Writer's plastic bag is lying on the ground. As they rise painfully to their feet, Writer predicts that they are in for another lecture, and we hear off-screen the sound of a large object falling into water, followed by ominous electronic rumblings and a brief shot of something splashing into what might be a well (possibly an anticipation of a later scene where Writer drops a rock into a well). Stalker cautiously edges along an unseen ledge while his thoughts are heard in voice-over; he joins his companions as they emerge from within a huge metal pipe. The voice-over asks for belief to be given to the other two, who should become helpless as children, for weakness is great and strength is worthless. Weakness, pliability, and tenderness express the freshness of existence, whereas strength, dryness, and hardness are the companions of death: what becomes hard will not triumph.

Professor wants to return to fetch his knapsack, but Stalker tells him this is impossible and sends Writer ahead down a ladder. Writer and Stalker are seen near the tiled wall; they then move past a series of archways to arrive at a large waterfall. As they begin to wade knee-deep toward the waterfall, Writer notices that Professor is missing; Stalker says it's too late to wait for him and urges Writer to hurry as the camera tracks in close-up over the embers of a fire and over shallow water covering a tiled floor on which a hypodermic syringe, some rusty metal objects, and pages from a book are visible. Writer emerges through the archway in the tiled wall seen twice already to find Professor calmly enjoying a drink from his thermos, with Writer's plastic bag on the ground beside him and a fire burning in the foreground. He tells them he "crawled" here to recover his knapsack; Stalker notices the nut and cloth and panics, saying they have fallen into a trap. He tells them to wait as the other two renew their feud and exchange graphic insults.

A mysterious and complex sequence follows, which is analyzed more fully in the chapter on *Stalker*. Color alternates with sepia, and the conversation continues uninterrupted while the positions and spatial relationships of the characters alter in a totally nonnaturalistic manner, and a dog mysteriously appears. At one point the camera moves off to examine a series of objects lying underwater in the manner of the previous scene. Biblical readings are heard, one in voice-over by what sounds like Stalker's wife and one spoken by Stalker himself. Pulsating electronic music intensifies the sense of strangeness and mystery. The dialogue, mostly from Writer and Stalker, deals mainly with the redemptive power of art, with even the cynical Writer paying tribute to this in words similar to Tarkovsky's own in *Sculpting in Time*.

A sudden cut from this setting introduces the "Meatgrinder," a dark tunnel lit at regular intervals by openings in the roof, its uneven floor dotted with puddles. Stalker tricks Writer into going first while he follows, huddled behind Professor. Tension is created by the sounds—the loud clatter of footsteps and water dripping from the roof—and by Writer's apprehensive features. When he reaches a door, Writer produces a gun, but the terrified Stalker persuades him to discard it. The door leads to a flooded interior; Writer wades chest-deep through the filthy water and climbs a flight of stairs. Professor and Stalker follow, the latter shouting for Writer to wait.

Writer is seen in a huge room filled with low sand dunes, with Stalker and Professor in the distance; Stalker hurls a metal nut, and he and Professor throw themselves to the ground. The nut lands, in slow motion, on a dune and unexpectedly bounces away from it; electronic music begins and Writer puts his hand to his forehead as if in pain. A long shot of the room shows a bird flying across it and suddenly disappearing halfway; another bird makes the same journey but lands safely on the far side.

Standing beside a well, into which he drops a large rock, Writer delivers a long monologue, talking, with intense self-disgust but also complete honesty, about the meaninglessness of his life and his work. What kind of a writer is he if he detests writing and experiences it as a torture, something shameful? He used to think his books helped people, but no one really needs him. Nevertheless, Stalker praises him, saying that he must be a fine person and that the "Meatgrinder" is the most terrible part of the Zone: Porcupine sent his brother, a sensitive, gifted person, to die there. He then begins to recite a poem—supposedly by this brother, but actually written by Tarkovsky's father—suffused with the bittersweet realization that a full life and the beauty of nature are not enough compensation for escaping one's true fate. Although no indication of a change of place has been given and the action appears to be continuous from within the "dune room," the ensuing scenes show the characters in a totally different space, with a series of rooms lining two sides of a sunken, half-drained pool filled with rubbish.

Saying that he knows he was tricked into going first, Writer calls Stalker a "louse" whose favorite is the Professor. As Stalker attempts to apologize, the dog appears and runs through the water. Another cut over uninterrupted speech now places the men inside one of the rooms, framed by the doorway and viewed in long shot. Stalker and Writer stand to either side of a brightly lit window, with Professor seated in the middle of the room and an old-fashioned telephone on the floor. (Audiences who have been told that the men's ultimate goal is a "Room" may assume at first that they have reached their destination; to avoid confusion, this particular setting will be referred to as the "telephone room.") In this 6 minute 50 second shot (the longest in the film) the lighting changes with intense subtlety, shading imperceptibly from very dark to very bright within the very restricted color range of the film as a whole.

In the discussion that follows, the tensions among the men increase, and some of their deeper motivations for the journey emerge. The apparently defunct phone suddenly rings—a wrong number—and Professor then uses it to call his laboratory. He tells his boss he has outwitted him and is no longer afraid of him: he has found "it" and is just a few paces away from the place itself. He hangs up and begins to muse on his own reasons for coming to the Zone: the gift the "Room" offers will be misused by politicians and megalomaniacs, all the "so-called saviors of mankind." When Stalker protests that he doesn't bring people like that here, Professor says he's not the only stalker in the world. Writer responds that Professor's real motivation is power and fame. When Writer turns on an overhead light, it flares briefly and goes out, providing a link with Stalker's house, as do the wooden floorboards and the sleeping pills that Writer finds on the window sill. As Stalker suggests it is time to go "there," Writer adorns himself with a crown of thorns that he has made from material found in the room and mockingly tells him: "Don't fool yourself; I don't forgive you."

After two or three brief shots (including one that shows the dog lying in the entrance to another room, with two skeletons lying in an apparent embrace in the background) Stalker leads the way to another opening in a wall at right angles to the one seen previously; the interior is hidden from view but is strongly illuminated. Speaking with great emotion and almost in tears, he tells them that they are now on the threshold, and this is the most important moment of their lives. Their most cherished desire, their sincerest wish, will come true here; if they think about their past it will make them kinder, but the most important thing is to believe. Who wants to go first? Perhaps Writer?

Writer refuses, saying he has no desire to humiliate himself by sniveling and praying, and Stalker turns to Professor instead. The latter, however, says he plans to destroy the Room with a bomb he has brought with him: his colleagues had tried to hide it, thinking that the Room "in a certain sense meant hope," but he found it and intends to use it, for "this place obviously won't bring anyone happiness" and he wants to ensure that the power of the Room will not be used by the wrong people for the wrong reasons. Stalker begins to wrestle with him for possession of the bomb and Writer intervenes, pulling Stalker away from Professor five times and attacking him with increasing ferocity, calling him a "hypocritical louse." When Stalker argues that Professor "wants to destroy your hope" and this is the only place people can come to when there is no hope left, Writer accuses him of being interested only in money and power: he is tsar and God here and can decide who will live and who will die.

Stalker tearfully denies this, saying that stalkers are forbidden to enter the Room or to have selfish intentions. He is a failure who has never achieved anything, but the Zone is all he has: everything else was taken away from him "behind the barbed wire." The people he brings here are as wretched as he is and have nothing to hope for; yet he, a louse, can help them. Speaking more calmly, Writer calls Stalker a *yurodivy* ("holy fool") and offers an explanation for Porcupine's suicide, even though his wish had apparently been fulfilled: the Zone responds to the *essence* of your nature, to what you *really* want, rather than to what you *think* you want. Porcupine's secret desire for money was stronger than his conscious wish to save his brother, and, realizing that, he hanged himself. Writer adds that he will not enter the Room: he doesn't want to pour the filth from his soul onto anyone else and end up like Porcupine. Does Stalker think this "miracle" really exists, and has anyone ever been made truly happy here? As Writer turns to look into the Room, he loses his balance and almost topples over the threshold; Stalker grabs his coat and hauls him back to sit on the ground beside him. The telephone rings again and is ignored. Meanwhile Professor, who has been fiddling with his bomb, glances into the Room, then starts to unscrew the cylinder and tosses the parts into the water.

A cut now places the camera *within* the Room, looking out at the three men and the pool behind them. Professor, continuing to dismantle his bomb, squats down beside the others, his back to them. Writer has meanwhile put his arm protectively around Stalker, and all three look toward the Room as the camera tracks slowly back to reveal the doorway and their reflections in a large pool of water in the entranceway. As the camera stops, framing them in the doorway, the light changes to an intense orange/gold glow and then fades slowly as Stalker wonders aloud whether he should come to live here with his wife and child, where no one would hurt them. A sudden interior rainfall begins, with the raindrops splashing loudly into the flooded interior and creating a band of rippling light as the men watch quietly. As the Professor tosses various objects into the water, the screen darkens once more and the rain slackens off to an intermittent dripping whose sound mingles with the splashing created by the Professor and then with the off-screen noise of a train.

As the sound of the train intensifies, a cut to an overhead position shows shallow water covering a cracked tiled floor, with part of the Professor's bomb resting on it. A fish floats slowly into view, with what seems to be blood trickling from its body; this substance then mingles with a black streak of oil that gradually spreads to cover the surface of the water as a discordant rendition of part of Ravel's "Bolero" is heard above the clatter of the train. These sounds continue briefly over a cut to black and white (or sepia) of Stalker's wife and crippled child, seen from within the bar, with a nuclear power station in the background. The wife enters the bar, where the three men are standing around the table almost exactly as before the journey started, except for the dog now sitting on the window ledge. Stalker tells his wife the dog "just tagged along," and the family leaves with the animal. Writer and Professor remain, both looking thoughtful and subdued, as if they have learned something, despite the apparent failure of their trip.

A foghorn sounds over a shift back to full color and what at first looks like a miracle—"Monkey" walking along the riverbank; a change of angle reveals that she is on her father's shoulders. The setting is the debris-strewn bank of a polluted river, with a distant power plant belching thick smoke. Back in his home (and in sepia) Stalker despairs over his failure: no one has faith any longer, no one needs him or the Room—it's all been in vain. His wife tries to comfort him, offering to accompany him to the Zone, but he refuses, asking what will happen if she too fails.

After a cut to a blank wall, the wife enters and starts to speak, apparently directly addressing the audience—though this self-reflective effect was not originally intended; the scene was shot in the bar, with the speech clearly delivered to Writer and Professor, and was moved to its present position only during editing. She says that her husband is "blessed," everyone used to laugh at him, he was a muddler; her mother was opposed to their marriage because he was a stalker, a marked man, and an eternal jailbird. Nevertheless she has been happy with him and has never regretted it: that was their fate, and if there were no sorrow in their lives, there would be no happiness either.

The final shot of the film, in color, begins with a close-up of "Monkey," wearing a headscarf, sitting reading a book. She is heard, in voice-over, reciting a poem by Fyodor Tyuchev and then appears to move, one by one, three glass vessels on the table before her by means of telekinesis (see the chapter on *Stalker* for a fuller analysis of this shot). A passing train then causes the table to shake violently, and the sound of the train mingles with a distorted fragment of Beethoven's "Ode to Joy"; the film ends with a fade on the girl's expressionless face.

Nostalghia (Nostalghia, 1983)

[*N.B.:* North American prints of the film omit the whole of the first half of Domenico's self-immolation scene. This synopsis is based on the British print and will indicate what is missing in the American version.]

The film opens in black and white on a landscape (later associated with Andrei's memories of Russia) shrouded in mist, with river and trees in the background, a telephone pole, and an almost immobile white horse. The credits begin as four darkly clad figures, an old woman, a younger woman, and two children, move away down a hill, followed by a dog, to the accompaniment of a woman's voice singing a melancholy Russian song. As they separate out and come to a halt, the image freezes and the music changes to snatches of Verdi's *Requiem.*

In muted color, a Volkswagen arrives in a misty Italian landscape; a man (Andrei Gorchakov) and a woman (Eugenia) get out and exchange a few words in both Russian and Italian, the man saying that he is sick of these beautiful sights. She sets off to see a painting in a nearby church and he starts to follow slowly. Eugenia is seen in the pillared and candlelit interior of a church with women in black dresses kneeling in prayer in the background; she has long, curly reddish hair and wears high heels and a black cape over a full-length, flowing white dress. In a conversation with the elderly sacristan she is politely reproached for lacking faith and is told that a woman is meant to have and raise children, in a spirit of patience and sacrifice.

Meanwhile the women have carried a life-size statue of the Virgin through the church and are praying before it; Piero della Francesca's *Madonna of Childbirth* is visible on the wall behind them. As a woman opens the statue's robes, a flock of small birds streams out. A series of virtual match-cuts takes us from a close-up of Eugenia's face to a slow track in to Piero's Madonna and then, in black and white, to Andrei, his hair conspicuously marked by a white streak (as was Stalker's). He looks up and then down as a white feather flutters slowly across the screen; he picks it up as it floats in a puddle. The sounds of running water and barking dogs are heard as he turns and looks across the landscape of the credit sequence toward a farmhouse. The sound of a Russian song is heard very faintly as an angel with large white wings walks slowly in front of the building. (The angel is barely recognizable on a first viewing and looks like two people walking side by side.)

A cut back to color introduces an interior eventually identified as a hotel foyer. Eugenia asks Andrei why he refused even to look at the painting they had driven so far to see; he responds only by asking what she is reading. She replies, "Tarkovsky," then adds, "Arseny" (the director's father). Andrei tells her that poetry is untranslatable and no one can understand another culture by reading its literature in translation. The only solution is to destroy the frontiers. As he turns to look back, toward the camera, the sound of running water again introduces a brief mental image in black and white: the head of a dark-haired woman, seen from behind against the background of the Russian landscape, as she breathes into and then wipes a glass while a dog barks shrilly. This is followed by a very brief shot of Eugenia turning away and tossing her hair back.

Still in the foyer, Eugenia asks Andrei about "his Sosnovsky" and why he returned to Russia; he responds by handing her a letter. We learn that Sosnovsky took to drink after his return and then killed himself. (Pavel Sosnovsky is based on Maximilian Beryozovsky, an eighteenth-century Ukrainian serf composer: see *Sculpting* 203; *TWT* 252.) The landlady enters and collects their keys; as Eugenia talks to her, the sounds of trickling water and a barking dog introduce another black and white memory/reverie of the dark-haired woman, the Russian landscape, and the farm, with the younger woman and the boy from the credit sequence running, in slow motion, after the dog. The dog splashes through a pond after a stick, the sound merging with the landlady's voice as she praises the beauty of the local landscape. Eugenia follows the landlady upstairs to her (separate) room, denying the woman's assumption that Andrei is her boyfriend.

A shot lasting 2 minutes 45 seconds (analyzed more fully in chapter 9) shows Andrei moving around his bedroom, switching lights on and off and examining its contents. A sound brings him to the doorway, where he finds Eugenia outside, clutching her book of poems. She asks him if he wants to phone his wife in Moscow; he shakes his head, takes the book from her, and returns to his room. Eugenia, still in her long dress and high heels, kneels and runs as if taking part in a race, but trips and falls. Apparently unhurt, she goes off laughing up the stairs.

In another complex scene, again analyzed in the chapter, Andrei sits and then lies on his bed; as rain begins outside, the lighting in the room darkens and the camera tracks slowly forward. The dog from the "Russian" scenes emerges from the bathroom and lies down beside the bed as the light brightens slightly to show Andrei apparently asleep, and the rain slackens to sporadic dripping. Shots in black and white follow of Eugenia and his wife embracing as the dripping continues and a Russian folk song is faintly heard; these are interrupted by a color shot of Eugenia looking down at Andrei. Back in black and white, Andrei's pregnant wife is seen lying on the bed as he looks at her; camera movement and lighting make it seem as if the bed is floating in space. As the light gradually returns, Eugenia is heard calling his name off-screen and telling him it is time for their visit to St. Catherine's Pool.

In this new setting the bathers taking the therapeutic waters discuss both Andrei (who, Eugenia informs them, is a Russian poet, working on a biography of a Russian composer called Sosnovsky who had visited this area) and a shabbily dressed middle-aged man (Domenico) who is walking around the edge of the pool, muttering incoherently, accompanied by a dog that looks exactly like the animal from Andrei's past. The bathers gossip about him, saying that he had shut himself up with his family for seven years to await the end of the world. Andrei begins to show interest when one of the bathers suggests that Domenico is a man of great faith. Domenico tells Eugenia an obscure anecdote about a conversation between God and St. Catherine. When Andrei says to Eugenia that Domenico can't be mad, for he has faith, she insists that he is just an ordinary lunatic and tells him of Domenico's latest fixation—repeated attempts to climb into the pool with a lighted candle and his ejections lest he drown himself. Andrei suggests that those we call mad are often closest to the truth, and says he wants to meet him as soon as possible.

Back in the darkened hotel foyer, Andrei briefly praises Eugenia's beauty, then asks if she knows why Domenico shut himself away; she responds coldly that she doesn't. The next scene shows them visiting Domenico, who is riding a stationary bicycle outside a dilapidated stone building. In the long (4 minutes 40 seconds), highly formalized shot that follows, the camera tracks in long shot from right to left and then left to right as Eugenia twice walks back and forth carrying messages from Andrei to Domenico and is rudely rebuffed by the latter each time. When Andrei asks if she has offended Domenico, she becomes angry and leaves, saying that she is going back to Rome. (It is only now that we learn that Eugenia is Andrei's official translator.) He approaches Domenico himself, but has no better luck in making contact before the man says abruptly that he is tired and goes off inside.

Nevertheless, Andrei is shown entering the building—in a series of reverse angle shots that create an unexpected and even bewildering confusion between exterior and interior space. We then see a black and white shot of what seems at first to be a landscape but is revealed to be a miniature, whose apparent rivers, valleys, hills, and trees (with bird song on the soundtrack) the camera explores in close-up before tilting up to show what seems to be a continuation of the model but is in fact a real landscape seen through a window. The sounds of dripping water and of a buzz-saw are heard as Domenico, off-screen and as if expecting him, invites him to enter.

The main furnishings of the room—gradually revealed as the scene proceeds—are a bed with a plastic sheet hung over it to collect rainwater and an empty, broken door frame; "$1 + 1 = 1$" is scrawled on the wall in huge figures, and objects singled out include a dusty mirror, books, photos, potted plants, a large green flask, an earthenware jug, and three bottles, two brown and one green, standing on the floor. The dog is also present, settling down on the flooded floor in a pose reminiscent of the swamp scene in *Stalker*. The sound of the buzz-saw is heard intermittently throughout, along with snatches of Beethoven's Ninth Symphony. Rain eventually begins to fall inside the room, collecting in puddles on the floor, and one long-held shot examines the rain bouncing off the surface of the bottles.

The two men move around, saying little at first. Domenico pours two drops of olive oil into his palm, murmuring, "One drop plus one drop makes a larger drop, not two." He offers Andrei some bread and wine and says that he was selfish in trying to save only his own family, for now the whole world must be saved. He picks up a lighted candle from a niche in the wall and blows it out, telling Andrei that he must carry a burning candle across St. Catherine's Pool for him, because he is prevented from doing so himself. He asks if Andrei has children, and Andrei describes his son and daughter and his wife—"like Piero's Madonna, but all in black." Domenico says that "we" are planning something big in Rome and then, almost sobbing, talks to the dog, saying he is scared of being alone.

The sound of the buzz-saw carries over from this scene into the next few shots, which mingle black and white images representing Domenico's thoughts and memories of his family's release from the imprisonment he had imposed on them, with brief color inserts of the continuing action in the present. The flashbacks include Domenico struggling with a man in a white coat and then pursuing his small son across some church steps, and his wife kissing a policeman's feet, a bottle of spilt milk beside her.

Among the color scenes are a shot of a car driving along a winding road with the dazzling white houses of a typical Italian hill town[19] in the background and (even though this too must be part of Domenico's memories) a small boy with a scab on the corner of his mouth who asks, "Papa, is this the end of the world?"

In color and in the same setting as the flashbacks, Andrei says goodbye to Domenico and is driven off in a taxi. Another black and white scene, in the same location and from the same angle, shows a crowd watching as Domenico's family are led down the stairs from their house toward an ambulance in the background.

Returning to his hotel room, Andrei finds Eugenia sitting on his bed drying her hair, saying that there is no water in her bathroom. When he offers no reaction and instead shows her the candle that Domenico has given him, she launches into a lengthy, increasingly hysterical tirade that continues, in one uninterrupted shot lasting 4 minutes 5 seconds, as she walks nervously around the room. She accuses him of being afraid, especially of freedom, and of being too much of a saint for "this" (baring her breast), for he is interested only in Madonnas; moreover he is boring and badly dressed. She tells of a dream about a soft white poisonous insect that she had tried but failed to kill, and finally breaks down in tears. Andrei, who has made virtually no response to all this, walks out of the room, muttering, in Russian, "She's mad."

Eugenia pursues him into the corridor, telling him to go back to his wife, and in the ensuing quarrel slaps him in the face, causing his nose to bleed, and goes upstairs. She returns, carrying a suitcase, and pauses in the foyer to read the letter that Andrei had given her earlier, while a male voice-over speaks its contents in Italian. The letter, written by Sosnovsky after two years in Italy, describes his feelings of homesickness and his longing for the birches and the air of his childhood. Andrei enters in the foreground during the final words of the letter, still nursing his injuries; as he lies down on a bench, another black and white dream/memory of his home and family follows (discussed more fully in chapter 9).

The sound of water continues from this over a brief cut to color and a shot of Andrei's head and shoulders as a woman's voice calls his name and he looks around and away again. There is a cut to the surface of a running stream, with the statue of an angel visible under the water, as Andrei's voice begins to recite off-screen, in Russian, one of Arseny Tarkovsky's poems, beginning, "As a child I once fell ill. . . ." The imagery of the poem associates an inaccessible mother with the motif of flying and also includes a white-clad nurse/angel. (A translation is given in *Sculpting* [91–92], with a brief scenario that includes the fluttering feather and distant angel of this film.) During the reading he is seen wading thigh-deep through a flooded, half-submerged cathedral-like building as a small figure moves around in the background. Sitting on a ledge beside a bottle of Russian vodka, some bread, a small fire, and a book, he pours himself some vodka and we hear his thoughts, in Russian: "I must go to see Dad. . . . I have a jacket in the wardrobe. . . . I'll put it on as soon as I get to Moscow." He wades off again, and starts to talk drunkenly—partly in Italian and partly in Russian—to a little girl sitting in an archway who tells him her name is Angela. Rain starts to fall as we hear in voice-over, but now in Italian translation, another of Arseny's poems, "Sight grows dim . . ." (*Sculpting* 215), with its imagery of life wasting away like a dying candle, only to blaze again "with posthumous light." Meanwhile the camera, in shots that recall *Stalker*, explores the debris beneath the water before cutting, on the last line of the poem, to Andrei, lying down on the parapet, with the fire and a burning book (the translation of Arseny's poems) beside him.

Dripping water introduces a scene in black and white (or sepia) that is discussed more fully in chapter 9. To the sound of the buzz-saw, Andrei walks through a garbage-littered street and passes a large mirrored wardrobe; as he examines himself in the mirror, voice-over and image combine to create a fusion of identity between Andrei and Domenico. Andrei is then seen, still in black and white, walking through a ruined, roofless abbey as a conversation takes place off-screen between voices representing St. Catherine and God, the former asking God to let Andrei feel His presence, while the latter replies that He always does this but Andrei is not aware of it. Andrei stops and looks upward as the sound of flapping wings is heard and, in color, a white feather falls from above him to land in some shallow water. He is then seen, still in color, lying beside the ashes of the now almost completely burnt book.

Andrei is waiting for a taxi in a hotel courtyard in Rome when he is told he has a phone call. The caller is Eugenia; she says she is about to leave for India with her lover, and Domenico is in Rome, taking part in some demonstration, and keeps asking if Andrei has done what he asked him to do. She asks how his heart condition is, and he says that he wants to return home. As Eugenia talks we see her lover, who is clearly some Mafioso figure, in the background. After the call, Andrei, who looks tired and ill, says he has to return to St. Catherine's Pool.

The scene which follows is omitted from North American prints of the film but is present in British prints. Domenico is heard orating off-screen as the camera explores a strange assortment of bystanders and apparent supporters, most of whom are either oddly dressed (for example, in pajamas), seem mentally disturbed, or stand in obviously artificial and immobile poses on a flight of steps with Domenico's dog also present. His speech is both ecstatic and incoherent as he urges a totally new way of thinking and behaving if we are "to stretch the corners of the soul" and the world is "to go forward." He is then seen standing on a scaffolding surrounding an equestrian statue. Tattered banners printed with incomprehensible fragments of slogans are visible behind him, and supporters carry placards while one man mimics his gestures as if reinforcing rather than parodying them. Most of the other bystanders show little interest in what he is saying as he continues in an odd mixture of forceful exhortation ("It is the so-called healthy who have brought the world to the verge of ruin") and disjointed raving.

The American prints resume with Andrei arriving by taxi at St. Catherine's Pool, which is now being drained and cleaned. The camera examines some of the objects retrieved from the water, including a bicycle wheel, a broken doll, a broken oil lamp, silt-covered bottles, and coins, and then, inside the pool itself, a bicycle with one wheel and a woman scavenging for other objects. Andrei, looking ill, leans against the parapet and slowly swallows a pill.

Back in Rome, Domenico, now standing on the statue of the horse, continues his harangue: "We must go back to the point where we took the wrong turn. . . . We must go back to the main foundations of life. . . . What kind of world is it if a madman has to tell you to be ashamed of yourselves?" He then calls for "music" and starts to pour gasoline over himself and fumble with a lighter. The mimic seen earlier repeats his actions. Finally the lighter works, and flames roar up around Domenico as the dog barks in frenzy and discordant bursts of music from a malfunctioning record player are heard. Shots of the bystanders emphasize their total indifference to what is happening.[20] Eugenia arrives, accompanied by some policemen, as the music becomes recognizable as Beethoven's "Ode to Joy" and Domenico's flaming body falls off the statue while the mimic writhes in simulated agony in the foreground. The music swells, then starts to scratch and skip, as Domenico crawls screaming past bystanders who make no attempt whatever to help; finally he lies still.

A cut to a close-up of Andrei's hands as he lights the candle introduces a shot in the almost drained St. Catherine's Pool that lasts 8 minutes 45 seconds. Andrei makes three attempts to cross the pool, carrying the candle; on the first two occasions the candle is blown out by the wind and he resumes, obviously ill and in pain. At first the only sounds are his footsteps, his groans, and a dog barking; as he reaches his goal on the third attempt, Beethoven's "Ode to Joy" begins very softly on the soundtrack. He places the candle carefully on a ledge, then groans and collapses off-screen; the camera stays on the lighted candle for a moment as the joyous music continues.

A man runs across the pool, which is now lined with onlookers, and the woman seen scavenging is shown in close-up.[21] There is a mingled sound of weeping and murmuring that continues, along with the sound of running water, over a black and white shot of the boy who plays both sons and here seems to represent Andrei's. A woman's torso comes into frame, wearing the white dress and black shawl of Andrei's wife, though we do not see her face. She puts her hands on the boy's shoulder.

There is a cut to a black and white long shot of the Russian landscape with the house, telephone poles, and trees in the background. Andrei is seated in the middle distance with the dog lying beside him and mysterious columnlike reflections in a small pond in front of him. The off-screen noises continue as the camera tracks slowly back to reveal the arches and pillars of the ruined cathedral on both sides and in the distance, enclosing and dwarfing the house and the woods. (For this shot a model of the dacha and the Russian landscape were built inside the ruins of an abbey near Siena: *Dossier Positif* 137.) The camera moves farther back and upwards to the sound of a dog barking and trickling water, and then the voice of a woman singing a Russian folk song. Snow, mixed with rain, begins to fall as the camera tracks farther back and stops as the snow swirls fitfully around and the voice too stops, leaving only the occasional bark of a dog. The title "Dedicated to the memory of my mother" appears on the screen, as the image gradually fades.

The Sacrifice (Offret, 1986)

The credits are accompanied by Bach's "Erbarme Dich" from the *St. Matthew Passion* and superimposed on Leonardo da Vinci's uncompleted *Adoration of the Magi*. As the credits and the music end, the sounds of seagulls and the sea are heard and continue into the opening shot.

The brownish tint of the painting is replaced by full color as a man of around sixty (Alexander) is seen planting a dead tree on the seashore, assisted by his son, a boy of around seven. He tells the somewhat inattentive child a story about a monk who told a younger monk to plant a dead tree and water it every day until it came back to life. The monk did this, and three years later the tree was covered in blossoms.[22] Otto, the local postman, arrives on his bicycle and gives Alexander a birthday telegram from friends addressing him as Prince Myshkin (the hero of Dostoyevsky's novel *The Idiot*). The camera tracks with them as Alexander and the boy walk away from the shore and Otto follows them, weaving in circles on his bicycle. We learn that Alexander is a literary and theatrical critic and lecturer. Otto says that he has spent his life waiting for something real to happen to him, and Alexander agrees that he may have done the same. Otto gets off his bicycle and the two men discuss Nietzsche and the nature of belief, with Otto commenting, "If I truly believe, it will be so." When he tries to ride off on his cycle he finds that the boy has tied the rear wheel to a bush, causing him to fall off; he pretends to be enraged. The child (who is wearing a white bandage around his throat and has said nothing so far) moves off as Alexander looks after him and muses, "In the beginning was the Word, but you are mute as a fish. . . ." (At 9 minutes 26 seconds this opening shot is the longest in all Tarkovsky's work.)

Alexander continues to talk to himself, saying that humanity is on a wrong and dangerous road, as a car arrives and a man and woman, both aged around forty, get out. They discuss Alexander, the man saying that he doesn't like his incessant monologues. The elaborately dressed woman is Adelaide, Alexander's wife and the boy's mother; the suave, handsome man is Victor, a doctor, family friend, and—as is hinted later—Adelaide's lover. He tells the boy that he will be talking again in a week. Alexander says he wants to finish his chat with "Little Man" (the boy) and the others leave. Sitting with his back to a tree and holding the boy on his lap, he tells how he and Adelaide discovered their house, quite by accident, though he knew at once that if he lived there, he would be happy till he died. He reassures the apparently frightened child that there is no such thing as death, only the awful fear of death. As he talks, the child slips away from him without his noticing. Strange shepherds' calls, which recur throughout the film, are heard faintly offscreen.

Alexander continues to talk, as if to the child: man has violated nature and we have built a civilization based on power and fear; our scientific discoveries are put to evil use and savages are more spiritual than we are; we have created a dreadful imbalance between our material and our spiritual development. If sin is that which is unnecessary, our whole civilization is built on sin. He then says he is tired of talking: if only somebody would *do* something instead! Becoming aware of the boy's absence, he calls out for him, and the child unexpectedly jumps onto his back. The two lie sprawled on the grass, and a loud thunderclap is heard as the kneeling boy wipes blood from his nose and Alexander stands up, then falls on his back, groaning, "Dear God, what is wrong with me?"

The shepherds' calls continue over a cut to black and white. The camera moves in a direct overhead shot over a courtyard littered with debris, including a burnt-out car lying on its side, with water flowing over a sidewalk. A rumbling sound and running water are heard, and the shot ends on a sheet of glass in which buildings are reflected upside down, and a slow fade to black.

A return to color shows Alexander's hand turning the pages of a book of Russian icons as he comments off-screen on their beauty, wisdom, and spirituality—all of which we have lost. He and Victor then talk in an elegantly furnished room, with antique furniture, a chandelier, a piano, a rocker, and billowing white curtains. The naturalistic color of the exteriors and the icons is now replaced by an almost, but not quite, black and white effect that continues for most of the next ninety minutes or so of the film: black, white, grey, brown, beige, and muted tones of green, purple, yellow, and blue are all discernible, but the stronger colors, especially red, have been drained from the image. Alexander thanks Victor for the book, and Victor asks if he has ever felt his life to be a failure. Alexander replies that, despite his love for his son, he had hoped for something "higher" in life and feels that he has put himself in chains, of his own free will. Yet he is happy. A young woman, dressed rather like Adelaide but with long frizzy hair, enters and coyly places a pear on Victor's knee. (As with the family in *Solaris,* the relationships between the characters are never fully clarified: the published "treatment" identifies this woman, Marta, as Adelaide's daughter by a previous marriage, but this is never spelled out in the film.)[23] Alexander reads them his birthday telegram and talks about his previous career as an actor; he is interrupted by Adelaide, who enters carrying a huge armful of flowers. They discuss his acting career; he says he abandoned it because there is something "sinful, feminine, and weak" in the way in which an actor's identity dissolves in his roles. Adelaide objects to his equation of sinfulness and femininity and says that the real reason he quit was that she liked him as an actor: he lured her from London through his acting, and then abandoned her. As she speaks, there is a cut to a woman in a maid's uniform who looks toward another woman in the background and says, "She will be his death." The women will be identified later as Julia, the housekeeper, and Maria, another servant, who does not live in the house. Both men seem embarrassed by Adelaide's behavior, and Victor says he will be moving to Australia soon.

Otto arrives wheeling a large object on his bicycle—Alexander's birthday present, a seventeenth-century map of Europe. As they admire it inside, Alexander protests that it is too expensive, adding strangely, "I know it's no sacrifice, but . . ." Otto replies indignantly that of course it's a sacrifice; what kind of gift would it be otherwise? He informs Victor that he has lived in the area for only two months and is a retired schoolteacher who works as a postman part-time.

Maria, the nonresident maid, enters and timidly asks Adelaide if she can leave now. Adelaide says yes, then finds three separate tasks that have to be done first; Maria humbly repeats all the instructions. Otto tells Victor that he and Maria, who came from Iceland some years ago, are neighbors. Alexander and his wife comment on how odd and even frightening Maria is. Otto talks about the relativity of truth, giving as an example a cockroach who thinks that its meaningless movements have a purpose. Maybe it's performing a ritual, Victor suggests, and Otto (echoing an earlier remark of Alexander to his son) says that anything could be a ritual. Meanwhile an exchange of glances between Adelaide and Victor hints at some relationship between them.

Alexander asks where Little Man is and goes off to find him. Victor tries to calm the worried Adelaide, and Otto begins to speak of his hobby as a "collector" of strange and inexplicable incidents. In a long and elaborate take (4 minutes 53 seconds) he tells a story about a widow whose dead son appeared on a photo taken twenty years after his death. When Victor expresses skepticism, Otto assures him that he possesses absolute proof and has a collection of 284 similar incidents. He walks off, saying that we are blind and see nothing; as he reaches the window the shepherds' call is heard, and he collapses suddenly to the floor. Recovering, he says that he was touched by "an evil angel passing by" and rebukes Victor sharply when he asks if he is joking.

Maria is seen walking rapidly away from the house across a barren, misty landscape. Indoors, glasses quiver and tinkle on a tray as a rumbling sound is heard offscreen, followed by the ear-splitting screech of a jet plane flying low overhead. Otto remains impassive as Marta and then Julia run from one side of the room to the other, the camera panning with them before it starts to track rapidly toward the open doors of a large cabinet where a pitcher of milk is shaking violently on a shelf. The pitcher falls and breaks on the floor.

Alexander is seen outside, in an image so drained of color that it appears black and white. The plane is no longer heard and he offers no reaction to it, studying instead an exact, small-scale model of their house on the flooded ground at his feet. Maria tells him that the boy made the house for him as a birthday present, with Otto's help, and he is now upstairs in his room. She seems nervous and embarrassed; after a pause she says she has to go and walks slowly off as a long-held note of music from a Japanese flute is heard and continues into the next scene. After a brief shot of Little Man's bedroom, Otto and Alexander are seen in Alexander's study discussing the reproduction of Leonardo's *Adoration*. Otto says that the painting is "sinister" and that he has always been terrified of Leonardo. Both men seem anxious and even frightened. Otto then goes to the balcony, climbs over a railing, and disappears from sight, presumably down a ladder or outside staircase.[24] As he leaves, a hesitant and agonized voice is heard off-screen talking incoherently about a military crisis and appealing to the citizens to keep calm. Alexander switches off a tape recorder; the flute music stops but the voice continues off-screen. Alexander, obviously agitated, has a drink, then goes downstairs, where Adelaide, Marta, Victor, Otto, and Julia are sitting around a table and the voice, coming from a TV, warns that war might break out at any moment. The speaker is never seen, and the broadcast ends with the countdown numbers of an end leader running down before the screen goes blank. Alexander appears dazed as he wanders around, muttering that he has waited his whole life for this.

When Otto attempts to comfort Adelaide, she jumps up and runs over to throw herself on her knees before Victor, pleading hysterically in a mixture of Swedish and English for him to "do something." He holds her in his arms as she says it's all her fault and her punishment and drags him down to the floor beside her; she begins to thrash her legs violently, screaming for Julia to fetch Little Man. Julia ignores her, but obeys Victor's request to fetch his medical bag; meanwhile Alexander, curiously detached from what is going on, offers Otto a drink, and takes one himself. Victor gives Adelaide an injection and lays her on the sofa, where she begins to calm down. Alexander walks outside and surveys the dark, barren landscape as a foghorn is heard along with the sound of tinkling bells.

In another very long shot (5 minutes 19 seconds) Adelaide speaks, almost in soliloquy (though Otto is standing nearby), asking, Why do we always do the opposite of what we want? She loved one man but married another. But love requires an unequal relationship where "one is strong, the other weak, and it is the weaker who loves without reservation[25] . . . how foolish we are anyway." Victor, who overhears her last words, says it's good that she has finally understood this. They agree that there is no point in trying to leave and go north to seek safety, and Adelaide embraces Victor affectionately as Alexander is framed between them descending the stairs.

Adelaide and Julia argue over whether the boy should be wakened, which Julia refuses to do, saying that, if Adelaide has to torture someone, let it be her or Mr. Alexander, not the child. Adelaide unexpectedly embraces her and asks her forgiveness. Alexander, looking very tired, takes a gun out of Victor's medical bag. The fact that there is a cut before we see Alexander replace the gun (he takes it out again later, before visiting Maria) may initially lead viewers to assume that he intends in the next scene to kill the child to spare him the suffering that a war would cause. In the child's very dark room (the image alternately lightening and darkening) a hand reaches toward the crib, then Alexander is seen leaving the room, carrying a bloodstained cloth, presumably the boy's shirt.

In his study, Alexander takes a drink and, obviously very distraught, begins to recite the Lord's Prayer. Sitting on the floor as the camera tracks slowly toward him into close-up, he prays for his family and friends, all who believe and all who do not believe because they are blind, all who have lost hope and feel the end coming closer, asking for them to be spared. For this is the ultimate war, and nothing will be left after it. He promises to give up his family and destroy his home, to be mute and relinquish everything that binds him to life, if God will only restore everything to what it was before and rid him of this deadly sickening animal fear. He crawls weeping over to the sofa, hauling himself onto it as the shepherds' chants are heard and Marta calls off-screen for Victor to help her. (The shot of the prayer and the vow lasts 4 minutes 46 seconds.)

The shepherds' calls continue as Marta undresses and then walks naked across her bedroom. A cut to black and white (the previous scenes, though dark, have still been in color) shows a man wearing a long coat running in slow motion along a corridor as rain falls on the shiny floor. (The published script specifies that this is Alexander, though it is impossible to be certain from the shot itself who the man is.) The dreamlike atmosphere intensifies with the sound of dripping water and the shepherds' calls, and a characteristic spatial paradox as Alexander is seen sitting indoors looking out of a window; the camera tilts up and tracks past him to show him outside walking past the window. A building which we later recognize as Maria's cottage is visible in the background. Feet trudge through mud and water, and a hand, in slow motion, picks up perhaps a wire and a bag of coins, then the camera tilts up to Alexander's puzzled face; he is next standing in a snow-covered landscape with trees, houses, and a large female statue. The camera tracks from overhead to show running water, coins, rotting leaves, rusty metal, mud and snow, then a pair of bare feet; the dripping water and chanting are joined by the tinkling of glasses, a rumbling sound like a jet plane, and heavy breathing. As Alexander says, "My boy," the feet disappear behind a wooden beam; the camera tilts up and over this and moves rapidly at ground level, with the sound of the jet growing louder, before suddenly tilting up again to show two wooden doors, one of which blows open violently to reveal a brick wall behind it.

Back in muted color, Alexander wakes up with light flashing intermittently over him. Jet planes are heard flying overhead, and the darkness gradually becomes lighter as dripping water is heard. Otto enters his room by climbing over the balcony, and a lengthy conversation follows (the whole shot lasts 7 minutes 12 seconds) in which Otto insists that Alexander must go to Maria, who is the only one who can help them: she is a witch "in the best sense," and if he lies with her and wishes for one thing at that moment, it will happen and all this will be over. The scene has an almost grotesquely comic element in Alexander's disbelief and his inability to understand what Otto is talking about, and in Otto's own furtive actions. Although the glass of cognac is still where Alexander left it, the sofa is now covered with a white sheet, and Alexander wears his wife's white shawl draped around his shoulders. A clock chimes two, but there is no electricity, and at one point they hear an unidentified woman's voice singing. Finally Alexander says he has understood, and Otto leaves after telling him that he has left his bicycle for him to use and has put a ladder against the balcony.

Alexander leaves by the ladder as Victor is heard below him, talking about art and acting. He hides from Julia in the living room, takes the gun from Victor's medical bag, goes upstairs, glances into the boy's room, then climbs back down the ladder and enters the porch. Still concealing himself, he moves past Adelaide, Victor, and Marta, who are sitting outside at a table, and collects the bicycle. He cycles unsteadily along a winding country road and finally falls to the ground. He seems about to turn back, but the shepherds' chants are heard and, as if responding to them, he continues slowly on his way. He arrives at Maria's house, and as she lets him in, a flock of sheep run past.

The furnishings inside include what looks like a religious painting, a crucifix, some family photos, a decorated tablecloth, and a mirror. Maria asks what has gone wrong at his home and says her television went dead at around eleven o'clock. She insists on washing his hands, which are dirty after his fall, and he then sits down at a small organ and plays a piece of music that he says his mother taught him. Almost weeping, he tells a story about how he tried to put his sick mother's neglected garden into order but, when it was ready, he discovered to his horror that he had destroyed it because all the naturalness had been lost. It was the same with his sister, who had her lovely long hair cut off in order to be fashionable; when his father saw her he began to cry.

As the clock strikes three, he says they don't have much time and kneels before her, begging her to love him and so save him and all of them, because he knows who she is. When she says gently that she doesn't know what he is talking about, he threatens to shoot himself. She embraces and comforts him as tinkling and rumbling are heard and planes scream overhead: "It concerns your home," she says. "I know her, she is wicked. . . . They have hurt you." She starts to undress him, then takes off her own clothes and lays him on the bed, repeating, "You poor, poor man." Her words continue over a shot of them levitating above the bed, draped in sheets. The shepherds' calls and flute music are heard over a black and white shot of the staircase and courtyard seen previously in Alexander's vision, now filled with fleeing people moving aimlessly in slow motion. Alexander's voice is heard, almost incoherent with fear, saying, "No, no . . ." as the camera moves overhead to the glass reflecting the buildings and then tilts down to show a child (presumably Little Man) lying with his face in a pillow.

A cut shows a landscape with a tower in the background. Alexander is lying on his back with a figure dressed like his wife and with her hairstyle beside him; as Maria's voice off-screen says, "Drink this," the woman turns and we see that she is Maria; his sobbing and the flute music continue. Another cut returns to full color with the picture of the Virgin in Leonardo's *Adoration;* the light dims as the flute music, the calls, and Alexander and Maria's voices are still heard.

A slow dissolve, still in full color (as the remainder of the film will be), introduces another dreamlike image of Marta running along a corridor naked, chasing chickens with a towel or cloth. As she runs off-screen, the flute music and calls continuing, Adelaide's voice is heard asking Alexander (who is still moaning) what has frightened him so. The camera tracks to pick her up and follows her to the entrance to the study, she stops, and the camera continues to show Alexander lying on the sofa and the electric lamp lit. Only the flute music is heard now as the room slowly brightens with no apparent cause and Alexander gets up, saying, "Mama!" He walks unsteadily across the room, bangs against the leg of the table, and starts to limp. He switches off the tape recorder and the flute music stops; bird song is heard as he closes the door of the cabinet. He tests the lamp, which works, and then makes a phone call. The person he speaks to tells him, "You can't imagine what things are like today," but otherwise everything seems normal and he is offered birthday greetings. A brief cut shows the child's empty crib with curtains blowing, and then Alexander turning off the lamp in his study. He stands in front of a mirror, puts on a robe with—as we see later—the yin-yang symbol on it, and leaves the room, sobbing.

He climbs down the ladder and works his way stealthily toward the bicycle as Adelaide, Victor, and Marta sit outside discussing Victor's plans to move to Australia. Victor tells them he is tired of the lot of them, and it becomes clear that mother and daughter are competing for his affections. Marta brings a note from Alexander, saying that the boy will show them the Japanese tree they planted yesterday and asking for forgiveness "even now." Adelaide muses on the reasons for this request as Victor reproaches the two women for their indifference to Alexander's kindness. As the boy cannot be found, they set off, along with Julia, to look at the tree, while Alexander moves back unseen to the house.

He replaces the gun and puts the bag in Victor's car outside, then starts to pile chairs and wicker armchairs on the table in the porch. After driving Victor's car some distance from the house, he sets fire to a tablecloth he has placed over the pile of chairs. Upstairs he switches on the tape recorder again and looks out over the partially flooded landscape before climbing over the balcony and down the ladder. The crackling of flames mingles with the sound of flute music.

In the distance the house is seen burning as Alexander watches. Victor, Adelaide, Marta, and Julia run toward him across the partially flooded ground; Victor reaches him first, and Alexander starts to speak to him before remembering his vow, saying: "No. Silence." Adelaide arrives and begins to cradle him like a child; the crackle of flames, bursting glass, and the intermittent sounds of the flute music and a ringing telephone are heard throughout. Alexander breaks away and limps toward Maria, who is standing watching as the fire begins to engulf the house; he falls to his knees before her and kisses her hands. Victor, Adelaide, and Maria engage in a series of tussles over him, and Victor finally leads him toward an ambulance that has arrived. Otto approaches, riding his bike, as Alexander breaks free again and is pursued by Victor and two men in white coats. Another series of escapes and recaptures follows, with Alexander embracing both Adelaide and Otto; when his wife tries to join him in the ambulance, however, he pushes her away. As the ambulance drives off, Maria rides after it on Otto's bicycle. The others are left watching the burning house as it finally collapses in a crescendo of flames and falling timber.

The child is seen, in sharply contrasting silence, carrying a bucket toward the tree Alexander had planted. The sound of the clanking bucket is joined by that of cows and then the shepherds' (or cowherds') calls. He puts the bucket down near the tree and returns for another one. The ambulance drives past him as Maria dismounts from the bicycle and watches at a distance. A high-angle shot shows the boy watering the tree, with the sea sparkling behind him; the shepherds' calls are heard, and the Bach cantata from the credits begins as he kneels down by the tree and looks upwards. Maria watches, then rides away. The boy is seen lying on his back with his head resting on the rocks at the foot of the tree. The Bach music continues as he looks up at the tree and muses, "In the beginning was the Word. . . . Why is that, Papa?" The camera cranes slowly up to the top of the tree, with the sea shimmering through the bare branches. The image becomes brighter, gradually washing out the sea and the branches, as a dedication appears: "To my son Andrei, with hope and confidence." The soaring music ends as the image comes briefly back into focus, then fades.

Notes

1. For the sake of convenience, we refer to what is now the former Soviet Union and to cities such as Leningrad (now St. Petersburg) by their older names, where these refer to events prior to 1991.

2. In our review essay on the main books on Tarkovsky to have appeared to date, in *Journal of European Studies* 20, part 3 (September 1990): 265–77.

3. During our research and interview trips in the Soviet Union, we were not granted access to archival materials on Tarkovsky at the Mosfilm studio where he shot all his Soviet films, but Tarkovsky's problems with Mosfilm, and the parent organization, Goskino, were recounted by many of our interviewees. Even allowing for natural memory lapses about events which took place from ten to almost thirty years in the past, we were able to piece together what we believe to be a reasonably accurate description of each film's history. Recent publications of memoirs and correspondence have also been helpful.

4. Some instances—though far from all that could be cited—are given in the chapters on individual films. A concise example of the problems involved, however, can be found in the *Monthly Film Bulletin*'s review of *The Sacrifice* (January 1987), which prints three photos, all of them purporting to represent images from the film and all given captions claiming that they crystallize something central to Tarkovsky's visual style. *None* of these images appears in the film! The first two present angles and composition significantly different from anything in the film itself, and the third example, on p. 8, captioned "A busy landscape," was clearly taken *before* filming began, as Susan Fleetwood is obviously applying her eye makeup and Allan Edwall and Filippa Franzén appear to be checking the script.

1. A MARTYRED ARTIST?

1. For example, *Iskusstvo kino* 2 (1989) and 4 (1992) and *Kinovedcheskiye zapiski* 9 (1991) and 14 (1992) each contain a number of articles on Tarkovsky and his films. The last of these (*K. z.* 14 [1992]) honors the sixtieth anniversary of Tarkovsky's birth with the publication of 26 papers presented at the First International "Readings" on Tarkovsky held in Moscow in April 1989 and includes our joint paper titled "Working with Tarkovsky in the West" ("Rabotaya s Tarkovskim na zapade"). Many recent articles are reprints of first-time publications of texts censored during the period of stagnation. One must not forget when dealing with criticism published in the Soviet Union before glasnost that the critical works about Tarkovsky's films were exposed to a similar kind of scrutiny and censorship as the films they were discussing.

2. Known as Irina Tarkovskaya while she was married to him, and acting under that name in *Ivan's Childhood* and *Andrei Roublev*.

3. By the early 1970s five categories of classification existed: highest, and 1 through 4. After the category had been assigned, the Printing Commission used this as the basis for deciding how many copies would be printed for national distribution and whether, in the case of a color film, all copies would be in color or whether certain more remote areas would receive only black and white prints. While blockbuster films might be released in 1,500–2,000 copies, most Soviet films averaged 100–300 (Golovskoy 48). After initial box-office receipts came in, a category could be changed, as was the case with *Mirror*, which was moved up from 3rd to 2nd.

4. Everyone was paid a fixed rate while working, but the real money came through the—often delayed—bonuses.

5. Babitsky and Rimberg state that only five feature films were produced in 1952 (243), while Peter Kenez offers what seems to be a more accurate count, based on the Catalog of Soviet Feature Films: seven films in 1951 and nine in 1952, if one subtracts filmed performances (211).

6. Goskino was not above causing considerable problems for foreign distributors who wished to buy or even see Tarkovsky's films: the French producer Daniel Toscan du Plantier gave us an amusing account of his attempts to see *Mirror* in Moscow in 1976, with a view to buying it for Gaumont (of which he was general manager at the time). After being given the runaround for several days (the film was still languishing under official disapproval) he was taken to a projection room in the suburbs at 7:00 A.M. The print was screened on the wall, and the translator left after three minutes, saying the film was incomprehensible! Toscan du Plantier was impressed by it nevertheless, but had to threaten Yermash with adverse international publicity before he was finally allowed to buy it (Interview).

7. Yuri Mamin, a director of pointed satiric comedies, recalls in interview the initial anger of Tarkovsky's students (themselves professional filmmakers) in the Advanced Courses for Scriptwriters and Directors (Vysshye kursy stsenaristov i rezhissyorov) at Goskino (1980–81) when he disdainfully dismissed all contemporary Soviet cinema, seeming not even to know recent films and filmmakers—though it eventually emerged that he knew much more about them than he had at first acknowledged.

8. Arseny Tarkovsky's third wife tells the following story (as do other Tarkovsky intimates): while making a telephone call from a public booth, Arseny met a woman who impetuously invited him for a ride in the country, and then helped her home when she twisted her ankle; he moved in and proceeded to live there with her and her husband. When asked how he could leave an intelligent, educated, beautiful wife and small children, his unchanging response was that he was totally bewitched by a "siren."

9. Other sources, however, including some of the contributors to the *O Tarkovskom* volume, present a somewhat less flattering picture. Accusations of financial irresponsibility (i.e., not repaying debts) and drunken abusive quarreling between him and his second wife may have some foundation in fact, but may also be exaggerated in order to discredit the latter.

10. *Martyrolog* was first published in German in 1989. Though no editor is named, Larissa Tarkovskaya takes responsibility for the selection in a foreword (7). An English translation, titled *Time within Time*, appeared from Seagull Books in 1991. Again no editor is named, and there is no foreword to this edition. Although the "original" German edition is credited, the actual selection of entries is often very different, ranging from occasional words and sentences to whole pages that exist in one edition but not in the other. For the sake of convenience we refer to the English edition (as *TWT*) except where the material quoted exists only in the German edition (cited as *Martyrolog*) or the German translation appears more accurate. The book has not yet been published in Russia.

The problems of establishing an "authentic" text in this case are reflected in other writings by Tarkovsky published under the auspices of his widow. We note elsewhere that there is no guarantee that the material altered or added to the revised English edition of *Sculpting in Time* was always approved or even written by Tarkovsky, and similar problems seem likely to occur with other posthumously published works (including the English version of the "script" of *Andrei Roublev*) that do not clearly assign editorial responsibility or state the basis on which a particular text has been established.

11. Alluded to in a diary entry of May 28, 1977 (*TWT* 145), but not limited to this one occasion.

12. In *Time within Time* this occcurs in an entry dated September 12, 1970 (p. 19); in *Martyrolog* it is part of a much longer entry dated September 14 (p. 51). The unex-

plained discrepancy is symptomatic of the differences in both text and wording between the two editions.

13. For a fuller discussion of Tarkovsky's attitude to women, see the section "All Unhappy Families Are Alike" in chapter 13.

14. To such an extent that even some of her detractors reluctantly admit that she may well have made it possible for him to continue working in conditions of extreme financial hardship during the 1970s. He pays frequent tribute to these qualities in his diary (which, of course, she edited!). Those who knew Larissa both in the Soviet Union and in the West discreetly note that she had "expensive tastes" and further developed Tarkovsky's own similar inclinations, thus being the cause of as well as the solution to his frequent financial difficulties.

15. A point lost in the English title (*Time within Time*), which is clearly intended to echo *Sculpting in Time*.

16. He was also spared the total hopelessness and wretchedness chronicled by Dziga Vertov in his diaries of the 1940s: "Most of my projects have not borne fruit, have not been finished. Nobody picked them up, hence they rotted. I have no powerful friends, nobody to go to for support. . . . Nobody wants to help me. Everybody is afraid of losing his head. But I am not afraid of losing mine" (quoted in Petrić, *Constructivism in Film* 67).

17. Cryptic diary entries for April 15, 1981, and April 6, 1982, suggest that he seriously considered defecting while on a visit to Sweden in 1981 (*TWT* 276, 312; *Martyrolog* 351).

18. These titles were cited, among others, by those we interviewed. *Hoffmanniana* is mentioned in Tarkovsky's diary for 1975 as a project to be made at the Tallinn studios in Estonia (*TWT* 106 and 117). Nothing came of this, however, though the script was published in *Iskusstvo kino* in 1976 (no. 8). A French translation appeared from Schirmer/Mosel in 1988.

2. SHAPING AN AESTHETICS OF CINEMA

1. In his lectures—as recorded in *Lektsii po kinorezhissure*—he analyzed Ioseliani's work and recommended that his students see all of both Paradzhanov's and Ioseliani's films. Most of his examples, however, came from the films of Bresson and Bergman.

2. Not all of them, of course, possess *all* these qualities; see, for example, Vance Kepley's *In the Service of the State* (Madison: University of Wisconsin Press, 1986) for an account of Dovzhenko's many compromises with state policy.

3. *Dossier Positif* 8; the original statement was made in May 1986.

4. He knew Paradzhanov well and visited and corresponded with him. In April 1974 he and the literary critic Victor Shklovsky wrote a letter to the Secretary of the Ukrainian Communist Party, protesting against the persecution of Paradzhanov, then on trial for illegal homosexual activities, but to no effect (*TWT* 93–95).

5. The publication history of the book in the West is quite complex. It was first published in German as *Die Versiegelte Zeit* in 1986, and then in an English translation from the Russian by the Bodley Head later that year. The American edition published by the University of Texas Press in 1989 uses the same translation but "in slightly different form." The French edition, *Le temps scellé* (Paris: Cahiers du Cinéma, 1989), includes a chapter on *The Sacrifice*, a preface by Tarkovsky's widow, Larissa, and, in an appendix, a bio-filmography, short credits, and two letters by Tarkovsky, one to the Iskusstvo publishing house in Moscow in 1980, and one to the head of Goskino, Filip Yermash, in 1983. None of this was in the original English edition. The revised English edition (London: Faber and Faber, 1989) has the chapter on *The Sacrifice* (finished, according to his wife, shortly before his death) and unspecified changes to the text (also attributed to Tarkovsky himself), but no preface and none of the material con-

tained in the French appendix. The notes for this English edition have also been revised, though mistakes in the translation (such as the confusion between "shot" and "frame"—the Russian word *kadr* means both) have been left unaltered. Given the fact that Tarkovsky was seriously ill during the time when the book was being revised, there may be cause for some doubt as to who was actually responsible for some of the changes and/or additions. For the sake of convenience, however, we use the 1989 English edition as our point of reference and, unless noted otherwise, quotations are taken from this.

6. Surkova was a student at VGIK and met Tarkovsky on the set of *Andrei Roublev*, where she was on a practicum. She became a close friend and collaborator on *Sculpting in Time*. According to Surkova, Tarkovsky had originally signed a contract with the Moscow publishing house Iskusstvo for a book in the form of a dialogue with the well-known film critic Leonid Kozlov. The book was to be titled *Sopostavleniya (Juxtapositions)*. When the deadline ran out on the first contract, Tarkovsky, this time with Surkova, signed a new contract. In 1979 the book was rejected for publication in the Soviet Union because, according to Surkova, it didn't have "enough of the standard socialist realist stuff" (Interview). Since both Surkova and Tarkovsky had emigrated abroad, they continued their collaboration on what was to become *Sculpting in Time*, adding the chapter on *Nostalghia* and the conclusion. Surkova is given copyright credit with Tarkovsky for the original English and American editions of this book, but not for the revised edition published by Faber in 1989. According to Surkova, her original contribution had been much more significant, as the book had contained her questions/comments on film, to which Tarkovsky then responded. When she agreed to remove her name from the title page before the original publication—i.e., leaving the book apparently all Tarkovsky's own work, with her contribution reduced to a brief copyright acknowledgment—she also removed most of her own formulations, thus leaving a somewhat haphazard composition for the published book (Surkova Interview, 1990).

7. Interviews Tarkovsky gave abroad in the 1980s as well as the *Lektsii po kinorezhissure* (*Lectures on Film Directing*, Lenfilm, 1989), which combine his series of lectures in the Advanced Courses for Scriptwriters and Directors at Goskino, USSR, with fragments from the previously published interviews and articles, demonstrate even more forcefully that Tarkovsky tended to recycle, rather than change, his ideas on the art of cinema. The lectures are, in fact, somewhat better organized than the book is, as they have been edited by the director Konstantin Lopushansky into five chapters: "Film as Art," "The Film Image," "The Script," "The Concept and Its Realization," and "Editing." The lectures are clearly also more specific and somewhat less theoretical and philosophical than *Sculpting in Time*.

8. To quote a typical example of this line of thought: "The quotes around 'Kleist' signify that his name does not refer to the author as a biological person but rather to the author as a discursive practice. In Harari's description of Foucault's definition of author, it is a 'function by which certain discourses are characterized'" (Mary Riehl, "The Author-Function as Security Agent in Rohmer's *Die Marquise von O . . .*," *German Quarterly* 64, no. 1 [Winter 1991]: 15).

9. This prose translation by Dmitry Mirsky in *Pushkin* (98) was adapted by Vida Johnson.

10. This is how the statement reads in the first British edition of the book; the revised edition omits the clause "that up till now has never been given expression."

11. Although this sentence, which appears on p. 50 of the first edition of the book, is omitted from the revised edition, it seems, nevertheless, to express a crucial aspect of Tarkovsky's concept of the moral function of art.

12. *Manchester Guardian Weekly*, January 14, 1990, p. 20. George Steiner likewise sees serious art as an encounter with the other, with "the unassuaged, unhoused instability and estrangement of our condition" (139).

13. The 1986 edition has "printed" rather than "captured."

14. From a 1984 talk on the Apocalypse at St. James's Church, Piccadilly, London. A transcript of this was kindly provided by Layla Alexander.

15. A. T., "My delayem filmy" 16–18. He owned a German Shepherd very similar to the one that appears in *Stalker* and *Nostalghia*.

16. Although Tarkovsky would certainly have studied Eisenstein's theories in film school, he mentions no Formalist critics apart from Vyacheslav Ivanov, though he knew Viktor Shklovsky personally. A fuller discussion of his imagery will be found in chapter 12.

3. WORKING METHODS

1. Material in this section is based on some forty personal interviews conducted by the authors with actors, cinematographers, scriptwriters, producers, editors, composers, and costume and set designers who worked with Tarkovsky in the Soviet Union, Italy, and Sweden. A full list of those interviews can be found in the Works Cited. This information is supplemented by the reminiscences published in the volume *O Tarkovskom* and various other published interviews. To avoid undue repetition of the names of sources, specific references will generally be given only for verbatim quotations.

We are fully aware of the dangers of relying on memories of events that took place up to twenty-five or thirty years ago and, equally, of the possibility that some of our sources may be—often unconsciously—accommodating their personal experiences to a semimythic concept of "Tarkovsky as genius" that existed during his lifetime in the Soviet Union and has taken even firmer root since his death. Usually, however, there is enough corroborating evidence among those who worked with him at different stages of his career, and even in different countries, to testify to the basic accuracy of the information provided here.

2. Nykvist was hired to work with John Huston on *The Last Run*, but Huston soon left the project (Niogret 26n).

3. Shortage of film stock may have been partly responsible for this in the Soviet Union, but in Italy and Sweden, where he had all the film he needed, he continued the same practice.

4. Although it is commonly assumed—and he did little in his public utterances to refute this—that Tarkovsky disliked and even despised science fiction, he in fact read quite a lot of it and was particularly fond of Ray Bradbury (Artemyev and Rausch interviews).

4. BEGINNINGS

1. It is symptomatic of the way in which factual errors, once canonized in print, are seldom rectified that Sartre's mistaken attribution of the original novella to "Cholokov" has never been corrected in subsequent reprints of this article.

5. *ANDREI ROUBLEV*

1. The script was published in two parts: *Iskusstvo kino* 4 (April 1964): 139–200, and 5 (May 1964): 125–58, with Andrei Konchalovsky's name listed first, probably simply in alphabetical order. This was a true coauthorship, and all critics in discussing the film would refer to "the authors." All further references to the script will be to the original Russian publication and *not* to the English version of what is called "Tarkovsky's original *kino-roman*" (screen novel) (A. T., *Andrei Rublev* 14). The English text is a translation of a clearly *reconstructed* script: the balloon sequence, for example, has

been moved from the beginning of Part II in the original Russian published script to the Prologue, presumably to reflect the change that was made in the film. Tarkovsky's second wife told us in interview that Tarkovsky was revising the Roublev script in the last years of his life.

2. See Shitova 18. Andron Mikhalkov-Konchalovsky has also used the náme Andrei Konchalovsky since the mid-1960s.

3. See Le Fanu 144–46; M. M. (Marcel Martin) in *Cinema 70* 143 (February 1970): 15–17.

4. Turovskaya gives October 19, 1971, as the release date and Le Fanu copies her, but Zorkaya and Yermash support Tarkovsky's own diary entry, which notes that the film was released on the "eve" of the New Year, which in Russian need not literally mean December 31.

5. Le Fanu lists only seven episodes, combining "The Passion" and "The Celebration" into one. Zak also lists only seven and omits "The Silence." The outline of the completed film is given in our synopsis.

The Russian script published under the title *Andrei Roublev* has the following structure: the prologue to Part I (the Kulikovo Field battle of 1380) is followed by nine titled episodes: "The Buffoon," 1400; "Theophanes the Greek," 1401; "The Hunt," Summer 1403; "Invitation to the Kremlin," Winter 1405; "The Passion According to Andrei," Summer–Autumn–Winter 1406; "The Blinding," Summer 1407; "The Celebration," April 1408; "The Last Judgment," Summer 1408; "The Attack," Autumn 1408. Part II's prologue was a peasant's attempted flight, not by balloon as in the film's prologue, but with wings. Then came three episodes: "Indian Summer," Autumn 1409; "Melancholy," Summer 1419; and "The Bell," Spring–Summer–Autumn–Winter–Spring 1423–24.

6. See discussion in Vernadsky 263–71. Vernadsky calls the defeat at Kulikovo Field a "severe blow to the Mongol power," but he also points out that the Tartars reestablished control over Russia almost immediately by sacking Moscow in 1382; the fourteenth and fifteenth centuries continued to be a time of struggle by Moscow and its surrounding principalities against the Tartars.

7. Tamara Ogorodnikova read aloud the full text of Pashuto's scathing letter at the First International Symposium on Andrei Tarkovsky, held in Moscow in April 1989. His suggestions included cutting Boriska's revelation that he had lied about knowing his father's secret; shortening the bell-casting scenes; and making clear "with some kind of technical aids" that certain scenes, such as the dialogue with the dead Theophanes, were not "real."

8. The historian Denise Youngblood points out that "Great Prince" is the correct translation of the Russian title, but we have opted to use "Grand Duke," the title more commonly found in history books.

9. Western critics too have problems here. Le Fanu, in his well-intentioned attempt to provide a historical context for the film and for Roublev's life (34–36), identifies the dukes as Dmitry Donskoi's "quarrelling sons Vasily and Yuri"—an identification that, like many of his "facts" about Roublev's life, would be disputed by many Russian historians. He then proceeds to call the deliberately *unnamed* characters of the film "Vasily" and "Yuri." In addition he misspells the name of the Kulikovo Field battle (as Kulikivo) and gives it the wrong date (1370 instead of 1380).

10. Tarkovsky seemed perfectly happy to cooperate with Columbia in cutting the film by "fifteen or twenty minutes": "I can certainly do so, starting with the balloon flight" (*TWT* 74)—a strangely offhand comment, given his five-year struggle against the Soviet authorities to preserve the film's integrity. No doubt he realized that he had no real control over a foreign company's decisions in any case. Columbia in fact cut the film by a good deal more than fifteen or twenty minutes—see synopsis for details.

Although his willingness here to eliminate the prologue suggests that he considered it dispensable, he nevertheless stressed in an interview with Michel Ciment that it had great importance for him as a symbol [*sic*] of the creative spirit and of the risks and the total commitment necessary if one is to create true works of art (*Dossier Positif* 92).

11. For typical responses see *Sight & Sound* (Summer 1969): 138; *The Guardian* (August 16, 1973); the London *Times* (August 10, 1973). The first detailed attempt in English to come to terms with the film was by Ivor Montagu in *Sight & Sound* (Spring 1973). Though his critical assessment of the film is sound and perceptive, his description of individual scenes is often inaccurate.

12. Tatyana Elmanovits points out that the emphasis on earth, roots, and fatigue in this scene contributes to the basic theme that art is (among other things) hard and painful labor (69–70).

13. See *Sculpting in Time* 119–20 and "Strasti po Andreyu" 78 for some uncomplimentary remarks on Eisenstein's historical films. A more freely acknowledged influence in this film was certainly Kurosawa, especially in the use of natural elements such as rain and mud as images "innocent of symbolism" (see *Sculpting in Time* 73).

14. According to the cameraman Vadim Yusov, Tarkovsky broke his own rule of "no surprises during shooting" by throwing the geese in front of the camera without warning (*O Tarkovskom* 76).

15. A similar example might be the confusing flashback to the blinding of the masons, where a failure to recognize the temporal shift may actually enhance a response to the sequence. As Herbert Eagle pointed out to us, "The viewer feels the painting in the cathedral and the blinding in the forest to be taking place *at the same time*. When Roublev smears the paint on the wall and weeps, he seems to be reacting to the terrible mutilation of the artists that *has just taken place.* . . . The fact that the events are likely to be understood as contemporaneous strengthens the viewers' emotional reaction."

6. SOLARIS

1. As the English and German versions of the diary offer a widely different choice of extracts here, these figures are put together largely from the generally more reliable German entries for October 2, 17, and 20 (*Martyrolog* 58–61). F. Yermash gives a somewhat different account, with Mosfilm requesting 1,850,000 and the Cinema Committee awarding a reduced figure of 600,000.

2. Tarkovsky's later coolness toward the film may have had its origin in his disappointment at its lukewarm reception at Cannes, even though it was awarded the Special Jury Prize. Important critics, such as Michel Ciment, were obviously unhappy with the film (*Dossier Positif* 96); M. A. (Mireille Amiel) in *Cinéma 72* 167 (June 1972): 56 contemptuously attacked it for not being Marxist enough and other "unpardonable weaknesses."

3. To such an extent that one British critic interpreted this phrase, which Lem originally intended as a criticism of anthropocentric thinking, as rousing "Sovexport rhetoric" (Philip Strick in *Sight & Sound* [Winter 1972/73]: 5).

4. Kris's ambiguous attitude toward both his parents seems to derive from feelings that Tarkovsky was confiding to his diary about his uneasy and difficult relationship with *his* parents during exactly the period when he was preparing *Solaris* (*TWT,* September 12, 1970, p. 19).

5. Other explanations of the ending include Philip Strick's belief that the planet has provided Kris with a "surrogate father" at the end (*Sight & Sound* [Winter 1972/73]: 5) and Kovács and Szilágyi's suggestion that "the changed environment around the house accompanies the interior changes in Kelvin's soul," and that "the psychic activity of Solaris comes to dominate everything until, finally, the whole universe becomes a part of the psychic universe" (100).

7. *MIRROR*

1. Wrongly given as "Maya Ivanovna" by Le Fanu (15) and the German *Andrej Tarkowskij* (181).

2. All film dialogue is translated by Vida Johnson from the Russian original and not copied from the subtitles. The metaphorical function of this scene might be compared to the balloon prologue of *Andrei Roublev*.

3. The English subtitles of the American version make the film needlessly confusing because they often fail to give the characters' names, as in this scene. This is especially important when the same actor plays two roles and the form of address can help the viewer to identify them correctly.

4. It is perhaps dangerous to try to read too much into the switches between color, black and white, and (more rarely) sepia. Dreams are generally in black and white, but this particular one is in color. Memories are usually in color, but the printing-works scene is black and white. The film's cameraman, Georgy Rerberg, told us that they were not given enough color film stock and thus had to fill in with black and white footage.

5. The figure we see here is that of Tarkovsky himself. He had wanted to show his face, but was dissuaded by his cameraman, Georgy Rerberg, who felt that this would make the film uncomfortably, and unacceptably, personal (Interview).

6. Here Le Fanu appropriates (without acknowledgment) information provided by Herbert Marshall (93), though he miscopies the Russian word as "Shralin."

7. So few critics—in any language—bother to correct even glaring mistakes when their work is reprinted that it is refreshing to see Eva M. J. Schmid, in her chapter "Erinnerungen und Fragen" of the German collection *Andrej Tarkowskij*, add an appendix correcting several, generally minor, factual errors from an article she had previously published on *Nostalghia* (79–80).

8. Maya Turovskaya's "three" children (68) in this scene seems to result from a mistranslation that confuses the genitive case of the Russian word for "those" (*tekh*) with that for "three" (*trekh*).

9. All the books mentioned indeed draw on the same dozen or so stills from the film for their illustrations, though few of them represent the film accurately. The strangest of these is a photo of the teenage Alexei (or, more likely, Ignat) in a ruined room littered with books, which is reproduced in *Dossier Positif* (37) and *Andrej Tarkowskij* (130): no such scene exists in the film. It even appears in Tarkovsky's own *Sculpting in Time* (127) and in the English edition of his diary (*TWT*, unpaged photo section), mysteriously captioned "Little [or Young] Andrey in his father's house."

10. See chapter 13 for a fuller analysis of the dream texture of Tarkovsky's films overall.

8. *STALKER*

1. There is contradictory testimony as to the extent to which Rerberg's footage was unusable: Feiginova, Rerberg, Knyazhinsky, and Kaidanovsky all assert that some survived into the final print, especially the waterfall scene.

2. The English translation (147) calls him "a slave, a believer, a pagan of the Zone," which makes little sense.

3. Kalashnikov worked only briefly on the film, shooting some 250 meters, but he was apparently called away by his long-standing director, Gleb Panfilov, to shoot another film. Tarkovsky provides no reason, just a diary note (April 7, 1978: 151) that he has "refused" to work on the film; on the other hand, Abdusalamov and Boym were definitely fired (April 15: 154).

4. Like Lem, the Strugatskys carefully avoid associating the characters and settings of their book with their own country. *Solaris* purposefully mingles different nationali-

ties among its characters, while *Roadside Picnic* is ostensibly set in Canada and the names are predominantly Anglo-Saxon, with some Germanic and Slavic elements. While Tarkovsky respects this convention of "anonymous" naming in both films, he is also following the common Eastern bloc practice of using ostensibly Western settings to criticize "their" problems when in fact the settings are unmistakably and purposefully Soviet and, in *Stalker*, so are the characters and the problems.

5. In the story this stimulates a *physical* response from the landscape and so warns of dangers to avoid. Tarkovsky's removal of these elaborately described perils makes Stalker's use of his nuts and bolts curiously haphazard: he seems to guide the others by a mixture of intuition and guesswork.

6. A typical reading of this kind, which makes some valid points, is offered by Gilbert Adair, though he goes too far in equating Tarkovsky with "the dissident underground." French critics also often saw a political allegory in the film: Danièle Dubroux's review for *Cahiers du Cinéma* 330 (December 1981) suggested that the Zone, protected by armed guards, might stand for the Eastern bloc in general, while the Room itself ("la chambre à désirs") could be seen as "the shop window that West Berlin is for East Berlin" (41).

7. Sources as different as the producer Daniel Toscan du Plantier and Tarkovsky's friend and fellow director Andrei Konchalovsky are united in stressing this (Interviews).

8. Another Christian interpretation, by Gérard Pangon (*Etudes cinématographiques* 110–11), is based on a different but equally incorrect description of the glasses and their movements, and where Amengual sees the jar containing the eggshell as symbolic of "dead matter" (33), Pangon interprets its contents as "signs of the rebirth/resurrection." Tarkovsky's antagonism toward symbolic readings of his films seems fully understandable in the light of criticism such as this.

9. De Baecque (25) suggests that their positions here imply their spiritual state (at least at this stage of their journey): the materialistic Professor fully on earth; the imaginative but skeptical Writer on waterlogged ground; and the spiritual Stalker almost enclosed by water. Less arbitrary than the attempts to find symbolic meaning in the three glasses, this interpretation derives some validity from the importance of water as a redemptive force throughout Tarkovsky's work (see chapter 12).

10. The fish, of course, was an important early symbol of Christ, accepted as such by both the Catholic and the Orthodox traditions. Here it is imprisoned; the fish in the shot that ends the scene of the men sitting outside the "Room" is bleeding and also perhaps being suffocated by pollution.

11. Interview in *Ecran* 78, no. 66, quoted by Pangon (*Etudes cinématographiques* 106 and 111)—who then goes on to ignore these statements in providing his own interpretation.

12. Although the moral significance of the film remained constant for him, he occasionally toyed in interviews with the idea that neither the Zone nor the Room really existed, and that Stalker "invented" them and their magical powers in an attempt to reintroduce a sense of faith and hope into a world that has lost these. He also thought seriously about a sequel in which Stalker lived inside the Zone with his wife and daughter and brought people there by force to try to make them believe, becoming a kind of "fascist" in the process. See *Dossier Positif* 125–29, interview with Aldo Tassone, originally published October 1981; and de Baecque 106–11, interview with Laurence Cossé, originally published January 1986. Also *TWT* 169.

13. Called "Scientist" in *Sculpting,* and by some critics.

14. As Jacques Gerstenkorn and Sylvie Strudel point out in their article "La quête et la foi" in *Etudes cinématographiques* (75–104), Writer's progress through the Zone involves the progressive discarding of all the protective coverings with which he shields himself from true self-knowledge: he has to leave behind a woman and his cigarettes, and during the journey he loses his liquor and his gun.

15. These are not from a poem by Tarkovsky's father, as Le Fanu asserts (96), but from Lao Dze (see the diary entry for December 28, 1977: *TWT* 147)

16. A point that is obscured by Peter Green (52) who says, wrongly, that we hear the train "at the beginning" of the scene.

17. In *Sculpting in Time* (193) Tarkovsky says that he "wanted it to be as if the whole film had been made in a single shot."

18. Some specific shot lengths are given in the synopsis. The first shot after the men's arrival in the Zone lasts 4 minutes 15 seconds; Writer's self-condemnation in the "dune room" is filmed in one continuous take of 4 minutes 30 seconds.

19. Le Fanu (93) fails to mention the crucially important electronic music ("the only sound is the clanking of the wheels over the sleepers"), claims there is no dialogue (there is some, at the beginning), and states that we watch the men's "tense and serious faces" throughout (rather than the backs of their heads or profiles).

9. NOSTALGHIA

1. The German edition prints this as a separate section, titled "Sketches from the *Journey through Italy*."

2. None of this information is provided in the English diary. Though the entries for 1982 are much fuller than in the German edition, they go only to May 4 and say nothing about the actual filming of *Nostalghia*.

3. Although she was finally allowed to leave, their son Andrei and her daughter Olga had to remain in the Soviet Union. See chapter 1 for information on Tarkovsky's lengthy and bitter attempts to reunite his family.

4. See Andrea Crisanti, "Le décor de *Nostalgia*," *Dossier Positif* 137; Tony Mitchell, "Tarkovsky in Italy." Mitchell's article, written *before* shooting began, should be treated with caution as a guide to the actual—rather than the projected—film. His later article, "Andrei Tarkovsky and *Nostalghia*," deals with the finished film and is more reliable, though it contains the puzzling assertion that Eugenia is pregnant by her lover (7).

5. Mitchell ("Tarkovsky in Italy" 54) gives a budget figure of £500,000. Toscan du Plantier, speaking from memory, offered a roughly similar figure, adding that Tarkovsky himself was paid around $100,000—the normal amount for a small-scale film of this kind. According to the latter, Tarkovsky tried (unsuccessfully) to dispense with an assistant director and claim the extra salary for himself. His wife Larissa is officially listed as an assistant in the credits.

6. Evidence for this seems to be based largely on Tarkovsky's own assertions and those of his wife. The film's coproducer, Daniel Toscan du Plantier, pointed out to us that the Palme d'Or at Cannes tends to go in any case to films with more commercial potential than *Nostalghia*, and furious politicking is a normal aspect of the decisions of any Festival jury.

7. Quoted by both Kevin Thomas and Yvette Biro, but with no source given (see *Film Review Annual 1985*: 981, 985).

8. The man who appears to be coordinating the demonstration is probably an exception and may be seen as cynically manipulating Domenico's actions for his own ends.

9. The sacristan's words about women (see synopsis) directly echo Tarkovsky's own diary entry for January 3, 1974: "What is the essence of woman? Subordination and humility [Unterordnung und Erniedrigung] for the sake of love" (*Martyrolog* 133). The English version gives a possibly less accurate wording: "submission, humiliation" (89). Tarkovsky's disclaimer—"whatever my main character's view of women may be, they are not necessarily my ideas about women" (A. T., "Between Two Worlds" 78)—seems rather disingenuous.

10. When she throws away her hairbrush, the sound of breaking glass is heard. A still reproduced in *Andrej Tarkowskij* (159) shows her standing in front of a cracked mirror, though this shot does not actually appear in the film.

11. This scene has been described in detail, partly because of its complexity and partly because—as with the final shot of *Stalker*—inaccurate descriptions of it have been used by French critics to impose a religious reading on the film. Peter Kral (*Dossier Positif* 44) sees only "women" (no son, daughter, or dog); misdescribes both their movements and those of the camera; and, instead of singing, hears a hoarse voice emanating from an off-screen loudspeaker, probably announcing the outbreak of war. The women then become "hieratic mothers or sisters" who represent the expulsion from Paradise, and the whole scene is claimed to embody Tarkovsky's vision of war as an unmotivated assault by inveterately hostile cosmic forces whose obscure purpose is to test human beings: "The gods . . . have taken possession of their lands."

12. The color insert of Eugenia looking down at him focuses mainly on her long, dangling red hair (an acknowledged fetish of Tarkovsky's own: see *TWT* 89). Although the shot is certainly sensual, it can hardly be described as depicting Eugenia "lying on top of him in erotic abandon" (Le Fanu 117).

13. See chapter 12 for a fuller discussion of the water in this and other films.

14. Although *Nostalghia* was shown at the 15th Moscow Film Festival in 1987, it has not—even now—been widely screened in the Soviet Union because of problems over rights to the film.

15. The reviews mentioned in this paragraph, apart from Canby's, are reprinted in *Film Review Annual 1985*.

16. In Domenico's room, the apparently monotone brownish colors are gradually revealed, as the scene proceeds, to be composed of infinitely complex gradations and variations. More than any other Tarkovsky film, *Nostalghia* needs to be seen in a very good 35mm print (or a perfect 16mm one) for its real visual impact to come through.

10. THE SACRIFICE

1. The film was a coproduction with Anatole Dauman's Argos Films in Paris, although all the creative and financial controls were in the hands of the producer and the Swedish Film Institute. Other financing was eventually provided by British, French, and Swedish sources, after some of the original Japanese funding fell through.

2. There are several clues that the country could *not* be neutral Sweden—among them the reference to missile bases and Otto's story about the soldier who was drafted and killed in 1940 in a city called Königsberg, which at the time was in the Soviet Union and was known as Kaliningrad!

3. None of this is intended to deny the fine work done by the actors whom he did use in the film, especially since Tarkovsky himself says that he rewrote the main parts for Erland Josephson and Allan Edwall ("Krasota spasyot mir" 145).

4. See Sven Nykvist's account in chapter 3 of how the desaturated color effects were achieved.

5. Readers may wish to consult the synopsis at this point, in order to follow the argument more closely.

6. There is no levitation in the treatment, and neither of the following two scenes is specified there. Alexander simply goes home, falls asleep, and has a dream in which he flies over a town of panic-stricken people who are fleeing either from him or from a mysterious dark cloud.

7. Philip Strick sees the visit to Maria (if taken naturalistically) as a symptom of "the intolerable tensions of living with Adelaide"; but "as guilt then overtakes him . . . and wife and mistress become interchangeable in identical clothes and hairstyles as

the night fades, all he can do for his life is burn it down and retreat, speechless, into remorse" (8).

Alexander, like some other Tarkovsky heroes, appears to suffer from unresolved guilt toward his mother (the point of the otherwise irrelevant story he tells Maria). Like Kris in *Solaris,* as he recovers from his dream/hallucination, he utters the word "Mama!" and, like the mother in that film, Maria washes his hands for him. What may be happening here is that too many of Tarkovsky's favorite wife/mother/mistress obsessions are intruding into a context in which they really have no business.

8. Marta is also seen naked between Alexander's making of his vow and his dream, in a scene which itself hovers between dream and reality. Whose dreams are these? Does Alexander secretly lust after his stepdaughter?

9. Although this scene is in stronger color than any of the others mentioned, this—as noted above—is no longer a reliable guide to its "reality." It follows on Otto's strange fit and his mention of an "evil angel passing by," and Otto offers no reaction as the women rush around in panic. Is Otto—or his "angel"—responsible then for everything that follows?

10. Later in the film Marta says that Alexander turned the tape recorder on "this morning" and later turned it off again, but this seems only to add to the questions posed by the film, rather than resolving anything.

11. Susan Sontag's comment on the structure of Bergman's *Persona* is relevant here: "For instance, the material can be treated as a *thematic resource*—from which different, perhaps concurrent, narrative structures can be derived as variations. Once this possibility is consciously entertained, it becomes clear that the formal mandates of such a construction must differ from those of a 'story' (or even a set of parallel stories). The difference will probably appear most striking in the treatment of time" (134–35).

12. The chapter on *The Sacrifice* in the revised British edition of *Sculpting in Time* (1989) makes the absurd claim that the shot of the house burning is "the longest scene in the history of cinema" (227). Interestingly enough, this particular statement is not found in the otherwise virtually identical essay by Tarkovsky published by the Swedish Film Institute in 1988 as part of the publicity material for Michal Leszczylowski's documentary *Directed by Andrej Tarkovskij*—which may suggest that it was inserted by someone other than Tarkovsky himself. (The added chapter on *The Sacrifice* was published posthumously.) The house burning lasts 6 minutes 50 seconds; Tarkovsky must have known that he had filmed two longer shots in *The Sacrifice* itself, not to mention the carrying of the candle across the pool in *Nostalghia.*

Philip Strick (8) claims the "opening and closing shots" of this film are both "ten" minutes long, seeming to mean by "closing shot" the house-burning scene (a slip often made in writing about the film), but overestimating it by some three minutes.

13. When Adelaide tries to burn Alexander's letter, near the end of the film, the lighter won't work and she crumples it up instead. Despite this, she tells Marta to put the ashes in a glass of wine and drink it: that way she will remember it all her life. Once again something seems to have gone wrong in the middle of a lengthy take (3 minutes 39 seconds), and Tarkovsky chose to ignore the incongruity rather than shoot the whole scene again.

14. Leszczylowski's documentary *Directed by Andrej Tarkovskij* records both filmings of this scene.

15. Riding his bike, which—as Strick points out (8)—was seen only a few minutes previously, propped outside the now-burning house, and thus not easily accessible for him to arrive on from the opposite direction. The bike's presence at the house seems to be another confusing clue establishing the possible "reality" of Otto's second visit and the scene with Maria.

16. He resembles, of course, Prince Myshkin—Tarkovsky's favorite character in the book he so much wanted to film. Both are good, kind, a bit mad, and basically weak, especially in their inability to fight for the woman they love. Alexander's ignoring of

the way Adelaide turns to Victor during her moment of crisis suggests a sad awareness of her infidelity, and the female statue in his dream perhaps represents the coldness of their relationship.

17. Her own view of Adelaide is that she is "destructive, but capable of enormous warmth and love . . . a dangerous woman, selfish because of her blinkered quality . . . she absorbed other people's energies and love" (Interview). Adelaide's hysterical fit bears obvious similarities to Hari's "resurrection" in *Solaris* or Stalker's wife's collapse after he leaves. Natalia Bondarchuk, who played Hari, told us that Tarkovsky's wife Larissa used to have similar "fits," on which the ones in the films were deliberately modeled. This has been confirmed by others who knew the couple well.

18. The Chinese scholar Liu Yan Pin discusses the film from this standpoint in "Simvolika Tarkovskogo i daoizma."

19. For sample English-language responses, see *Variety* (May 14, 1986): 14, *Films and Filming* (September 1986): 43, *Sight & Sound* (Autumn 1986): 284–85.

German critics, who were generally those most sensitive to the philosophical nature of Tarkovsky's work, also found his last film disappointing: "a failed masterpiece" (Andreas Kilb, *Die Zeit* [January 1, 1987]); "on the border of vulgar expressiveness and pseudo-philosophy" (Klaus Kreinmeier, *Frankfurter Rundschau* [January 10, 1987]: 36). While most critics failed to note the film's incredibly personal thematics, Kreinmeier perhaps pointed to the heart of the film and its problems when he criticized Tarkovsky for turning his back on history and looking for salvation in his own purified self (36).

11. IMPRINTED TIME

1. Tarkovsky's figure (*Sculpting* 117), confirmed by our own count.

2. Andrei Konchalovsky quotes Tarkovsky as giving this rationale for increasing the length of shots: a slight increase leads to boredom; a longer one creates new interest; and an even longer one creates "a special intensity of attention" (*O Tarkovskom* 233).

3. Tarkovsky certainly would have been familiar with Viktor Shklovsky's concepts of "defamiliarization" (*ostranenie*, literally "making strange") and *zatrudnenie* ("making difficult"), which formed the foundation of the new Formalist theory of literature and art in the 1920s that explored the relationship between and the transformation of "life" into "art" (see Eagle, "Introduction").

12. THE IMAGE

1. A more schematic way of putting this might be to use the categories established by semioticians such as Lotman (43):

"1. Comparison of the visual image/icon with a corresponding event in real life" (i.e., the horse as a real animal).
"2. Comparison of the visual image/icon with another such image [in the visual arts]" (i.e., metaphoric and mythical associations of the horse).
"3. Comparison of the visual image with itself in a different time unit" (i.e., the horse from one Tarkovsky film to the next—"intertextual coding"—or within a particular film such as *Andrei Roublev*—"intratextual coding").

Generally, however, we will use our own, less technical, terminology.

2. Zholkovsky defines the poetic world of an author as "the hierarchy of his invariant motifs (situations, objects, linguistic structures—[we might say images]), which is crowned with the central invariant theme and accounts for all that the author's texts have in common" (75).

3. This particular combination (earth and water) is discussed at some length by de Baecque (23–26).

4. Here Tarkovsky seems to reverse Bachelard's observation that "in the life of every man, or at least in the dreamed life of every man, the second woman appears: the lover or the wife. The second woman will also be projected on to nature. The wife-landscape will take her place beside the mother-landscape. Doubtless the two projected natures will interweave or overlap" (171). Although the mother is associated with nature from her very first appearance, Natalia is exclusively identified with a monotone, claustrophobic apartment interior, reflecting the narrator's inability to complete the projection of the mother's image onto that of the wife. When the narrator tells his wife that when he remembers his mother she always has Natalia's face, his obvious present unhappiness—and his poor relationship with his mother in the present—have perhaps seeped back to contaminate his memories.

5. Tarkovsky specifically acknowledged this link in interview with Michel Ciment: "I never see mud, I see only earth mixed with water, the source from which things grow" (*Dossier Positif* 92).

6. Early Christian writings contrast the Tree of Knowledge which led to the Fall of Man with the "tree" on which Christ suffered to secure mankind's redemption.

7. *Sight & Sound* (Spring 1990): 140. The image was originally to be part of the scene immediately after the visit to Maria when Alexander dreams of Maria dressed in his wife's clothes and with her hairstyle.

8. Le Fanu obscures the effect of this by misdescribing the scene, inventing a nonexistent rider. He also says, wrongly, that the horse first "mount[s] the wooden steps of the belfry" (49).

9. Followed, rather strangely, in the next shot by a different angle on the table in which some of the objects are still there (the cup and saucer) but others have disappeared or been replaced by something else.

10. In the documentary on the making of *The Sacrifice*, Leszczylowski's *Directed by Andrej Tarkovskij*, he is seen demonstrating to the actress who plays Marta how to perform this action.

11. The dacha in *Nostalghia* doesn't really seem to resemble any of the others, but its spiritual connections are clear. According to the film's set designer, Andrea Crisanti, it was based on a photo of Tarkovsky's own (presumably present-day) dacha in Russia, but "of course it became something different in the film" (*Dossier Positif* 137).

13. LIFE AS APPEARANCE, LIFE AS A DREAM

1. Although, as we argue in our final chapter, Tarkovsky's characters both need and distrust words, speech is ultimately essential for human communication. Even so, there are times when a respectful silence (that of the three men outside the Room) or a resort to action rather than verbal self-absorption (Andrei carrying the candle across St. Catherine's Pool) is both meaningful and necessary. (For further discussion of this theme, see Karriker 188–90.)

2. The two possible, and minor, exceptions to all this are the brief cuts to hands outlined against a fire, and a fire burning in a field; but these seem to exist for poetic and rhythmic effect rather than to enhance meaning.

3. Herbert Eagle's comments on the "semiotic time" of Dziga Vertov's *The Man with the Movie Camera* could intriguingly be applied to the very different structure of *Stalker*: "The organization of space and time and the visual characteristics of the shots themselves move the 'narration' forward. Time is present primarily as tempo and rhythm. Thus . . . semiotic time dominates both the time of the story (a story may not even exist) and the time of the perceiving subject" (42).

4. During this sequence, Andrei is seen saying goodbye to Domenico and embracing him, but the reticent older man has made it very clear that he has no intention of

discussing his private life with anyone. We are unlikely then to be seeing a "visualized" version of their conversation here.

The scenes of Domenico's self-immolation in Rome are not witnessed by Andrei and thus also take place beyond his inner world; yet they seem somehow to be "sensed" by him and inspire him to complete the other man's mission.

5. Although Petrić is a more scrupulous and accurate "reader" of the films than most, his analysis is not without errors: he makes the usual confusion between Ignat and Alyosha in the "earring" scene, saying that it is the former (rather than the latter) who watches the extinction of the sputtering oil lamp ("Tarkovsky's Dream Imagery" 32); and in the dune room in *Stalker*, the two birds do not fly simultaneously across the screen, as his description implies (31). First one flies, and disappears, then the other appears and safely crosses the same space.

14. A DIALOGUE WITH ART

1. They are usually kept in the far background and are not always easy to identify. A viewing on a Steenbeck machine, however, reveals that two of them change places from one shot to the next!

2. Olga Surkova asserts that she researched and provided many of these references; even so, Tarkovsky clearly desired to work within the classical literary tradition, both Russian and Western.

3. Although intellectually Tarkovsky retained a strong interest in Western art, literature, and music, he became increasingly contemptuous of Western materialism and lack of spirituality. While he attempted to remedy this to some extent by turning to Eastern philosophy and religion, his deepest allegiance remained with Russian culture as a source of true spiritual values.

4. When we discuss the work of Tolstoy and Dostoyevsky we are conscious of operating, like Tarkovsky himself, within the clichés and the generalities of the Russian literary tradition and make no attempt to "correct" his interpretation.

5. Though we are not told which part he played in *Richard III*, the obvious assumption is that it was the—surely inappropriate—title role (unless Alexander's renunciation of the stage is meant to derive from his having to adopt an alien identity of this kind). Perhaps Richard II might have been a better, more Myshkin-like, choice.

6. The poem is found in a cycle from 1941–62 called *Before the Snow* (*Pered Snegom*), published in the collection *Stikhotvoreniya* (*Poems*) (Moscow: Khudozhestvennaya literatura, 1974). Arseny Tarkovsky's published creative output is quite modest, with the period 1929–1974 represented by this one volume. (All quotes are translated by Vida Johnson.)

7. Even the names of the main poetic cycles from 1929 to 1974 point to the significance of nature in Arseny Tarkovsky's poetry: *The Guest-Star* (*Gostya-zvezda*, 1929–1941), *Before the Snow* (*Pered snegom*, 1941–1962), *To Earth—the Earthly* (*Zemle-zemnoye*, 1941–1966), and *The Messenger* (or *The Harbinger?*) (*Vestnik*, 1966–1971).

APPENDIX

1. I.e., a film longer than ninety minutes. The division into two parts was normal practice for prestigious films in the Soviet Union and allowed the budget to be doubled.

2. Possibly dying, as some critics believe (*Andrej Tarkowskij* 97), but equally likely simply enjoying itself and calmly indifferent to the demise of Tarkovsky's "Icarus" (cf. Brueghel's painting *The Fall of Icarus* and Auden's poem "Musée des Beaux Arts"). The balloon flight must have been influenced by Yuri Tarich's 1926 film *Wings of a*

Slave (*Krylya kholopa*). In Tarich's film the flight is made by means of wooden wings, as in Tarkovsky's original conception of this scene.

3. This shot derives from a preliminary version of the script describing a rebellion led by the mayor of Novgorod, who is the victim here. As this subplot was dropped from the film, it is probably sufficient to see him as another unfortunate victim of the pervasive violence of the times. He is certainly, however, neither the buffoon (de Baecque 67) nor—even less—Roublev himself (*Dossier Positif* 79)—identifications based on a misleading production still.

4. Gaston Bachelard, in *The Psychoanalysis of Fire*, presents the action of a young woman jumping over a fire as a traditional fertility rite in many cultures (Boston: Beacon Press, 1964; paperback edition 1968: 34).

5. The flashback is not immediately identifiable as such, even to a competent critic such as Gauthier, who describes all the scenes that follow as if they continue in time and location (the cathedral) from what has preceded them (64). The blinding white interior of the two different settings—*both* the Duke's palace and the cathedral—and the lack of any obvious transitions make this one of the most difficult episodes to decipher. In the script the palace is being rebuilt and repainted after being burned down by a peasant—hence the charred tree or pillar. The script also separates the two episodes chronologically, with "The Blinding" coming first and "The Celebration" intervening before "The Last Judgment."

6. Like almost every published still ostensibly from this film, the picture of Roublev holding this icon and looking at it—reproduced in Le Fanu (35), Turovskaya (illustration 6), and even *Sculpting* (39)—is not an image that appears in the film itself. This is true also of the stills "from *Andrei Roublev*" in Gauthier (60, 71, and 77), Le Fanu (43), *Andrej Tarkowskij* (107), *Sculpting* (48 and 52), and *Dossier Positif* (78 and 85). As most of these appear in more than one book and even in the English version of the published script, they perpetuate a false record of the film.

7. Seryozha was seen in the previous episode on the boat as one of Roublev's apprentices. Assisted by the dates in the published Russian script, it becomes clear that this flashback is set *before* the "Celebration" episode and that Roublev befriends the boy after the blinding and takes him with him on his next journey to Vladimir, to work on the cathedral. He is one of those killed in the Tartar raid, and when he mentions this to the ghost of Theophanes, Roublev adds, "And what a day I found him on!" referring back to the blinding scene.

8. She is usually referred to as "the dumb girl," "the mute," or "the deaf-and-dumb girl" by Western critics. In the script she is called the *durochka*, meaning "little fool," though she is also referred to as *blazhennaya* ("blessed"), thus taking on some of the attributes of the "holy fools" so respected in Russian tradition for their instantly recognizable goodness and spirituality beneath a veneer of seeming madness. We will normally refer to her as the "Fool."

9. A major city and independent principality at the time, it was destroyed in a Tartar raid in 1238. It was attacked again in 1408 and the cathedral burnt; the historical Roublev was not a witness to this raid but was summoned to the city the same year to restore the cathedral's paintings. His work was severely damaged when the Tartars attacked the city again in 1410.

10. Irma Rausch, who played this role, explained that her part was much more fully developed in the original script. She was supposed at this stage to be pregnant (not by Roublev, though he accepts the blame for it in recognition of his sinful nature) and was to give birth to a child and recover her senses afterwards—hence her mysterious reappearance toward the end of the next episode, in a scene that was one of the first to be filmed and that Tarkovsky decided to retain even if her presence was not readily explicable (Interview, 1989; also in published script). Traces of this original concept remain in the men's reactions here.

11. The Duke has Italian guests with him who discuss, in their own language, how

unusual it is for Russians to display technical accomplishment of this kind. Tarkovsky, as Gauthier suggests (76), may be alluding here to the way in which the Tartar occupation prevented Russia from participating in the Renaissance—a theme that was taken up by Pushkin and is echoed in *Mirror*.

12. The "Old Testament Trinity" was a standard motif of Russian icon painting and depicted Abraham entertaining the three angels (simply called "men" in the King James version) who visited him and foretold that Sarah would give birth to a son (Genesis 18:1–19). It was regarded as a symbol of the Trinity, and Abraham and Sarah were usually depicted as part of the scene. According to a Russian book-length study of this work (*Troitsa Andreya Rublyova. Antologiya*), Roublev's version differs from the traditional treatment in leaving out Abraham and Sarah and offers "an absolutely different interpretation of the legend. The icon's purpose is not to depict the appearance of the Trinity to Abraham, nor to extol his hospitality; rather, it gives expression to the philosophical ideal of the unity and unseparateness of the Three Persons of the Trinity" (208: English-language summary). It was presumably this emphasis on unity, together with the serenity, harmony, and gentleness of the figures themselves, that attracted Tarkovsky to the work. A widely held view is that the figure on the left is God the Father, the central one Christ, and that on the right the Holy Ghost (Smirnova 277).

13. Turovskaya (81) says it is in black and white, as does Barthélemy Amengual (*Dossier Positif* 84). Le Fanu has the horses "running free" (42) rather than standing still swishing their tails. A French critic, Jean Delmas, sees "three peaceful horses" which he interprets as "the Trinity of horses which echoes the Trinity of angels" (5–6).

14. This helpful information is not translated in the British or American subtitles. Many critics therefore assume that the woman is the father's second wife, or even Kris's mother. The film's script identifies the girl as a neighbor's child, and thus not, as some critics understandably believe, Kris's daughter; but the boy (Berton's son? his grandson?) is never properly accounted for, even by the script. This vagueness as to the exact relationships between characters is found also in *The Sacrifice*.

15. Identified as such for us by Mikhail Romadin. Despite the specific Soviet associations here, there is, as in Lem's novel and in much Soviet and East European science fiction generally, a calculated mixture of nationalities and settings in the film: the dacha is obviously Russian but the city into which Berton drives is Japanese—"futuristic" from the point of view of the average Soviet viewer of the early 1970s. Among the main characters, only Gibarian's Armenian name links him unambiguously with the Soviet Union.

16. According to Vadim Yusov, the alternations between black and white and color resulted from a shortage of color film (Interview).

17. Tarkovsky's plot logic is confusing here: Gibarian says in his videocast that strange things are *already* going on, and that the only way to deal with them might be to apply radiation to the ocean—which contradicts what Snaut says here. Lem is much more consistent in saying that Gibarian and Sartorius illegally submitted the ocean to radiation (35) and that "the phenomena here began to manifest themselves eight or nine days after that X-ray experiment" (77).

18. Most critics refer automatically to Hari as Kris's wife. In the novel, he identifies her to Snaut (Snow) only as "a woman who. . . . She died" (73), and there is likewise no evidence in the film that they were actually married. Turovskaya carefully avoids using the word "wife," referring to "the woman he once loved" (51) and "His old love" (55). Russians will commonly refer to a live-in "significant other" as a "wife."

19. Strangely identified as "the Grail" by Turovskaya, whose book also incorrectly gives the boy's question as, "Is this the *edge* of the world?" (128).

20. The continuity here is odd, especially with the dog, which is restrained by a leash in one shot, but not in others.

21. A *mea culpa* is due here from one of the authors (Petrie), who misdescribes the sequence of events here in *Magill's Cinema Annual 1985*.

22. Tarkovsky quotes this story in his diary for March 5, 1982 (*TWT* 303), attributing it to an unidentified *Lives of the Fathers.*

23. The treatment can be found in the version of the script published (in both French and German) by Schirmer/Mosel (1987). The normally reliable *Monthly Film Bulletin* (January 1987) incorrectly calls Marta "Julia" (the name of the housekeeper) and Julia "Marta" in its plot summary (7).

24. The location of the study in relation to the remainder of the house remains puzzling throughout. Exterior shots show an outside staircase at one corner, but one would not normally have to climb over a railing to reach a permanent stair, and Otto, on his next visit, says explicitly that he has brought a ladder with him this time. He seems as reluctant as Alexander later is to use the stairs within the house.

25. Here she paraphrases Tarkovsky's own ideas about love: "what nobody seems to understand is that love can only be one-sided, that no other love exists, that in any other form it is not love. If it involves less than total giving, it is not love" (*Sculpting* 217).

Filmography

Credits are based on those given in Maya Turovskaya's *Tarkovsky: Cinema as Poetry* and the British Film Institute's *Monthly Film Bulletin*, supplemented and occasionally corrected by checking against (a) the credits listed on the individual films, (b) the information provided in our interviews, and (c) the credits in the German volume *Andrej Tarkowskij*. Unless otherwise noted, dates given are release dates.

Abbreviations: *P.C.*—Production Company; *P.*—Producer; *P. Sup.*—Production Supervisor; *P. Manager*—Production Manager; *Asst. D.*—Assistant Director; *Sc.*—Script; *Ph.*—Photography; *Camera Op.*—Camera Operator; *Ed.*—Editor; *A.D.*—Art Director; *Sp. Effects*—Special Effects; *M.*—Music; *M.D.*—Music Director; *Cost.*—Costumes; *Sd.*—Sound; *L.P.*—Leading Players.

THE STEAMROLLER AND THE VIOLIN (KATOK I SKRIPKA), 1960

P.C.—Mosfilm (Children's Film Unit). *P. Sup.*—A. Karetin. *Asst. D.*—O. Gerts. *Sc.*—Andrei Mikhalkov-Konchalovsky, Andrei Tarkovsky. *Ph.*—Vadim Yusov, Sovcolor. *Ed.*—L. Butuzova. *A.D.*—S. Agoyan. *Sp. Effects*—B. Pluzhnikov, V. Sevostyanov, A. Rudachenko. *M.*—Vyacheslav Ovchinnikov. *M.D.*—E. Khachaturian. *Cost.*—A. Martinson. *Sd.*—V. Krashkovsky.

L.P.—Igor Fomchenko (*Sasha*), V. Zamansky (*Sergei*), Nina Arkhangelskaya (*girl*), Marina Adzhubey (*mother*)

Length: 46 mins.

IVAN'S CHILDHOOD (IVANOVO DETSTVO), 1962 (AMERICAN TITLE: MY NAME IS IVAN)

P.C.—Mosfilm. *P. Sup.*—G. Kuznetsov. *Sc.*—Mikhail Papava, Vladimir Bogomolov. Based on Bogomolov's novella *Ivan*. *Addit. Sc.*—E. Smirnov. *Ph.*—Vadim Yusov. B/W *Ed.*—G. Natanson. *A.D.*—Yevgeny Chernyaev. *Sp. Effects*—V. Sevostyanov, S. Mukhin. *M.*—Vyacheslav Ovchinnikov. *M.D.*—E. Khachaturian. *Sd.*—E. Zelentsova. *Military Advisor*—G. Goncharov.

L.P.—Nikolai (Kolya) Burlyaev (*Ivan*), Valentin Zubkov (*Captain Kholin*), E. Zharikov (*Lieutenant Galtsev*), S. Krylov (*Corporal Katasonych*), Nikolai Grinko (*Lt.-Col. Gryaznov*), V. Malyavina (*Masha*), Irina Tarkovskaya (*Ivan's mother*), D. Milyutenko (*old man with hen*), Andrei Mikhalkov-Konchalovsky (*soldier with glasses*), Ivan Savkin, V. Marenkov, Vera Miturich.

Length: 95 mins.

ANDREI ROUBLEV, 1966 (USSR RELEASE 1971)

P.C.—Mosfilm. *P. Manager*—Tamara Ogorodnikova. *Sc.*—Andrei Mikhalkov-Konchalovsky, Andrei Tarkovsky. *Ph.*—Vadim Yusov. Scope, b/w, and final reel in Sovcolor. *Ed.*—Lyudmila Feiginova. *A.D.*—Yevgeny Chernyaev. *Sp. Effects*—V. Sevostyanov. *M.*—Vyacheslav Ovchinnikov. *Cost.*—L. Novy, M. Abar-Baranovska. *Sd.*—E. Zelentsova.

L.P.—Anatoly Solonitsyn (*Andrei Roublev*), Ivan Lapikov (*Kirill*), Nikolai Grinko (*Daniil the Black*), Nikolai Sergeyev (*Theophanes the Greek*), Irina Tarkovskaya (*the Fool*), Nikolai (Kolya) Burlyaev (*Boriska*), Rolan Bykov (*the buffoon*), Yuri Nikulin (*Patrikey*), Mikhail Kononov (*Foma*), Yuri Nazarov (*Grand Duke/his brother*), S. Krylov

(*bell-founder*), Bolot Ishalenev (*Tartar Khan*), Sos Sarkissian (*Christ*), Tamara Ogorodnikova (*Mary*), N. Grabbe, B. Matisik, Volodya Titov.
   Length: 185 mins. (See synopsis of *Andrei Roublev* for variant versions and lengths.)

SOLARIS, 1972

P.C.—Mosfilm. *Asst. D.*—A. Ides, Larissa Tarkovskaya, Masha Chugunova. *Sc.*—Andrei Tarkovsky, Friedrich Gorenstein. Based on the novel by Stanislaw Lem. *Ph.*—Vadim Yusov. Scope, Sovcolor. *Ed.*—Lyudmila Feiginova. *A.D.*—Mikhail Romadin. *Sp. Effects*—V. Sevostyanov, A. Klimenko. *M.*—Eduard Artemyev, J. S. Bach (Choral Prelude in F Minor). *Cost.*—Nelly Fomina. *Makeup*—V. Rudina. *Sd.*—Semyon Litvinov.
   L.P.—Natalia Bondarchuk (*Hari*), Donatas Banionis (*Kris Kelvin*), Yuri Yarvet (*Snaut*), Anatoly Solonitsyn (*Sartorius*), Vladislav Dvorzhetsky (*Berton*), Nikolai Grinko (*Kris's father*), Sos Sarkissian (*Gibarian*).
   Length: 165 mins. (See synopsis of *Solaris* for variant versions and lengths.)

MIRROR (ZERKALO), 1975

P.C.—Mosfilm, Unit 4. *P.*—E. Vaisberg. *P. Manager*—Y. Kushnerov. *Asst. D.*—Larissa Tarkovskaya, V. Karchenko, Masha Chugunova. *Sc.*—Andrei Tarkovsky, Alexander Misharin. *Ph.*—Georgy Rerberg. Sovcolor, with b/w newsreel sequences. *Camera Op.*—A. Nikolayev, I. Shtanko. *Lighting*—V. Gusev. *Ed.*—Lyudmila Feiginova. *A.D.*—Nikolai Dvigubsky. *Sets*—A. Merkunov. *Sp. Effects*—Y. Potapov. *M.*—Eduard Artemyev, J. S. Bach, Giovanni Batista Pergolesi, Henry Purcell. *Cost.*—Nelly Fomina. *Makeup*—V. Rudina. *Sd.*—Semyon Litvinov. *Poems*—Arseny Tarkovsky, read by the poet.
   L.P.—Margarita Terekhova (*Masha, Alexei's mother/Natalia, Alexei's wife*), Filip Yankovsky (*Alexei, age 5*), Ignat Daniltsev (*Alexei/Ignat, age 12*), Oleg Yankovsky (*Alexei's father*), Nikolai Grinko (*male colleague at printing shop*), Alla Demidova (*Lisa*), Yuri Nazarov (*military instructor*), Anatoly Solonitsyn (*doctor passing by*), Innokenty Smoktunovsky (*voice of Alexei, the narrator*), Larissa Tarkovskaya (*rich doctor's wife*), Maria Tarkovskaya (*Alexei's mother as an old woman*), Tamara Ogorodnikova (*woman in Pushkin-reading scene*), Y. Sventikov, T. Reshetnikova, E. del Bosque, L. Correcher, A. Gutierres, D. Garcia, T. Pames, Teresa del Bosque, Tamara del Bosque.
   (The major published credits for the film in English [*Monthly Film Bulletin*, Turovskaya, Le Fanu] all perpetuate the young Alexei/Ignat confusion by crediting Filip Yankovsky with the role of Ignat age 5, rather than Alexei age 5. Similarly, all credit Larissa Tarkovskaya [Tarkovsky's second wife] with the role of the old mother, though the part was played by Tarkovsky's own mother, Maria. Larissa plays the role of the doctor's wife in the "earring scene.")
   Length: 106 mins.

STALKER, 1979

P.C.—Mosfilm, Unit 2. *P. Group*—T. Aleksandrovskaya, V. Vdovina, M. Mosenkov. *P. Sup.*—Aleksandra Demidova. *P. Manager*—Larissa Tarkovskaya. *Asst. D.*—Masha Chugunova, Yevgeny Tsimbal. *Sc.*—Arkady and Boris Strugatsky. Based on their novella *Roadside Picnic*. *Ph.*—Alexander Knyazhinsky. Color. *Camera Op.*—N. Fudim, S. Naugolnikh. *Asst. Camera Op.*—G. Verkhovsky, S. Zaitsev. *Lighting Sup.*—L. Kazmin. *Asst. Lighting*—T. Maslennikova. *Ed.*—Lyudmila Feiginova. *Asst. Ed.*—T. Alekseyeva, V. Lobkova. *P. Designer*—Andrei Tarkovsky. *Sets*—A. Merkulov. *Artists*—R. Safiullin,

V. Fabrikov. *M.*—Eduard Artemyev. *M.D.*—E. Khachaturian. *M. Sup.*—R. Lukina. *Cost.*—Nelly Fomina. *Makeup*—V. Lvova. *Sd.*—V. Sharun.

L.P.—Alexander Kaidanovsky (*Stalker*), Anatoly Solonitsyn (*Writer*), Nikolai Grinko (*Professor*), Alyssa Freindlikh (*Stalker's wife*), Natasha Abramova (*Stalker's daughter*), F. Yurna, E. Kostin, R. Rendi.
Length: 161 mins.

NOSTALGHIA, 1983

P.C.—Opera Film (Rome), for RAI TV Rete 2; in association with Sovinfilm (USSR). *Exec. P.*—Renzo Rossellini, Manolo Bolognini. *P.*—Francesco Casati. *P. Exec.*—Lorenzo Ostuni (RAI). *P. Sup.*—Filippo Campus, Valentino Signoretti. *P. Admin.*—Nestore Baratella. *Asst. D.*—Norman Mozzato, Larissa Tarkovskaya. *Sc.*—Andrei Tarkovsky, Tonino Guerra. *Ph.*—Giuseppe Lanci. Eastman Color. *Camera Op.*—Giuseppe De Biasi. *Ed.*—Erminia Marani, Amedeo Salfa. *Asst. Ed.*—Roberto Puglisi. *A.D.*—Andrea Crisanti. *Set Dresser*—Mauro Passi. *Sp. Effects*—Paolo Ricci. *M.*—extracts from Verdi, Wagner, Beethoven, Debussy. *M. Consultant*—Gino Peguri. *Cost.*—Lina Nerli Taviani, Annamode 68. *Makeup Sup.*—Giulio Mastrantonio. *Sd. Rec.*—Remo Ugolinelli. *Sd. Mixer*—Danilo Moroni. *Sd. Rerec.*—Filippo Ottoni, Ivana Fidele. *Sd. Effects*—Massimo Anzellotti, Luciano Anzellotti.

L.P.—Oleg Yankovsky (*Andrei Gorchakov*), Erland Josephson (*Domenico*), Domiziana Giordano (*Eugenia*), Patrizia Terreno (*Gorchakov's wife*), Laura De Marchi (*woman with towel*), Delia Boccardo (*Domenico's wife*), Milena Vukotić (*town worker*), Alberto Canepa (*peasant*), Raffaele Di Mario, Rate Furlan, Livio Galassi, Piero Vida, Elena Magoia.
Length: 126 mins.

THE SACRIFICE (OFFRET), 1986

P.C.—Swedish Film Institute (Stockholm)/Argos Films (Paris). In association with Film Four International. Josephson & Nykvist, Sveriges Television/SVT 2, Sandrew Film & Teater. With the participation of the French Ministry of Culture. *Exec. P.*—Anna-Lena Wibom (Swedish Film Institute). *P.*—Katinka Farago (Farago Film). *P. Man.*—Göran Lindberg. *Casting*—Priscilla John, Claire Denis, Françoise Menidrey. *Asst. D.*—Kerstin Eriksdotter, (Postp.) Michal Leszczylowski. *Sc.*—Andrei Tarkovsky. *Ph.*—Sven Nykvist. Eastman Color, b/w. *Camera Op.*—Lasse Karlsson, Dan Myhrman. *Ed.*—Andrei Tarkovsky, Michal Leszczylowski. *Ed. Consultant*—Henri Colpi. *A.D.*—Anna Asp. *Sp. Effects*—Svenska Stuntgruppen; Lars Höglund, Lars Palmqvist. *M.*—J. S. Bach, "Erbarme Dich" from the *St. Matthew Passion;* Swedish and Japanese folk music. *Wardrobe*—Inger Pehrsson. *Cost.*—Inger Pehrsson. *Makeup*—Kjell Gustavsson, Florence Fouquier. *Sd. Rec./Rerec.*—Owe Svenson, Bosse Persson, Lars Ulander, Christin Lohman, Wikee Peterson-Berger. *Interpreter*—Layla Alexander. *Technical Manager*—Kaj Larsen.

L.P.—Erland Josephson (*Alexander*), Susan Fleetwood (*Adelaide*), Valérie Mairesse (*Julia*), Allan Edwall (*Otto*), Gudrún Gísladóttir (*Maria*), Sven Wollter (*Victor*), Filippa Franzén (*Marta*), Tommy Kjellqvist (*Little Man*), Per Kallman, Tommy Nordahl (*ambulancemen*),
Length: 149 minutes.

Works Cited

PRIMARY SOURCES: WORKS BY AND PUBLISHED INTERVIEWS WITH TARKOVSKY

Andrei Rublëv. Trans. Kitty Hunter Blair. London: Faber and Faber, 1991. Filmscript.
Andrei Rublyov. Original script of *Andrei Roublev* published in two parts: *Iskusstvo kino* 4 (1964): 139–200 and 5 (1964): 125–58. Afterword ("Vozrozhdyonny Rublyov") by V. G. Pashuto, *Iskusstvo kino* 5 (1964): 159–60.
Bely, bely den [Bright, Bright Day]. Moscow: Mosfilm, 1973. Director's script for early version of *Mirror*.
"Between Two Worlds." *American Film* (November 1983): 14, 75–79. Interview.
Ekran 65: Sbornik. Moscow: Iskusstvo, 1966. Interview, pp. 154–57.
"Entretien" with Boleslav Edelhajt. *Cahiers du Cinéma* 392 (February 1987): 36–39, 41. Interview.
Hoffmanniana. Munich-Paris: Schirmer/Mosel, 1988. In French. First published in *Iskusstvo kino* 8 (1976): 167–89. Filmscript.
"Krasota spasyot mir" ["Beauty Will Save the World"]. *Iskusstvo kino* 2 (1989): 143–49.
Lektsii po kinorezhissure [Lectures on Film Directing]. Ed. Konstantin Lopushansky. Leningrad: Lenfilm, 1989.
Martyrolog: Tagebücher 1970–1986 [by Andrej Tarkowskij]. Trans. Vera Stutz-Bischitzky and Marlene Milack-Verheyden. Frankfurt am Main/Berlin: Limes, 1989.
Mashina zhelaniy [The Wish Machine]. An early version of *Stalker* by Arkady and Boris Strugatsky published in *Sbornik nauchnoy fantastiki* 25 (1981): 7–39.
"Mezhdu dvumya filmami" ["Between Two Films"]. *Iskusstvo kino* 11 (1962): 82–84.
Mirror. For early filmscripts see *Bely, bely den* and *Zerkalo*.
"My delayem filmy" ["We Make Films"]. *Kino* (Lithuania) 10 (1981): 16–18. Interview.
"O kinoobraze" ["About the Film Image"]. *Iskusstvo kino* 3 (1979): 80–93. Interview.
Opfer. See *Le Sacrifice.*
Le Sacrifice [The Sacrifice]. Munich-Paris: Schirmer/Mosel, 1987. Published in German as *Opfer.*
Sculpting in Time: Reflections on the Cinema [by Andrey Tarkovsky]. Trans. Kitty Hunter-Blair. 1986. Revised edition, London: Faber and Faber, 1989. Cited as *Sculpting.*
Solaris. Moscow, 1972. Unpublished montage script.
Stalker. Moscow: Mosfilm, 1978. Director's working script. See also *Mashina zhelaniy.*
"Strasti po Andreyu" ["The Passion According to Andrei"]. *Literaturnoye obozreniye* 9 (1988): 74–80. Interview.
"Tarkovsky." In *Kogda film okonchen [When the Film Is Finished]*, pp. 137–71. Moscow: Iskusstvo, 1964.
Le temps scellé [by Andrei Tarkovski]. Paris: Editions de l'Etoile/Cahiers du Cinéma, 1989. French translation of *Sculpting in Time.*
Time within Time: The Diaries 1970–1986 [by Andrey Tarkovsky]. Trans. Kitty Hunter-Blair. Calcutta: Seagull Books, 1991. Cited as *TWT.*
"Vsesoyuznaya pereklichka kinematografistov" ["An All-Union Filmmakers' Discussion"]. *Iskusstvo kino* 4 (1971): 50–51. Interview.
"Vstat na put" ["Taking the Right Path"]. *Iskusstvo kino* 2 (1989): 109–30. Interview.
"Ya chasto dumayu o vas . . ." ["I Think of You Often"]. *Iskusstvo kino* 6 (1987): 93–105.
"Zachem proshloye vstrechayetsya s budushchim?" ["Why Does the Past Meet the Future?"] *Iskusstvo kino* 11 (1971): 96–101.
"Zapechatlennoye vremya" ["Imprinted Time"]. *Iskusstvo kino* 4 (1967): 69–79.
Zerkalo [Mirror]. A version of the filmscript cowritten with Aleksandr Misharin. Pub-

lished after the fact in *Kinostsenarii* 2 (1988): 122–54. Moscow: Goskino SSSR. Introduction by Aleksandr Misharin. See also *Bely, bely den.*

SECONDARY SOURCES: WORKS ABOUT TARKOVSKY AND GENERAL CRITICAL LITERATURE CONSULTED

Abramov, N. "Dialog s A. Tarkovskim o nauchnoy fantastike na ekrane" ["Dialogue with A. Tarkovsky about Science Fiction on the Screen"]. In *Ekran 1970–1971*, pp. 162–65. Moscow, 1971.
Adair, Gilbert. "Notes from the Underground: *Stalker.*" *Sight & Sound* (Winter 1980/81): 63–64.
Andrej Tarkowskij. Reihe Film 39. Munich: Carl Hanser Verlag, 1987. Essays by various authors.
Anninsky, Lev. *Shestidesyatniki i my* [*The Sixties Generation and We*]. Moscow: VTPO "Kinotsentr," 1991.
Babitsky, Paul, and John Rimberg. *The Soviet Film Industry.* New York: Praeger, 1955.
Bachelard, Gaston. *L'eau et les rêves* [*Water and Dreams*]. Paris: Librairie José Corti, 1942.
de Baecque, Antoine. *Andrei Tarkovski.* Paris: Cahiers du Cinéma (Collection "Auteurs"), 1989.
Baglivo, Donatella. *Andrei Tarkovsky: A Poet in Cinema.* Ciak Studio, Italy, 1983. Documentary film.
Batkin, Leonid. "Ne boyas svoyego golosa" ["Unafraid of One's Own Voice"]. *Iskusstvo kino* 11 (1988): 77–101.
Bordwell, David. *Narration in the Fiction Film.* London: Methuen, 1985.
Carroll, Noël. *Mystifying Movies.* New York: Columbia University Press, 1988.
Clark, Kenneth. *Leonardo Da Vinci: An Account of His Development as an Artist.* 1930. Revised edition, Harmondsworth: Penguin Books, 1967.
Cohen, Louis Harris. *The Cultural-Political Traditions and Developments of the Soviet Cinema, 1917–1972.* New York: Arno Press, 1974.
Delmas, Jean. "' . . . comme un fleuve,' Andrei Roublev" ["' . . . Like a River,' Andrei Roublev"] *jeune cinéma* 42 (November–December 1969): 3–9.
Dempsey, Michael. "Lost Harmony: Tarkovsky's *The Mirror* and *The Stalker.*" *Film Quarterly* (Fall 1981): 12–17.
Dossier Positif. Ed. Gilles Ciment. Paris: Editions Rivages, 1988. Essays titled *Andrei Tarkovski.*
Dyomin, Viktor. Article in *Pervoye litso* [*The First Person*], pp. 263–73. Moscow: Iskusstvo, 1977.
Eagle, Herbert. *Russian Formalist Film Theory.* Ann Arbor: University of Michigan, Michigan Slavic Publications, 1981.
Eberwein, Robert T. *Film and the Dream Screen.* Princeton, N.J.: Princeton University Press, 1984.
Eisenstein, Sergei. *Film Form: Essays in Film Theory.* Ed. and trans. Jay Leyda. New York: Harcourt, Brace and Co., 1949.
Elmanovits, Tatyana. *The Mirror of Time: The Films of Andrei Tarkovsky.* Tallinn: Eesti Raamat, 1980. Unpublished Russian translation of Estonian original.
Etudes cinématographiques 135–38. Ed. Michel Estève. Paris: Lettres Modernes, 1983. Essays by various authors titled *Andrei Tarkovsky.*
Film Review Annual 1985. Englewood Cliffs, N.J.: Jerome S. Ozer, 1985. Contains reviews of *Nostalghia* from American and British newspapers and periodicals.
Gauthier, Guy. *Andrei Tarkovski.* Filmo 19. Paris: Edilig, 1988.
Gershkovich, Alexander. "Proshchaniye s 'Zonoy' " ["Farewell to the Zone"]. *Novoye russkoye slovo* (November 13, 1984): 5.
"Glavnaya tema—sovremennost" ["The Main Theme Is Contemporaneity"]. *Iskusstvo kino* 3 (1975): 1–18.

Glück, Gustav. *Pieter Brueghel the Elder.* Trans. Eveline Byam Shaw. London: A. Zwemmer, 1951.

Golovskoy, Val, with John Rimberg. *Behind the Soviet Screen: The Motion-Picture Industry in the USSR 1972–1982.* Ann Arbor: Ardis, 1986.

Green, Peter. "The Nostalgia of the Stalker." *Sight & Sound* (Winter 1984/85): 50–54.

Hollander, Anne. *Moving Pictures.* New York: Alfred A. Knopf, 1989.

Hyman, Timothy. Review of *Solaris. Film Quarterly* (Spring 1976): 54–58.

Johnson, Vida T., and Graham Petrie. "Andrei Tarkovskii's Films." *Journal of European Studies* 20, pt. 3 (September 1990): 265–77.

Karriker, A. Heidi. "Patterns of Spirituality in Tarkovsky's Later Films." In Graham Petrie and Ruth Dwyer, eds., *Before the Wall Came Down: Soviet and East European Filmmakers Working in the West,* pp. 183–201. Lanham, Md.: University Press of America, 1990.

Kenez, Peter. *Cinema and Soviet Society, 1917–1953.* Cambridge: Cambridge University Press, 1992.

Keppler, C. F. *The Literature of the Second Self.* Tucson: University of Arizona Press, 1972.

Klein, H. Archer, and Mina C. Klein. *Pieter Bruegel the Elder: Artist of Abundance.* New York: Macmillan, 1968.

Kovács, Bálint András, and Akos Szilágyi. *Les Mondes d'Andrei Tarkovski [The Worlds of Andrei Tarkovsky].* Trans. from Hungarian by Veronique Charaire. Lausanne: L'Age d'Homme, 1987.

Kroll, Jack. Review of *Solaris. Newsweek* (October 25, 1976): 104, 107.

Le Fanu, Mark. *The Cinema of Andrei Tarkovsky.* London: The British Film Institute, 1987.

Lem, Stanislaw. *Solaris.* Trans. Joanna Kilmartin and Steve Cox. 1971. Harmondsworth: Penguin Books, 1981. (First published in Polish in 1961.)

Leszczylowski, Michal. *Directed by Andrej Tarkovskij.* Swedish Film Institute, 1988. Documentary film.

Leyda, Jay. *Kino: A History of the Russian and Soviet Film.* Princeton, N.J.: Princeton University Press, 1973.

Liu Yan Pin. "Simvolika Tarkovskogo i daoizma" ["The Symbolism of Tarkovsky and Daoism"]. *Kinovedcheskiye zapiski* 9 (1991): 154–65.

Lotman, Jurij. *Semiotics of Cinema.* Trans. Mark E. Suino. Ann Arbor: Michigan Slavic Contributions, no. 5, 1976.

Loysha, Viktor. "Takoye kino" ["That Kind of Cinema"]. *Druzhba narodov* (Moscow) 1 (1989): 214–32.

Marshall, Herbert. "Andrei Tarkovsky's *Mirror.*" *Sight & Sound* (Spring 1976): 92–95.

Mikhalkovich, V. I. *Andrei Tarkovsky.* Scientific Popular Series. Moscow: Znaniye, 1989.

Mirsky, D. S. *Pushkin.* New York: E. P. Dutton and Co., 1963.

Mitchell, Tony. "Andrei Tarkovsky and *Nostalghia.*" *Film Criticism* 8, no. 3 (1984): 2–11.

———. "Tarkovsky in Italy." *Sight & Sound* (Winter 1982/83): 54–56.

Montagu, Ivor. "Man and Experience: Tarkovsky's World." *Sight & Sound* (Spring 1973): 89–94.

Niogret, Hubert. "Entretien" with Sven Nykvist. *Positif* 324 (February 1988): 25–27.

O Tarkovskom [About Tarkovsky]. Ed. Marina Tarkovskaya. Moscow: Progress Publishers, 1989. Reminiscences by various friends and coworkers.

Petrić, Vlada. *Constructivism in Film.* Cambridge: Cambridge University Press, 1987.

———. "Tarkovsky's Dream Imagery." *Film Quarterly* (Winter 1989–90): 28–34.

Petrić, Vlada, ed. *Film and Dreams: An Approach to Bergman.* South Salem, N.Y.: Redgrave Publishing, 1981.

Ratschewa, Maria. "The Messianic Power of Pictures: The Films of Andrei Tarkovsky." *Cineaste* 13, no. 1 (1983): 27–29.

Rogers, Robert. *The Double in Literature.* Detroit: Wayne State University Press, 1970.

Rycroft, Charles. *The Innocence of Dreams*. London: The Hogarth Press, 1979.

Salynsky, Dmitry. "Rezhissyor i mif" ["Director and Myth"]. *Iskusstvo kino* 12 (1989): 79–91.

Sartre, Jean-Paul. "Discussion sur la critique à propos de *L'Enfance d'Ivan*" ["Discussion on the Criticism of *Ivan's Childhood*"]. *Les lettres françaises* (December 26, 1963–January 1, 1964). Reprinted in *Etudes cinématographiques* 135–38 (1983): 5–13, and Sartre's own collection *Situations VII* (Paris: Gallimard, 1965), pp. 332–42.

Shitova, Vera. "Iz zemli, vody, i ognya" ["From Earth, Water, and Fire"]. *Sovetsky ekran* 3 (1989): 18–19.

Smelkov, Yu. "Katok i skripka" ["The Steamroller and the Violin"]. *Iskusstvo kino* 8 (1961): 25–26.

Smirnova, Engelina. *Moscow Icons 14th–17th Centuries*. Leningrad: Aurora Art Publishers, 1989.

Solovyov, Vladimir. "Semeynaya khronika ottsa i syna Tarkovskikh" ["The Family Chronicle of Tarkovsky Father and Son"]. *Novoye russkoye slovo* (May 12, 1989).

———. "Zamysel, poetika, film" ["Concept, Poetics, Film"]. *Neva* (Leningrad) 10 (1972): 194–201.

Sontag, Susan. *Styles of Radical Will*. 1967. London: Secker and Warburg, 1969. Essay on Bergman's *Persona*, pp. 123–45.

Steiner, George. *Real Presences*. Chicago: University of Chicago Press, 1989.

Stenograma zasedaniya khudozhestvennogo soveta [*Typescript of Artistic Council Meeting* (on *Ivan's Childhood*)]. March 1, 1962. First Creative Unit, Mosfilm.

Strick, Philip. Review of *The Sacrifice*. *Monthly Film Bulletin* (January 1987): 7–8.

Strugatsky, Arkady, and Boris Strugatsky. *Roadside Picnic/Tale of the Troika*. 1977. New York: Pocket Books, 1978. (First published in Russian in 1972.)

Surkova, Olga. "Avtobiograficheskiye motivy v tvorchestve Andreya Tarkovskogo" ["Autobiographical Motifs in the Creative Work of Andrei Tarkovsky"]. *Kinovedcheskiye zapiski* (Moscow) 9 (1991): 187–93.

"Talisman Andreya Tarkovskogo" ["The Talisman of Andrei Tarkovsky"]. *Sovetsky ekran* 2 (1990): 22–23. Interview with Nikolai Grinko.

Tarkovsky, Arseny. *Stikhotvoreniya* [*Poems*]. Moscow: Khudozhestvennaya literatura, 1974.

Troitsa Andreya Rublyova. Antologiya [*The Trinity of Andrei Roublev: An Anthology*]. Ed. and with an introduction by G. I. Vzdornov. Moscow: Iskusstvo, 1981.

Turovskaya, Maya. *Tarkovsky: Cinema as Poetry*. London: Faber and Faber, 1989.

Vernadsky, George. *The Mongols and Russia*. Vol. III of *A History of Russia*. New Haven: Yale University Press, 1953.

Vinokurova, Tatyana. "Khozhdeniye po mukam 'Andreya Rublyova' " ["The Tormented Path of *Andrei Roublev*]. *Iskusstvo kino* 10 (1989): 63–76.

Yermash, Filip. "On byl khudozhnik" ["He Was an Artist"]. *Sovetskaya kultura* (September 9, 1989): 10 and (September 12, 1989): 4.

Zak, Mark. *Andrei Tarkovsky: Tvorchesky portret* [*Andrei Tarkovsky: An Artistic Portrait*]. Moscow: Soyuzinformkino, 1988.

———. Article in *Kinorezhissura: Opyt i namyok* [*Film Directing: Experience and Allusion*], pp. 98–127. Moscow: Iskusstvo, 1983.

Zholkovsky, Alexander. *Themes and Texts*. Ithaca: Cornell University Press, 1984.

Zorkaya, Neya. "Filmy i rezhissyory" ["Films and Directors"]. In S. I. Yutkevich, ed., *Problemy sovremennogo kino*, pp. 63–70. Moscow: Iskusstvo.

———"Zametki k portretu Andreya Tarkovskogo" ["Remarks toward a Portrait of Andrei Tarkovsky"]. *Kino panorama* 2 (1977): 144–65.

INTERVIEWS CONDUCTED BY THE AUTHORS
RELATING TO TARKOVSKY

Akimov, Vladimir (scriptwriter). September 1989, May 1991.
Alexander, Layla (translator). June 1988.
Artemyev, Eduard (composer). October 1989.
Bondarchuk, Natalia (actress). October 1989.
Borovsky, Victor (opera voice coach). June 1988; June 1991.
Brown, Irina (opera producer). June 1988.
Burlyaev, Nikolai (actor). October 1989.
Demidova, Alla (actress). October 1989.
Dvigubsky, Nikolai (set designer). March 1990.
Feiginova, Lyudmila (editor). October 1989.
Fleetwood, Susan (actress). June 1988.
Fomina, Nelly (costume designer). October 1989.
Gerber, Alla (film critic). October 1989, May 1991.
Gordon, Alexander (director, Tarkovsky's brother-in-law). May 1991.
Josephson, Erland (actor). March 1988.
Kaidanovsky, Alexander (actor). September 1989.
Kimm, Fiona (opera singer). June 1988.
Kleiman, Naum (film historian). October 1989, May 1991.
Knyazhinsky, Alexander (cinematographer). October 1989.
Kochevrin, Yury (Tarkovsky's high-school friend). May 1991.
Konchalovsky, Andrei (director, scriptwriter). May 1991, June 1991.
Lawless, Stephen (opera producer). June 1988.
Leszczylowski, Michal (editor). June 1988.
Lloyd, Robert (opera singer). June 1988.
Lopushansky, Konstantin (director). October 1989.
Mamin, Yuri (director). July 1988.
Misharin, Alexander (scriptwriter). October 1989.
Nykvist, Sven (cinematographer). May 1988.
Offroy, Martine (former Director of Public Relations, Gaumont, Paris). March 1990, June 1991.
Ogorodnikova, Tamara (production manager; actress). September 1989.
Ovchinnikov, Vyacheslav (composer). October 1989.
Ozerskaya, Tatyana (translator, Arseny Tarkovsky's third wife). May 1991.
Rausch, Irma (actress and first wife of director). October 1989, May 1991. (Also known as Irina Tarkovskaya while married to Tarkovsky.)
Rerberg, Georgy (cinematographer). September 1989.
Romadin, Mikhail (set designer). October 1989.
Sokurov, Alexander (director). July 1988.
Surkova, Olga (film critic). May 1988, July 1990.
Tarkovskaya, Larissa (second wife of director). March 1990.
Tarkovskaya, Marina (sister of director). October 1989, May 1991.
Terekhova, Margarita (actress). September 1989.
Toscan du Plantier, Daniel (producer). March 1990.
Turovskaya, Maya (film critic and scholar). July 1990.
Wibom, Anna-Lena (producer). June 1988.
Yankovsky, Oleg (actor). October 1989.
Yusov, Vadim (cinematographer). October 1989.
Zorkaya, Neya (film critic and scholar). July 1990, May 1991.

Index

VIDA T. JOHNSON, Associate Professor of Russian at Tufts University, has published on Yugoslav and Russian literatures and Russian film. She has coauthored, with Graham Petrie, a chapter on Andrei Tarkovsky in *Five Filmmakers*, edited by Daniel Goulding.

GRAHAM PETRIE, Professor of Drama at McMaster University, is the author of *The Cinema of François Truffaut; History Must Answer to Man: The Contemporary Hungarian Cinema;* and *Hollywood Destinies: European Directors in America, 1921–1931*. He has also published several short stories and a novel, *Seahorse*.